Setting the Tone

NED ROREM

SETTING THE TONE

ESSAYS AND A DIARY

LIMELIGHT EDITIONS

NEW YORK

First Limelight Edition, October 1984

ISBN 0–87910–024–9

Manufactured in the United States of America

Library of Congress Cataloging in Publication Data

Rorem, Ned, 1923–
  Setting the tone.

  Reprint. Originally published: New York : Coward,
McCann & Geoghegan, c1983.
  Includes index.
  1. Rorem, Ned, 1923–   . 2. Composers—United
States—Biography. 3. Music—Addresses, essays, lectures.
4. Authors—Addresses, essays, lectures. I. Title.
ML410.R693A33   1984   780   84–4374

To James Holmes
as to the sun.

CONTENTS

Prologue   11

I DIARY

The Piano in My Life   17
Of Vanity   32
Being Ready   39
Paris in the Spring   49
Nantucket Diary, 1974   60
On Edmund White's States of Desire   86
Setting the Tone   90
Being Alone   99

II PEOPLE

Women in Music   123
Misia   127
Remembering Janet   132
Cosima Wagner's Diaries   135
Boulanger as Teacher   138
Thomson as Teacher   144
Messiaen and Carter on Their Birthdays   146
When Paul Jacobs Plays Debussy   149
Thinking of Ben   153
Testimony: The Memoirs of Dmitri Shostakovich   160
Boulez   165
Cocteau and Music   172
Vera Stravinsky's and Robert Craft's Stravinsky
    in Pictures and Documents   186
Stravinsky at 100   190
An Auden   200
Courageous Coward   209
Shaw: The Great Composers   215

III THE MUSICAL VOICE

Teaching and Performance   221
The American Art Song   225
More Notes on Song   240
Fauré's Songs   247
The Mélisande Notebook   251
Fauré and Debussy   259
Considering Carmen   262
Notes on a French Bias   273
A Triptych Notebook: Reactions to the Theater Pieces of
    Ravel, Poulenc and Satie   278
Thirteen Ways of Looking at a Critic   292

IV EARLY PIECES

Writing Songs   299
Song and Singer   310
Listening and Hearing   316
Composer and Performance   324
Arthur Honegger   334
The Beatles   337
The Avant-Garde as Démodé   346
Around Satie's *Socrate*   351
Paul Bowles   355
Remembering a Poet   358
Remembering Green   361

Index   369

PROLOGUE

Do you still keep a diary? people sometimes ask.

Yes, insofar as a diary (as opposed to a memoir) is on-the-spot reaction to professional concerns. But no, insofar as a diary is a gossipy confessional or a platform for keening.

I began in 1945, as a release from shyness, to investigate on paper what I could not say aloud. Over the years the journal absorbed more than mere outpourings of love, vicious envy or depressions oozing from the gray corners of alcoholism; it grew into a travelogue, a recipe carnet, a social calendar with notes on works in progress. Indeed, the book became a catchall for my virtually every preoccupation except the main one—musical composition.

I was a musician who happened to write, not an author who happened to compose. Thus the diary, being random and bloody and self-indulgent, answered to different needs than the music, which was planned, pristine, objective. Or such was the case until 1966 when my first book, *The Paris Diary*, was published. At that time I had already been a professional composer for twenty years. Suddenly I discovered that the reading audience was far different from the listening audience, that the two did not overlap, that neumes and nouns excite separate nerves and that a composer's notoriety will never equal an author's. The "public" ascribes less responsibility to a composer than to an author, for literature can wound where music cannot. True, when Proust lamented that the upper-crust fauna to whom he mailed galleys of *Swann's Way* never reacted (Madame de Chevigné, the model for the Princesse de Guermantes, confessed that she "caught her feet" in Proust's prose), Cocteau pacified him: "Do you ask ants to read Fabre's studies in entomology so as to learn more about themselves?" But I had written of people by name and was stunned to learn they didn't appreciate it.

"Did you originally keep a diary in order for it to be read?" people then ask.

Everything written is meant to be read, if only by the writer at another time. But if I were to continue to publish words, I realized that I would have to bear the consequences. Gradually, like amoebas merging and then separating, or like two Ned Rorems passing each other as they enter a mirror, my joint professions exchanged focus. If the writing today has become more planned, pristine and objective, the music, though not exactly random or bloody or self-indulgent, is, I like to think, more imbued with the kind of ugliness which is as crucial as beauty is to art. Two careers run parallel. Can I really know if they infringe upon each other, any more than general practitioners can know where the path of specialization might have led them? Most who read my words have never heard my music, while musicians are usually surprised that I have written books. Books about what?

The question is academic. Those three diaries which brought a brief though golden fame are long since out of print, as are the five collections of essays. Meanwhile musical life prevails as it did before I ever published books. Yet I still write prose—as the present volume attests—branching out now beyond my navel, with articles mainly on matters artistic commissioned by, and tailored to the requirements (sometimes even aping the tone) of, specific periodicals. And I still keep a diary—though what author's work, or indeed what composer's, is not to some extent a diary? The mood is quieter. After a certain age, certain subjects become embarrassingly dull and no-body's business. One of these is sexual intercourse, another is the injustice of personal sorrow. Could the same be said of a composer's palette? Will I hold to such a principle a decade from now? These paragraphs, in guise of a preface, are themselves as inconclusive as diary entries.

The diarist years later cannot be sure if he is recalling an actual occurrence, or what he wrote about the occurrence. The composer endures no such confusion: he never knows, in vision or in verbs, what he's composing "about."

Bon mots in writing, like percussion in music, are effective in inverse proportion to their frequency. Thus I can't condone, on technical grounds, certain repetitions within the overall text. (While correcting the galleys, for example, I found three statements of "Critics of words use words; critics of music use words.") If I did not remove some of these repetitions it was partly because in different contexts they took on different emphases—or so I prayed—and partly because redundant obsession is the woof of the diaristic mode.

Most of the pieces in this book have appeared elsewhere during the past two or three years, generally in a different shape.

"The Piano in My Life" is from a volume of miscellaneous essays called *The Lives of the Piano*. "Being Alone" was first published in *The Ontario Review*, "Paris in the Spring" in *Antaeus* and "Nantucket Diary, 1974" in *Tri Quarterly*.

Since 1979 I have contributed regularly to *Christopher Street*, and the following articles were first printed therein: "Of Vanity," "Setting the Tone," "When Paul Jacobs Plays Debussy," "Thinking of Ben," "Boulez" and "More Notes on Song."

Other articles were commissioned as book reviews: "On Edmund White's *States of Desire*," "Misia," "Vera Stravinsky's and Robert Craft's Stravinsky in Pictures and Documents" were in *The Washington Post Book World*, and so was "Being Ready." "Cosima Wagner's Diaries," "Shostakovich," "An Auden," "Courageous Coward" and "Shaw" were in *Chicago Tribune Book World*. "Boulanger as Teacher" was in *The New York Times Book Review*.

Still others came out first as record reviews or as liner notes. "Fauré's Songs" was in *Stereo Review*, while "Fauré and Debussy" and "The American Art Song" graced disc jackets for, respectively, Columbia Records and New World Records.

Five pieces were originally conceived as lectures: "Women in Music" was delivered at a feminist symposium organized by Francine du Plessix Gray at Rutgers and later was published in *Vogue*. "Thirteen Ways of Looking at a Critic" was for a critics' panel in Santa Fe. "Teaching and Performance" was a commencement address at the Curtis Institute, refashioned from a similar address at Northwestern five years earlier.

"Messiaen and Carter on Their Birthdays" was broadcast as an homage on the BBC in London, then published in *The Spectator*, while "Stravinsky at 100" was spoken before the Chamber Music Society of Lincoln Center, then published in *Opera News*.

Opera News also published "The Mélisande Notebook," "A Triptych Notebook" and "Considering Carmen."

"Cocteau and Music," commissioned by the French-American Foundation for an upcoming retrospective, first appeared in *London Magazine* and then, in America, in *Keynote*. "Notes on a French Bias" was in *Stagebill*, "Remembering Janet" in *Gaysweek* and "Thomson as Teacher" in a program of Virgil Thomson's music at Yale.

All the "Early Pieces" are from long ago ("Writing Songs" in 1959 was my first essay on a musical subject) and are here reprinted from former collections, some with a blush but none with apology.

1983

ONE

DIARY

THE PIANO IN MY LIFE

1.

I am my ideal pianist.

Quick, an explanation.

If I'd rather hear myself play than anyone, it's not that I'm better than anyone (there is no "better than"); it's that my fancy fills in missed notes, the inner ear camouflages mere sloppiness. I play just well enough for perfection, while virtuosos play too well for perfection. Most great pianists perform the same repertory. They can't all be right. But I am right for me. Perhaps the gambit should read: The only pianist for my idealized performances is me.

I have never needed to lament, "If only my parents had forced me to practice!"

In 1972, when I was forty-eight, I wrote in my diary on April 30: "Margaret Bonds is dead. So closes the miniature dynasty of female piano teachers who taught me all I knew by the time I was fifteen. Nuta Rothschild, Belle Tannenbaum, Margaret Bonds, two Jews and a Negro, all dead. In this day or any other it's scarcely revolutionary for a pupil to have a woman tutor. But for a white child to have a black music teacher was not standard practice in Chicago during the 1930s, and is there a reason not to be proud of it? (Margaret was only ten years older than I.)"

In 1975, while working on a "memoir" for Maurice Ravel's centenary, which occurred March 7, I made this aside: "Needing tangible references I remove from an old storage box, labeled *Ravel: Piano*, dozens of crumbling Durand editions procured in high-school days. Keyboard facility then was a curse; wanting quick results I acquired early the skill of fakery, and never practiced. Today my hands recall like yesterday how I counterfeited fingerings. I still play the music in *the same wrong way*. Would it have been so painful to have learned it right? (Recurring dream. Jailors tell me: Sight-read this unknown Ravel scherzo an augmented fourth higher than written, without an error, and you will go free. Miss one note and you are burned alive . . . But who is the judge?)"

In 1978 on the sixtieth anniversary of Debussy's death, I talked with a friend, and later noted: "JH takes exception to the remarks on Debussy,

17

refuting my claim that melody, like sex and food, is actual experience, enjoyable in the present as it unfolds. JH contends that *harmony* is Now; that melody depends on what has happened while harmony is what is going to happen. Well, both reflections—they are reflections, not assertions—hold water. *Reflets dans l'eau.*"

Six years after Debussy died in Paris, I was born in Indiana where my father was teaching accounting at Earlham College. At the age of eight months I moved to Chicago, taking the elders with me. My parents, then financially lower-middle class (on a professor's salary), were culturally highbrow, and as liberal citizens they were already what they remain today: well-read left-of-center Quaker converts. Mother (Gladys Miller), whose younger brother had been killed at Belleau Wood in 1918, bore that trauma by joining the Society of Friends and becoming a "militant pacifist." Father (Rufus Rorem), the first in his enclave of Norwegian farmers to receive a Phi Beta Kappa, was fomenting the notions on medical economy which—once maligned as Socialized Medicine—would evolve into Blue Cross.

Although not specifically musical, our parents "exposed" my sister Rosemary and me to concerts, mainly high-class piano recitals.

I recall the hoary sight and sound of that archetypical genius, Paderewski, furrowing his brow 'neath a snowy mane and curving a digitus o'er his own Minuet in G. (Did you know that Paderewski's heart—his pickled heart—reposes in a Brooklyn bank vault, deposited there by patriotic Poles when he died in New York in 1941, a relic not only of the man as musician, but as first premier of the newly created Polish nation in 1919?)

I recall the giant specter of Rachmaninoff, his salt-and-pepper crew cut set off by a military tux, hovering over his inevitable Prelude in C-sharp minor which he deigned to offer as *bis* after a gorgeous version—and my first hearing—of Beethoven's Opus 31, No. 3. I wasn't yet aware of Rachmaninoff as final embodiment of the nineteenth-century virtuoso wherein pianist and composer were one, the composer being not only his own best interpreter but a finished performer of other men's music. Nor was I aware of Rachmaninoff's self-destructive youth by which I would later justify the poignance of my own.

 I recall the businesslike stance of Josef Hofmann, acolyte of the legendary Anton Rubinstein, seated at his forty-five-inch Steinway keyboard specially built to accommodate his little hands. Hofmann too was a sometime composer (pseudonym: Michel Dvorsky) and a sometime carouser who in 1926 became for twelve years the director of the Curtis Institute among whose students I would eventually be listed and among whose faculty I currently preach.

Was it not meet that, on reaching the age of reason, the artistically disposed son of intelligent parents should commence formal training in music?

All piano teachers are women, and they are all called Mrs., the noun—or is it an adjective?—of the safely mated or widowed. There exists no such breed as the male music instructor for beginners, men having more solemn concerns.

Such misconceptions are no less prevalent today than in 1930 when, age seven, I began to "take piano" from the first of seven women who would represent Art in my early life. Mrs. Pickens, who lived two blocks away on Chicago's Kenwood Avenue, wore purple, and served tea brewed from senna leaves after each lesson. With her guidance I quickly mastered "Cherry Blossoms," all on the black keys, and another more complicated number named "Mealtime at the Zoo" in which I *crossed hands*. Soon I graduated to Mrs. Hendry, befriended by my parents at Friends' Meeting. At her students' recital on Blackstone Avenue I played, badly, the Brahms A-flat Waltz, after which I felt undeserving of the hot chocolate and oatmeal cookies served to the assembled families. To this day I'm queasy about eating if I've not worked well, and I still nurse a vague guilt—increasingly vague, thank God—about taking money for the exhaustingly agreeable task of composing music.

After Mrs. Hendry came Aunt Agnes—Mrs. Thompson—who was considered the musician of our clan. (Her daughter Kathleen became First Viola of the Toledo Symphony, married the First Flute, and their son Ross Harbaugh is the Cello of the New World Quartet.) But Aunt Agnes lasted for only an Oberlin summertime. In the autumn I began "taking" with Mrs. Davis, spouse of a paternal colleague, and in the spring came the luminous Mrs. Rothschild.

Now, none of these women, before Mrs. Rothschild, provided a sense of need. I may have been learning piano but I was not learning music. Nuta Rothschild was the Russian wife of art historian Edward Rothschild, and like many a sensitive university wife she had time on her hands. Our first meeting opened the gates of heaven. This was no lesson but a recital. She played Debussy's *L'Île joyeuse* and *Golliwog's Cake Walk* and during those minutes I realized for the first time that here was what music is supposed to be. I *didn't* realize that this "modern stuff" repelled your average Music Lover, for it was an awakening sound which immediately, as we Quakers say, spoke to my condition, a condition nurtured by Mrs. Rothschild who began to immerse me in Impressionism. With Perry O'Neil, our grammar school's official genius (he had a scholarship, and was elsewhere a pupil of Rudolph Ganz), I would go Saturdays to the record booths of Lyon & Healy, and listen and listen and listen. Debussy led us forward to Ravel and Stravinsky, not backward to Brahms and Verdi, and I was unquestioningly at home with the garish roulades of *Scarbo* and the so-called percussion pianos of *Noces* before I'd ever heard a Chopin Nocturne. (I say "so-called percussion" because Stravinsky, like Copland after him, is said to have fostered a new approach to the piano. In fact, Mozart and Beethoven and Liszt and Mussorgsky all treated the piano for the percussion that it is. The difference between the keyboard of Stravinsky and, say, Rachmaninoff is not that Stravinsky treats the piano as a percussion instrument, but that, with his leaner harmonies and dearth of pedal, he treats it more *percussively*. Both are composing percussion music. A piano is always a piano until physically modified, as by John Cage's "preparations," when it becomes a new instrument, but still a percussion.) Such scores and discs as we could not afford with our allowances, we stole. I devoured Romola Nijinsky's dubious portrait of her husband, and Lockspeiser's biography of Debussy which remains, alas, with its mean inexpert biases, astonishingly the only extant book on the subject. I had half-learned all of Debussy's piano repertory when Mrs. Rothschild, upon the death of her young husband, left Chicago forever.

Like every child I hated scales. As soon as I was able to get around the keys I became more intrigued by improvisation than by practice. I spent whole days pounding our baby-grand Starck, making up pieces but not writing them down. (Except for the titles: "Tragic Bubbles on the Ruby Lagoon," "Corpse in the Meadow," "A Streamlined Carol.") Most parents do not have a pre-adolescent son who prefers Scriabin to softball, nor does every son assume that his classmates rush home after school, as he does, to listen to Delius.

"How do you plan to make a living?" asked Father, on learning I wanted to be a composer when I grew up. Apparently I replied, "What difference does it make, if I can't be a composer?" That answer was so un-American as to impress Father who, although a breadwinner, was also a not-so-sublimated baritone. To his eternal credit he agreed then and there to be supportive of the family freak. He has never been a Stage Mother, but Father nonetheless believed in work. It was time for a real teacher.

The Julius Rosenwald Fund in Chicago was not only the backbone of the Committee on the Cost of Medical Care of which Father was coordinator, but sponsor for Negro fellowships in the Arts and Sciences. Among the beneficiaries in those days were Katherine Dunham, W. E. B. Du Bois, Marian Anderson, Howard Swanson, Margaret Bonds. The last-named at twenty-two was a middle-western "personality," having played Carpenter's *Concertino* with the Chicago Symphony under the composer's direction, and being herself a composer of mainly spiritual arrangements and of original songs in collaboration with Langston Hughes. It was Margaret Bonds—*Miss Bonds*—who was to be my next piano teacher.

Every Saturday morning I boarded the streetcar for her house on South Wabash. At our first lesson she played me some ear-openers, *The White Peacock* by Griffes, and Carpenter's *American Tango*. Had I ever heard American music before? Fired by my enthusiasm, she assigned the pieces on the spot, with no talk of scale-and-trill practice.

Margaret Bonds played with the authority of a professional, an authority I'd never heard in a living room, an authority stemming from the fact that she herself was a composer and thus approached all music from the inside out, an authority that was contagious. She dusted off the notion that music was solely for home use. She also showed me how to notate my ramblings ("Just look at how other composers put it on the paper"), hoisting the ephemeral into the concrete: once his piece is on the page a composer is responsible for it, for it can now be reinterpreted by others, elating or embarrassing its maker.

The first piece I wrote down, "The Glass Cloud," was influenced by Margaret's other prize pupil, Gerald Cook. Gerald was a pop pianist and serious creator who would soon spend a term with Nadia Boulanger. In the years to come his identity with Margaret would shift from student to colleague as the two-piano team, Bonds and Cook, became a glamorous enterprise at Cerutti's in New York, and at Spivy's Roof. When Margaret went her separate way to marriage, motherhood, documentation of Negro song, opera writing, and death, Gerald turned into the greatest living accompanist of the Blues, working first with the lamented Libby Holman, then—and still—with Alberta Hunter. (Accompanists dislike that word and call themselves pianists. Once I identified Song as: "A lyric poem of moderate length set to music for single voice with piano." If the definition holds for everything from *Der Doppelgänger* to *Le Bestiaire*, with my own songs thrown in—and I don't write "accompaniments," I write integrated piano parts as important as the vocal—it must be expanded for the Blues which by their nature never repeat themselves the same way. Then what is Gerald Cook? A contradiction in terms, a composer of improvisations, a jazz accompanist who repeats himself literally, and whose repetitions become Art? Hear the discs with Holman and Hunter: how, beneath their subjectively raw but subtle and moaningly spoken incantations, he weaves an icy, classical, velvet, inexorable web to encase and soothe forever the open wound.)

Did I outgrow Margaret Bonds? Why were lessons discontinued? If there was an objection to a seeming glib jazziness *chez elle*, Margaret thought of herself as classical and deep. (Conversely, I feel as influenced by prewar jazz as by "serious" music. Not the tune itself but Billie Holiday's *way* with a tune taught me to knead a vocal phrase, just as Count Basie's piano playing still shapes my piano composing.) In any case Margaret and I lost track of each other until we had all moved East during the war. Then we remained close friends until she died.

Only last year I went back to Chicago—to accompany a vocal recital, as it happens. Not one old friend remains in the city which was once my world. The weird thing is how little has changed; a new cast of actors in the same old décor. Or almost the same. Nothing, nothing is left of the brief block of one-story artist studios just east of the I.C. tracks on Fifty-seventh Street. That was once Hyde Park's Montmartre. Rolf Beman, Georg Redlich, Gertrude Abercrombie, how many vanished painters, brought to the fore by the WPA, were toiling and giggling and drinking and dying within a Bohemia that casually bisected the university milieu of my parents! Charlie Biesel was the crosspoint. At one of his parties early in 1938 Mother and Father met and liked Belle Tannenbaum who became my next piano teacher.

Belle was a bigtime local virtuoso and free-lance professor, bitter rival of Molly Margolies who was Ganz's tenured assistant and scapegoat. She immediately tried to discourage my French disposition in favor of the more "honest" repertory of Haydn. Coincidentally, I got special dispensation twice weekly from gym to attend harmony classes in the Loop with expert Leo Sowerby, another stickler for basic training. Belle was maybe fifty, four feet eleven, plump with spindly calves, platinum hair, a huge bosom and tight black dresses, a coarsely amicable social style and the keyboard technique of Horowitz. I adored her. Thanks to Belle we cashed in the old Starck and invested in a new Steinway "B." I can still see us that afternoon in Lyon & Healy's vast storeroom crowded with instruments like wingèd horses, Belle testing the mahogany lids with her tiny fists, kicking at the brittle wooden legs which she likened to her own "piano legs" (though aren't true piano legs those foot-thick cylinders found on earlier models?), sitting now at this keyboard, now at that, each time easily playing—as though opening a faucet of nectar—the infinitely melancholy Prelude in G by Rachmaninoff.

Under Belle Tannenbaum's tutelage I memorized the first movement of Grieg's Piano Concerto which, on June 21, 1940, I performed, in my white graduation suit, with the American Concert Orchestra, a subsidiary of the WPA's marvelous Illinois Symphony, with one William Fantozzi, conductor. That is the only time in my life I have played with an orchestra.

Also that month, age sixteen, despite low grades, I emerged from U-High (in the white suit), and the following autumn I was accepted at Northwestern University's School of Music, despite the same low grades, on my creative potential.

All through high school, and indeed through grammar school, it had been Perry O'Neil, not me, who was the star pianist; I was known at best as a "dreamer." To be a Composition Major now seemed eerily official. However, I remember less about the lessons with tiny Doctor Alfred Nolte (himself a former protégé of Richard Strauss) than about lessons in my "minor" with Harold Van Horne, my first male piano teacher and the impulse for my first intense piano practicing. Suddenly I dwelled in a competitive world of pianists better than me, who practiced nine hours a day on the standard classics. That none of these wunderkinds was obsessed with, or even really knew the music of, Debussy and Stravinsky, was no less bemusing than my ignorance of Schumann and Mendelssohn. The target of my new concentration was not cheering crowds but repertorial lore. In two years at Northwestern I learned all thirty-two Beethoven Sonatas and the entire keyboard catalogue of Bach and Chopin. Today I have a wider range than most pianists because I never bogged down in perfecting any one piece. (Oh, I *did* give a pretty accurate rendition of Ravel's Concerto in "Solo Class," with Van Horne at the second piano). Indeed, it's shocking how *few* pieces most successful pianists have in their fingers; after a point in their careers they're stuck with two or three recitals, two or three concertos, and have no more time, or seemingly curiosity, to revive more warhorses, let alone to learn contemporary works. But by the same token my appreciation—my "whistling knowledge"—of basic symphonic and operatic chestnuts is surely narrower than your average Music Lover's. And if once I lusted after the French esthetic, and later tried to keep up on the output of my fellow creators, today as a composer I'm less and less interested in the music of other people. As a pianist I'm more and more interested in the hours I spend alone with the Bach Inventions which I first enjoyed with Harold Van Horne. He was a quiet, charming, black-haired, thin, bespectacled family man whose robust pianism belied his outward passivity. He committed suicide in 1959.

The year 1943 was spent at the Curtis Institute in Philadelphia on a scholarship with Rosario Scalero whom I despised. The study of composition, to bear fruit, must be solely with a successful practitioner, one who has himself learned from hearing his music frequently rendered by the best executants. True, Scalero had in the 1920s been an exemplary professor for Barber and Menotti, but they were younger then than I was now, and I had ideas of my own. That old Scalero should proscribe original work, and prescribe only counterpoint and more counterpoint (which I'd already had to excess at Northwestern), meant that he, like Nolte, had failed. For the record my "secondary" piano teacher was Freda Pastor. What I retained from Curtis was not the wisdom of a dusty maestro but the still vital friendship of young pianists, notably Eugene Istomin and Shirley Gabis Rhoads, but also the rich flock of wartime *jeunesse:* Gary Graffman, Seymour Lipkin, Jacob Latiener, Theodore Lettvin.

Then 1944 brought me to the magic of the Empire City against the better judgment of my parents, still in Chicago, who stopped my allowance. I have never regretted the crucial step from Scalero's security to the adventure of Virgil Thomson. The first year in New York I acted as Virgil's copyist in exchange for $20 a week and orchestration lessons, learning more about the real world of music in that short time than in all my twenty years. Through his friend E. Robert Schmitz, Virgil found me yet another piano instructor. The intelligent Betty Crawford imparted the Schmitz "method"—"natural" hand position, thumbs on the black keys, etc.—which, for better or worse, I'm still stuck with. One thing leads to another. Betty, with whom I gave the first public hearing of my Four-Hand Piano Sonata (at a Regional Meeting of Blue Cross in the Statler Hotel, no less, thanks to Father who was passing through town), got me a job as accompanist for Martha Graham's classes. Martha thus became my first official employer for whom I drew out Soc. Sec. # 091-22-5307, and earned two dollars an hour.

Next, 1945 saw me back in school, this time at Juilliard, urged by Father, always the academician, who felt it more honorable to have a degree and pooh-pooh it than not to have a degree and pooh-pooh it. The name of my "secondary" piano teacher at Juilliard I've forgotten, but I played better than her, and she was the last I've ever had.

Father maintains that when I was four I stood at the piano one fine day and to everyone's surprise played, *lentissimo* but without missing a beat, "My Country, 'Tis of Thee" in C. Obviously I was imitating some grownup. Since then, most of what I've learned about piano playing has come from emulating peers. The same goes for composition: I've gleaned less from formal lesson than from piracy. (Charlie Chaplin, on being complimented for his singing voice, answered, "But I don't sing at all. That was an imitation of Caruso.")

Do I play in public these days? Not as often as I'd like. When I do it's always as accompanist to my own songs, and to those of French masters. Not that my solo works are necessarily too hard for me, but they were mostly conceived for other hands with different shapes and more experience.

The five most urgent pianists from my generation (urgent, because they've cared enough about my music to play it) are: Eugene Istomin, a Serkin pupil, who once, while attempting a vibrato on ivory as though it were catgut, said he'd learned as much from Heifetz as from any pianist, and who, in his record of my *War Scenes* with Donald Gramm, proves again that the greatest "accompanists" come from the ranks of great soloists; Leon Fleisher, a Schnabel pupil, who offered the 1950 premières in Paris of my Second Sonata and *Barcarolles* (Shirley Gabis Rhoads gave the first *Moroccan* performance of these), and whose record of the *Barcarolles* is a moral in how underplaying can break the heart; the late Julius Katchen, pupil of Yves Nat, to whom I owe the existence of my Second Concerto, and of the exemplary record of the Second Sonata, and who belied the small-repertory-syndrome of virtuosos by having in his fingers, at a day's notice, any one of thirty recital programs and thirty concertos, and was learning new ones all the time; Jerome Lowenthal (younger than the rest, but a pupil of their colleague, William Kapell), whose blinding disc of my Third Concerto shows his seniors that intellect and fire are the same thing, and whose vision of my chamber works exceeds what composers find (so rarely) merely satisfying.

Who is the fifth pianist? She is a secret.

2.

A hundred and fifty years ago Composer and Performer—hitherto, often as not, the same person—began, for whatever reason, gradually but inexorably to turn their backs on each other so that they now face in opposite directions. That situation is unique to music, the other arts having kept pace with the moment. Books reviewed in this morning's *Times* were published this year; movies showing around town are by definition contemporary; most choreography today is by living persons, and most galleries exhibit mostly living painters. As for theater, "legitimate" and otherwise, it is so regularly the work of active playwrights, that when a drama of O'Neill comes along we speak of a revival. But we do not speak of a Beethoven revival where Beethoven is the rule. Music is the sole art which still hovers over the fading past.

Nineteenth-century repertory which dominates our orchestras looms even more darkly over small instrumental ensembles and piano soloists. Ninety percent of the works of ninety percent of their programs are a century old, while the Bartók quartets and Prokofiev sonatas generally proffered as token modernisms are from fifty to seventy years old. American music is almost nowhere played, even by serious young American virtuosos whose equivalents in the pop world, whatever their worth, quiver with the pulse of the times. That this active malady should forever come as news—bad news—to the pedantically powerful peddlers of musical flesh who presume to know what audiences want is degrading to living composers, on whom it has formed a deep wound.

The wound was temporarily salved for me last summer in Santa Fe where, during an exceptional fortnight, I was a "public guest" of the Chamber Music Festival. Old and new works of mine were maximally rehearsed and glitteringly dispatched by first-rate general practitioners, as distinct from first-rate Modern Music Specialists so often met in academe. I was also displayed, for better or worse, as pianist and speechifier, and surely got as good as I gave. With a kind of morose joy I discovered that general practitioners, no less than the general public, when they think of composers at all, still think of them as in the grave.

My new work, *The Santa Fe Songs*, tailor-made for baritone William Parker and Piano Quartet, was premiered at the festival. One stipulation by the commissioners of this piece was that I myself act as pianist in the first performances. During an Open Discussion Rehearsal for the nonpaying public I announced that although I'm vastly experienced in hearing my music performed and in performing myself as accompanist to singers, I have never, never played with a chamber group. (Whispers of disbelief from the audience.) Turning to my strong-playing colleagues, Ani Kavafian, Heiichiro Ohyama and Timothy Eddy, all vastly experienced themselves, I asked if any of them has ever performed—not coached, but actually played—with a composer. Silence. (More whispers of disbelief.)

In retrospect I realize that the unusual inclusion of a live composer at the Open Rehearsal had seemed, both to the artists and the listeners, so uncoercively logical that I was momentarily regarded less as a talking dog than as a functioning member of the musical community. That such a community in America should be an exception and not a rule is outrageous. That for the Santa Fe Chamber Music Festival it should now be a rule and not an exception suggests that, gradually, Performer and Composer may be turning around to face each other again.

In 1945 when I moved into my first apartment alone (one large room on West Twelfth for $20 a month), Virgil Thomson lent me an antique upright. That piano, like an elderly foster child, had been kicking around among his friends for years; now, five feet high and embellished with a pair of triple-pronged candelabra jutting from the music board, it filled my room. Everything functioned except the E-key a thirteenth below middle C, which did not exist. In 1949 before leaving for Paris I gave the piano (to Virgil's annoyance) to the Salvation Army. During the intervening years all my music was composed in reference to—or, as choreographers say, was made on—this instrument, a series of pre-opus ones which had nothing in common except for a notable lack of low E's. (Coincidentally, my current piano, a mellow Baldwin bought from Earl Wild twelve years ago, is faulty on the same low E.)

Which brings up the question composers hear most often: *Do you compose at the piano?* They react uneasily, since a method is less important than its outcome.

Some composers always use the piano, some use it part-time, some never. To the layman, music being *the* intangible art because it is heard and not seen, the composer's workshop is more intriguing than that of other artists; and there's a vague notion abroad that something's wrong with a musician who composes at the piano, even if the composition is *for* the piano. The notion results from the image of Hollywood Beethovens ambling through fields with the muse and penning inspirations on the spot as full-blown overtures. Yes, music did use to be simpler; harmonic relations were heard by the inner ear without need to confirm them at the keyboard. But today's knottier sonorities aren't dictated by the muse alone. If Britten claimed that the discipline of avoiding a piano sharpens the fancy and precludes superficial solutions to profound conundrums, Stravinsky claimed that it is unmusical to write *away* from the keyboard, for music deals with sound and composers ought always to be in touch with *la matière sonore*.

Now musical composition, though always dealing with sound, does not primarily deal with sound but with the cohesion of ideas eventually expressed through the language of sound. Ideas can occur today in fields as they did yesterday; the difference is that as they seldom occur fully formed their ultimate usefulness might not be ascertained until they are remodeled at the piano. Which doesn't mean a composer rambles over the keys hoping to hit the Lost Chord. It means that once an idea is found, immersion in the sonic element will indicate the natural "tone" of the idea by subjecting the tone to the artifice of form.

Music designed to be played on a piano is certainly more effective when contrived for what that instrument can do. All masters of virtuoso keyboard writing, from Scarlatti through Chopin to Rachmaninoff and Ravel, "realized" their material in keyboard contact. Can you imagine the source of Liszt's glittering fountains as being mere silence?

These aperçus apply to the so-called creative act, not to orchestration. (To the second most-asked question—"Do you do your own orchestration?"— the only answer is: Who else would be more qualified?) Orchestration at the piano makes no sense since it requires extraneous choices of color. Unlike composition, orchestration is a craft that anyone can learn.

It does not follow that to compose "tellingly" for an instrument one must know how to play it; and if composing for a group of instruments there is even less reason since no one can play them all at one time. A musical author is trained to orchestral theory—the physics of sound as pertaining to relationships of balance, weight and hue of various solo or choirs of instruments. He is also trained to write characteristically for individual instruments according to their possible range, their happiest tessitura within this range, their shading potential and dynamic restriction. No one has time to wholly master each instrument and still to compose, while half-mastery inhibits.

Nor does a composer who is a proficient performer necessarily write best for his instrument. Facility in performing, hence in writing gratefully for an instrument, may induce casualness about structure. Meanwhile a composer who does not play a given instrument might happen upon usages that would not have occurred to the specialist. Hindemith, a violist who never composed at the piano, wrote keyboard works which don't sound hard though they don't always "feel right" under the hand. Accidents of instrumental dialect are like the writings of Conrad and Dinesen and Nabokov who, because their native tongues lay elsewhere, lent our language a dimension unimaginable to authors raised in English.

How does it feel to hear your own music?

I'm aware only of what goes wrong, not of what goes right. I'd rather accompany my own songs than sit impotent in the hall; that way I concentrate on the business at hand. I do not feel to be the composer while playing my own music, so am not prey to "composer's nerves."

Nerves apart, composers do have a postpartum elation that other artists don't; their product alone involves a "double emergence": subjective birth through mind to page, objective birth through sound. Indeed, music, like plays, has two existences while visual arts have one; the passive existence on paper with unlimited potential; the active existence in sound which is singular and absolute.

Successful composer-singer teams the past fifty years have been rare and strictly from overseas. Who can you name beyond Britten & Pears from England, or Poulenc & Bernac from France? Is it more than coincidence that Benjamin Britten and Francis Poulenc were the greatest voice composers of our time and also intensely accomplished pianists? If tenor Peter Pears and baritone Pierre Bernac enjoyed careers distinct from their composer-colleagues, still their way with *all* music stemmed from constant truck with these active inventors rather than with "mere" accompanists or, indeed, with mere great pianists. The two *équipes* performed naturally the works of the *maîtres;* and Pears and Bernac each have written the last word on how to interpret, respectively, Britten and Poulenc. (Did Bernac & Poulenc ever perform Britten? I wonder. Did Britten & Pears ever perform Poulenc?) Yet the whole spectrum was fair game for each pair, the mode of execution in Schubert and Debussy and Purcell and Fauré fermenting through the decades into flawless unities.

No American equivalents. Samuel Barber and Leontyne Price were an item for gala moments, mainly at premieres of cycles by Barber for Price. But when they went on the roster of Columbia Artists Management as a duo for sale, they had no bids. (Nor were there buyers for Donald Gramm and me on the same roster ten years later.) *Americans do not know what a composer is.* If they can raise the money for a prima donna, they're not about to waste it on a crank piano player who demands equal billing.

In 1926 Eugene Goossens conducted the first English performance of *Les Noces.* Stravinsky's score is, of course, notable for its four pianos, manned on this historic occasion by four composers: Georges Auric, Francis Poulenc, Vladimir Dukelsky and Vittorio Rieti. Last night I phoned Rieti to ask how it went, fifty-five years ago. "It was a publicity stunt, a bad performance. We had done it pretty well in Paris the week before with Marcelle Meyer instead of Dukelsky on Piano III. When Dukelsky joined us in London it turned out he'd been practicing Piano II, which was my part, but he wasn't quick enough to switch parts, so I took over Piano III, which I hadn't rehearsed, and he played Piano II. The ensemble was shaky, but got better in Belgium when we did it in concert without the ballet. I later played it in Spain with three other composers—Count Chigi, I think, and Nino Rota, and I forget who else."

The piano is Auric's instrument, but he's not a soloist. Poulenc was a soloist, but not an ensemble player. Dukelsky played piano but was not a pianist. Rieti is a pianist in private (he says) but has stage fright. As for the spectacular Marcelle Meyer, she was not a composer but a composer's servant who, like Ricardo Viñes, Jacques Février, Marguerite Long, Wittgenstein, Gieseking, even Arthur Rubinstein, and how many others, specialized in new music during those old gold days. (Have we their parallels? William Masselos, perhaps? Paul Jacobs? Anyone else?) No doubt Madame Meyer single-handedly—or eight-handedly—held the piece together in Paris. Yet one ponders how bad or how revealing the London version actually sounded. Did Stravinsky like it? Years later he himself conducted a recording with four American composers as his pianists: Copland, Barber, Sessions and Foss. Whatever is lost by the disparity of egos is perhaps regained by a sense of homage.

For two hundred years the instrument known as the pianoforte has evolved according to the composer's needs, not the pianist's. If today composer and pianist are generally separate concepts, the "pianism" of a given piece results from the composer's, not the pianist's, ingenuity. No evidence remains of that first notorious *Noces*, but we do possess mementos of still earlier masters. Before he died in 1915 Alexander Scriabin recorded himself (i.e., his own music) with hair-raising precision. "When Scriabin played his Fifth Sonata," wrote Prokofiev, "every note soared. With Rachmaninoff all the notes lay on the ground."

Maurice Ravel, on the other hand, played poorly. Photographs of Ravel's studio display Moreau-like exotica, checkerboard tiling, nonfunctional globes supported by twisting brass snakes, accouterments of the sort Napoleon rifled during his Egyptian campaign and which remained *à la mode* until after the first World War when style turned sparse and "modernistic." Ravel's piano music bridged the period. *Gaspard de la nuit* alone, with its burning sprays and waves of flame, exhibits every shimmering convention of the improvisatory past, yet is "modern" in its economy, with not one note too many. His Tiffany-like structures being compact as marble, it comes as a surprise to hear Ravel's own mushy executions, left hand forever anticipating right hand in the hiccupy manner of, say, Paderewski's *Moonlight* Sonata.

If Ravel's piano music closed the door on nineteenth-century France by funneling all of Liszt into the smallest possible space (as Schoenberg funneled Wagner into a somewhat larger space), Debussy, fourteen years Ravel's senior, opened a door onto the twentieth century with his once-ambiguous harmonies and so-called fragmented forms. Even if composers had the last word on how they should be heard, Debussy's own surviving interpretations are too blurred for much use. Recording in 1902 with Mary Garden he sounds merely remote, and *D'un Cahier d'esquisses* is most memorable for wrong notes. Nevertheless Debussy clearly played his own pieces straighter than Ravel played his. Misty music to sound misty must be played without mist, whereas pristine music to make its point must be played pristinely.

If these "impressionists" seemed to be sabotaging their own music the explanation lies partly in fashion (possibly all nineteenth-century music was played half as fast and half as rigidly), partly in the player-piano rolls from which their performances are transcribed. But what of a living master like Messiaen whose performance refutes his notation? A two-piano recital with his wife, the expert Yvonne Loriod, is like Beauty and the Beast, so oblivious is his account and so accurate is hers of the intricate rhythmic patterns engraved on the page. And I have seen Virgil Thomson raise his hands over the keyboard and let them fall with great authority on all the wrong notes. These men are not out to undermine themselves, they are playing what they heard while composing. Their music is on the paper, not in the performance, and although they have a right to play it as they wish no professional would think of imitating them.

Still, one always learns from a composer at the piano, especially when he's playing someone else's music. He is less maniacal than "real" pianists about the technique of trills, and about historical truth (which is never true and never historical). Hence he gets to the quick more quickly—speaks, so to speak, with colleagues long gone. Virgil's version of Mozart's K.330 is a primer in human relationships, the inevitable *vocality* so rife in Mozart's piano pieces coming immediately to the fore.

If sometimes composers' bloopers exude more authority than "real" pianists' accuracy, while "real" pianists play subtler accompaniments than professional accompanists, nothing is more rewarding than a composer who is also a real pianist accompanying other composers' songs. Listen to the discs of Jennie Tourel "supported" by Leonard Bernstein and savor the sense of each song's skeleton. Bernstein is deferential without being cowed, acting the piano's role with a composer's knowledge, not with the soft-pedal furtiveness of an illegal alien.

A composer is often pestered with "Come on, play us your symphony," and when he explains that his symphony was not conceived for the piano, and that anyway he doesn't recall how it goes, there's a bemused reply: "You wrote it, so you of all people should know it." But on completing one piece he leaves it to begin another. It's his interpreter's job to master the problems, memorize the notes. Composition and execution, though not mutually exclusive, do not go hand in hand. Some fine composers do not play any instrument competently. The true virtuoso-composer really has two professions: he must sit down and *learn* his own music as he learns anyone else's, by practicing.

The piano is the least expressive of all musical instruments, and the most popular.

Insofar as expressivity is measured in ratio to the human voice (that vibrating primal force and ultimate criterion) the piano, by way of all media—bowed, blown and banged—is as far from a soprano as you can get. Even a kettledrum with its intrinsic quiver resembles a singer. (I discount the non-pitched percussion which, though probably as old as, and surely the original supporters of, organized chant, are today mainly decorative.)

Insofar as its popularity rests on the potential for being complete unto itself, the piano is second to no contraption, even the guitar, in being all things to all musical men. More than any single instrument it contains means for rich harmony, counterpoint, rhythmic variety and color complexity. Only the violin supersedes it in melody, but lacks the dynamic range. The piano is the most useful of instruments because it can *counterfeit* expressivity, thanks to its pedal facilities, and because it can emit any number of notes up to eighty-eight at one time. That is why composers work it as a tool, and why of all solo vehicles it has the widest first-class literature.

Nevertheless, America today, unlike Europe of yesterday, is a land of specialists in music as in all else.

Composers who are also pianists? At random, a few: Leon Kirchner, Robert Helps, David Del Tredici, Charles Wuorinen, Lukas Foss. They all play their own music dazzlingly, as well as that of contemporaries. I can think of but one—Lee Hoiby—who feels compelled to specialize, as Rachmaninoff did, in standard fare.

Pianists who are also composers? At random, fewer: Glenn Gould, William Bolcom, Leo Smit, Noël Lee, each no less serious than their predecessors Busoni, Schnabel, Casadesus, Steuermann.

Francis Thorne has earned his living as a barroom pianist, like Erik Satie of yore. Other composers, other instruments. David Diamond has worked as a violinist; David Amram as a french horn player; Barbara Kolb as a clarinetist; Daniel Pinkham as an organist; Lou Harrison as a sitarist, not to mention tack-pianist and any number of Korean instruments including jade flute; Conlon Nancarrow as confectioner of études for piano rolls to be inserted into the old-fashioned player piano, études too elaborate for living hands; Harry Partch and Lucia Dlugoszewski as players on instruments of their own manufacture, instruments never before seen on earth.

But your average American composer—if there is such a thing—gets along as a normal pianist, and will even accompany his songs if called upon. George Perle and Miriam Gideon, Jack Beeson and Hugo Weisgall, do not as public pianists betray the products of their private selves. At the same time they do not have the souls of hams, the extrovert-introvert flamboyant reticence of a Gershwin who, it could be argued, was at once the most "modern" musician of his era and the last of a race of full-time composer-pianists.

A note on notation. Unlike the painter's action which produces an absolute product, transcription of musical ideas from mind to paper is only approximate. Which is why there are as many interpretations of a given work as there are interpreters; why composers themselves, even the most accomplished, veer from the text; and why, according to trends, pieces are played faster or slower or stricter or freer. The simpler the music, the harder to notate; there is more variance in Haydn-playing than in Schoenberg. Metronome marks don't help much, except in practicing. The only precise tempo indication is *presto possibile*. The vaguest is *con moto*. Meanwhile the Mona Lisa smiles unchanging through the centuries.

Long ago Lou Harrison picked up some money working on a jazz book for author Rudi Blesh. Lou's job was to notate for posterity the rags of Jelly Roll Morton by listening to old records and writing down what he heard. Since Jelly Roll never played the same piece the same way, Lou wrote down only the passing version captured on disc. Now jazz, as everyone knows, is rhythmically rigid, its nature emerging from—being defined by—how much freedom a soloist (or a right hand) dares, while still jibing within the measure (or with the left hand). Lou's transcriptions of this music, so easy to listen to, looked as elaborate as Stockhausen, and would have been impossible to play except by piano roll, never by Jelly Roll.

In 1948 I was interviewed by Alfred Kinsey (and so, later, were my parents; when he could, Kinsey liked to keep it in the family). He was plotting a book on the sexuality of the artist. After the interview we had an off-the-record chat about other musicians, in particular and as a breed. I offered my considered opinion about the penchants of male, as opposed to female, pianists, concert tenors as opposed to operatic baritones and as distinct from pop singers of both sexes, solo string players versus orchestral string players, drummers and harpists versus choristers and organists. But I could absolutely not formalize about the sexual makeup of composers. Now, thirty years later, I still cannot. The sexuality of performers, however, remains fairly predictable if not identical to the old days. Kinsey never completed the book. But just as his treatise on The Human Male should have been specified as The Human *American* Male, so his new book should have been named The Sexual Life of the American Artist. I was to discover that just as *genus homo* was sexually another species abroad than at home, so *genus musicalis* followed other patterns in Europe (where, for example, organists are mainly heterosexual). The sexual life of human pianists—are there other kinds?—is varied enough today to inspire an essay of its own.

The ugly turn beautiful while playing the piano, the drab become desirable, as though lit by a halo or hit by Cupid's arrow. But only momentarily. When they stop, they revert. The beauty, the carnality oozing from an artist at work is due to concentration on something not himself. The concentration is the one refuge from ego, from the mask, from the hurly-burly, and is never visible on the face of a mere audience which displays the stupor of ecstasy or of boredom. Not that geniuses in their daily lives are selfless. Heaven forbid that they be loving and sweet like everyone else! But the *act* of genius is selfless. And so is the act of interpreting genius, which ironically is more often found with amateurs in the parlor than with virtuosos in the concert hall.

New York, January 1981

OF VANITY

For months the tub faucet has leaked with a fragile steady flow finally forming an ineradicable brownish path through the porcelain. Sadness seeps from the spout, oozing there always, whether anyone's home or not. Yet I am unable to summon Manuel with his inexpert tools and recalcitrant Puerto Rican sass. The leak, like the poetic gladiator's slow and wasted hemorrhage, chides me for increasingly sloppy habits. Facts of life leak all over every day yet I'm no longer drawn to channel them quaintly, through prose or notes, so they streak down shapeless to the sea and are absorbed. Yet what's there to record? Brown leaves swirling in Central Park are now too much, while even Mozart and Ravel are now not enough. Nor do I in aging any longer *understand* our so-called finer stuff. I mean this literally. Hoping to model a new piece on "Sunday Morning" I've mulled the Stevens poem for hours, but can't begin to comprehend a single verse, a single image, while both Father and JH after one reading proffer their legitimate *comptes rendus*. Or Sondheim's simple "Send in the Clowns," so plaintive and evocative as a whole, in detail eludes me: what do those figures relate to? who are these people? why do average listeners nod knowingly while I stay in a cloud? All meaning and value and nuance of love and art and casual life escape uninterpreted through extravagant space, while one rude word from the checkout girl at the A&P can wreck my day.

People as they get older seem to ask themselves why they are alive. But more and more I know—feel—why I'm alive; the knowing is the feeling. Admittedly the life, by my own arranging, is ever more fenced in; I shy clear of the unpredictable adventure. No longer like young Narcissus do I contemplate the still pond, but like a castrated satyr catch the reflection in a rushing brook. That image stays fixed. Could the brook drag it rippling away? Oh, now I see: the brook's what the pond was: the ripples are wrinkles, the bottom's eroded, and yes, the face stays put, while all this flow is so fresh, so fresh. (The mirror becomes Narcissus's pool, so absorbed in reflection it stagnates in lovesickness and grows immune to medicine. Otherwise stated: message supplants catharsis, idea precedes style, and we live in a most Romantic Age.)

Visit from a youngish reporter planning a biography of Truman Capote.

32

Disconcerting, the number of years and anecdotes surrounding my tangential acquaintance with that unsatisfactory author, from our first cool meeting with Jane and Paul Bowles in Tangier in 1949, through hectic Paris evenings that autumn, then in New York, then France again with Jack Dunphy in further seasons, and the ballet *Early Voyagers* with Valerie Bettis, to the last ugly contact in 1968. Today Truman's is a name uttered in hushed tones by the likes of Cher and Johnny Carson: he's the poor man's thinker, *le savant des pauvres* who are mostly quite rich. Not that the real intelligentsia is contemptuous, they just have nothing left to say. Truman sold his talent for a mess of pottage. (When later I tell JH how disconcerting it was to dredge up the past, he snorts, "The past? You have no past—you sold it for a mess of pottage.")

Question of ethics: Should a living subject of biography be paid? Should people being interviewed be paid? The biographer, after all, gets a fat advance and the publisher stands to make millions off the exploited subject. But we who were there did all the work.

(The first time I ever saw Marie Laure, months before actually meeting her, I was in the Pont Royale bar with Truman Capote who waved to her sitting across the room with a redhaired fellow who later turned out to be Tom Keogh. Recalling this today makes me feel warmly toward T.C.)

At X's party this afternoon a young Apollo comes up and declares: "I'm a poet." Is it wrong to smile? The announcement seems so somehow superfluous.

Thirty-two years ago, at one of Bu Faulkner's gin-soaked bashes in a featureless room of the Chelsea, I approached John Latouche with the words: "I'm Virgil's copyist, and I just made the parts for his Second String Quartet which is dedicated to you." "Really?" said John. "I didn't know people who looked like you ever did anything."

Frank O'Hara, telling about his first visit to Auden, described a sty with intimidated kids at the great man's feet. He whom Chester Kallman called Miss Master, smelling peculiar and four sheets to the wind, at one point quashed a brash quipster by saying: "You've got to be an Auden to get away with that remark." An Auden! thought Frank, gazing at the poet whose bourbon dribbled from an unshaved chin onto a maculate tie, from there into his lap, and thence down to his humid socks.

Sometimes when least aware of how we look we're told how well we look. The compliment's appreciated, one is grateful for the unexpected. We're at our most interesting when least conscious of appearance.

Beauty is never unaware of itself. Italians, so vain, are also so fair. Contradictorily, once they're dressed up and raring to go, knowing themselves fair, they concentrate on *you*. Young Americans today are unlovely moving as they do in collective anonymity, yet concentrating on just themselves.

The above re-emphasized: All young people are beautiful except those who think they are. That statement's probably false. Beauty, like intelligence, is never unaware of itself; good features are good features, facts. But a beautiful expression is (sometimes) unconscious, and we are often complimented on how well we look when we think we're at our worst. Naturally some stupid people think they're intelligent, but nobody intelligent thinks he's stupid. Detectable are those, both stupid and unlovely, who sit around looking intelligent and lovely.

Any poor, ugly or stingy person can imagine himself as rich, pretty or generous; but it is impossible, claims Auden, to imagine oneself as either more or less imaginative than, in fact, one is. "A man whose every thought was commonplace could never know this to be the case." (*The Dyer's Hand*, p. 97.) Now, almost anyone who reads that will agree, and in agreeing will place himself among those who do not have commonplace thoughts.

I cannot concur. I have never had an uncommon thought. I state this with neither fake humility nor a wish to seem quaint. I know—as far as anyone can, according to Auden's claim—that my every thought is banal. Being intelligent (am I?), I suffer from this, and in swiping uncommonplace thoughts from others (such as Auden) I fool some people some of the time while knowing in my heart I'll go to the grave as a mediocre thinker, perhaps even with a mediocre heart.

But can a person's music—his talent, gift, "creative" genius—follow this pattern? Have there been great creators with so-so intellects? (Certain great interpreters, like chessplayers—Toscanini and Bobby Fischer, for example—would seem to be infants when off duty.) Art renders the obvious unique, and in turn renders the unique contagious. Art is a healthy disease.

My logical instincts as a composer sometimes clash with Auden's uncommonplace ideas about music. For instance, his notion (not all that uncommonplace) that film music "is bad film music if we become consciously aware of its existence" is refutable. Such music is not "bad," it's just not film music according to the function assigned it by Auden. No musician in the audience will ever be unaware of film music, no matter how "good" it is. Elsewhere Auden tumbles into the comparison trap, dangerous where the arts are concerned whether the comparison be of likenesses or distinctions. (There are seven arts precisely because they fill seven needs; if the arts could express each other we'd need only one.) Auden shows the difference between ear and eye by demonstrating the difference between motion in what he calls musical space and visual space. "An increase in the tension of the vocal cords is conceived in musical space as a going 'up,' a relaxation as a going 'down,'" says the poet, and continues: "But in visual space it is the bottom of the picture (which is also the foreground) which is felt as the region of greatest pressure and, as this rises up in the picture, it feels an increasing sense of lightness and freedom. The association of tension in hearing with up and seeing with down seems to correspond with the difference between our experience of the force of gravity in our own bodies and our experience of it in other bodies." Etcetera. No musician could have spun such words. The bass is as much a weighted foundation in music as in painting. The lowest-sounding strings on fiddle and guitar are the highest placed. Are sopranos, by virtue of being on top of the basses, performing the male's sexual role, or do they emerge from down under and rise toward heaven? In which case, doesn't their very lightness, their lack of tension, allow them to float upward? Meanwhile, in the visual, who agrees that the bottom is pressure? Is the acrobat hurled from above, or sucked from below?

Auden elsewhere and often is the canniest layman I've ever read on music, and then he becomes an Auden.

I never mean literally what I say, including this sentence.

Having met Elizabeth Hardwick at a party and very much felt a reciprocal rapport, I phoned to invite her over next Saturday. Without the slightest pause she said, "I couldn't possibly, I've much too much work." She proceeded genteelly to talk about the work, and filled out our conversation with this and that, but didn't mention a raincheck. Such a rebuff can set me back years, to when I wasn't accepted by "popular" classmates. But their rejection was in favor of their own sporty gorgeousness as against my eggheaded effeteness, while Hardwick and I are theoretically cut from the same cloth. That she should consider me a lesser cut cast an unredeeming shadow across the afternoon.
Obsequies as social: I'll go to your funeral if you go to mine.

The reason that good movies aren't often made from good books (or that, when both are good, they don't contain the same *kind* of goodness, and the author's first smell isn't brought to the film) is not that movies are condensed, condescending, unfaithful or vulgar. It's that books feed our personal imagination while movies do not. Thus the Absolute General (Josef K. or Everyman) can only disappoint when materialized since we've already envisaged him as ourself, and the Absolute Particular (Jesus C. or Charlus) can only shock, since we've already visualized him as himself.

Is there the phenomenon of pretending to live, as opposed to living? Who dares define it? An example: Robert de Montesquiou (model for Charlus) whose biographer, the canny (and now late) Philippe Jullian, wrote: "The anguish of being forgotten which haunted the poet's last years is that of a man who, instead of living, has given a good performance," and went on to equate living with participating (mainly in love and sex) rather than observing two-dimensionally. Now, who can prove that participator is more vital than spectator? and what indeed is participation? Is listener more passive than player? It takes two to tango. Everything alive *wants* to exist, even the iridescent orchid or amoeba, even the suicide in midair.
One does know what Jullian means. Life can seem over before it's over, when quips fall flat, flesh decays, and trends of the day pass you by. Still, can he show that life is less acute, less "real," in the idiot's focus on a birdsong than in Einstein's focus on . . . Life is no prelude, but a contrast, to death. Life is no defined activity. Life is life.
I'm now old enough, but perhaps you are not, to observe my own baby pictures as period pieces: those long nightgowns and bunting caps and sepia-toned smiles all chubbily posed. Similarly, looking back—*hearing* back—to my first French years with Marie Laure, there was a certain tonality, a phraseology, in the uppercrust male voice (hetero as well as homosexual) that was rarefied and raspish, fusing high-class English R's with French lisps. Cocteau had it, and Charles de Noailles, and they heard it from Proust and

maybe from Montesquiou. Who talks that way now? How the generations shift, substitute for each other, and have no reference, beyond perhaps quality, for goodness or badness of interpretation! The work itself (by Bach, say, or Tolstoy, or even Picasso) may be fixed, impermeable, but our viewpoint ever fluxes. My God! if I can't know what your green is, or your way of hearing ninth chords—and you're right here beside me—how much less would I know how Bach wants himself played. Not, surely, worshipfully. What stays? Does greatness stay? If viewpoint swerves, how can that *about* which we have viewpoint not also swerve? Who says Bach's so great?

How could a movie of Proust be anything but small? Pinter's screenplay is in itself the finished work of art. But understatement is not an American gift. Whether dealing with whales or the human heart our literature has always been outsize. Our pictures too, especially ones about nature, incline to editorialize. It's hard for anyone to let a sunset speak for itself. And Americans are literal: big things they make bigger, small things smaller. But with the 1930s came the subtle shove of France. If the inherently little, as given (through enlargement) new dimensions of horror in the dolls of Balthus, has influenced the foodstuffs of a Roy Lichtenstein, then the inherently huge, as given (through reduction) a new sense of wonder in the townscapes of Jean Hugo, has influenced the landscapes of a Wesley Wehr.

(I shan't pursue this unstable course, it's forced. Americans have always made miniatures, while Europeans invented *the fact of size* with all those cathedrals. True, certain Americans like Brion Gysin—he's Canadian, actually—paint the whole Sahara on a six-by-nine-inch canvas, while Alfonso Ossorio—he's Filipino, originally—paints microbes on a six-by-nine-*foot* canvas.)

How many angels dance on the head of a pin? Twelve, said Thaddeus. Twelve trillion, said Theobald. Thaddeus was wined, dined and sainted for his piety. Theobald was burned alive for his presumption.

If I grind axes as a composer in the world, as a composer composing I do not. In composition I've no method, have invented naught, have offered to the earth no *means* for producing; indeed, I allow myself to produce according to that most dangerous of all means: tailored impulse. Neither leader nor follower nor textbook maker, I am judged only as good or bad, not by whether through learned exegesis I conform to my own graphic system. Since critics don't know bad from good, they have difficulty assessing, much less (and this is the critic's chief chore) describing, me.

Ives, whom I despise, has in form if not in texture very much influenced me.

All writing, first and foremost, evokes. Some bad writing draws forth a "How true" while some good draws false conclusions. But the false and true are reactions to what the writing evokes of our own—not the writer's—experience. Scanning Susan Sontag's last photography essay, I read: "The primitive notion of the efficacy of images presumes that images possess the qualities of real things, but our inclination is to attribute to real things the qualities of an image."

*

Darius Milhaud in the late 1960s, although humorous and alert in his wheelchair, had long since given up on medicine. Milhaud's current consultant, a sort of diviner, was able by means of a scanning rod to examine a group photo in the day's paper and determine not only who among those featured had what disease, but even diagnose those (unseen at the extreme right or left) who had been cropped from the portrait. He did stress that the picture had not only to be recent (the image of a person now dead was useless) but reproduced by a small-circulation press (the more editions or replicas, the more evanescent the subject's "readable" specter).

Swing Band men of the thirties were famed through recordings. When hired for a hotel dance they felt obliged to recheck their own discs and to imitate by rote their recorded improvisations, so that the college kids would not feel cheated by living variations.

". . . our reluctance to tear up or throw away the photograph of a loved one, especially of someone dead or far away." Aren't we equally reluctant to throw out letters, or books, or quilts or locks of hair? Yet we do—and are instantly less bereft, more secure in what we call our memories.

One page of Susan elicits this page from me. If her evocations in themselves are not particularly sentimental, the reactions they call up, at least in me, are strong, and that is good for us both.

Cruelty in the name of truth, serpentine candor entwines the pillars of society. To tell someone (whether or not "for his own good") that someone else has slandered him, or that his nose is grotesque, or that his sister is a dyke (which maybe he never knew), is to relate facts (when in fact these are only facts), not truth. Fact is the odd side of fiction, while truth is the odd side of lie. A fact is not necessarily necessary; even truth need be called up only to set a fiction straight, when that fiction has been uselessly disruptive.

The contempt I can feel for even my closest friends.

Most of what we think about each other we don't say. Curiosity, hostility, lust, those suggestions "for his own good," or above all, boredom—these impulses, with the years, are kept more or less consciously quiescent, while amenities increasingly satisfy. The surface delight of regarding those bright persimmons on that deep blue plate, of regarding them with or without you, seems more urgent than falling in love again, or than working for justice in the world. Do I want to know you better? There is no better.

JH explains that suicide by throat-slashing results in an instinctive but vain attempt to rejoin the severed arteries gushing and then flowing and then dripping slowly, for months, like the bathtub faucet, eroding forever. The fact of Paris today: there's no point of reference (except the defunct past) in all these so-familiar lanes that yell for recognition.

On Dick Cavett's show Truman Capote, looking like that extraterrestrial embryo from the end of *Close Encounters*, posits the same defense of his upcoming nonbook as he posited last year and the year before: "Well, Marcel Proust did the very same thing." One might quickly reply: Yes, and so did Hedda Hopper. Every writer—or interpreter or conversationalist or archeologue (to avoid the word artist)—depicts reaction to milieu; there is literally no other material to work with, on or off the earth.

And what makes Earth turn?

Dream of an insomniac. Earth grinds to a halt. Peering now through his closed window as through a lens, he perceives that the world outside has stopped. Not stopped merely as in a photograph (in this case caught on the window's retina), for the immobile subject of a picture, while being scrutinized, still exists in time; but stopped utterly, the inanimate stopped, and the numberless molecules revolving at infinite speeds have also ceased to budge. The world's frozen in time. Except for him. He remains free to pace the interior of this fractured moment, to observe from his perch the gelatinized pedestrians, mouths half-opened on an unfinished verb, stopped, all stopped in this split second and caught forever in transparent lava.

He draws back from the window. With the hesitant élan of one who has made a distasteful choice and now must see it through, he lies flat as upon an auction block, fully clothed, and starts to onanize. From a swamp of thorns growing sadly desperate like the Leaning Tower of Pisa stuffed with the steaming custard of the sort they used to serve in kindergarten, friction begins slowly, mouth closing, opening, closing, descending along that female beach like a pear-colored peach, a hot Saint Bernard, a scorched leaf. Heated by his own blood, he does not increase, but as though caught on a fishhook moves his sweaty head from side to side, and tears gush.

Suddenly his fantasies are deflected by the breeze of an angel's wing, a memory of magic: here I am in my prime, with maybe just a few more months. The thought excites him so that a smoking liter of bloody mucus spurts all off-white toward the dark hairs of his belly like infected buttermilk. Silence.

Silence as in the subway. Stock still, mummified on the bed.

Now the fragile room quivers, so slightly. As in a swoon he turns his head again, only his fevered head softly, and gazes toward the open window more dejected than ever in his shortish life. From outside a spring wind brings sounds of forsythia blooming, the chirp of sparrows, the tingle of Good Humor wagons mingling with giggles of faraway children playing hopscotch on the wet pavement. Then softly he stirs his body through the sheets and closes his eyes, as the world gradually begins to move again.

Not intellect but sex, however paltry, in its thorough self-interest, makes the world go round.

Having now culled these presumably random but actually oh so alike posies from a diary of the last three years, I'd be tempted to beribbon the garland as "vanity" did that not apply finally to any collection, to any art, to indeed any effort by Caligula or Karl Marx, from childbirth to war, because, as the Preacher saith, all is. Not truly all perhaps, for beasts aren't vain—not in either sense of futile or conceited under the sun. Vanity is the paper-thin placenta of civilization that protects us awful humans, with a delicate transience, against the mad logic of the sky beyond the sun.

1978

BEING READY

"What on earth are we going to tell them?" I ask Russell Oberlin, the famed countertenor, as we gather with colleagues at one of those benighted roundtables. Tonight's subject, to abet young hopefuls in the hall who will model themselves on us, is: To What Do You Owe Your Success?

"God knows," said Russell. "I've always had it easy—but we're not supposed to tell them that. From the instant I began as a choirboy everyone knew I was good. I've never had to pull strings. But have I been successful? Does anyone think of himself as that?"

It's been sort of the same with me. Had I not been encouraged from the start (encouraged not with love but with performances, commissions, reviews), I could never have persevered. Even today, if a month passes with no evidence that I am admired, I want to throw in the sponge.

Beginners do like recipes. But with so-called creators, by definition (or non-definition), each case provides its own recipe. What worked for us might not work for you. All one can suggest is: Move to New York, know the right people, and your talent, if you have any, just may help you.

My musical background is one of inversion, the earliest exposure having been, by some happy error, to the sounds of my time. In early adolescence I owned complete catalogues of Griffes and Harris and Carpenter and Copland (not to mention Ravel and Stravinsky), yet knew no note of Beethoven nor even Tchaikovsky. I had to accustom myself—indeed, brace myself—to classics, as others, from duty, attend to what they call "moderns." Since in matters artistic the rugged American grain still runs toward the European past rather than the local present, my stance was quite unpatriotic. Yet in all centuries but ours musical standards were everywhere based on the contemporary. Which is as it should be. Music most comprehensible to people of today is music of today because it is penetrated by today, and literally no one can fail to perceive this on some level. Today's music may feel hard because it lives, and life is hard. But the hardness speaks, even when we don't like what it says, while the classics drift forward with the pacifying mutism of cadavers. We can know the past only through current interpretations which change each day. The static known is judged by the fluid unknown.

39

My greatest thrills were my youngest thrills: seeing Mary Wigman dance when I was ten, discovering *Le Sacre* at eleven, reading Gide at twelve, falling in love for the first time at thirteen, dying of a broken heart at fourteen. I have never been more ready. Life ever after has been spent in trying to reanimate, and to skewer with a five-pronged staff, those moments that made my hair stand on end.

Do not judge others by yourself.
Then by whom shall I judge them?
Don't judge at all.
Right. I'll condemn.

How would you introduce a novice to modern music?
By playing it.
What pieces would you have him listen to?
Those to which his curiosity draws him. If the lust isn't there, chuck the whole matter. Who says we must all love music, or presumes with biased conjecture that the unmusical are missing something? James and Kafka and Picasso despaired of music, yet were not slouches any more than the entire Surrealist Party which categorically banned the sonic art.
How should children learn about music?
By being taught to compose in the nursery. If infants were given the basics of musical notation, along with shaping mudpies and rhyming cat with rat, their parents would stop asking the composer (on those mythic occasions when they meet fact to face) how he hears all those notes in his head. They don't ask the painter where he finds an image, or an author where he finds a plot—because they too have their images and plots.

On Being Ready

Rehearsing with Donald Gramm for our Texas recital I'm dismayed at how much worse I play than during our concerts two years ago; even then I played less well than for our recording fifteen years ago. Yet the repertory is the same. Of course, you must run ever faster to stay in one place, and I do practice less. Still, not only my brain but my hands now forget how to hit the right note with the right tone at the right time.

Practice may make perfect (oh dull perfection!), but overpractice makes stale. Interpretation does not with the years automatically improve, grow more right, more "telling." Serkin's recital last night was a freak show of swollen detail, of fragment construed as monument, each purling droplet so lovingly traumatized that no further flow was permissible. Serkin has the Midas touch, alas. Age, with a healthily advancing artist, simplifies complexity.

Teachers so often admonish: Don't touch this until you're ready. (When are you ready? Suppose you die first?) Students who technically play rings around their teacher concur: The notes aren't tough, but oh, those profundities! We dare not yet tackle this. (The "this" is inevitably Beethoven, never Poulenc.) Awe of the deep past knows no bounds.

Now, maturity does not come with maturity. Maturity is here, you have it or don't. Unready at twenty means unready too at fifty. Progress in itself is not always positive. Disease progresses.

"How," loadedly asks Rudolf Serkin of the young pianist, "is your *Waldstein* coming?"

"I think I've finally got it under control."

"Really? I've been playing it all my life and still don't have it under control."

Young player, learn this: If you're the real thing, you're real now. You'll spend the next six decades treading water in the fountain of youth. Are there any first-rate eighty-year-olds who weren't first-rate at twenty? And how many virtuosos augment their repertory after they've made it big? Master everything today, think it out tomorrow.

October 1952. Hugues Cuénod and I have a date to record some songs of mine, which he's never seen, at Vose Greenough's studio. "Let's sight-read the first take," suggests Hugues, "and see what happens." The ensuing performance turns out better than all further takes. Nervous tension, intelligence, métier, seizing the nature of the moment, these cut through detailed years of study like the sword of Perseus.

Practice makes imperfect.

Until a hundred years ago the composer was mostly his own performer. Today not only do creator and interpreter face opposite horizons, they seldom meet—mainly because the interpreter is busy interpreting composers of a hundred years ago.

One summer I was Token Composer at Marlboro, that Edenic site in the heart of Waspland staked out by Rudolf Serkin and some fourscore nonpaying guests, successful heterosexual Jewish instrumentalists under thirty practicing on nineteenth-century German scores. At a public recital a token piece of mine was played. Later at The Party young Peter Serkin, whom I'd never met, failed to react either to my music or to my person. Since he's more than a merely adroit executant, though not quite dripping with whimsy, I tried all sorts of chitchat but got no rise. Desperate, I resorted to crossing the crowded room by walking on my hands, the one thing I can do that nobody else can. He melted.

Voici les moeurs du meilleur monde.

Language

Où se trouvent les toilettes? These are the first words the infallible John Simon spoke to me, after introducing himself in the waiting room at La Guardia where we were to catch the same plane. Now *toilette,* of course, means attire; what Simon meant was *lavabos.* Such are the false friends grammars speak of. Words resembling English are always weaker in their French context. *Malicieux* means sly, *sinistre* means dreary, *formidable* means swell, as does *chic* which never means chic.

We were seeking the adjectival equivalent for *evil* in French, and concluded it doesn't exist. *Mauvais* and *méchant* may refer to a rotten fruit or a nasty kid, but not, theologically, to wickedness. To declare someone evil one must use the noun. *Il est le mal*. Francine wondered if there were any one person about whom we might say that. I thought for a while, then brought out: *Boulez c'est le mal*. Through charm and guile and force and intellect Boulez has brainwashed two generations, setting back, not forth, the state of music.

American première of *Pli selon pli*. During the entr'acte there again rose that sacred buzz which has continued for days in some circles, though not in mine, to the effect that we were present at the biggest event since *Le Sacre*. Actually Boulez's "plea" now sounds like what it precisely is: smallish, easy on the ears, the sole example of what has emerged in an unbroken stream from so-called French Impressionism. The highlighting and lowlighting of color, yes color, is not, as with Stravinsky, a mere offshoot of Debussy but a continuation of Debussy.

For three decades I've thought of Boulez as my contrary in that he was order & ice while I was heat & folly. But the contrariness is contrary to that. Ironically he is the sensual one, though never never sad. I could not, for example, give in to paraphernalian exotica, wind chimes and kotos and bells and Chinese cymbals and that whole family of hammered keyboards like marimbas and vibraharps and such, which Boulez seems partial to. Being the dance, I dread being known for the dancer. He speaks a lush tongue for the serene statement; my language is pared, the result opulent.

Language is a system of symbols about specifics. Whether *tree* or *last* or *when* conjure up the same images for all, we all agree on how to use them. Music would seem to fit that definition, except music's symbols are not of specifics; indeed, they represent nothing—they themselves are the end sought. Music is said to conjure up images *different* to us all.

Because writing is something everyone learns, many an amateur effort is as historically secure as the professional—Madame de Sévigné, Emily Dickinson, letters and poems of prisoners and children. Musical composition is not something we all learn. There has never been an amateur composer of any interest. The prose of composers ranks high: Wagner, Debussy, Virgil Thomson, Paul Bowles. The composition of non-specialists falls flat: Lionel Barrymore, Benjamin Franklin, Ezra Pound, Adolf Hitler.

When Francine called Jane Bowles a minor writer, she seemed surprised when I said that, by and large, I prefer minor art to major art—that I have more *need* for, say, Fauré than for Schumann, while admitting that Schumann dug deeper. It seemed never to have occurred to Francine (any more than to up and coming Freshmen) that so-called secondary artists could be more satisfying than those making the Big Statement. Of course, my examples were frail; how can one argue two composers of such different time and place? And maybe I am missing something. But don't we all miss something by not being each other? Still, in art the Big Statement is ofttimes a political blinder.

(Did Schumann dig deeper?)

Charm

What's missing from his pictures? I ask as we leave X's vernissage. Without missing a beat JH answers Charm. Well yes, I guess so, though Beethoven made it big without charm. Ah, but Beethoven *did* have charm, rustic and pompous though he sometimes seemed.

Charm alone cannot a masterpiece make, as witness nineteenth-century French music. Yet to a very real extent there exists no big work that lacks charm. That is precisely why Kafka is great where Borges is not, Mahler is great where Bruckner is not, Manet is great where Courbet is not. (Find your own examples. Mine may weaken the argument for you—you who find Borges charming.)

With Barbara Kolb to rehearsal of Thea Musgrave's new opera. Barbara's not one for lenience toward a sister; spite splays forth like shrapnel at the least whisper of other female composers. Before the lights dim Miss Musgrave, who will conduct her own work, enters the pit and begins informally to go over a few thorny measures with the orchestra. Twelve seconds later Barbara declares: "I can't bear it, it's all sound effect, no trace of tune, no sense of theater, she's only here because she's foreign and a woman, I'm leaving." "But Barbara, she's only sketching backgrounds. After the curtain rises, you'll see: solo human voices will sing pretty lines against these colors." In fact, after the curtain rose, the colors leaked, discoloring all, and the pretty lines never did emerge. We both left at intermission.

An hour with Twyla Tharp on Public Television—not, I trust, a wasted hour, since the next three sentences derive from the program. Tharp's dancers, and she herself, all do the same thing: the goofy loose-jointed slurred rag-doll shake. And they all do only that, they do it all the time, always the same way. Tharp's dancing is all about charm, though she herself has none.

Similarly Musgrave's opera is all about mystery, though her music is open and flat.

A commissioner, to whom I send a progress report describing the piece as a divertissement, replies: ". . . divertissement seems to indicate something frothy, light, charming. Jeanne's performance fortes [the work is a Double Concerto for cello and piano, to be played by him and his wife] are poetry, elegance, liquidity, nuance, color, insight and dramatic power. I am serious, emotionally profound—although, alas, not sufficiently profound intellectually—and I am most comfortable with material of substance. Do we have a problem here?"

JH advises me simply to change the title to *Concerto Profundo*, since the commissioner and I, though perhaps musically sympathetic, don't speak the same English, and since music (which is never too vague for words, but always too precise) only "means" whatever the composer tells you, in words, that it means. Meanwhile, what's wrong with froth, light, charm? Emotional profundity is for sophomore bull sessions. Since everyone imagines himself to be emotionally profound, conscious frivolity, i.e., comedy (which, at its most "profound," comes only through, and thus comprises, tragedy), is what must be cultivated. Depth is there, or it isn't, but it can't be bought.

Make an essay on the virtues of superficiality, on whether art cannot be snared and frozen in a sad clean ray of red light or in a tight flock of feathers as well as in a Greco crucifixion or in a Bach mass. No one's glibber than he who sees forever deep. Tragedy examines two sides of one mask, but comedy examines three.

Re frivolity. This moment—the *value* of it—can never come again, whether it be savoring a lime sherbet in Piazza Navona at sundown as we gaze into each other's features, or learning the horrors steaming on Three Mile Island. The star of an Antonioni movie is not the groaning heroine but the waving trees.

Learning

Ever so rarely performers turn around to face composers, seeking advice from the horse's mouth. What to answer them! It's all there on the staff. Teachers know, composers know how. But if composers could explicate their music they'd be authors, not musicians.

Good performers don't need coaching. When they're bad no coaching helps. Good ones have shown *me* a thing or two about points I've missed. Bad ones forever miss the point. Good ones can't "save" bad music, they bring out the badness in gold relief. Bad ones make even good music sound bad, but the badness is blamed on the composer.

Once in my nervousness, like many an oaf, I started clapping before the piece was over—and the piece was my own.

The composer-as-teacher runs a danger. Teachers repeat themselves. After the first year they not only believe what they say, they believe *in* what they say, so they say forever the same thing. Nice for the syllabus, not for a sonata. And the compulsory magnanimity, dealing with other people's music, encroaches on the composer's solitude—his leisure to work. The composer-as-teacher is effective only when being just a composer, an example, leading his life, erring, involuntarily emitting an education in the guise of a healthy infection. The horse's mouth spits. To teach is to lead other horses to water and to make them drink.

Art is clarity. The most complicated statement, if it is art, is the simplest form for that statement. That one statement is all there is. Another statement, if it is art, is independent of the first, and indeed of all other statements.

Eggs make chicks make eggs make . . . So turns the tedious wheel. Humans too, spawning themselves, clone eternally. Only works of art, even bad ones, grow from a kernel toward a unique bloom signaled by a singular Stop.

Given this conclusion one cay say: *Le Sacre du Printemps* or the *Quartetto in Modo Lidico* reflect the essence of economy, while your average pop song is more lavish than its content. The process of distillation—that's all any artist can learn from any other. So far as the process can be imparted through demonstration rather than through imitation, only a Nadia Boulanger turns pedagogy into art. And Boulanger very early forsook all notion of herself as a composer.

*

With discouragement I reflect, after coming home from bouts at colleges around the land, on how despite the richness of the ivied halls the poorness of instruction runs rife. If I'm the guest of one member of the department, other members testily arrange to grade papers in their offices during my public talks and tunes. Now, supposing it is not intramural rivalry but scorn of me that's behind the boycott. Shouldn't they still attend me in order the better to scorn me? I may never come again, yet their poor papers are always with them.

Seemingly complex questions generally have plain answers. The riskiest advice is also the only advice.

How, asks a student, do you compose a piece? Answer: By making it up as you go along, how did you think? Carissimi and Chopin, no less than John Cage or Judy Collins, proceeded by putting one foot before the other. Not that they stumbled through a maze of Self-Expression. Merely to express yourself is to betray what you have to say. We are all self-expressive but our Self-Expression is not our identity. Identity is manner—hearty-hewn manner—of delivery for Self-Expression. To feel deeply is not necessarily to articulate with the economic urgency of art. To discourage Self-Expression is the teacher's chief task.

How, continues the student, once you've channeled Self-Expression, do you compose a *perfect* piece? Answer: By imitation—using a model you love. If, as Radiguet contended, a true artist cannot copy, he has only to copy to prove he's a true artist. (Radiguet produced two flawless novels, then died at twenty. Ironic America, land of youth, never produced a Radiguet. Of course, music is finer than prose, and Mozarts are rarer than Radiguets. Yet Russia, not America, produced a Shostakovich whose first symphony, written at nineteen, is a masterpiece.) Now, a perfect piece, which any well-schooled hack can learn to make, cannot be guaranteed to bleed and breathe, and even God just hopes for the best.

After two minutes in the new Saratoga Bookstore I had to leave. The place was well stocked and with pleasant ambience (a fire blazed, a woman with braids sat reading Kafka), but the radio blaring country music was too intrusive for concentrated browsing. In New York too I've noticed this: hangouts like health stores and head shops you'd think would be opposed to such digestive hindrance to hearing yourself at any price.

I don't know why, but young people today who read their Kafka (as well as Shakespeare) and who look at de Kooning (as well as Raphael), do not listen to the "equivalent" music. Never in a bookstore or art gallery do we hear Monteverdi or Machaut or Webern or Weber. Ideally, of course, one would prefer silence in these locations, and I'm opposed to Rizzoli's policy of "good music" as background for buying.

O the dithyrambs I confected around the Beatles years ago! Today I'm more than indifferent, I'm hostile. Pop is inherently wrong by being preemptive. Each summer the Schaefer Festival in Central park not only drowns the contiguous opera concerts in another part of the forest (like a great sow who, oblivious to her runts, smothers them), but forty thousand West Side families become captive audience to the din. This is no comment on the quality of the music, although overstatement is always suspect.

On Being Artistic

> I used to give my heart and soul to my dancing
> To keep the wolf from the door,
> But now I'm a lady,
> Ain't got to dance anymore.

Thus crooned Mae West, as I, a child, thrilled to her success, never thinking that that to which one gives one's heart is perforce more than a makeshift trade, or that if dancing is but a means to a financial end, why give it your soul? But if I ignored the meaning of art in America, neither did I know what a lady was, though I was glad Mae had become one.

And I thrilled too at the unexplained contradiction of the Saint Louis Woman who, despite "all her diamond rings / Pulls that man around by her apron strings." When Mae West got diamonds, surely the aprons (if there ever were any) got thrown away.

Yet again am I invited by "a practicing psychologist" to participate in a panel about "Psychology and the Creative Process," and yet again, with a sigh, I try to explain: "Creativity is not a word in my vocabulary. If it were, I would apply it solely to productive (as opposed to interpretive) artists, of whom I know a goodly number. Not one of them has ever expressed interest in what you call 'the psychology of creation.' Indeed, the meaning of art seems of more concern to outsiders than to artists. And why should a composer like me wish to tell you in words precisely what he exemplifies in music? If he could tell you, he wouldn't need to be a composer . . . The only absolute rule about 'creative people' is that they are more practical-minded than is generally believed. Surely I am not the first to ask what the fee will be for participation on your panel."

The psychologist: "I wasn't asking you to tell me in words what you exemplify in music. I was inviting you to join in an exploration of the creative *process* in yourself and others. I would be surprised if you were not interested in the manner in which you come upon your own creations. Other creative artists are. You *are* the first to ask what the fee would be for participation on my panel."

How can one win when the other makes the rules? He invites me, presumably because I am a "creative artist," but when I can't concur with his definition I err. Now, if by the nature of things I am the one to define the process, he paradoxically rejects my opinion even as he solicits it.

What such romantic laymen refuse to grasp is that the "creative process" (if that's the term for the action of making so-called art) is no more and no less than hard work. Well, everyone on earth has something to say and everyone knows the feeling of hard work, everyone wishes to communicate and, indeed, many "untalented" people are able to "feel" more deeply than "real artists." The fact that one hard worker produces something expert that catches fire while another produces something equally expert that's stillborn is what makes this one an artist and that one not an artist. No other century than ours is further concerned with the question. Artists understand me. Psychologists don't, or won't.

Elsewhere we read of a team of canny psychologists who are "onto" the mystery of "creativity" because they're studying children—all children being, as everybody knows, imaginative and fantastic and uninhibited until the growing-up process puts a damper on their Self-Expression. What the canny psychologists won't face is that children are also un-self-critical. If it can be argued that a great artist is one who, among his other blessings, has happily retained his childlike knacks, it cannot be argued that a child, by virtue of his knacks, is a great artist. Children may well be "artistic," but art is restraint, not excess. Until a child learns to chisel inspiration into singular inevitable shape he cannot be termed an artist. Nowhere does history give us an example of the child-as-great-artist, although the great-artist-as-child is everywhere. Well, not quite everywhere.

In 1953 in France a nine-year-old girl named Minou Drouet was "caught" writing marvelous poetry. Her fame rose even to the Académie Française which, while allowing that her verse rivaled Rimbaud's, suspected that maybe her parents were writing it for her. She was thus put into experimental isolation, but even alone in her cell she wrote great poems. Jean Cocteau, who despised the whole business, declared: "All children have genius— except Minou Drouet."

(14 September 77) Deaths today of Stokowski, of Gustave Reese, and especially of Callas and of Robert Lowell. With all his discontent and sadness Lowell *left* something, whatever it is, and isn't that the point? Artist's sorrow pays. Can they thus be said to be sorrowful when they are capable simultaneously of notating the sorrow, since the act of notation is, while it lasts, a removal from sorrow—from, that is, active life? And how much of JH's anxiety is not itemized for heaven? He contends that we are all deluded, except the insane. Delusions are a keel. The person who convinces friends of his delusions, functions. He who convinces strangers of his delusions achieves prosperity, and (if the delusions are couched in notes or paints or verbs) posterity. The public, feels JH, is deluded by the geniuses' delusions. For there is no such thing as Good Art in the absolute.

Melomaniacs sigh in contained exasperation as though I had uttered a pseudo quip, but I am dead serious: You don't have to love a piece to play it well (some pieces don't concern love); you have to know what it's about. Conversely, to love a piece, even to know what it's about, doesn't mean you'll play it well. The French play their own music less well than outsiders do. Do they not "understand" their own music? (Ravel didn't understand Ravel, judging by how he played himself.) I don't much like Schubert, but I do know how he should "go," and play him well. Probably the rule is that a certain sort of objectivity obtains in all true—not to say great—interpretation. Merely to feel something doesn't mean that the feeling can be transferred to an audience, or that, if it can, it's the right feeling.

*

In my diary I don't seem to need to detail important events surrounding my musical works, not even to report on the glamour of their worldly launching. Is this because such works represent my unverbal side? Because such works are diaries in themselves?

Nor do I relate reaction to current politics. A Sartre would denounce this as invalid. Can an artist in the glow of Watergate focus only on his navel? Yet is not any diary, by virtue of recording the present, a political document? Avoidance of the specifically political is itself a political stance. (Or is it rather societal, like despair among our Indians? People confuse these notions.) I don't record much about astronomy either, or about high fashion or chicken breeding.

Paul Goodman once reproached certain radicals for spreading their worthy acts too thin. To support blacks this month and abortion next month is to abandon blacks. I state this not to justify but to define my manners. The poor are always with us, but artists' truths are uttered only once.

Such truths as may lurk in the preceding notes seem nonetheless uttered, as I reperuse them, over and over. Is it a cop-out to justify their fragmented redundancy by stating that unique art, like the drabbest existence, is accomplished, indeed survived, by repeating, in slightly different vocabulary, the same old four or five maxims, day after day after day?

Nantucket, July 1979

PARIS IN THE SPRING

Years after I'd come back to New York for good, I wrote Virgil in Paris to ask if he'd seen my lost youth. "There's plenty of lost youth around," he answered, "but I don't know if any of it's yours."

A city's staying power—its ability to inflict pain—lies less in intrinsic beauty than in the force of faded friendships. Yet Chicago, the town where my every First Time occurred, is no graveyard; it is I who return from the grave into a vital center that has no room left. And so today in Paris, where once I loved and lived, I'm lonely not so much for dead friends as for my own mislaid corpse.

What hits most about a childhood spent in Hyde Park is not specifics, like walking home from the Midway age nine on ice skates because shoes had been lost and being limp with iodized welts for a week, but the sun, the heavy western sun flooding the concrete between Dorchester and Lake Michigan in any season. What hits most about seven French years with so much to recall that's now congealed into a single flavor as hours and years bubble by is not famous meals and heads tasted and observed or heady hearts, but a single stifling afternoon reading *Howard's End* to the smell of tuberoses in Marie Laure's garden, Place des États-Unis.

. . . as an adolescent scanning Balzac with a map of Paris to pursue the circuities of Vautrin. Brought up a Quaker, meaning in silence, needing noise, meaning music, and by extension, France (certainly not Germany) and the bejeweled Catholicism of the Mediterranean . . .

Like Guitry's *tricheur*, all unknowing I plucked that poison ivy for the Boy Scout, after he relieved himself in an Indiana glade, to use as toilet tissue. God guided my last Parisian visit in 1969 to say adieu to Marie Laure a month before she died. This week I re-return, three years after her death. Paris: is what no longer contains Marie Laure. The presence of her absence is so everywhere apparent. Paris, filled by a void.

"I will love you forever" may be said by one person in honesty to many, since one person *is* many, though not at once. If he is many at once he could only collectively say "I will love you forever," and collectivity isn't love. Take a dozen cherished skeletons, grind to powder, add a quart of adrenaline laced with Chablis, strain and refine until the liquid thins down enough to immerse a metropolis with invisible atomic silk. Observe through tears from a distance of twenty light years, and you'll see Lutèce as it looks this morning.

38 Rue des Épinettes. Of course it's as though I'd never left, rain and cold, but a warm supper chez Édouard Roditi and his circle of eccentrics—a mother hen in the Tower of Babel.

It's easier to love the stupid than the bright. The word *France* strikes terror in the hearts of homebound Americans, but there's no rent to pay, taxis are cheap and meals cost about the same while being superior, so I spend dollars on posies for ladies. Exhausted, constipated.

Sunlight peeks furtively now around corners in the seventeenth arrondissement where each humble grocery on the Avenue Saint Ouen upstages with bloody roses and giant tomatoes the equivalent on Madison Avenue. Protective wrath of Nora Auric over the telephone, she having misread a reference to Georges in *Critical Affairs*.

When people ask if during my years in Paris I ever met *Les Six* I like to say, "Yes, I knew all five." How? Through knowing their music—that's the way to a composer's heart. Thus in 1949 toward dawn on a stool of La Reine Blanche I hummed to Auric, whom I'd just met in the bar, themes for each scene of *Sang d'un Poète*. Thus, when we played guessing games at Lise Deharme's with Milhaud I tested his tunes by heart to him—tunes he'd forgotten. Thus to Germaine Tailleferre I sang *Madame n'est pas là* on Pinget's poem. Thus to Honegger the theme from *Pastorale d'Été*. And thus to Poulenc . . . It's not so much that I knew these people's music, or even that I knew it well, as that I was a Young American Composer who knew their music. A Y.A.C., then as now, was a contradiction in terms to the French, and if they weren't particularly interested in my music they were interested in my interest in theirs. And . . . Not that I was their type.

I'm 5 feet 10½ inches and since age twenty have weighed seldom less or more than 150 pounds. Dark brown eyes and hair, though the latter was bleached during the early 1950s (the French still think of me as blond). Slim legs have turned skinny, though my shoulders remain good-shaped. Hands, especially the right one, begin to spout liver spots. Extreme nearsightedness such that I've turned—with glasses—quite farsighted, and can read now only with the naked eye. Externally slim ass (internally bloated with what would appear to be swelling brains) and fairly flat stomach. Small nose, selfish lips, as yet no double chin nor much gray hair, but sagging ears and eternal dandruff. Have never had a venereal disease. Was once extremely pretty if you like the type, which I detest. With magnetic charm, which others name crass monopoly, I pontificated forever, having long since coldly concluded that shyness is never rewarded and that I was no dumber than other pontificators in the room. Where's the silver infant who once monopolized by silence? who (so he thought) made philosophy futile in the face of lust? Longing at once to be guiltless and guilty, passive and active, ravished in flesh and dominating in mind, I simply never get laid.

My major weakness during the "Paris Years" was believing flattery (that I was cute, talented, etc.). My strength was in work. But if I never let flattery stand in the way of work, clearly I did work because I was flattered. After a point the goose of Encouragement is more needed than the gander of Fancy. Fancy is the *donnée* of any artist; obviously he would never have been encouraged if he had never produced to start with.

Certain behaviorists claim the contrary—that inside every banker is an artist struggling to get out—and their nurseries swarm with toddlers urged to "express" themselves. But where, pray, are the artists who get out? More cogent: Inside every artist is a banker struggling to get out.

Conversation is neither an art nor a graceful fashion for English-speaking peoples. Americans mean what they say though they sometimes struggle to say what they mean. The French do finally say what they mean though they seldom mean literally what they say. Despite their indirection, their metaphor and irony, the French are succinct; Americans, despite their one-track-mindedness, their clumsy longing for a bull's-eye, are convoluted. This dogma is French but I am American. Therefore . . .

Marie-Louise Bousquet has finally died. No American who knew Paris did not know Marie Louise: the very soil and fluid of two cultures, in her sandwiches and daiquiris, merged every Thursday at the sun-filled flat in Place du Palais Bourbon. American specialists, mainly of *Harper's Bazaar*, learned about General Practice by drinking with the French. We met our countrymen (Jean Stein, Thornton Wilder), and those whose country we were visiting (Cartier-Bresson, Josette Day). Not that a party's as good as the guests, it's no better than the host. Knowing who she herself was, Marie Louise had the freedom to learn about you, and that was great fun for her. But such salon life, never a part of America, is ended forever in France. Marie Laure, Marie Blanche, now Marie Louise—*les trois Maries*, as they were called—have flown the coop.

More than any female of my generation I loved most, during the early fifties, Heddy de Ré. Brief hour in the Orangerie where Degas's *Absinthe* again reminded me of us then, then two hours with Heddy herself. Absent, still pretty, disappointing, asks me nothing of me after sixteen years and, with her friend, drinks Calvados, claims to have forgotten English.

Why when today's so dull should dredging yesterday prove less so? Yesterday, when as an adult I returned to Chicago—that sole shelter and thus sole menace of youth—I was struck not by what my mind once learned there but by what my body had felt: smells of leather in Woolworth's Bookstore, of summery debris in October underscoring anxieties of forgotten homework, and especially of sex forcing itself from behind every door on Kenwood, on Blackstone, in Mandel Hall: every bush in Jackson Park seemed witness to our virginity perpetually lost and found, as every bar on Rush Street hosted our sprees.

Paris becomes the Chicago of my maturity, a maturity which shows nothing of "culture." There from the Reine Blanche (Christ, it's a milk bar!), kidnapped to Morocco by Guy Ferrand twenty-four years ago this month. There near the famous Observatoire *pissotière* (vanished!) was the encounter with Henri Fourtine, April 1952, whose peasant hands, like later those of P, bruised month after month the spermy sheets of the Rue de Vaugirard, sheets spilled with Cointreau, and eventually with the welcome stains of melting croissants from the bakery downstairs. The uncontaminated carnality of France! Hôtel de Lille where beneath a window of that ground-floor room we screwed one afternoon to the sound of strangers one yard away. Past ghosts frighten us as we frighten them, dissolving with a screech. France is only possible when one is in one's twenties.

Once with Heddy, as we drank deep into the night, we listened wide-eyed while the now-defunct Robert LeMasle (one of several self-proclaimed models for the *Nightwood* doctor) declared: Hangovers are needles thrust full length into unanesthetized flesh, and I'm a tattoo from sole to scalp with no space left, yet I remember every one.

Friendship for Eugene Istomin led me to hear his Trio play the sort of program (all Brahms) I rarely attend. That they should begin an hour late (because, as it turned out, Isaac Stern had overslept) and then perform routinely (except for Eugene's cohering excellence) didn't lighten matters, particularly since during the wait a couple in my overcrowded loge were necking with a sound like the squashing of hot peanut butter in armpits. Despicable public shows of love! What do they do privately then? In the Théâtre des Champs-Élysées the pleasure of newlyweds should dwell in the complicity of knowing what's coming later or what just came. But to come now, in the open, is to come for us—and we are less jealous than offended: it interferes with our rhythm.

People always say: Write what you know. Is anything in me unsaid that needs saying? Any old notions with new stresses? The only way to recount the very same thing to different people is to change form for each person. Yet when the page is printed, the score sounded, doesn't the "art" freeze? No, each listener alters the form for himself. Art paints particulars so strongly that the generalities from which they emerge gleam through. Obviously the Sahara can't be depicted on a canvas the size of the Sahara; when Jean Hugo paints those scenes from French life, his format is a postage stamp. How many angels dance on the head of a pin? Nathaniel says thirteen, Sarah says ninety. Assuming that Sarah and Nathaniel are observing the same pinhead, do their two sets of angels look alike? Might Sarah's angels be heftier even than Nathaniel's?

Write about what I can't write about.

(Seventeen years since I permanently left Paris. In October 1957, the Claude episode closed, I returned to America "to start a career," as Virgil put it, revisiting France only in 1964, briefly again in 1969 and now in 1973. Yet during intermission people say, "It's been ages! Have you moved?" And in New York, meeting me for the first time, someone asks, "But don't you live in Paris?")

Slowly, into Place de l'Alma, uphill, savoring and withholding, away from the Théâtre des Champs-Élysées (little in common now with the *gratin*, ignorant of our Watergate) into Rue Freycinet, disturbed by the shadows. As though I were walking home, like ten thousand times before, with the intention of crying when I emerge into Place des États-Unis. But home's now a huge hollow tombstone. How long did I stand there in the inky frost, watching the so familiar leaves quiver so late in the night over the wall as I had watched the leaves outside Polignac's mansion fifteen seasons ago, watching the still, still, still house behind whose boarded windows no light flickered? All Paris has become a cemetery where this Magritte-like monument dominates, and, finally, without life, looks foul. Quickly I walk away and will never return.

Sleepless night, dreams like daydreams, nocturnal daydreams. In blackness the door opened to Marie Laure's house which became a box of sunshine. Entering there with the white-haired Roro, we walked among white roses wide awake, and way back there another door opened and four beautiful women emerged, two with blond and two with black hair. They strolled toward us but did not (or pretended not to) notice us. Returning through the house alone, I reached the first door which reopened back into this black bed. Wallace the cat whined continually. And as if that weren't enough, I kept getting ideas (mostly on how to contain French Music into a definition) and had to turn the light on to record them, then turn it off, then on. A sleepless night—*une nuit blanche*, as the French say.

Nuit blanche. Once in the dear dead days of long ago Gordon Sager visited the Turkish bath of Harlem. Next day he announced, "The only other customers were Caucasians. *J'ai passé une nuit blanche.*"

New York, with the singular virtue of expanse, lacks, by virtue of that virtue, the exterior intimacies of Paris. A French dusk, for instance, is heartwarming: On a rainy afternoon we watch the *tabacs* on the Rue du Bac switch on their lamps and fill up with clients pausing for a *coup de rouge* on the way home; later we peek into windows where families sit down quarreling to their lentil soup; or, from indoors, in any season we look out onto passing heads of lovers and sycamore leaves and hear the clink of *boules*. In Manhattan we eavesdrop by phone, nor is it a city of easy cafés, of Peeping Toms, of (as Robert Phelps calls them) followers.

Dull brilliance of liquor, dull pleasures of a sauna, sharp dullness of health. If vice were replaced by intelligence! Yet in a sense, vice *is* intelligence. Along the mall in Central Park, observe the homely Hare Krishna youngsters dancing their uninventive dance. (Mother drops coins in their cup, then asks: "Now will you give me some coins for peace?" They look through her, uncomprehending, and dance off.) A few yards farther, see the health-nut kiosks replete with signs informing you what not to eat so as to "gain a heightened consciousness"—this accompanied by five simultaneous transistors blaring rock.

It proves little that no mutual friends visit her grave (they're permanent residents, after all), or that I, who never do such things, do. But always one to do things halfway I do not, in the taxi to the Cimetière Montparnasse, clutch the cluster of custard-colored roses dreamed of. Nor do I expect, as the caretaker leads the way, to end up at the Caveau Paine-Bischoffsheim (the Caveau Noailles being in another part of the forest) where, if you stand on tiptoe and peek through the vines you perceive not a quarreling family but, next to Marie Laure, the stone coffin of Oscar Dominguez. No morbid tone, no sensation of what Henny Penny called "The Distinguished Thing." Annoyance, on the contrary. To be dead is unlike you, animated witch. Come out from under there, be yourself! Your silence makes a wild noise in me now. You were the only French person who cared about America.

Satie's the most overrated of the underrated composers, yet when you speak with the avid Satilophiles you often discover they've never heard of *Socrate*, the composer's sole piece which might remotely aspire to grandeur, in itself and without quaint appendages, on strictly musical terms. Fifteen years ago Poulenc was in a reverse position but for the same reason: of all the overrated composers he was the most underrated. His piano miniatures and most harmless songs were done to death, yet the existence of his major works (meaning, for once, larger works—the religious and profane operas and cantatas) was ignored, at least in the U.S.A.

. . . like Gide who, the one hour in his life he lay with a woman (on the beach at Hyères, according to Marie Laure), sired a child, Poulenc became the father of a daughter.

. . . not that he idealized men, but his ideal man was Governor Dewey.

. . . the rocky, inexpert French of those longtime expatriate females haunting, drunkishly rich, the Rue de Rivoli in 1949. Esther Arthur, Mrs. Forrestal. A language when mastered is mastered in a year or less, the rest is nuance. Yet the nuance already caught by a native child of five will never be caught by you, foreigner. Gift for tongues is unrelated to gift for music.

We each speak our personal sub-tongue. Except for a widening vocabulary, there's no "improvement" past a certain point. Our French is our French. Desiring, when I first lived here, to transport my English to my French—to seek the inevitable equivalent for each Nedism—I merely applied myself. My French is as good as any foreigner's, yet in grade school, seeing no future in French, I was, despite my musical talent (my "good ear"), the worst in class.

. . . from the window, *ô délire*, while writing, I can look over there into another morning window giving onto the court from the Rue J. Keller where a man, mirror propped against the pane, shaves, stripped to the waist, biceps at play, black curly hair on scalp and chest, the works, *quoi!*—while behind in shadow the visage of a red-haired woman. The Paris of Gabin, which, having never been known, is most missed like—do you recall?—that May day in 1953 when Georges Geoffroy met James Pope-Hennessey for the first time, yet had dreamed of him the night before and in the dream reproached him for not appearing years sooner, so much time's wasted . . .

Paris, the place where she isn't. Paris, a disease once had. There remains a glamorous contagion like the perfumed maze through which Gide's Theseus rambled. Heavy rain. Lunch chez Lily Pastré, prey now to gaps of memory, and Boris Kochno, so warm. The ease with which they speak of funerals. Boris retains the guile of alcoholics—their childlike wish to provide antidotes to being a pain in the neck. He's Russian too, of course, and who can resist that spooky thrill, his great . . . The past presses in like a mean tea cozy. I ache to be in this very room as it was years ago. Yet the room hasn't changed. Unless caught quick it's lost for good, but it's never quick enough, and always wrong. Rain. Not a foreign country but a homeland whose patois I've forgotten. Two Mormons just knocked on the door.

The Épinettes is a cobblestone quarter sufficient unto itself, as remote from central Paris as . . . Wooden shoes, window boxes with leeks and zinnias of every color, a bandstand in the adjacent Rue Collette. Am vaguely superfluous, like those French journalists living permanently in New York, but are invisible to New Yorkers. Except that their *raison d'être* is to report on the present, mine is the past that grows more labyrinthine than the future. Everywhere mirrors in which to seek a friendly reflection, always more distant, less intriguing.

Robert Phelps, lunch in nearby bistro, Rue Lantiez, then, beginning with the Cité des Fleurs, a seven-hour promenade. Manic and vicarious, Robert plays the role of professional loser whereas he's a true winner of sorts, being unique in what he does and which he does well: to fix situations through the lens of the brief word: the French gift, bestowed on a Yankee, of the spoken photo. But the gift's not no-strings, flashed in my vision. Unrecapitulatable is to be these three things: in love, in Paris, in your twenties. Poor Robert cannot be twenty. He sees the city as I saw it then, inconveniences are quaint, all crotches godly, ashcans are Greuzes and advertisements pure Corneille. Thanks alas to (they say) Madame de Gaulle not one *pissotière* remains, so that particularly art nouveau mystique which represented the compleat eroticism of a not so distant day's defunct for Robert.

He asks what three things I'm most ashamed of. Quick retort: 1) Sugar, 2) certain sexual attitudes and 3) my best songs—as though what feels good must be contemptible. Yes, expatriation does not make Americans more French, it makes them know increasingly how American they are.

One thing may lead to another but art runs faster than beauty, said Paul Goodman and Jean Cocteau. Well, art may run faster than beauty, but one thing leads to another. On April 3, 1952, the first time I ever was in Grasse, Charles de Noailles invited me and Marie Laure (his spouse) to lunch with Cocteau. Afterward the four of us visited Marie Laure's mother, Madame de Croisset, who lived in a nearby rust-colored stucco villa which contained a Pleyel, so that—at Marie Laure's insistence—I could play the ballet *Mélos* for Cocteau. I recall two things mainly: 1) On arriving, Cocteau announced to Madame de Croisset, "It seems like yesterday that I was bringing Marie Laure back from our outings." (He'd not been in this house since the summers of World War I when the adolescent Marie Laure began nursing the love-hate she never forsook.) 2) Rather than do it herself, Madame de Croissay rang for a servant to open the drapes in the *salon de musique*. Oh, there were other things too. (Cocteau wore a white leather jacket; drank straight gin before eating; talked movies with Charles de Noailles as though Charles cared. Wasn't there also a feeling that, although he'd probably made the brief trip from Cap Ferrat mostly to see me again and to hear the music— we'd met only once before—he was disappointed to find me in the company of the Noailles? As he said good-bye, taking his seat beside the curly-haired chauffeur of the white Porsche, he immediately drew forth a notebook and began to work, having already lost an afternoon with the likes of us.) But what is forever striking is that nothing is as (complex as) it seems. To discover that two people whose milieu is presumably identical have not met on home ground for thirty-five years! An outsider concludes that famous contemporaries spend their lives mutually hobnobbing. (When, the outsider might well wonder, do they do the work for which they're famous?) As for Madame de Croissay with the curtain, it was not I (a bourgeois American) but Marie Laure herself who later remarked, "Couldn't she have pulled it herself?" (M.L. added that she'd not realized Cocteau didn't know English. Her surprise surprised me: how could she not have known?)

That same year I first saw Nathalie Sarraute, at the Catalan restaurant, deep in conversation with a mutual friend, Dora Maar. Marie Laure and I watched from across the room. They later joined us. Sarraute appeared to be what I already knew Dora to be: a no-nonsense hardworking reasonable left-wing artist as contemptuous of frivolity then as Women's Liberationists are contemptuous of it now. Thus it seemed contradictory, a week later, to receive Sarraute's novel, *Portrait d'un inconnu*, amicably inscribed. Frivolous act.

Twenty-two years later, at George Braziller's in New York, I reintroduced myself to Sarraute, reminding her of that other time and place. She said: "You know, that's the last I ever saw of Dora." For two decades I'd assumed they were friends. Actually I know them both better than they know each other.

Dali exhibit. Exhausted, he now imitates himself to where only the signature, which literally never alters, breathes life.

Petit Palais, exhibit from Maoist China of ancient art works and crafts. Impossibly crowded and reeking. So with a catalogue I withdraw to a sunny cloister to examine photographs of the artifacts which surround me. (This trip's a macrocosm of the experience? In an actual teeming Paris I'm enlivened only by memories.)

Eugene's touching solicitude of ailing John Trapp as they cross Avenue Marceau, holding hands, on way to restaurant. Eugene disabused about Hurok. "Managers do little beyond providing a mailing address. Dates are gotten through personal contact." Professional criticism. My unfabulous but literal memory retains less what critics have written about me than about others. Even when good (even when bad) reviews of my work or words bore me. I already know, deeper than they, how good (bad) the work or words are. If the review itself is literature (Mazzacco on Diaries or Flanagan on Cycles), I'm more intrigued by how it's written than in what . . .

*

Five o'clock at Nathalie Sarraute's. In the late sunshine of her wide high parlor, a stone's throw from Marie Laure's, we talk pleasantly about our countries for five quarter-hours and drink Fresca. She doesn't feel cordial toward Susan Sontag (who once introduced her at the YMHA, then didn't stay to hear her speak), but loves Mary McCarthy. McCarthy and Sontag are the only American representatives in Paris at present, but I've yet to find a Frenchman who, in his darling insulation, has heard of either.

Sarraute, when I confess that *Tel Quel* and company is just too thick and cold, suggests I look into Butor's nonfiction, especially his words on music. And kisses me good-bye.

Hôtel Biron, gardens and nursemaids, specter of Rilke. Again, museum as environment, as place to inhabit, but only incidentally to look at pictures in. Rodin's pictures, superior to his strangled sculpture.

"Pour Ned Rorem avec une amitié et une admiration qui pour une fois est vraie." Does he recall having thus inscribed the flyleaf of his short stories in July 1957? With the same eyebrow-raising candor I inscribed *Critical Affairs:* *"Pour José-Luis de Vilallonga avec une amitié et une admiration qui pour une fois est vraie,"* presenting it to him last night in his Neuilly apartment, which has black walls and a mirrored floor, before we went forth with his very new youngish spouse, Syliane, not pretty but with *chien* in gold lamé turban and white lamé pants and plenty of gold-and-silver accessories, and whose baby (not José's) was born last month during a seven-minute labor. (*"Sept minutes d'horreur,"* she adds.) We dined at the Sept, which is "where one dines," and were joined by a Guy Monréal whom José had said *"meurt d'envie de te revoir,"* but who showed no sign of ever having heard of me. Despite this false situation—is it a Spanish situation?—one likes José for his unlikely combination of hyper-intelligence and hyper-chic, not to mention his kind, kind eyes with which through his sangría-colored glasses he once gazed down on us from the screen in *Giulietta degli Spiriti* and now gazed at me, while over there with a covey of young beaux dined ageless Danielle Darrieux in yellow. I'm not what Vilallonga remembered; lacking *mondanité* now, I bored him.

Pop music, all of it, here is still in ¾, so I grow testy, fevered, and they drive me home to the sticks of Épinettes. Retire late with sore gums, sore finger, sore foot . . .

Familiar streets, Varenne, Grenelle, with no longer a lustful rendezvous while waiting in the rain to cross with the green light—green fire, as the French call it—just dates with sentimental agony, for instance Lise De-harme, bejeweled, the same, all in orange. Invited for tea, yet offered nothing but her husband, Jacques Perrin, kept in a side room, and the plump pink pussycat. Nothing has changed except everything. Old friends are reruns with new wrinkles. Only JH, who phoned last night in tears, remains always new.

Rereading Butor, his essay on music. The question is not does he date—everyone dates—but does he date well. Too soon to know, but not too soon to know he dates soon. His whole tonality, like that of current French music (if one can speak of non-tonal music as having tonality), seems a decade off. Of course this judgment is by the same American scale as in 1969 when I last reacted to the music of Paris, and different lands flower differently, some never. Russia never had painting, but did have the novel-of-frenzy and the music-of-frenzy a century before Germany. Germany never had cooking. Italy never had song (as opposed to aria) and England had no music at all during twenty-five decades though her poems and pictures then . . . etc. *Mais Butor!* When non-practitioners (even Huxley or Mann or Proust) write about music, musicians (even second-raters) twitch. It's hard to learn exactly what point Butor is pushing as he speaks of music as a realist art. To a professional his essay reads (like Pound's essay on harmony) as an obvious conclusion reached the hard way—by hit or miss. Butor seems to have talked to Boulez or someone and then come home to note his own reactions, naïve but hardworking.

"Music is indispensable to our life," says he. Why?

"One need not be concerned with political implications in music," says he, "whereas in other realms it's clearly established," etc. How?

In other realms, too, the stronger the politics the weaker the art.

Butor willfully refutes Stravinsky's notorious *mot*, "music is incapable of expressing anything," while alluding to all music as song. Now, all music is not song, but since all song is a musicalizing of words it does gain literary sense and "expresses" something. Yet Butor goes on to claim that unless we know the convention we cannot grasp more than a part. His statement's right but the conclusion is wrong—that "a man who knows nothing of classical Arabic can still delight in the calligraphy, but he resembles a museum viewer who can contemplate only the shadows of statues." There is no single way to love anything; but as soon as we *comprehend* a language we lose its beauty, visual and sonic. A Frenchman can no longer *hear* French.

". . . transcription . . . the possibilities of literal imitation which music possesses are vastly richer than the onomatopoeias of spoken language. . . ." Butor is speaking of musical grammar which has "acquired an enormous range of flexible discourse: the noises of machines in Varèse, the songs of birds in Messiaen." Yes, but do Messiaen's birds fool real birds? Are real machines taken in by Varèse? In seeking "the fundamental connection that unites music and words" Butor becomes the hopeless researcher. Why not seek the fundamental disparity? (for if the arts all "meant" each other we'd need only one), or posit a thesis on the rapports between rhythmic shapes and colors (though not meanings) of a given nation's music—which came first, the talk or the tune? "If I hear a Schubert song without understanding German," says Butor, "I may find the music wonderful . . . but only when I have understood the poem's meaning shall I appreciate its fitness to the words." Supposing another composer used the same text with equal, but contrasting, fitness? If Butor insists on "that formative process we call rhyme, which in music is generalized into recapitulation, variation, development," how would he compare music to prose?

"Immature poets imitate; mature poets steal." Eliot in 1920.

Inexorable dirt of the nostalgia is less like Proust than like the going-back sequences in *Our Town* or *Un Carnet de bal*. Or is it that these works themselves are so far away, while the situations within them now return? More quickly than the sight or sound, one can retrieve the smell and taste of a *flic* or *ouvrier* long ago adored and now doubtless decrepit or dead. First hot days, daffodillian, and prenubile girls, as they always have in this season, like white bats swarm the byways squeaking offensively in first-communion garb. First hot evenings, orchidian, and muscled paragons, as never before in old seasons, like butterscotch statues avoid the streets in favor of the working-class gay bar, Rue Davy, in their *salopettes*. And one goes to bed, alone, disturbed.

Long ride through torrential downpour to Villejuif in Jacques Dupont's car with Sauguet back-seat-driving all the way. (The reward was Jacques's décor for *Les Contes d'Hoffmann*, yet only the French could feel rewarded, as the French do, about a new production of *Les Contes d'Hoffmann*.) They tell me of my "enemies." Sauguet's right-wing royalism is too extreme to take seriously, yet oozes (as how can any conviction not?) onto his music, sometimes profitably (like Wagner's beliefs) as in *La Voyante* and the *Cello Concerto*, sometimes hatefully, as in . . . Conversations do give hangovers, but they don't make you vomit.

We read papers in the subway, they read books.

Nora Auric has retained a kind of beauty like that of a statue in a garden, fashioned first so skillfully by man, but carved and curled thereafter by nature, by mellowing dews and healthy mold and lively rot. (That is a writerly depiction of a sort I've never never penned—or typed—before, but is it not apt?) She is alarmed by this diary, mistakes it for autobiography, chides me for being démodé with words like *surrealist*, and yes, no doubt I've hurt them all. And yes, I play at being "older" because of course I don't feel older.

Tired of being tired, do the old welcome death as the young welcome sleep? I think not. The young despise going to bed. And the old think always in terms of tomorrow, even of "tomorrow when I'm dead."

A diary is harmony, a memoir is counterpoint. My words are vertical smacking isolated chords which describe, as snapshots describe, quick moments. But even the horizontal narrative misrepresents, since it's only one man's fancy. (Yet what does it misrepresent?)

What now at almost fifty have I made that counts? The future's not ahead, it's here. Let's go home and work.

1973

NANTUCKET DIARY
1974

20 June

Airborne, confined to his box, Wallace arrived petrified, in a pond of urine, shit and vomit. Within twenty minutes he was at home on West Chester, licked sleek, proprietary.

Static-y transistors, unmuffled motorcycles, noise for noise's sake is not the final insult for some, but a surreal burlesque.

Once we were installed in the house, our landlady showed up to show us a few ropes. She turned on the electric dishwasher and left it on, so we talked a little louder. Proudly she turned on the laundry box and then the dryer and left them churning, so we talked louder still. Calm as you please, she switched on the radio (already set to a "good music" station, perhaps for my benefit) to show how she used background music. By the time she demonstrated the furnace adjustments we were all merely answering each other's mouthings, unruffled as in a silent movie.

Conservatives say: "We notice that those in favor of abortion are so often the same as those against the Vietnam War. Isn't this a contradiction?" Liberals reply: "We notice that those against abortion are so often for the Vietnam War. Isn't that a contradiction?" Both arguments are specious, the contradiction being that Vietnam and abortion are unrelated.

24 June

It seems unfair to judge by first reactions, yet for me in matters of art those reactions seldom alter with time. Occasionally I'll come round, as with Brahms and Beckett, though whenever I stab anew at George Eliot, at Faulkner, at Schubert, at Berlioz, I'm baffled, not at what they are in themselves, but at what other people—delicately intelligent people—find in them.

Last night masochism urged me to reconsider *Le Partage de Midi*. Claudel, too, remains what he always seemed: a sophomoric *composeur* with no sense of shape. The lavishness of his banality! The sexist simplicity of his Catholic heart! Pushed to such limits, triteness turns special. That he allowed no abridgments of those redundant ohs and ahs, that he lived to such a ripe age, are because he "got out of himself" by sitting through his endless plays. Only economists die young.

Unlike inspired cuisine from mediocre food, a good production cannot hide faults of a "literary" play; it can only heighten them. But that marvelous production at the Comédie Française—was it 1954? There, like yesterday, stands Edwige Feuillère, whose slightest pattern moves mountains, and there is Félix Labisse's décor for the first act. Was ever a set more apt? Few. Balthus's maybe, for *L'Île des Chèvres*, or Noguchi's for Martha Graham's dance about Saint Joan, or Bill Ritman's for the second scene of *Tiny Alice* . . .

25 June

Darius Milhaud is dead at eighty-one. The headline strikes ironically after what I wrote yesterday of Claudel, collaborator in Milhaud's happiest works.

Did Darius die "fulfilled"? Does anyone at that age? Fulfillment comes with youth, while age poses pointless questions. *Faute de mieux*, he did continue and had a following. I, for one, would be quite another musician today were it not for adolescent obsessions with his *Création* and *Choéphores* and the contagious *Chants hébraïques* which Nell Tangeman sang so often and so well.

Personally, I knew Milhaud far less than I knew Auric, but he influenced me far more. How could Auric's music influence any composer? His greatness lies not in his music but in the intelligence which produces the music. Like too many intellectual artists (like Bill Flanagan), he thinks before he speaks, then fails to write it down afterward. Motto: make first, censor later. By this motto Milhaud made junk, but his pile is far higher than Auric's, and contains some sizable pearls.

Like great chess players, certain geniuses are social dolts with one-track minds. I doubt that Beethoven was "well rounded," that Bach was "cultivated." Breeding, reading and charm infringe upon the necessary narrowness of great acts. Humor is decadence pure. Why suppose that the key composers are any more literary than the monumental authors are musical?

Half the Groupe des Six has vanished.

28 June

I'm awakened by a fierce, nagging screech. Is it Wallace the cat scratching his litterbox or clawing his log in the kitchen? Has Con Ed again set up rivets in the street? No. It is JH grinding his teeth. Painful. Imagine the wear on JH's gums, as he noisily crunches diamonds into the jawbone night after night. My own teeth were filed years ago.

Ten days on this island—raw, windy, with ropes of rain thick as the bars in a zoo. Restrained by the weather from the joys of the beach, I've been orchestrating eight hours a day and have sties in both eyes. JH meanwhile has been reading on Africa—*everything* on Africa—and our only company is each other. Mutual entente is somewhat of an invasion of privacy. Yet do I know what privacy is?

Left to my own devices I'm a shell.

At dawn JH went into New York, where he must remain for a week. With his departure the ironic sun emerged, and here am I at loose ends, dreading the virtue (chore) of creation. Two big orchestral works are commissioned, paid for; yet I've spent the morning baking a *clafouti aux cerises*, keeping my mind as far as possible from the needs of my métier.

Clafouti Limousin

1 cup flour
¼ cup butter
2 eggs
½ cup granulated sugar
½ cup powdered sugar
1 cup boiled milk
Pinch of salt
3 cups pitted black cherries

Mix flour, salt, granulated sugar and butter. Add cool milk and eggs, and mix to produce a smooth dough. Line a buttered flan case with half the batter, sprinkle cherries with powdered sugar, cover them with the other half of the batter. Preheat oven, and bake at 400° F. for 30 minutes.

Pears may be used instead of, or along with, cherries. Brown sugar may be used instead of, or along with, granulated.

29 June

The Paris Diary is quoted in Darius's long obituary. (". . . Rorem described the Milhaud home in Paris as 'a barren apartment on the Boulevard Clichy looking down onto the million wild lights of Pigalle's merry-go-rounds.'") What nature of work would I now be most concentrating on were it not for Robert Phelps's perseverance in getting that little classic printed? Could I have written (and published) six more books, thus gaining the authority to be heard as a critic whose quaintness makes other critics climb the wall? Would I have centered more on musical composition? Would the composition have been "better"? Deeper? Idle conjectures. But in the less than eight years of this new career I've become, with the accompanying slight notoriety, sourer. That may be age.

I am growing more superficial. "Why" interests me less than "what." Surfaces are all: the smell of roses or peanut butter, the story line in Kierkegaard. How these things came to be, what *forms* them, no longer intrigues me.

Profundity is for the young. It has little to do with being alive, though it has much to do with being human. (Ironically sex, which has everything to do with being alive, preoccupies me hardly at all, not even vicariously. In *Deep Throat* the orgies are continually slowing down the plot.)

Will I, did Darius, do people die because they've said all there is in them to say? Style remains. Yes, but that point's been made too.

Last night, alone in this ocean, after a supper of yams, fresh tomatoes, and oatmeal bread (one dollar a loaf), I took a stroll at the hour between dog and wolf, overcoming the honeysuckle and foghorns, but not the non-melancholy void which seems to indicate: Why even bother to kill yourself?

This morning I feel all right again.

30 June

Preview last month of Jim Bridges's new movie. Afterward, small party at the Sherry Netherland for the prima donnas, including John Houseman with whom I've always found conversation hard as with a statue. Fate arranged that the two of us leave in the same elevator and, finding ourselves on the same street pursuing the same taxi, we shared the vehicle with strained civility. Houseman, as it happens, is the best thing about *The Paper Chase*. With expertise and diligence Jim Bridges has confected a film which ridicules diligence and expertise. Personally affable, Jim asks that his work also be taken affably. Result: the story is recounted in an antiseptic voice having nothing to do with its *auteur*. I recognize this the more quickly in that the virtue of likability is my vice too. The Houseman character, a grumpily skillful law professor, is made to seem unsympathetic because he places hard work higher than personality interplay.

I blew my nose in the paper napkin, then wadded the napkin and, as an afterthought but within the same gesture, reached across the table to polish some dust off the brass lamp. Jim Bridges reacted only by stating, "Now, that would be filmed, not in three shots, but in one." My reaction, had he done this, would have been: "He blows his nose in G-flat major."

Howard Moss came over to show us his pastiche of my journals—the parody of a parody, you might say—before publishing it in *The New Yorker*. He calls it "The Ultimate Diary." I had no reaction. It didn't seem amusing, but I'm too close or too far for focus. Then again, maybe it's just not amusing (although JH laughed). Howard, with his catholic verbal gifts, has never struck me as a humorist. But if satire is not my dish, glory is, and to be satirized is *the* glory. Howard himself once wrote: "The parody is an unconscious compliment: To have read someone closely enough to produce an acceptable imitation, to have become obsessed to the necessary degree requires an attention and concentration the works of most authors never receive."

A reassuring wonder, Howard never changes. In 1946 when we first met he looked fifteen years older than he was, today he looks fifteen years younger. He remains thirty-seven. His poet's quality too is stationary—which is to say high. If there've been no tidal waves, neither have there been droughts, and he's one of the few versifiers who can write prose that's prose (although he can't write theater—or, of course, pastiche). All this—his appearance, his talent's stance—is due, I'd say, to psychoanalysis. With his furrowed Noël Cowardian smile and his unwillingness to utter a banal quip, Howard's the "therapized" model, the precise contrary of the current New

York school (all those Anne Waldmans), whom one might call The Pseudo-Unsophisticated.

A souvenir persists. Was it in 1950, after having lived already one year in Paris, that I ran across Howard briefly one summer night at Saint Germain des Prés and, according to Howard in later years, was cool to his warm greeting? True, expatriated Americans were proprietarily inclined against old friends as new interlopers. But in this case coldness came from being taken unawares (just as we are cold to those we'd prefer to be in bed with, but, from shyness, haven't yet met): I happened to be wearing a black-and-white broad-striped polo shirt which Howard had loaned me three years earlier.

1 July

For whom do I compose? For the listener within me. Sure, I hope other listeners may find a sympathetic point of contact, and I need those listeners. But I don't know who they are. There are as many audiences as there are pieces, and the audiences don't necessarily overlap. "The" audience is neither vast nor wee. Mick Jagger's audience is not *La Traviata*'s, and hers isn't Billie Holiday's, and hers isn't Mélisande's, and hers isn't Berg's, and his isn't Webern's, and Balanchine's isn't Martha's, and hers isn't Twyla's, and Twyla's isn't mine. Does art soothe death, or the death of love? Not much. The cause of art is never enough. Art is usually about love and death, but death and love are not art, nor even about art, not even Mishima's. Priority: anyone can die of love, but only I can pen my tunes.

If Nantucket is made up of right-wing Gentiles, comfortable but not super-rich, and no artists, none at all, but some good journalists, is it the Jews of Martha's Vineyard who lend to its higher artistic gloss? They're comfortable but not super-rich either, and Gentile.

The argument of *Equus* comes too close to comfort to the dream recounted on page 34 of *The Paris Diary*, published in England in 1967. The playwright credits his source as being an unnamed man, now dead. Well, I am sort of alive, but the author of my old diary is in a sense dead, though not his copyright.

Toothpick limbs descended from the terry-cloth robe which, when he removed it, revealed a smoothly hairless belly looking less like a pot than a pillow case of mauve silk stuffed with mashed potatoes. He eyed us, not cruisily, but with that sidelong Neronic leer meaning "I recognize you but I don't recognize you."

2 July

Our world is mine as well as yours. Anxiously each morning I realize that before nightfall there will be two bombardments of noise pollution from North Church, day after day, month after unquiet month. I do not, as a citizen, challenge the genuineness of motive in bestowing upon Nantucketers these "carillon concerts" (actually commercial discs emitted through loudspeakers). I do not, as a Quaker, primarily object to the Congregational bias in program selection, though it does exclude the island's Catholics, Jews, Buddhists and atheists. Nor do I, as a professional composer, necessarily resent the quality of the "arrangements" flowing like tasteless treacle through my study.

I do complain that a church can be so arrogant as to presume I enjoy these broadcasts, and that I have no choice in the matter. Whatever other townspeople's reaction may now be, they were not consulted beforehand and are a captive audience. Suppose they in turn, through religious (or even lay) affiliations, broadcast far and wide their personal convictions! Imagine the din! Yet what prevents them? Who sets examples in taste?

Taste is a personal affair; to impose it upon others is to insult them, whether the imposition be that of a rock band or a Bach mass. Painting (fortunately for many in Nantucket) is a silent art: we can look away when it offends us. But since we cannot "listen away" from music, its public emission becomes an invasion of privacy.

Should a vote be cast? Perhaps. But not on whether to continue the North Church recitals, nor indeed on whether they should ever have begun, since most voters wouldn't care (there is too much approved noise everywhere to assume that the inured ear actually listens rather than merely hears, viz, the constant Muzak at the A&P). The vote should be on the more tenuously moral question of whether the pleasure some find in certain public sound is worth the pain this sound causes in others.

Can it now be observed that Schoenberg, like Gertrude Stein, evaded the problem of making art by allowing himself to become snared by his own design for making art?

To complain about the Pan Am Building is to miss the point of Manhattan. The Pan Am Building doesn't block the view, it *is* the view. By the same token, to complain that one performer betrays the composer while another illuminates the composer is to assume that there is one way only. The composer himself might be surprised by this. Still, there are differences that have less to do with interpreting specifics than with music generally. The difference between E. and G. as pianists is that there is nothing "wrong" with G. His one identifying mannerism is his lack of mannerism. Perfection palls, beauty limps, greatness contains the tragic flaw. Paradoxically, the flaw of perfection is not tragic.

Tears didn't blind her, they acted as magnifying glasses. Seen through salt water her own mistakes looked like the faults of others. (Or: Tears don't blind, they enlarge. Seen through salt water, our own mistakes look like others' faults). Yes, the world is according to our humor and locations. If I see that field with my eyes, but cannot see my eyes, can I see the field?

Who is Plato? He is Satie's librettist. Stella Adler? Ellen's mother. Jesus Christ? A character in a tale by Anatole France. Poppaea? Charles Laughton's wife.

They've grown diamond-bright and too strong. I can no longer compete with my imitators.

3 July

Are there, this hot afternoon in Chicago, ten thousand youths masturbating to Michigan breezes in a blazing room, as we learned to masturbate there thirty-six years ago? By the average law, my life's two-thirds done.

He has led—*comment dirai-je?*—a dead life. A dead life. How flat falls the phrase.

Let *brilliant* be banished from literary commentary. Can they still, those in the highest places, permit this meaningless adjective?

The large kitchen has passed from yellow to gray even as I've typed these few words, and the lanes of Nantucket begin again to resemble those of Tangier as night falls, with the hills and cranberries charging through the window, and the hour turns sad again, as though JH, son and father, had died.

One's happiest days are those when one was saddest—that is, most open to reaction, to new experience and heartbreak, the first long journey away from home.

4 July

On the beach this morning a retarded (what used to be called feeble-minded) woman of perhaps thirty-five, flanked by patronizing kin, was patting her sand castle with unlovely hands and giggling—her drooping lower lip incapable of enthusiasm, the lusterless mongol eyes unfocused on her work. What does she *know*? Where are her answers? Who guides her?

All day I observe the *va-et-vients* of Wallace the cat, and wait for his secrets. Is he a sage or an idiot sphinx? Maybe just a baby? But babies know what we've long forgotten?

You know that ghastly look some mashed potatoes get, of cheap white soiled satin? Well, that's how my abdomen's beginning . . .

The Cincinnati piece is nearly done. The overall title of the ten separately named sections is *Dreams*.

5 July

We had decided on Nantucket for three negative reasons: no mosquitoes, no need for a car, no social temptations. The positive virtues are those of many a New England area: clean air, swimmable sea, homegrown tomatoes. The house, rented from a Miss Melva Chesrown, charming and comfortable, two floors quaintly furnished, and a geranium garden. Before my parents come tomorrow, let me assess the first nineteen days.

Community is 101 percent heterosexual WASP, non-intellectual well-off republicans with too many children of whom the females are prettier than the males. The food (like the painting in the clever wharf galleries) is blandly costly, and the movies are safe, chic revivals: *Million Dollar Legs*, which is surrealism for the unwashed—or rather, for the overwashed—and *To Have and Have Not*, which holds up neatly, Bacall being that contradiction: a human star. Bogart/Bacall has nothing to do with acting, everything to do with presence.

In the Unitarian Church there is a conventional concert series run by cultured behatted matrons who do not know my name. In the charming bookstore there are shelf upon shelf of best-sellers dusted daily by macrobiotic thirty-year-olds who do not know my name. So much for a life's work.

I've been alone here half the time (JH must return intermittently to New York). Black nights no longer afflict mornings' start at eight, and the weather's been perfect: a level, silky 72 degrees.

On the new vast sheets of prepared onionskin, with a special soft lead, I've orchestrated forty *tutti* pages; this comes to about five hours a day and a callused thumb. (Oh why, in this large cottage, does Wallace in the middle of the night choose to climb onto the kitchen table and sleep precisely on top of the smudgeable manuscript?)

Of the three books I've finished reading—the Claudel play, *Maigret et le fantôme* (even my precious Simenon seems watery on this island) and *Claudine en ménage*—only the last was worth it. But what worth! In that Claudine series, which readers overlook, the good-natured and all-wise Colette argues a stronger case for women, and two generations earlier, than *A Room of One's Own*.

Gay Sunshine, in a joint issue with Boston's *Fag Rag*, has appeared, containing the interview Winston Leyland taped with me last October. It's inordinately extended, and could surely be as informative at half the length. Yet there's no rule for interviews and, if cut, the content might remain, but my snappish aura would fade with the conversational tone. I do make an issue of how I don't make an issue of homosexuality, and I must say that, within the context of the rest of the magazine (those close-ups of cocks, those manifestos of faggots, those dirty poems), my statements seem reactionary. Yet compared to these islanders I'm an insidious radical.

The islanders, meanwhile, without exception possess the Gentile hemophilic lassitude of the unliterary *gratin* (as opposed to Jewish *nouveaux riches*) which folks like me seldom come across anymore except in Marx Brothers revivals. Yet my loneliness led yesterday to the Harbach's cocktail party at which, through throngs of martini drinkers in the clean old American décor, I was approached by a lady—yes, lady—whose name I didn't catch but whose posture—slim, high-society, handsome, fifty, white marcelled hair and long amber skirt—looked cool as a foaming beer. Heat rose only in a declaration about her native Washington, D.C.: "It's all taken over by the darn Negroes!" I don't necessarily resent her prejudice. I resent her country-club presumption that I, a perfect stranger, share her prejudice.

Depressing fireworks on the public beach.

Why do I write all this? Why persist? For whom? It's not particularly unusual. I write it all because I know who I am, and that is unusual. If from the start *je me suis fait un personnage*, I know who that personnage is.

Thus (and I state this seriously) I am drawing for posterity a situating portrait that plainly does portray.

Meanwhile in the oven across the room cooks a Nectarine Crumble, same recipe as for Joe LeSueur's Cherry Crumble, but with the dangerous addition of one egg. Will it turn out?

6 July

For an autobiography, a logical and legitimate scenario could be built from other people's letters, especially love letters. Who has the courage to plunge into those tear-filled trunks? To spend too long there means that one's life is past. Yet such letters, at least in my case, make landmarks. Who was I, or who did I think I was, when A thirty years ago sent those unhappy words, or B twenty years ago or C ten? Alone, the box filled with mementos from Marie Laure provides a portrait of both her and me at a fixed point in French history.

Love letters are the food of retrospect, introspect and extroversion. And what about hate letters? And business letters?

11 July

Monet's *Regatta à Trouville* is my favorite painting because it evokes some satisfied geography from my own past, a geography I can't elsewhere relocate. Was it on the beach of Lake Michigan that I first knew that untroubled combination of color and temperature? Or the beach at Safi? At Paestum? Saint Tropez? Fire Island? A late summer cloudless sky, a tulip garden filled with hoopskirts at water's edge, money, calm, a chill in the breeze. Such a scene was this afternoon's at the Nantucket jetties, with JH, recalling the sailboats from Scheveningen beach in 1956, when elegant wolfhounds fled through the snow as the sky darkened.

Other pictures by Monet hold little interest for me. Vuillard is my favorite painter.

Did the Ark of Noah provide for fish, or for the larger mammals of the oceans? It did not.

My favorite painter is Caravaggio because he makes me long to live on his stage. That's the sole criterion by which I can judge art, including the art of tragedy.

18 July

The Cincinnati commission is coming nicely. Nine of the eleven movements are composed and orchestrated. What shall I name it? JH suggests *Music for Money*.

Finished *After Leaving Mr. McKenzie*, which in its lumpy style and subject is identical to *Good Morning Midnight*. No American writer has ever, as Jean Rhys does, centered on the mistreated lackluster female caught in unlikely sectors of foreign cities. (What about Maeve Brennan? asks JH.)

The Sting. Some folks got together and said, Let's make a movie about whores and hire two whores to star in it. There's not a frame of the film that doesn't pander.

Lost Horizon (revival of Frank Capra version). How could we once have so thrilled to this sexist, racist cant, this admonition to "Be Kind" by the same Sam Jaffe who presumably sanctioned a pilot's murder and kidnapped these unwilling passengers to fertilize his Caucasian Utopia, where Jane Wyatt (who, with Isabel Jewell and Margo, is the only woman of any race in sight) teaches Tibetan children to sing Brahms in English?

Current reviews of Kate Millett's *Flying* make me uneasy about the reception (if there is one) of my *Final Diary* this autumn. Millett is chided (at least by Lehmann-Haupt) for being homosexual ("the book should appeal to others with her hangups") and, worse, for mixing trivia with deep thinking. As though the very nature of diaries were not based on the Importance of Unimportance.

But humor can't go hand in hand with revolution. Humor means multiple viewpoint, which revisionists cannot afford. Humor has always been for the comfortable. Because they are healthy and their world is new, children view with blinders—they laugh at nothing. Humor is the beginning of decay.

23 July

Finished *Eugénie Grandet* late last night in discouraged astonishment. Ineffable Balzac! Without him, would Mauriac or Green or Gide be as they are? Could they even exist without his example of high strain in the provinces?

This morning I again take up Henry James (he in whom I so drowned in the early 1950s), this time with apprehension. To peruse his introduction for *The Awkward Age* is to laugh with despair. Could I really understand all this in 1952? Today Henry James reads like a parody of Henry James.

You cannot write a tone of voice. Nor can a composer compose his interpretation. Hearing today, over the years, those stern words of Miss Burris— that fourth-grade teacher who made me cry—I cry again at what made her make me cry.

25 July

JH returns this evening from four days away in the cold, according to his call last night, while Nantucket finally bursts into a conflagration of good-natured jonquils. His voice is so always defeated that I protect myself by impatience rather than by sympathy. Yet if JH's woes are continual, I tell myself that I grow less pessimistic with age, that I have more to hide behind than JH, notably a screen of appreciation without which every infant and man is only half himself. Yet what is appreciation but another transient luxury, while JH's sadness, if I were to admit it, is the purity of logic: a necessity. Our planet has no escape. Hope of outer space? Heaven's an endless cemetery. As far as eyes can see, and forever beyond, shine stars by the quadrillion, each one a tombstone.

Clearly I am not endowed with what once was called a poet's eye. I see what is. Waiting last month on Morris Golde's Water Island porch I observe acres of shrubbery, the beach beyond and the ocean. I find what's there, not clusters of throbbing emerald plush or masses of lavender talcum stained with blue champagne, but shrubbery, the beach beyond and the ocean. Although reared within Freudian metaphor I lacked the imagination to see Mother as Jocasta, buttocks as breasts, cocks as snakes and vice versa, or art as depiction of anything beyond itself. Perhaps such literal-mindedness, coupled with lazy half-knowledge, becomes the specialty that turns into Me.

Morris's shining virtue: wishing to be loved, he's willing to love others by giving them the benefit of the doubt. His shining vice: expecting rhetorical questions to be answered. ("Isn't that the most gorgeous sunset you've ever seen? Hey, isn't it?" "Yes Morris, yes it is.")

Morris, to whom I explain that I never made it to Jane Wilson's opening, answers: "Neither did I. How was it?"

27 July

The obituary page was meaningless once. Now I turn there daily with the nausea of anticipation. If no one has died, I sigh with relief (and disappointment). Yet hardly a week passes but the hyper-private news spits from the public pages, as we tremble from the banality of it. This morning: Parker Tyler. Again the review of a lifetime flies by in a minute, as for a drowning man.

We are not who we think we are. But then who are we? This persona—contrived with our bare hands early—is indeed what we think, though its *effect* we can never be sure of. The difference between sane and insane is that the one knows himself and the other doesn't. Which one? The contrivance, so human, we've forced on beasts. Wallace, our Russian blue feline, the apple of JH's eye—fat, spoiled and domesticated there on the gray lawn—is *a part of our lives*. He too, when the bomb explodes, explodes. And the *natural* world? We humans precisely have *made* it natural and in our image, reconditioned. We are who we think then.

Parker was seventy. I'd have thought younger, despite his pasty look during our *croisements* of the past year, mostly in the elevator of my parents' building where he too lives—lived. The excruciating familiarity of that elevator where Parker will nevermore set foot. The lavish art nouveau of the Nantucket Sweet Shop on Main Street. I could immortalize it on this page, as in *L'Eclisse* Antonioni immortalized a bus stop where his stars met. The film ends at the bus stop, abandoned, not even haunted, ours now. Should you visit the Sweet Shop, where nightly I now sit, you would recognize that bric-a-brac from my accurate description, but you'd ask, Where's Ned? Nothing remains but place. Finally it goes too. Battlefields of hell bloom bright with posies.

28 July

Over thirty years ago I left Chicago, and with it the Fifty-seventh Street meeting of the Society of Friends, into which I'd been bred by converted parents. Because the general past is always golden, because this particular group seemed, to my family, lively and liberal (flourishing as it did on the twigs of Hutchins's imaginative nest), and because every gust but this one from the Windy City has ebbed, what more natural than to retain member-ship in absentia? This I do with an annual contribution, receiving in return the *Newsletter*, virtually my sole lien. Now, although the *Newsletter* does not purport to be a literary monthly, I see no reason why, when for once I send a message (an articulate complaint against one Reverend Greeley, whose ma-cho pap in an earlier edition had outraged me), this message should be revised by the editors into the garbled smarmy cant typical of this periodical's tone. Etcetera.

That paragraph opens an unfinished missile to the *Newsletter*. But then—sigh—O why? The recipients do not recall the saucy little boy in their halls, do not know "who" he has become, do not see Quakerhood my way, and why bother? Three weeks ago, when Mother and Father were here on Nan-tucket, we attended meeting (I for the first time in a decade) on Fair Street, and each of us was "moved" to speak regarding the self-congratulatory mood about us. In my case, this was self-congratulation on how un-self-congratula-tory I am, but I was proud of *them*. How, they asked, can we sit here and benefit from this peace, which you say we owe to George Fox, when in fact there is no peace?

Having paddled out of the preface to float swiftly now in the mainstream of *The Awkward Age*, I've cracked the nut—or grown a 1974 vintage—of Henny Penny (as Robert Phelps calls him). The novel is camp, so high that Wilde by comparison joins Neil Simon. (Those characters of every sex and age are never at a loss for original *répliques*!) Now, if the text proper is camp, so by extension is the preface, on a stratosphere level—a triumph not only of style, but of style-as-wit. Consider, then, the whole oeuvre of HJ (JH reacts with bored laughter) and how very coarse in his wake become his immediate American predecessors.

Parker Tyler's obituary (he deserves a more comprehensive one) places his major—his *known*—works as from an early period. Shuddering, I realize that most of what most of us have to say is said before fifty. Fortunately, at least in the area of "art," for every Rimbaud there is a Verdi.

How, I've been trying all day to recall, did I first know Parker? Through John Myers during those fruitful *View* years? I do recall that through Parker I met Tchelitchew. Indeed, it was my urging (having, like all nineteen-year-olds, become bewitched with Tchelitchewiana at MOMA) that prompted Par-ker to choreograph a meeting, realized at the Russian Tea Room, where a fourth joined us (Perry Embiricos?).

Dawn Angel, composed in 1945, predates *The Lordly Hudson* by two years, and is my first post-juvenile song. Before musicalizing the verses, I asked Parker to read them aloud, during which process I recorded in my mind the nuances of his careful voice, then set the poetry according to the poet's personal rises, falls and pauses.

The chore of correcting two massive sets of proofs just received from Boosey & Hawkes! *The Poets' Requiem* (1954–55, Rome) and *Little Prayers* (1973, New York), my only large works for chorus and orchestra, both with soprano solo, and both—perhaps not coincidentally—on poetic compilations of Paul Goodman. A page of music proof, as opposed to the less complex prose galley, requires about ten minutes' reconsideration. Here are 150 pages. How uninterested I've grown in the old *Requiem* and new *Prayers*, which already have little to do with me.

29 July

Monday night. Robert Phelps phoned late yesterday from Hyannis, where Becki has been hospitalized for a week following a major car crash. (At fifty we change our minds, yes, but if we refuse to change our bodies, engines and oak trees change them for us.) Glad to offer Robert, who ferried over for the day, a perfect temperature, healthy lunch (with JH and Gustavo Vega, who's visiting for a few weeks), and a Chekhovian stroll—*des journées entières passées sous les arbres*.

With righteous indignation we follow the impeachment ceremonies on the clear-cut cable TV with which this house is endowed, while through the window creep new-mown hay and goldfinch chirping—and Becki's bones are broken on Cape Cod. Nixon's initials are mine backward. (My middle letter is from Miller, Mother's maiden name.)

The one person on the island—perhaps because I've vaguely known and liked her earlier and elsewhere—with whom fraternity would seem plausible is D. D. Ryan. So when she accepted my invitation for a drink, I went to some effort to prepare for a nice visit. When, after an hour, she hadn't shown, I phoned, to learn she'd simply forgotten. I am very, very, very paranoid, and this is no help.

It is misleading for any workman to pretend that the reputation (whatever it may be) gleaned from his work doesn't grant both carte blanche and noblesse oblige, although these attitudes, in principle, are extraneous to the work. (Protection's needed from too much public if one is to create the very work which creates that public, but one still craves appreciation in order to feel that the work is worthwhile. Only amateurs champion value in a vacuum.) When D. D. simply forgets, what's the use?

The rich make their own rules, more tiresome here than in France where the rich have been rich longer, so you don't constantly have to prove you love them for themselves, as though money had nothing to do with the grooming of those selves. Admittedly, the European rich I once knew were only through Marie Laure's association (though I knew *her*), while in America I know almost none, and those "almost" are past episodes, all female, with marriage in mind.

1 August

Is the theater of the quotidian more active in the rural summer, or just more sharply focused? Mother called to say that Father fell from a curb, suffered a chipped hip, will remain in Saint Vincent's for three weeks after a pin is affixed to the bone. She adds (not knowing I know) that Parker Tyler is dead, that a few mornings ago, as coincidence would have it, she was at Saint Vincent's visiting a patient who said Parker was in the next room. She entered there, greeted Charles Boultenhouse *qui veillait*, and shook the pallid hand of the patient, who *maybe* recognized her, though he seemed "lost," and who died that evening.

Mother and Father waited five hours in Emergency before Father was examined—Father, who co-founded Blue Cross and who for forty years was America's most distinguished medical economist, who lies now in a ward, Father who will be eighty in November.

Whatever became of rough trade? Already in the 1960s there had emerged a type far too sveltely masculine to be anything but queer, while the straight hard hat was too potbellied to be appealing. Today—after flower children, "passive" husbands and unisex—one may well ask, If opposites attract, who is one's opposite?

2 August

Here is your past, pronounced the voice, and a door opened into the gloom of our Chicago apartment. It had been stripped bare, as by bandits.

Before falling to sleep (from which I was, at 2:30, to wake up screaming from that nightmare too clear for comment), I savored the habitual skilled intensity of Pauline Kael in her diatribe against the "moguls." She does skirt one point: that people get (as Nixon got) what they deserve. And though she allows that better movies are being made now in America than at any time anywhere, and reaffirms the obvious—that hits are not to be confused with art—she avoids admitting that the vast movie public never was or can be, by definition, discriminating. (The young, as she claims, may have had their taste waylaid in the past two years, but have they ever really been *nuancés*, as she gives them credit for? On summer beaches now, as from winter porches then, show us one, just one, of those thousand lovely children attending to the Debussy Trio as he would to the rock background. *Le Sacre* could fill their every visceral requirement, but where is it?) Otherwise, of course, she's right about moguls slapping poets for being poets. In music the moguls (i.e., performers' impresarios) are unaware of the very existence of poets (i.e., composers), and the word *artist* has come to mean performer, entertainer.

To be a movie critic is to investigate, like a telescope, the inherently expanding; because film, no matter how "fine," is through its size construed for *le grand public*—the collective eye. To be a music critic is to examine, as under a microscope, the infinitely small (and how many contracting universes float on that lens!), because a piece of music, no matter how gross, is construed for the unique ear. Only when music relinquishes its function as an aural art (something to be attended) and caters to the whole body (an accompaniment) does it cease being a fine art.

9 P.M. After twenty minutes of *Blazing Saddles* we leave the theater, dis-

couraged. There's still enough calm afterglow on South Water Street for our stroll toward the wharves to watch the sunset, balanced this evening by the moon, which has become a perfect lavender globe. This cheers us up. Then we stop by the Hub to buy ten postcards.

"That's fifty-two cents," announces the salesgirl, one of the prettyish Vassar types who swarm the island in summer to learn about life by getting a job.

"Why fifty-two? How much is one card?"

"A nickel."

"Then if I buy each card as a separate purchase, they'd only come to fifty cents."

"You'd be ripping us off by avoiding the tax."

"On the contrary, you're ripping me off by manipulating the tax."

"Are you speaking to me, personally?"

"I'm saying the policy is unfair. Usually to sell an item in quantity is to lower the price. Here the more I buy, the more you charge, yet you say I'm ripping you off. The customer as usual is wrong, and I resent it."

Yet I paid what she asked, and went off feeling awful. Returning with Gustavo to the safety of the house on West Chester Street and the purry welcome of Wallace, I finish the peach cobbler made this afternoon and begin the penultimate piece of my Cincinnati opus—a scurrying toccata called *Apples*, for three oboes and three violas.

(That loathsome new verb—*to rip off*!)

7 August

JH returned from New York Sunday with a headache. By last night the ache had turned to what he felt was a cerebral hemorrhage after three days of high fever and near-constant delirium. I waited in the emergency ward of Nantucket's Cottage Hospital while JH was being inspected this morning at dawn. And I inspected the flow of the very young in other emergencies—mostly long-haired children with ticks in their ears or gashes in their poison-ivied toes. One young couple brought in their son Brian, age two, who since yesterday had refused to open his eyes. There he was in his mother's arms, silky skinned, unsmiling and unprecedented, shrieking when prodded, the parents more innocent than he in his sophisticated visual autism. What became of Brian I do not know. JH emerged, after sinus X rays (negative), diagnosed as a flu carrier and told to take two aspirins and rest. He's sleeping now, thank God, silently.

8 August

Twenty years ago tonight I first met P at a long-since-vanished *boîte* in Cannes. Of that, nothing remains, though I can recall, as clearly as though it were a large-print version of the Bible in my lap, each phrase and motion of that two-year episode. But I only recall; I do not reexperience. The body's intact without the blood. Still, the past looms ever larger as the future recedes. (Is *recede* the word? I mean to get smaller, *rapetisser*.) And if love affairs of the past are unnourishing, affairs of the past stick and twist, entertaining endlessly. Nobody, except JH (who, when he goes off, leaves me bereft), means much today.

10 August

We can sympathize with, but not feel and so not weigh, another's pain. The hurt which for days JH has borne is almost too much for me, yet I don't ache. We can "project into," but not adopt and so not judge, the flesh of the opposite sex. No man or woman will ever know from inside what is a woman or man. Nor can we be readers of our own writing, and music composed in a swoon is sneered at. We might know the facts of our youth, but can only repeat them blurred on the edge of an expensive coffin. . . . What a wind. And so clear. The first morning of a new president's reign, Mother's and Father's fifty-fourth anniversary (to be toasted tonight at Saint Vincent's Hospital) and the day I completed the orchestration on what now is named *Air Music: Ten Variations for Orchestra*. Methodic folly.

Could one wish for more unflawed mornings, windless clovered cobalt air at body temperature? Jane Bowles's *Plain Pleasures* extols the virtue of "simple things," those little joys that make life worthwhile. I wouldn't dare today, as I dared a year ago, to be bored, to wish tomorrow would come, to "kill" time, because the only delights in the present are bromides. Yet such perfect sunlight only helps to focus on tombstones, like naked light bulbs in a concentration camp.

Plain Pleasures, in fact, is a sordid tale, and I do feel at loose ends, notwithstanding Mother Nature's inexplicable splendors, when I've finished a long piece. Which is worse: the distraction of not working or the anxiety of work? Thank God, I've two more deadlined commissions, one for North Carolina's orchestra, the other for harp solo. *Je suis un mauvais oisif*, a bad idler. Lacking the imagination for just living, I'm forced into art.

How can I know if my prose and music interfere with each other? Without the prose would the music be better or just thicker? Without the music would there be a subject for the prose?

Only as a composer am I qualified to soliloquize, since my life is no longer amorous, garrulous, or drunk, and since I've no more friends—certainly no new ones. (Who would they be, and what could they give me that I couldn't find in their works? Except maybe a taxi ride to the hospital in moments of need—moments, however, growing paradoxically fewer as one gets feebler.) Killing time. Now that I am allowed to speak, I have no more to say.

Of my six books published since 1966, none has been reviewed by the national weekly press, and only one, *The Paris Diary*, in the Sunday *Times*. Reasons for this I will never be told. Clearly they have little to do with my two "categories" of book, since Nin's and Muggeridge's diaries are all reviewed by all the press, and essays by, say, Haggin or Porter are also decently covered. Nor is it because of my value as a littérateur, since those who do not review me (*Time, Newsweek, Esquire*) do often quote my opinions, and since those authors who won't supply blurbs for me (Calisher, Purdy, Robert Craft) do often use my blurbs for themselves.

A seventh book is coming forth. The resignation in midstream of Aaron

Asher includes most support for my *Final Diary* at Holt, Rinehart. Their logistics to the contrary, publishers who do not show interest in their own books, specifically through advertising, will hardly fire the public's interest, since the public will not know the books exist. With a sigh I see the *Diary* relegated to the also-ran column of the ad brochures, and foresee the usual pipe-smoking disinterest from the *Times*, which prefers its latter-day Saroyans.

With music I have no complaints. Whatever my music *is*, whatever it represents for various levels of consumer (from fellow composers of all persuasions to choir directors in Idaho), it is *available*.

Julien Green's endless examination of faith, tiresome as it is, gives motivation and body to his journal. Green's glue is God; mine is bitterness. I'm not contemptuous of the deserving, or even of the nondeserving (Casals, Schweitzer) in themselves. My hate is centered on the unfocused adoration of gurus at the expense of the intellect.

23 August

Sweep terrace, bake peach pie, empty cat pan, water marigolds, spend long hours at beach without a book—anything to avoid typing these paragraphs. Type these paragraphs, strain for "perception," concoct some gossip, reflect on horrors of creation, think up "telling" epigrams—anything to avoid real work. Really work, spend long hours at keyboard, fill notebook with notes and their inversions, copy and orchestrate, make it legible—anything to avoid that strain of concentration which is the stimulation of a true creative bowel. Stimulate a true creative bowel and forget the pies and pans.

But nowhere here anymore will you find moaning for sex—for wasting time performing the (perhaps) one act worth noting.

To have said this before is not to have said it, since I've not said it at this age. All's the same, but different; the blank page is the same, but the anxiety's quicker, with less time to fill the page.

There are no fascinating people, only their works are fascinating. *Et encore.* I don't interest myself now, only my work does that. *Et encore.* (I picture her cold eyes falling by chance upon such words, hear her superior sigh of pity at the poverty of my invention, O friendly diarist. Yet in fact, America has no art.)

The telling sounds savage, although the "reality" of the dream seemed sad. Wallace, his Russian blue fur on fire, clenched teeth with his double, except that the double had no eyes. Slowly he absorbed Wallace, and a single beast was formed with black bloodless sockets "looking" at the moon, and I awoke to a bleak whine. Neighbors explained: all local cats were having their eyes cored by the maniac.

In fourth grade I saved my allowance to buy a tiger-eye bracelet. Within this bracelet I stored the playing cards (the trading of which was all the rage with fourth-graders then) and hid them in my school desk. Miss Burris, discovering this, observed that the bracelet was too valuable for such service and called my home.

I love my friends because I need them, not the other way around, and begrudge each second of the time they take. A composer cannot be a host, at least not this one. I'm so easily swayed, yet I blame you, not me. Could I live with just the cat as though he were a friend? Possibly. Provided JH were there.

Morris Golde has come and gone after an agreeable four-night stay, one of several we've had since June 17, reconfirming the yawning disparity between a dinner guest and a weekend companion. It's not that I haven't the time, as the clock goes, to isolate myself while friends are here. It's that I haven't *the leisure to work*—the ability (so pronounced when I was thirteen) to shut myself off from family. On the incomparable caramel sands of Cisco we observe a bevy of muscular red-haired paragons whom I imagine, as with a scythe, decapitated. Brilliant. (How can intelligent commentators use that meaningless adjective anymore?)

I am not intelligent, I am brilliant.

And yet we are planning to buy a house. If we do (assuming there's no crash), and my life savings become land, it will effect my third major relocation in a half century.

24 August

Welcome damp day, early cool, dead maple leaves all over. Fog of churning butter. Shirley's about to arrive from Martha's Vineyard for an all too short week.

28 August

For Shirley's distraction and our emancipation we invited three guests for Tanqueray gin at six: Rosette Lamont, platinum blonde in bright blue, bringing her essays on Ionesco; Eugénie Voorhees, bracelet of gold and silver (a merging which, like brass and bronze or sequences and cloisters, satisfied me utterly), bringing her calm beauty; and Rex Reed, with an expensive red sweater, bringing his brash and never-still tongue. My standards are perhaps no higher than Rex's, but my criteria are different. When he exclaims about Nantucket's being "divorced from reality," I picture him back in Manhattan at those private screenings, those cocktail parties where he's the cock of the walk, those *têtes-à-têtes* with Angela Lansbury.

I tell them I've just finished an extended piece, which Rex takes to mean journalism—*piece* having replaced *article* in literary jargon. Do I, he wonders, ever write fiction? No. My life is my fiction.

30 August

Herpes simplex is virulently recurring. For two decades, three times a year, it has arrived at an hour's notice—a fragile tingle at the base of the spine; a flowering of pustules that expand into blisters, secrete, burst; a hyper-sweet pain through the buttocks dissolving into a raw wound. The attack runs its course in twelve days.

Cervical *herpes* may lead to cancer, though rectal *herpes* (far rarer than genital *herpes*, or shingles, or cold sores) is, in males, just what it is—a virus with no antidote. Nonetheless, last winter Dr. Webster experimentally submitted me to six smallpox vaccinations in six weeks. Shots in the dark that didn't take.

Labor Day

Before leaving on her ferry yesterday, Shirley strolled with me (like characters in each other's dreams, stunned from the heat in slow motion) through the little pair of cemeteries on New Lane, where the stone-marked graves of the Folgers and Coffins and Gardners revived my Chicago Quakerism. Thirty-five years at most, Shirley contends, and we'll both be stashed in that ground.

JH feels that my condolence letters never quite hit the mark. But what should I write in such letters? That I wished it were me? If we were guaranteed a longer life—another hundred years, say—but knowing what we know, would we accept? Of course. We can quickly get used to anything, including mint-new dimensions.

2 September

Brooding on yesterday's cemeteries. The fact that I will not survive is intolerable. Fear of death lies not in that my work might be lost, but that myself will be lost. If the work survives, it will be as misconstrued, or at least as reinterpreted as Chopin's today. But what of the person, Chopin? The man is superfluous to his art: the art sheds the body like a lizard its skin. People who may love my music look into my eyes and are . . . what? . . . unaware? . . . dare I write uninterested? Yet I live in this body, and am afraid of being abandoned underground. With a magnifying glass let me focus on Nadar's famous photograph and ask, "Who are you? Tell me, who are you? Because your music can't answer any more than mine can."

We are not our art. I entreat the eyes of Chopin. But they do not answer.

Of everyone I know H.B. most plays the genius and has the least to show for it. I wish that barking dog would stop barking so that I could write about that barking dog that won't stop barking.

Allergy frightful. For two years it's been quiescent. Since Mother's hay fever vanished with menopause perhaps here was one change of life for the better. But it returned full force. Chlor-Trimeton and Afrin give all the bad side effects without good benefits. A drowsy numbness fills the soul but my nose remains blocked.

Despite these increasingly savage bouts which always rage during the pre-frost sodden days of late September, especially on Nantucket, which (though advertised as pollen-free) is adorned with eighteen cruel varieties of goldenrod which goes to seed during weather too sweet to be true, autumn is visible, most particularly through the total darkness which now covers the town like a giant tea cozy by 7:30 P.M. That was the hour when last evening, humanly alone in the house and washing dishes, I heard a crash. The front porch door was shattered. My two simultaneous reactions: something had been thrown in; Wallace had jumped out. I do feel despised by locals who find me cranky about the carillon and are capable of harassment, yet no rock or beebee shot was on the inside porch floor. I do know that Wallace had been excited by the sight of a rabbit on the lawn at dusk, but no bloody fur was on the outside grass. A neighbor who heard the noise appeared a minute later, but said she'd seen nobody running off. On the other hand, a cat just doesn't dive with impunity through plate glass, especially a sedentary nine-year-old urban beauty like Wallace who's never been outside without a leash. Yet that's what he had done.

For three hours I patrolled the area with a flashlight. Nothing. JH phoned back from New York, distraught. (Though perhaps no more lovingly attached to the animal than I, he surely is more anthropomorphically so, and for him it was as though an offspring had been kidnapped.) Sleepless night, cups of snot pour from itchy eyes, delayed reactions setting in, visions of Wallace stunned and scraped, devoured by foxes, demented by famine, incapable of coping.

In the thick mist of dawn he materialized on the front lawn, no worse for wear, and I phoned JH who was so relieved he wept. Wallace has consumed two packs of Tender Vittles, and now, at noon, slumbers atop the piano, his nocturne vanished, but not my hay fever.

Although antagonistic to dream interpretation, to mysticism, to ESP, even to practical analysis of events beyond the five senses, I've long since ceased being surprised that dreams, far from symbolizing what in fact occurred yesterday, represent fairly accurately what will occur today. Paradox. For the future does not exist. If the future existed it would not, by definition, be the future.

The French, who have no word for mind (as distinct from brain or wit or intelligence) sometimes say soul, as in *état d'âme*, the equivalent of state of mind. Thus, when I raised a table knife, not to eat nor yet to test the sharpness but to examine in its gleam the reflection of myself, Marie Laure would say, *"Tu t'occupes moins de ton état d'âme que de ton état de corps."* Preoccupation with a "state of body" has switched now from concern with beauty to concern with collapse. This Nantucket summer has strayed unnoticed when, faithless to work and play, day after opaline day, I keep to my room in suicidal panic, self-absorbed utterly, gasping from all-consuming asthma. With ill health, the first thing to vanish is objectivity—seeing three sides of the same coin which defines humor. The funniest thing JH, in his infinite patience, has uttered these past weeks is, "Your sense of humor will see you through."

3 September

No one has written, but somebody should, an esthetic history of movie music. Seeing *Of Human Bondage* again (what bromidic marshmallows we swallowed once from the lips of Leslie Howard, yet what matchless techniques had Bette Davis even then!), and all to the afflicting notes of Max Steiner, I realized how inappropriate such music had become. Music makes or breaks the weakest, the strongest, film. The sixties' taste of the European masters: Antonioni used only the sound of factory whistles or "source" tunes from radios; Fellini, only Rota's jaunty scores for even his saddest tales; Bergman, with his sense of the apropos in *Cries and Whispers*, Chopin and Bach; Bertolucci, the languorous Delarue. The most avant-garde use the most arrière-garde music (Satie). Cocteau's taste. Use of jazz in the fifties' tragedies. Why they worked, why they didn't. Etc. Endlessly complex as a study on the employment of form and color in the Renaissance.

✳

Cold, wet, end of a season. The weather smells of Fez twenty-five Novembers ago, the premature African snow, burning logs, dampness that makes my music paper curve and and the crackers soggy.

4 September

From Sauguet in Coutras, and from Roro in Majorca where he's bought a house, I learn that *"la grande, la grosse, la bonne Lily Pastré n'est plus."* Well, she'd have been well over eighty, so it's no surprise, though there does come the question, With what do all those recollections rhyme, alone and unversified in my brain, and to be scratched out thoroughly when my body too *"n'est plus"*? It's here in this paragraph? No, sir. The flavor of her lawns—those eighty-acre lawns of Montredon where we played croquet, where I completed the second act of *Miss Julie*, where Lily's indiscriminate generosity was manifest in five full meals a day on a garden table set for twenty and conversation (not probing but still urgent) solely on music, and those granddaughters gorgeous as hyacinths or fawns, and where I was warmed by the sentiment of knowing that she, whom I'd known longer than Marie Laure, would stick—the flavor of those lawns is gone.

Something is seamy about the presence of Rex Reed. Has it to do with high intelligence congealed around projects so flippant, or with his soft black hair framing those unfocused eyes? When I announce I might buy a house here, he says: "You must be very very rich. Imagine what it's going to cost you, those shipments from Bloomingdale's on the ferry?" When I answer that I'll paint the rooms white, and that such furnishings as are needed will be found at the local Sears, he gazes at me from those gorgeous empty orbs with disbelief and pity.

5 September

Alone again this week, and the temperature's turned almost to freezing. Still, with a sweater on, I water the lawns while the evening stew stews, the invisible sun sets, and out through the door and up to the cloudy heaven floats the simmering onion. My frame of reference, ever narrower, is me, me, me. This diary, though compiled by a sure intelligence, seeks vainly for intelligent observation.

A call out of the blue from Martin Peretz invites me to organize a panorama of the current musical American scene for *The New Republic*'s sixtieth anniversary. This will take me away from myself, thank God.

Since for years I've derided Hemingway, last night, to refresh my mind for future derision, I reread a dozen of his stories. I liked them. Suddenly they're in context, classic, assessable (*Up in Michigan*, for instance, was composed three years before my birth). He wasn't a poet, or even somehow a novelist, but a playwright who didn't write plays. His gift, his unmistakable quality, was a good ear—that is, an absence of imagination.

7 September

Despite the continuing knots of rain, Rosette and I went last night to the White Elephant to hear Frank Conroy play piano. This he does with the lean skill of those black thirties' soloists but not (so far as I hear) with much personal necessity. Like his book, *Stop Time*, Conroy's musicality is undeniably affable: it holds your interest even when nothing is happening, which is most of the time. But it lacks the fever of art. His intelligence, his neuroses, his acute sensitivity are all quite predictably normal. His pianism, like his literature, feeds on the past (a narrow past) more than you'd think for one his age—an age, however, more advanced than it looks. For he's not twenty but thirty-eight, with a brief catalogue, and a face which, like Jackie Onassis's, resembles, because of the extremely wide-set eyes, a bewitchingly lovely embryo.

Later. Advance reviews of the *Diary*, just received, are more snide than for previous books. "The self he exhibits," declares the Kirkus Service, "belongs to a world of artifice, finds Rochas cologne truer than roses, and seems to require the diaries for completion." Yes, that is so. I prefer perfume to plants just as I prefer Frescobaldi to folk song. I am not attracted to raw material, but to what can be made from it. More disconcerting is to be taken literally, to have each phrase humorlessly deciphered as though I had *meant* the phrase. "For how much longer can he entice the boys with his black T-shirt?" the review asks (the boys, indeed, as though that slur were still in coinage!), and goes on to say, "An involvement for consenting adults."

But if there's a grain of truth in every lie, there's a sackful in any opinion, no matter how stupid. Perhaps, simply, my book does not give off the tone I intend. With all the contrivance, the tears are real, but I cannot bear to have my sarcasms taken sarcastically. Nor, alas, can I with any potency defend my diary within my diary.

Night. The rain forms a cage around the house. Not with displeasure have I been shutting myself off more and more from all art and all attitude, even from the day. I wait to sleep. Unfortunately for my moneymaking, I'm no longer convinced, American style, that a "productive" life need be spent in producing. My life's sole variety is in the never-the-same flame patterns there in Melva's grate.

8 September

Shouldn't there be second thoughts on Frank Conroy as for Jim Bridges? Isn't the heel of Achilles precisely his most identifying trait? Could not our faults be more special—indeed, more purposeful—than our virtues? (Cocteau is generally credited with Picasso's famous remark: *"Ce que les autres te reprochent, cultive-le, c'est toi."*) On a Tuesday night instead of a Thursday am I not capable of finding in Frank Conroy's *Honeysuckle Rose* an ordinariness so unique as to become great art? On a Thursday night instead of a Tuesday am I not capable of finding that Jim Bridges's weakness—charm in lieu of statement—is in fact his strength, his statement? Frank says that a person in deep depression, by dint of never giving but ever taking as into a bottomless pit, becomes finally less touching, less fascinating, than, *pace* J. D. Laing, just boring. His piano playing like his single novel, although both concern madness, is sanity pure, and lovable. As for Jim Bridges's movies, it is only because their obsession with the Practical Joke goes against my upbringing that I chide them and not him.

Can a composer know what his music connotes? Some of my merriest moments have been heard as macabre, while other heart-burning songs are termed (and by paid men of sense) icy.

. . . although at this writing I've yet to attend a first rehearsal. The meaning implicit in the hot live sound may stray from what, even to me, it said on the inscribed cool page.

Wildly rainy, with lightning way out there, yet the sun shines and everything's diffused (is that the word?) in a pink glow. To awaken inside a rosebud couldn't be too different from this . . .

Insomnia. As though this shimmering bed were the sole wakeful object in the universe, alit, radioactive, shuddering. How to summon sleep! Will sleep ever arrive, like astronauts gauging that frail slit in the envelope of space through which they must reenter Earth's orbit?

Ned Rorem, b. 1923. Like everyone whose birthday comes in the fall, I'm forever recorded as being older than I am—as being, for example, thirty instead of twenty-nine during most of 1953, or forty-two in 1965. Indeed, in 1923 I was reported as being a year old before I was born.

Robin Morgan proposes that in these troubled times women too should be drafted. Well, yes. But if conscription is our world's sole indignity wherein men have it worse than women, why should women apply for equal rights under a stupid law? Would it not be purer to work together to abolish that law? Or is such reasoning pacifist rather than egalitarian?

Yet again this morning the radio talks of "innocent victims," meaning women and children. Is the implication that the soldiers—those teenage boys who have little choice but to fight—are guilty?

The fetus in a repressive society. Suppose a woman were pregnant with what she knew to be, for whatever reason, a homosexual. Has she the right to wilfully miscarry this infant, knowing that in the adult world it would eventually be legally executed? In a repressive society, which is stronger: the horror of abortion or the horror of inversion? If a fetus is a creature with rights, why do we not sing a requiem for a miscarriage?

JH came into the room a moment ago and said: "I was just at Grandma Moses' vernissage where I overheard one eight-year-old say to another, 'What junk! My old grandfather can paint better than that.'"

9 September

The sun's come out after two weeks. The sky looks washed. Off for a long bike ride to Polpis.

News about my upcoming book is bad. Holt, Rinehart conspires against the likes of my style in favor of machismo and moneymaking. Adding injury to insult, Marian writes that Robert Craft, upset by a reference in an advance copy which fell into his hands, has requested (with the gentle threat of litigation) that the phrase be removed. Everyone likes everything about the book except the niggardly sentences on himself.

Deaths of Marcel Achard and of Harry Partch, the arrière-garde of France and the avant-garde of America.

Why am I less attracted to a contemporary artist's work after he dies? When friends die, the excruciation lies in knowing we'll never see them again. Precisely that "never" is what leaves me cold when artists die (artists, that is, who are not necessarily friends). The fact that their catalogue is now complete dulls, rather than quickens, my interest. (Do an essay on this. These words are too rusty and the idea's shiny.)

For Rosette Lamont, when she interviews me as a new resident of Nantucket: The local concert series? It's profoundly superficial—to coin an oxymoron—because in its super-safe concentration on established nineteenth-century German masterpieces the programs become expendable; they go in one ear and out the other—at least my ears. The performers are as much to blame as the ignorant organizers. Virtuosically speaking, the performers are good: they are all first-rate second-raters. But from a composer's standpoint, concerts worth going to are concerts of his time and place. There's really nothing more to get from these eternal hearings of Schubert and Beethoven. Of course, that's why people go to them.

Bitter? Sort of very. But it's glib: a lifetime spent on what is unappreciated. I'd have liked to be, but am not, a celebrity American style. My nature demands it, but the nature of my work does not. There I am. Now it's too late, nor will I concede—for I could never talk on a talk show about all those passing fancies meant to be seen and not heard.

The Final Diary's a grave. I remain living. That book houses a fictitious animal I chose to name Ned.

There is no posterity anymore. Why should I, then, not collect my own letters, and publish while alive my posthumous works?

12 September

(Re Jay Harrison's funeral)

Those deaths which "don't come as a surprise" surprise us most. Being expected, they are written off before they occur. When they occur, we're doubly saddened. No gulf is wider than that between almost dead and dead.

15 September

Mother and Father went home by way of the ferryboat to Hyannis yesterday after a week of indefatigable talking and walking, though between them they count 160 years while I am forever thirteen. Who could not envy their rapport, the continual conversation and mutual consideration, the active participation in Quaker Meeting and radical politics, when so many couples well before their golden anniversary adopt policies of exhausted silence?

Summer visitors. Those fogbound morning conversations that so eat into the energy of the day. I keep wanting everyone to stop talking, so that I can go write about what they're saying—to stop living, so that I can write about living.

The composer in me could never have written that paragraph. No one can prove, nor do musicians necessarily claim, that music concerns living.

There *is* accounting for taste. Everyone likes raspberries and ice cream, everyone likes the smell of pine, everyone likes the touch of silk and the sound of Ravel, everyone likes (in body, if not in mind) to get blown. Not everyone likes leeks and sour cream or barnyard smells, not everyone likes thistles or Schoenberg, not everyone likes to blow.

Were there fish on Noah's ark?

Why do I write music? In order to "show" those bullies in grammar school, with whom I was in love . . . Well, at least I'm free now from the thrilling monotony of being in love, the wasted months of being in love, the gorgeous nightmare of being in love. But not free from writing about it.

I often think about how seldom I think about sex.

Rich socialite Joan Crawford to poor violinist John Garfield in *Humoresque*: "You don't like martinis? Well, they're a cultivated taste. Like Ravel." (But didn't I just say that everyone likes Ravel?)

17 September

Everyone's gone. Even D. D. Ryan (the Pop Art devastation on the interior of whose innocently old-fashioned brick house provides, they say, an ideal clue for how to make a sow's ear from a silk purse) is gone. Nantucket now, after the season, would resemble *Death in Venice*, except that only in America will you find a breeze so pure, so rich in bluebell cloisonné, etc., etc.

"Bang, you're dead!" and the fictive victim obligingly falls to the ground during this child's game.

"But what if the fictive victim coincidentally has an infarction and actually does fall dead?" asks gifted little Claudinette while explaining her new novel's plot, and so doing, imitates the fictive victim. But the book never gets written, since Claudinette too falls dead.

Anachronisms in the movies: Jeanette MacDonald's wristwatch in *Naughty Marietta*. The seagull that flies across the lens in *On the Beach* when the San Francisco Bay is supposed to be devoid of life.

JH just came into the room and said: "I've been rereading all of Shakespeare. He doesn't hold up."

20 September

Back in New York I am able finally to play the new Desto recording of my *Night Music*, which was issued several months ago. I put on the record. Displeased, I stop it midway and turn on the radio, where *Night Music* is playing at exactly the point I had turned it off.

It's already been ten years since I've felt a strong need for novelty, for possibilities around the corner—love affairs, world travel. Gradually the efforts outward, the planet's potential, have dwindled, and for several months now the corners I've turned are internal. My living area grows smaller and smaller, from city to armchair to my myopic frosted-over lenses. All my gymnastic is in thought. Unhappily I'm limited to myself, smugly, knowing that just that rose petal there has so much more variety than my poor fancy.

On Edmund White's

STATES OF DESIRE

TRAVELS IN GAY AMERICA

In a famous poem fifty years ago Kay Boyle summed up homosexuality as engrossing as bee-raising and as monotonous to the outsider. Well, monotony is perhaps not quite the reaction today of, say, Anita Bryant whose belligerence reflects the old tack of the ignorant. More disturbing is to find that tack still taken by cultured "outsiders." Male homosexuality is currently treated by Mary McCarthy as silly, by Hilton Kramer as corrupting, by Norman Podhoretz as dangerous, and by William Styron as makeshift (although to his credit, the sole character in *Sophie's Choice* with a touch of grandeur turns out to be lesbian). Indeed, no first-rate heterosexual thinker has ever dealt at length intelligently with this increasingly visible matter.

If outsiders are those shunning tenets of a prevailing group, the term would seem more apt for homosexuals themselves were they not continually functioning within a straight milieu. As to how monotonous *they* might find the upcoming Talese report on straight sex will depend on how restrictive the survey and how skillful the prose. The prose of Edmund White, meanwhile, as he recounts his travels in gay America, glimmers and surges into channels far wider than his stated theme, and in a mode that could make even bee-raising a hit course at West Point.

"I looked everywhere for the tinted windowpanes I remembered from a childhood visit," notes the author toward the close of his book, during an excursion in the line of duty to Boston's Louisburg Square. "At last I discovered two panes, one pale amethyst, the other purple; I was reminded that glass is a liquid that continues to flow (that's why it warps with age). Perhaps if I return after another hundred years those panes will be violet puddles on the cobblestones." Boston was the last lap of a twenty-city investigation pursued by White, age forty, with an adolescent's horny zeal. The investigation is no more a queer tour of the United States than Gide's journal is a gay guide to France (oh, just a bit more), although it poses as a documentary—

narrated from a thoroughbred horse's mouth—on our national gay bour-
geoisie. Actually it's an artist's selective vision (through purple panes, if you
will) of human comportment which is and is not his own, mulled over,
distilled, then spilled onto the page with a melancholy joy like "violet puddles on the cobblestones."

First stop, Los Angeles, which like every city boasts its "body type, the
Platonic form for that locality. . . . Since most people's parents are heterosexual (so much for the role-model theory of sexual orientation), and everyone is raised to be straight," gays, once they discover their nature, must
invent themselves. Here the self is "silken, tan, hairless . . . a trail of golden
dust shading the hollow just above the coccyx." In San Francisco, where at
least 20 percent of registered voters are gay, the body is "trim, five-foot-ten,
and the face wears a dark beard and mustache below warm brown eyes
radiating good will." SF minds shift from est to S&M, such a contradiction,
"where the society against which a young homosexual might rebel is itself
largely homosexual," endorsing gay unanimity as the only strong policy.
"The progressives of Seattle keep looking back over a shoulder . . . convinced they are more elegant than their Portland neighbors to the south," a
perception corroborated by one case history here, another there, both with
"very handsome" men (few of White's interviewees are physically plain). In
Santa Fe "chastity is now suspect, and bisexuality has been declared a form
of rank hypocrisy," because the Liberation Movement, otherwise noble, does
discourage the rugged individualism of yore.

So flows contrast across the land. If sodomy to Salt Lake City is as witch-
ery to Salem, Denver gaywise seems easygoing as Athens. If Houston is the
friendly town where "machismo still stands as much for honor as for violence," Dallas is "snobby, pissy, phony elegant, up-tight." If Kansas City is
"the Fifties in deep freeze" where "marriages" betwixt Older Man and Beautiful Boy still prove the norm, Cincinnati is not far ahead when "no one has
stopped to ask if respectability is a valid standard." If Gay Liberation is a
feeble affair in Chicago, which is nonetheless "the chief oasis between the
coasts," blame it on Mayor Daley's Machine ploughing up the city too deeply
for grass-roots activity to sprout. Florida, meanwhile, like all the South
where Gay Lib has made few inroads, adores drag and "nelly behavior . . . as
the only available means of expressing distinct identity. . . . Gay anger is not
directed against Anita Bryant but against the radical gay leader, Bob Kunst."
Key West ("the rate of violence is lower than in any major city"), Memphis
("all the men here are femme," claims a denizen), New Orleans ("like Venice,
a poetic city with prosaic citizens"), Atlanta ("no one ever wants to leave,"
although the black and white gay worlds are utterly separate): each center is
classified, replete with interviews (occasionally with intellectuals, mainly
with white-collar fauna), and with no sexual holds barred. Yet always rising
above the opinionated babble or murmuring through the moans of an "orgy
room," transliterating the lingo of bigoted queens or miming the wisdom of
Castro Street theologians, we hear the private voice of Edmund White,
humanist yet unsentimental, tough but never cynical, luscious though not
campy.

However, we also hear the risky whisper of generality, the undifferentiation common to documentaries where there is no "building toward," no climax, only comparisons, and where ten examples seem better than one. The constant slant provokes indigestion: surely there's more to homosexuality than being homosexual! "I am trying," claims White early on, "to describe the styles of life that are unique to a city, not those that could be lived in any city." Still by the time we reach Manhattan, after two hundred pages wherein White has played scribe to endless middlebrow bull sessions, we are told that the cliché gay Westsider is in his late twenties, works as an architectural assistant, gets stoned with friends on Friday while watching old movies on TV, wants a new apartment, a new job, a new lover, works out at the Y, digs ballet and brass bedsteads, is in group therapy and convinced he's "making progress." Is the gay Eastsider so far away? or even the straight Washingtonian? What we learn about lifestyle is finally less singular than the terse interpolated essays—some a mere two sentences—on politics ("Unlike other minority groups, homosexuals through liberation . . . are becoming more idiosyncratic and less assimilated to the general population"), on pedophilia ("A great deal has been written about the havoc pederasty may or may not wreak on the young, but little has been said about the disorder it introduces into the life of the lover of boys"), on sexual violence (which has "broken the tyranny beauty used to hold over us," but which seems to be mainly symbolic, not harmful, like ritual fights between male wolves), on the dissolution of the Protestant family, or on the Proustian yearnings within White's own case history, much of it having nothing to do with sex, still less with homosex; for his treatise is more a diary than a Baedeker, being at once too special and too general for reliability.

I once argued that Edmund White's chief theme in literature, like Antonioni's in movies, was Responsibility—or rather, the lack of it. Was not the hero of *Forgetting Elena* (the first of White's three previous books) exempted, by his amnesia, from the chores of his mannered entourage? Did not the narrator of *Nocturnes for the King of Naples* kill off his lover before the curtain rose, thus eluding the question of fidelity while affording himself the leisure to intone an elaborate elegy? Was not *The Joy of Gay Sex* by definition an advocacy of promiscuity—an evasion of the "serious" ménage? I posed these questions not to judge but to locate the tonality over which the author piped his friendly tunes. (Though surely the questions camouflaged a suspicion that something was not quite right: If even a sinful French Catholic like Huysmans punished his protagonists for their carnal doings, how could Edmund White—like me, an American WASP—let his characters off scot-free?) "Perhaps sex and sentiment *should* be separated," suggests White. "Isn't sex, shadowed as it always is by jealousy and ruled by caprice, a rather risky basis for a sustained, important relationship?" Maybe too White's friendly tunes were precisely that—tunes—not dutiful discourse. In only one brief paragraph of the present book, when a young host dies in Georgia shortly after White leaves that State of Desire, is there a hint of more than fleeting fondness for any of the myriad contacts formed during business hours. But after all, to discuss with strangers what used to be called the "intimate moments" (and this, while enjoying, unlike the clinical Kinsey, their hospitality, and sometimes their carnal favors) calls for a certain cool.

Now, if I argued that White dealt with a general avoidance of responsibility, might someone else argue that homosexuality is a particular avoidance of responsibility? Had I missed the point? Was the point that Edmund White always, in fiction as in reportage, elucidates (as distinct from advocates) a view of our times as a sort of Erotics of Morality, promoting the cheerfully disinterested use of the body? "I can picture," says he, "wiser people in the next century regarding our sexual mania as akin to the religious madness of the Middle Ages—a cooperative delusion. I feel that homosexuals, now identified as the element in our society most obsessed with sex, will in fact be the agents to cure the mania. Sex will be restored to its appropriate place as a pleasure, a communication, an appetite, an art; it will no longer pose as a religion, a reason for being. In our present isolation we have few ways besides sex to feel connected with one another; in the future there may be surer modes for achieving a sense of community."

It's unclear if "our isolation" here means mankind's, or gaykind's, since often in his book White, an English teacher by trade, employs—as do many gay writers succumbing to the exigencies of non-sexism—the ungrammatical formula of substituting "our" for "their" (e.g., "Narcissism is an insult that has been hurled at gay men for decades because of our supposed fascination with our looks.") He is otherwise a true stylist, and like all true stylists he gets away with murder, the special brand being a rococo suffocation undared since Pierre Louÿs. Is this opulence one that insiders so loosely name Gay Sensibility? If such a thing could be pinpointed through example rather than through definition, then yes, doubtless a Gay Sensibility does elusively ooze from the pages of Edmund White. His rhapsodic preamble to the San Francisco chapter, for instance, contains not one straightforward sentence among the fountains and dreams, fuchsia and tears, beige-gold living rooms and Sung landscape poetry. Not that the tone is devious, for there is nothing to hide; but declarative information does get waylaid by ornamental orchestration. His trick is to avoid amateur gush. My having thus limned Gay Sensibility, will Noël Coward's terse high camp rise up to disqualify me? But if Coward pens never a word too many, neither with all his fioratura does White. Both are good writers in that they do not overwrite. (Wilde had it both ways—the sumptuosity of *Salome*, the aphorisms of *Earnest*—though never simultaneously. Similarly Hemingway. For the sensibility is not restricted to merely avowed gays.)

Whatever the style, this book tenders its subject without apology, and with the cultured clarity of an address to peers. Perhaps the book's wholesomest reminder to our permissive-robot era is that the homosexual has earned the right to be ordinary. In no way is he worse or better, and therefore more inherently interesting, than any other offshoot of Adam's breed. Indeed, if his "condition" defines itself simply by what goes on in bed, then like heterosexuality it can be monotonous even to the insider.

December 1979

SETTING THE TONE

I am a composer who also writes, not a writer who also composes. The distinction is because I make a living as one, and not as the other.

For longer than I can remember the two strings of my bow have played different tunes. My music at first filled a need for order, was dry and clean, well-bred and spare; and though I may have felt it to be sensually Catholic and French, the French themselves found it restrainedly Quaker and mid-western. My diary meanwhile, filling a need for chaos, seeped venom and sperm, blood and gin, with asides of unchanneled gossip and effusions on True Love.

In 1966 when my first book appeared I had been for twenty years a professional composer, in the sense that my music was paid for and published. Suddenly in a few weeks I received more public attention as a diarist than in my whole life as a musician. This was due to the then-unprecedented literary format, and to the fact that I led a double life which in America, land of specialists, seemed deliciously unpatriotic.

Since 1966, while continuing as a full-time composer, I have published seven more books. Thus I practice two professions. Do these professions interfere with, or nourish, each other? They still fill separate needs but the needs are reversed. After that first diary came out it was no longer feasible to scribble "Be still, o heart," not just because the phrase grew less becoming with the passing years, but because print made my privacy your business, and I'm a recluse. So gradually my nouns and notes, like night and day—or like giant amoebas within my sievelike brain—oozed *through* each other, emerging on opposite sides. (The two Dorian Grays nod coldly in passing, as they simultaneously enter and leave the mirror.) Today I could hope my music's grown wilder and vaster, my writing more objective and leaner. Indeed, my prose is now mainly essays on esthetics with never (how times change) the pronoun *I*.

Do I still keep a journal? Yes, but more sporadically, and no longer with a tragic—that is, a narcissistic—sense. I mean no more and no less than I say, and shun hidden meanings. Mostly I type sharp jottings on matters musical, and by culling from these this column will be hewn.

To compose is not to express oneself at the moment; rather it is to release oneself from the moment into a timeless limbo. To compose is to notate what one has learned over the years about the nature of things (including self-expression). Thus one can make sad music during a tranquil period, or happy music during periods of horror.

Gazing into Mr. Cavett's features I refrain from saying: I am not the person you invited, just a shell representing that person. A composer is a composer only when he's composing. Yet here I sit in my party clothes, with my special charm (or lack of it) and knack for talking *about* my work. Isn't that talk dry air if the work can't speak for itself? To object that my music was just heard, and that I myself performed, is to bring forth this reply: I performed Ned's songs, but had to sit down and relearn them like any other pianist, and played them perhaps less well than another. Were I underground they'd sound the same.

That which exists in the present moment—like food or sex as opposed to memory or anticipation—is the making of art, and especially the fear of death. Obsessed with being lost forever before learning what it all meant, can we find balm in this filmed banter? It jells us, you and me, throughout eternity, though we ourselves will wither and vanish, perhaps even before the show is aired. Death is not delayed, but waylaid, by this interview.

In belaboring the question "Is Musical Comedy the Same as Opera?" no correspondent has yet hit the nail on the head. The difference between the two species is not esthetic but practical, not a matter of art-versus-entertainment but of the kind of voice a composer has in mind. No Merman or Donna Summer could ever perform Carmen or Donna Anna, any more than a Horne or a Sutherland could belt real pop. True, an Eileen Farrell is occasionally cited as a "convincing" jazz singer, but the inverse convinces no one—witness Streisand's trammeled pretensions in "The Classical Barbra."

Substitute an unmiked diva for Lansbury in *Sweeney Todd* and you'll hear inappropriately slick vocal "placement" and touristy R-rollings. The recent *Mahagonny* fiasco is proof that legit voices can't cope with even so historic a white elephant as Weill. It's not that pop singers haven't the scope of op singers (though they haven't), or that op singers can't learn to fake a bluesy whine. It's that the *need*, and hence the literature, of each genre is disparate. This need dominates the earliest training of each kind of vocalist. Thus composers are faced with separate constructional considerations for each genre.

The genres, like church and state, have run forever parallel, and in Europe—less specialized than we—have sometimes merged. Poulenc in Paris wrote the same sort of music for all occasions, sacred and profane, merely trimming tessitura for chanteuses who lacked the range and breath of opera pros. Blitzstein in New York altered his language for each occasion, using simple tunes and chords in his theater pieces for untrained voices, and dissonant fioratura for his one so-called opera. Yes, some hybrids (though not *West Side Story*) use both type of singer: John Reardon or Barbara Cook are not, with their high-class stylization, embarrassing in *Oklahoma* or *Candide*. But would any opera from Monteverdi to Berg be conceivable with your typical Sondheim cast?

Whatever the musical speech or philosophical sense of a lyric theater piece, that piece's definition rests on the composer's technical intent: it may be termed opera only if composed for operatic voices, and musical comedy only if composed for musical comedy voices.

The two genres might be termed Variable and Invariable. Insofar as "Lonely Town" or "Send in the Clowns" or even "Summertime" are plausible as sung by any sex in many settings and keys and in a variety of arrangements, they are variable, and so the context from which they spring is not opera. Insofar as *"Or sai chi l'onore"* or *"Voici ce qu'il écrit à son frère Pelléas"* or even "Pigeons in the Grass" are not plausible except as sung by the sex and voice they were conceived for, in one key and setting and orchestration, they are invariable (set arias, if you will), and so the context from which they spring is opera.

Only in America could this argument rage, amongst letters to the *Times* about the foreign takeover of national orchestras. If our cultural inferiority complex, still at this late date, is salved by hiring Europeans for our symphonies, the same inferiority asks us to dignify a recent and unique commodity—musical comedy—with the name Opera, as though opera with its long and tacky history were a serious sign of worth.

Music cannot lie, though it can speak a banal truth.

The piano tuner has come and gone. As always, when rising from his finished work and before accepting payment, he expects you to "try out" the keyboard. Now, when "you" are presumably an inventive musician, what do you try out for this artisan's approval? Annual quandary: What to play for the tuner to assure him the job's well done! It's the piper who pays.

Why repeat that even the wisest aren't wise to themselves since the issue is endlessly demonstrated? The sole point shared by the wise Susan Sontag and the wiser Gore Vidal is a misconception about their own work. Both rate their fiction above their journalism.

Difference between critic and reviewer? You can be a critic, but not a reviewer, of your own work. (That's an example of one difference.) Having last week assembled some journal extracts under the title *Of Vanity*, I now find them poetistic and mawkish. Or: they just miss being mawkish and poetistic because, *dans l'ensemble*, they succeed.

If a writer does have the right to find his own work poetistic and mawkish (though he should reread the work ten years later before making his opinion public), he does not have the right (not even ten years later) to claim that his works "just miss," much less that they succeed; it is not for him to know what vibrates for others.

A claim is wishful thinking, not the staff of life. Even when concocting *War and Peace* the author can only keep his fingers crossed.

The most profound statements are always the most obvious. To put down Rod McKuen as "America's most understood poet" is less witty than dumb. Whatever McKuen's worth, the notion of comprehensibility-as-suspect is old hat. Great poets don't argue against clarity.

*

Whenever during a speech about composers in modern society I bring up the subject of money, people either chuckle (they know I'm not serious) or stare at me as though I'd said fuck.

Music cannot be owned. An American painter of my age and reputation earns ten times more than I earn; paintings, being an investment, can be rebought and resold indefinitely. But beyond what a composer receives for a commission (and the price of, say, an opera, which takes three years to write, is about what a prima donna makes in three nights) there is little income from any one work.

Professional artists together seldom discuss esthetics (having reached their own conclusions and formed their own secrets, they put esthetics to silent work and leave discussion to sophomores), they talk about money, since that's the most vital form of appreciation and their main salvation. Write essay on The Economics of Creation—except that Virgil Thomson's autobiography is already that.

A professor from Maryland phones to ask if I'll participate in what he terms an Art Song Symposium next season, and if so, what is my fee. How much (I inquire) did you give Elly Ameling last year? Well—er—we gave her forty-six hundred. Good (I reply), I'll take that too. The professor says he'll speak with the board. That was two months ago and I've heard no more. How dare a composer presume to rate with a diva! Since composers don't have agents they must deal with these matters personally. Still, no host should require a potential guest to name a fee, then reject the guest on the basis of that fee. The host names the fee . . . to be accepted or not.

Cézanne: another of the universal geniuses whose genius and universality elude me. Balthus too. The latter's retrospective has all New York agog; that I actually knew him makes me privy to the magic. Now, it is pleasant to boast, evoking the hundred meetings, retinting the past. But it all meant little to me then.

So much of what we like to call Greatness depends on conditioning. Would I realize, if confronted with an anonymous Rimbaud, that he was great? Now that Picasso is dead, Martha Graham is our only surviving *monstre sacré*—certainly our only sacred *American* monster. Thomson and Copland don't fit the concept; indeed, they've worked all their lives to dispel that nineteenth-century Great Master syndrome.

Don Pasquale at the Met. One may object less to Sills's bronxiness than to the nineteenth-century direction imposed onto an eighteenth-century situation. A soprano in a bustle is Puccinianly romantic, and by definition tragic; for her to sing that which is by definition "reasonable" (though farfetched and burlesque) is to confuse the eye by the ear.

Were I asked what I most strive for in music, I suppose I'd say simplicity. And I suppose Elliott Carter would answer much the same. (I name Carter because he seems on the farthest pole from me. His music proposes a Gordian Knot of logic, threads leading back to his Minotaur.) An artist tries to say in as few notes—or words, steps, shots, strokes—as possible what only he can say. Bach's first cello suite is in five movements because he didn't need six. The first movement is built from 42 measures because he didn't need 43, and they contain a total of 672 notes (I just counted them) because he didn't need 673. A work of art is unique, a one-shot deal, in that it cannot be otherwise than what it is. No matter how complex, it is the essence of simplicity. Now, simplicity is precisely the element lacking in pop music. Undeniably it is simple so far as sophistication is concerned (it doesn't "développe"), and it is sometimes simpleminded. But when it has said what it has to say it doesn't stop, it keeps on going, and thus is needlessly complicated. Etcetera . . .

Self-cannibalism sounds frightful, yes, but fruitful too. To feed off yourself is also to feed yourself. With art this is not only phylogenetically and ontologically the case, but—what's the proper adverb?—narcissistically. Just as no one speaks a language without having learned, and then rejected or accepted, the language of his forebears, so no specific art work would be quite this way without the artist's own preceding work. Even within a given painting each element "works" according to other elements. In music a note makes sense according to notes above and beneath and before and beyond it. (Including the first note?) Look at Beethoven's Fifth, nothing if not an object feeding on, and feeding off, itself. Or my own *Water-Hyacinths*, an endless snake (or ought one say a golden cord?) unwinding, doubling back, coiling ever higher, swallowing its tail while still expanding. In art, the procedure cannot reach a dead end—that is, cannot end in death; nor yet, like the amoeba, ceaselessly divide. The end result, unlike a baby, is an end in itself, and Life. Etcetera . . .

Those 672 notes, incidentally, would seem to be evenly balanced, at the rate of 41 measures each containing 16 notes, and a final measure of one note. Actually the twenty-second measure contains just 15 notes, and so does the twenty-ninth, while the final measure—the only one with a vertical harmony—is a three-voiced chord, the triple-stop having caught up the two notes lost in the above-mentioned measures. Etcetera . . .

When Casals, or indeed any professional student, professes daily dedication to Bach on the ground that a Bach suite comprises unlimited information and can thus be studied inexhaustibly, one wonders if Bach agrees. If Bach agrees that a certain suite comprises unlimited information, why, then, did he compose six suites? Put another way: If any work of art, big or little, contains the whole universe, why do those cellists not study contemporary music along with their Bach? Etcetera . . .

The etceteras terminating the above four entries must mean: there's more to say, perhaps, but not by me.

Enigma. When we do not know a foreign tongue we hear it for a sonority, which appears lovely or ugly or clipped or rippling or guttural or "musical." Once we master the language we no longer listen to it, because we understand it. We hear it for sense, not sound. To know what someone is saying is to no longer appreciate his timbre; meaning takes precedence over sensuosity.

Does this contradict the common preaching about Modern Music—that familiarity breeds (not contempt, but) only familiarity, and finally love? Once I began to *know* music (forms and styles and periods and especially the details of instrumentation—that is, to be aware of what woodwind or combination of brass was in utterance) I heard it differently, and maybe with less carnal joy.

There is no one Right Way to listen. Are there wrong ways?

Judy Collins took me to hear *Adriana Lecouvreur*, of all things. What could have led one (her fat photos?) to imagine that Caballé was stentorian? She's a two-ton Cuisinart exuding only egg-whites, and the adulation around this tedious invention only reconvinces me of the average Opera Buff's misdirection. Or am I misdirected in feeling that all feeling for all music must be focused on, and judged from, the composer's vantage? Yet by any vantage Caballé, since her vehicles are so weak (i.e., choice of repertory and physical stamina), should be billed as no more than a latter-day Teresa Stich-Randall.

A whole afternoon at the Metropolitan Museum reveals once again that artifacts, no matter how sumptuous, are no rivals for art. The so-called Age of Spirituality (early Christian exhibits), no less than Diana Vreeland's hokey Vanity Fair (badly lit clothes, accompanied by incense and Muzak) made me want to cry, after quitting the signed trophies of Vermeer and Manet and Tiepolo.

Waning powers of concentration. Little retains the attention now as when I first "loved" art. As I stroll from frame to frame my eye is not so much diverted by as centered upon other strollers. It's the pictures that are distracting. If in the novels of Wharton and James strangers meet cordially beneath public gallery portraits or in foreign cathedrals or even in teahouses, I, who am (was) dissolute, notorious, unprincipled, have never in my libertine timidity picked up anyone through proper conversation in a sober décor. I envy the freedom of action of actors in books—even the freedom of their restraint—when my own ways (as much yesterday as today) are bounded by fear, fear of boredom as well as rejection, and hence of paths not taken. Is it wishful to think that the *rencontre de musée* is a figment of everyone's imagination? In fact, I once knew the public tearooms of Europe's leading museums more intimately than those museums' exhibits.

I hate Pollock. Can I not be right in my wrongness? Artists are often less right about their contemporaries than are laymen, or even critics. But they are often right too, and toward painting I am a layman. Pollock in his emperor's-new-clothes seems no better clad than Boulez.

Ceaseless agreeable thick rain. Around noon an ambulance screams to a halt across the street. A hundred pairs of eyes including mine look down into the slush, and wait, until finally, stretcher-borne, an octogenarian cardiac is hoisted forth. I raise my gaze to that of a man in the window over there, and think how we resemble those gaping reporters in *I Want to Live* watching

Susan Hayward gasp her last. We're glad it's not us. Anita Ellis can ping out
a note as tersely cruel as an icicle which in one second melts into a blue-hot
tear.

A day seldom passes when I don't at some point, however brief, feel like
crying. The feeling is never desperate, not stronger in rainy weather, nor
does it stem from any of a dozen daily rejections: at Food City where the
checkout person rings me up with a sneer; on the subway where an old man
(unintimidating because unappealing) accepts without a thank-you the seat I
tender; in the sauna's damp shadows where, on bended knee, I glance up to
see that venerated twosome link arms and walk off, leaving me with egg on
my face, a lump in my throat—though what seems a tear in my eye is just a
crystal of steam. No, the desire to cry seems sparked instead by a sense of
well-being, of sunbeams and birdsong, of things going well. But since
"things going well" are in the long run meaningless, I don't in fact cry.
Earth's mediocrity, more than its meaninglessness, is deadening, yet I am
part of Earth and I don't want to die.
     Francis Robinson did die last night. I learn this from the latest of my ever
more friendly treks to the obit page which set the morning tone, and en-
viously I surmise that Francis will be remembered as "well liked." At least *I*
have been well loved, though such intensities seem confined to earlier years
in other lands, and it's been a long time since I've heard the words *je t'aime*.
     "How long ago!" I mutter, noting that John Ashbery's touching verses
called *The Idiot* date from 1957, but forgetting that that was the summer I
gave up France forever, with a decade of my best songs behind me. Most of
us are far closer to death than to birth, with perhaps our strongest work—
however weak—behind us. Yet JH has been forty for thirteen months now,
and those months are the wisest I've seen in him: he seems to have come to
some sort of terms.

Situation: A schoolteacher's moral standing is wrecked when it's learned
he has slept with a pupil. And his health is wrecked by a disease caught from
the pupil.

Originality, advancement, novelty—these are minor sides of music. Progress is not of itself a benefit, since we refer to the progress of a disease.
Twenty chefs, using the identical recipe with the identical ingredients in the
same kitchen with the same utensils, will turn out twenty separate soufflés.
The touch of the chef, like the pianist's touch, is his identifying property, not
his sieve.

To reread my diary is to cringe. Yet I hold to every banal word, and am
forever governed by a distaste for the serious.
     Barbara Walters to Nixon: "How do you feel, Mr. Nixon, about being
thought personally cold and impermeable?" Richard Nixon to Walters:
"Come on, Barbara, let's be serious." Is Mom's apple pie a mere dessert to the
broccoli of battle, or might our ex-president allow that peace is more serious
than war? Does bombing the East make a more precious West where we will

not only bake pies but pen tales of past wars without fighting new ones, and maybe even finally sit down to crack *Swann's Way* again?

Cocteau said: "Proust used to read to us every night from *Swann's Way*. He would start anywhere, begin again, break off to explain that the doffing of a hat in the first chapter would reveal its significance in the last volume, and he would titter behind a gloved hand, a titter that smeared all over his beard. 'It's too silly,' Proust kept saying, 'no, I won't read any more. It's really too silly.'"

Cocteau also claimed to have been on the set of *Frankenstein* where, between takes, Boris Karloff roared with mirth at the slapstick. And Kafka, according to Max Brod, considered himself "the Offenbach of fiction." Of course the reverse intent-and-effect is more usual: the proposed serious taken as comic, as in a Susan Sontag movie.

On a Cavett rerun Edward Albee tries the Gore Vidal stance: loftily lenient, world-wearily witty, one-of-a-kind yet out for mankind. He doesn't make it. Albee's complaints are personal (about his critics, which oughtn't so outwardly to nettle America's "leading playwright") while Gore's are general (about the state of the Union, with practical solutions advanced). He also flings forth too many sputtering firecrackers:

"Did you know, Dick, that under Nixon more money was allotted to the arts than under any other president?"

"Gee, Edward. Why was that, do you suppose?"

"I have no idea."

But the Why is no mystery. Nixon's donation to art was sand in the eyes of detractors. Then too, the arts always fare better under reactionary than under liberal governments. Meanwhile Edward, not rising to the bait, allows Cavett to drop the word *fag* not once but thrice. Now, although Cavett's social role is that of court jester who dares deferentially to outrage the king without risking decapitation, it's doubtful if he'd bait, say, Jimmy Baldwin with the word *Nigger*, or Adrienne Rich with the word *chick*.

The reason for my (shall I say profound?) attraction to French as opposed to German culture lies in terseness. Does the peacock's rainbow fan reveal less than his heart and lungs? Surface is as telling as depth, the casual as touching as the Big Statement, and nostalgia is the bread of creativity. Surgery clarifies, yes, but it also kills.

Both here and abroad, many critics tend to equate the serious with the complex. Today even in France—indeed, especially in France—that is true. And what is serious? Are Wilde and Chaplin and Copland serious, or the ultra-simple Mondrian or Erik Satie? Is Schoenberg more serious than Ravel by virtue of being harder to grasp—of having a "system"? Once *serious* is defined, who decrees that art must be serious?

I have never concocted an apology for my musical language; have compiled no syllabus for critics to hang their prose on; nor, when writing program notes, have I felt that words speak as clearly as the music they purport to describe. It is time, though, to advance a motto:

I believe in the importance of the unimportant—in the quotidian pathos.

Like sex and food, music exists in the Now (as distinct from love, which, like power and philosophy, exists in retrospect or in anticipation), and this Now must always be pleasurable, even when it hurts. The pleasure comes from economy. I do not know what meaning means, except that it is instantly recognizable. All of this will not justify my credentials (only the music can do that), but it will explain an esthetic which already sounds more important than I intend.

Seemingly random, the foregoing notes actually contain in microcosm all that has ever concerned me. Nothing's writ here that I've not writ before, nor will I e'er write of aught else.

It is not what you say or even how you say it, not the skilled sentence nor the sculpted tune in themselves, but the placement of the tune or sentence within the paragraph or madrigal. An author, no less than a composer, asks himself: Should I end loud and slow, or fast and soft? start with a bang or a whimper?

If these entries began on a biographical tone—"I am not a writer who also composes but a composer who also writes"—must they be balanced by the same? Or by some "affirmation"? Or maybe a downbeat? How to choose?

It is not his ideas but the sequence of his ideas that doth a poet make.

1980

BEING ALONE

Public Passports

No matter how tenacious or, indeed, victorious in the ring, the bull is never spared. Though he fell the torero to become champion, the bull is doomed. Why? His use is used up. At a second "go" the animal knows the tricks, and like the wiliest pacifist he'll turn and run off. Similarly, we spectators are irreparably conditioned by our first corrida. You are deflowered only once.

I've attended two bullfights. The ordeal in Arles in 1952, with six consecutive *mises à mort*, was so gorgeously stigmatizing that I hadn't yet healed when, sixteen years later in Acapulco, I saw my second. Still, the first steeled me for the next. Forced to witness death, over and over in twenty-minute segments of identical choreography, one turns self-protectively blasé, even in a concentration camp. Or does one? Perhaps no amount of experience will ever immunize us to certain things: bullfights, sunsets, starvation, love.

I note these paragraphs while reading *Christopher and His Kind* with a disapproval of Isherwood's assumption that readers not only know but have cared about knowing his whole previous catalogue. An anxious nostalgia threads this presumably "honest" reweaving of old themes. Nothing is riskier than for an artist to set the record straight years after. Late truth lacks the energy of early distortion. And who, one might well ask, will in forty years reshuffle these currents facts of Christopher? Art always hits the nail on the head, but accuracy for its own sake cannot guarantee art.

Delving further, disapproval gives way to bafflement: How, in the company of the major minds of his time, Christopher's unabashed carnality remains his sole subject matter! (Auden writes usually on ideas, Christopher seldom.) How, lest his public for one instant forget it, he repeats his name constantly, thereby paradoxically, unlike Proust, lending a vague impersonality to his narrator! (I always hesitate to speak my own name, feeling somehow that I am dropping it.) How, in his tastes both cultural and tactile, he is German as opposed to French! Am I in my Frenchness so far from him? Now, when the chips are down, what I deplore in his writing is what I defend in my own: the unembellished given of the self as subject. But there remains the nagging question: Can one's own behavior, and even one's presumable objectivity toward that behavior, be fair game on the literary racetrack?

"Life," claims Eric Bentley, "is seldom simple; art never." I reply: Life is never simple, art always. With its curving paths through multiple layers art nonetheless follows the straightest line between two points. How an artwork works is the only way for that work, whereas living is nothing but alternatives. Art is economy and shape, life is waste and disorder.

Happily it is not for an artist to define what he does. An artist doesn't do art, he does work. If that work turns out to be art, that is proclaimed through the judgment of lesser lights.

Virgil Thomson (calmly to Hortense who is annoyed that guests ignore him): "When I find myself among those who don't know my name, I know I'm in the real world."

My fame, modest though it be, establishes a security which (were that fame withdrawn tomorrow) cannot withdraw tomorrow, because the remaining years—hours?—are fixed, and we readjust to every minute. Now, the more secure I grow, the less I feel urged to wax brilliant. (Was it 1954, Cannes, that I observed Van Johnson and Jean-Pierre Aumont soberly double-dating, with, on their arms, gyrating before the paparazzi, two obscure starlets *being brilliant?*)

Secure and *brilliant* are words I don't enjoy. *Brilliant* is so overused ("a brilliant young author") as to be meaningless; *secure* reeks of the analyst's couch. I avoid formula phrases more assiduously than mannerism phrases, formula phrases (*nuclear family, middlebrow, New Left*) being confected by individuals whose bandwagons joggle uncomfortably, mannerism phrases (*like I mean you know*) being folklore, anonymous.

I ask Francine what *nuclear family* means. Doubtless thinking me square, she explains that it's the immediate nucleus of parents and children. Well, of course. Isn't that just plain family? Global village, Third World, collective unconscious, these are "spinoffs"—ugh—of family.

In the dream this question was posed: Why are we alive? Quick the answer: Creation. Does my unconscious sprout such corn? By daylight, of course, I can thresh that to signify anything. We aren't alive to express ourselves—to be "creative"—or even to wonder why we're alive. We have invented our own existence so as to exist. We have been created because we have been created. Do not read this as redundant; we are Scotch tape over a black hole.

In those dangerous hours of early morning when one awakes and realistically dwells on growing old alone, ill and penniless, and like a drum the thought crescendoes to a burst of tears in which we fail to drown because the rising sun parches them, and maybe lights the path to a bit more darkness and sleep—in such hours I used to come to the notion of you finally, and be saved. Now that's past. Either I must reach another notion, or avoid the dangerous hours.

If it's really so bad, why not kill yourself. And he killed himself . . . This literal reply to a figurative query has been, more than a smarting transient slap, a Promethean punishment which no one deserves.

*

Morris being back from a brief expensive stay in Paris I plead with him to describe the odor of the Seine, of the Boulangerie du Bac, of the sun on the Luxembourg gravel, of the pubescent students at the Flore, of the granite on the house where I lived. I can't return. But as I practice (as I'm doing now) Debussy's *Ballade de Villon à s'amye* I simultaneously ascend the Rue Mouffetard in the body I inhabited twenty-nine years ago tonight, and descend on the dark intimate regions of human mates now dead.

"I'd always adored playing the wisp of mauve fluff into which some coal miner rams his frame."
"Perhaps the mauve fluff role should now be shifted to another."
"Another? Never! How dare another. Either I play the mauve fluff or nobody plays the mauve fluff. Though turnabout is unfair play, if it *were* fair, the parts in the play shouldn't depend on the age of the victims—I mean of the participants."

Some people twenty or forty may seem to be thirty or fifty, but no one fifty or thirty truly looks forty or twenty. JH insists that we all look our age, but some look it better than others.
People say my face belies my years. Why is it a compliment to look young? What's wrong with looking one's age? True, to "look old" is to slim down the chances of getting laid. But what are these "chances"? Are they American only? Is sex just for the young? Yes, maybe.

And so tomorrow, at the vast party planned by JH here, I turn fifty-five, and not only youth but the past as concept slide into a new dimension. On the day you discover that grown-ups don't have the answers, you yourself have become grown-up.
Francine and I are both now hesitant about losing our heads through our bodies: great sex takes so much time. The more fools we—in our flight from folly.
Insomnia's the negative side to that coin which depicts the fight betwixt the flesh and the intellect of a single person. Sex is the cure for insomnia. They say.
(Sketch a profile of Francine: her suave naïveté, her "Malheurs de Sophie" nose, her literary wisdom and lacunae, her beauty at forty-eight.)

Watching friends survive and push, guided solely by the velvet leash of delusion, have I too then been had? The delusion is that we are indispensable, that we have something unique to say. It's nice to hear someone remark, "You write marvelous music," but saddening too. Is the delusion more than high-class horniness? Music is made by another me who accepts the compliment and who wants to be loved for the self alone, as though there were such selves. JH maintains that his mental impotence arises from an incapacity for accepting self-delusion. Is that maintenance against the final embarrassment not itself a delusion? Art's the grand illusion. Even the greatest, in order to proceed, must leap before they look. (Yet some of these greatest have killed themselves.) Well, if we are not indispensable, we *are* irreplaceable, even when moldering in the grave, for our chemical swervings keep Earth in balance. End of lesson.

20 December 1977. With Robert Phelps I went this snowy afternoon at five, armed with white roses and Godiva chocolates and a copy of my new *A Quaker Reader*, to visit Janet Flanner whom I'd not seen *dans l'intimité* since two years ago when she came to dine with Lillian Hellman, and, on leaving, had a heart seizure in the elevator. We were four (with Natalia Murray filling the chasms of Janet's lapses by regaling us with tales of de Pachmann, one of those mad geniuses who, when divorced from his métier, seems merely moronic), and stayed perhaps three hours. Janet's already half in heaven, her every hesitant phrase and gesture being made in souvenir of ancient gestures and phrases, and one feels her hang on. For she forgets who we are from one five-minute period to the next; and after the several times she goes to the bathroom (she has many stiff drinks), imagines herself to be home in the Ritz again. (Like Elizabeth Ames who at ninety talked in the next room with her mother and sister, each dead for fifty years.) Yet I am at ease and learn from her, and admire her staunchly no less for yesterday than for today. Senility is surely agonizing for them too, who cannot help but know they're lost.

I am still hoping to retrieve that person (the one with the iron-blue hair) I was too drunk to accept in Jackson Park thirty-eight summers ago when now I enter this uptown bar. Or to relocate this person (the one with the strident nape muscles) whom I shunned gratuitously in the Luxembourg Gardens twenty-four autumns ago when now I enter that downtown café. Or that other paragon. Or this certain-to-be-love. And do you know? They can be found. Their actual flesh and blood can be found, but as overwhelmed by the passing ages as my own. Yet I still pursue the longed-for pursuers whom I'm certain could have given me that which is never given. I am still . . .

Virgil comes to dine, and as always his table talk shimmers. Afterward when we all adjourn to the parlor he as always falls asleep. Conversation turns to classical music. Virgil awakens.
"What are we discussing?"
"Beethoven."
"Top drawer," says Virgil, and drops off again.

Of Country Matters
To the young, sex is what grown-ups do. To the elderly, sex is what the young do. Sex is all-consuming while it thrives, and is the subject (if not the source) of most art. But sex does not cause suicide, and must be put aside in order to write about it. To be appreciated is the primal need.

The cliché that homosexuals don't like women blinds us to the fact that homosexuals do appreciate women differently. Colette: *Les vacances, c'est là où l'on travaille ailleurs.* It could be argued that a gay man savors a woman's beauty the more purely in not being deflected by sexual yearnings. He can "see her," not "see her in bed."

*

Although sex and love need not be mutually exclusive, neither are they mutually inclusive, but folks confuse them. Such folks, known as puritans, are actually impuritans blending oil with water. Love can add elegance to sex, but sheer sex unenhanced in the abstract and alone is therapeutic. Sex can add sorrow to love, but platonic love unenhanced in the concrete and shared is fulfilling and durable.

What is a human being? A human being is the substitute for a melon.

Surely there exists more mundane frustration about artists than about gays in the world's eyes. I'm less defensive than Isherwood—less "moralistic"—about queerdom than about musicality, for musicality in this world is queerer than any kind of sex.

Straight men, often intelligent ones, are wont to reach two conclusions, jointly contradictory, about the gay male: 1) that he would like to bugger them, and 2) that he is a woman trapped in a man's body. More confounding is the supposition about a gay conspiracy in which all homosexuals are organized in hating all heterosexuals and have amassed stockpiles to prove it. (JH contends that these are *my* conclusions, and propagandistic hogwash.)

Sexuality is more a matter of how X feels about Y than of how X feels about himself. Homosexuality, unlike negritude or womanhood, is a part-time job.

In his interview last night with William Buckley, Cavett asked, "Have you ever, thinking back, found yourself to have been wrong?" Needless to say Buckley never answered, never at least with a yes or no. But it's a good question, and in posing it of myself I quickly reply yes.

Is the reply defensive? What in fact have I found myself wrong about? (Not, certainly, musical tastes—if tastes can be thought of as right or wrong—although my tastes have grown narrower, excluding what was once acceptable while retaining the same *type* of preference.) Well, I've changed about women. Raised in a profoundly unprejudiced milieu I was taught to accept Negroes, artists, the "poor" as equals. Yet women always appeared to be of a lesser caste. I am not stupid, yet the only females I could tolerate were precisely those whose so-called female traits were underplayed. Baudelaire wrote that the appreciation of intelligent women was the pederast's prerogative. He was not wrong, but I was.

Is there a homosexual sensibility? people still ask. Why yes, no doubt. But one would be hard put to show that sensibility defined, say, by the homosexual's musical composition or poetry or law practice or medical notions, as distinct from the sensibility of one who screws too seldom or too often or is redheaded or over fifty or is more interested in microscopes than in love or is dumb.

The trouble here is that "homosexual sensibility" is a slogan masked as an idea. Until semantics are settled, perpetrators will cram the work of gays into pigeonholes by cutting off limbs. Meanwhile, if there *is* such a sensibility, dare you include Whitman (said to be queer) with his careless macho rhapsodies to the great outdoors? Dare you omit Beardsley (rumored to be straight) with his quaint sonatinas to a vast powder puff?

Is there a gay sensibility? Define it, then I'll tell you if there's one.
Does God exist? Define him, then I'll tell you if he exists.

The other boys thought it was sissified for our gym teacher to go around
with that dame in the fur coat. Girls were nowhere. Little did the boys know
that in just a year or so they too . . . But I, oh I, adored the female eyes like
gunshots through the black foam, adored the boys too (their tang, their
marble thighs) and the gym teacher most of all.

If I cannot let you know I wish to go to bed with you—or you, or you, or
you, or you—it's because I can't face your saying No. Title: *Sleeping Around*.
". . . if I cannot be gay let a passionless peace be my lot."
                                        —Tennyson, *Maud* (part I, ix)

Homosexuality? Oh no! What can one now add to this plot, saturated and
draining into popular journals? One can add only, as with any art or history,
one's singular experience, cast the home light.

(Write an exegesis on Kay Boyle's "A Defense of Homosexuality" from *A
Glad Day*, if it can be retrieved, at the risk of passing for a mad nabokovian
pedant. She speaks of it as "a thing with a future as yet badly done by
amateurs neglecting the opportunity to be discriminating." But all that was
fifty years ago. Well, bee-raising is fascinating to outsiders no less than
homosexuality, but outsiders don't laugh at and burn bees.)

X hates niggers and kikes and . . . *heterosexuals!* No, there's no wounding
slang for a power group. Slang, yes, but not wounding. *Honky* doesn't hurt
unless you're white alone in Harlem. "She's a dirty straight" flows inanely off
a queer duck's back, while "goy" has no strength to shame. Coldly amusing.

No less than many another intelligent alcoholic I've ceaselessly asked myself why I drink (drank). I do know why I used to think I so easily first drank:
shyness, and guiltlessly to justify the longing to be (what then was deemed)
sexually passive. But such reasons explained nothing. (More on shyness,
which anyone intelligent is, yet which is never rewarded. Those witty others
were in fact no less dumb than I.) Unlike physicians or A.A. addicts I'm not
too intrigued by either the ounce of prevention or the pound of cure; and
unlike the head-doctors, I realize that to learn the reason is not to stop the
continuation. Well, I don't know the reason for homosexuality either, but
homosexuality is natural and healthy, while drinking isn't.

"Some of my best Jews are Friends," said the rabbi of his flock defecting to
Quakerism. Ah, Jews like homosexuals, but unlike blacks or Females, can
largely choose their own flow, for their "state" is a frame of mind.

Some Jews contend that in every Gentile there's an anti-Semite longing to
get out. By that token there's a touch of anti-gay in every straight. The anti-
Semite does not feel inferior to Jews so much as he resents their high pose
("They think they're better than we are"), while the anti-gay pictures himself
in a physically clumsy posture with an unappetizing person. Is the reverse, in
either case, the case? Are Jews anti-goy from sheer fantasy? Are gays anti-
straight from carnal revulsion? And are anti-black whites more or less vir-

ulent than anti-Semites or anti-gays by being (if they are) from a lower class?
If blacks are hated for being inferior and Jews for being superior, homosexuals are hated for being both. There are, of course, no doubly-hated Jewish
homosexuals, since a homosexual Jew in the act of love has discarded his
heritage and become a gay goy, which blacks cannot do, which makes their
lot inflexible and thus the more terrible.

Our world, we are told, expands with information, with ever more available culture, and with permissive "democratic" sexuality. Yet a mere nudge
of the Rock of Reason reveals the maggots. Observe the resurgence of
pogroms, of anti-black Puerto Ricans, of Professional Jews like Norman
Podhoretz and Joseph Epstein and Meyer Levin (and they are the most
sinister because the most cultured) who aren't about to let gays off the
hook—or rather, onto the hook. If poor minorities are logically unsympathetic to each other because misery does *not* love company, ignorance of
homosexuality in high place is more bemusing.

Now, if no first-rate American heterosexual thinker has ever dwelt at
length on this increasingly visible matter, could it also be argued that whites
don't write right about blacks either, or men about women? Perhaps homosexuality doesn't need to be written "about," it being as natural in its highs
and lows as heterosexuality, and no one uses heterosexuality *as a subject*—
only as a given. But whereas men *are* concerned with women (and can project
into women), and whites are concerned with blacks (and blacks with whites,
of necessity and at all times), straights aren't really interested in the so-called
gay question.

If none of them speaks wisely about homosexuality, they speak of music
not at all. But this proves nothing, since certain straight authors (who?) write
lovingly about so-called good music (inevitably Mozart), while certain gay
authors (Isherwood, Vidal) are dull on the matter.

(Morris says I'm wrong about no first-rate American heterosexual thinker
dwelling at length on the subject, and cites John Lahr's book on Joe Orton.
And I've just finished a charming little novel by Barry Gifford about what
Gide called *la chose*.)

I am not a gay activist, I am a gay pacifist.

Gay is a term I shun. Unlike *fairy* or *faggot*, the term was always used by
gays themselves, so perhaps it's nice that now it's settling into the lingua
franca. Yet *gay* is a post-Freudian colloquialism which, though possibly useful even for, say, Dag Hammarskjöld, seems jarring for such pre-twentieth-
century homophiles as Socrates or Tchaikovsky or even Forster. What have I
against the term? Not, certainly, its implication of merry for something so
"serious." I prefer *queer* because that's how I was raised. Terminology's
regional. Just as I never tasted pastrami or sour cream before moving to New
York, so I never heard *dyke* or *straight*: Chicago Wasps didn't eat Mediterranean dishes, and Chicago queers referred to minty and jam. Individual jargon is to be cherished. But if Paris is worth a mass, and if now I say *black* for
Negro, I stick to *queer*, and that's my right, since . . .

JH tells me to stop declaring that I've not suffered from the stigma—that
I've felt less discriminated against than for being a composer. He feels the

declaration is, first of all, untrue, and also that, like an unscathed graduate of
Buchenwald who found it "not so bad," I cheapen the very real agony of
others.

The vast collective horror that awaits us is so marvelous that all art pales in
the possibility. Unless, of course, it's the very stuff of art: the universe
becomes a dragon's maw. The destruction is real. But since the universe, or
our concept of it, is balanced, who still talks of miracles? Could there, in a
real sense, come a miracle? What might it be—since who can speak of Hope,
Love and Charity, or even avalanches of wheat and honey? Can nuclear
benefits compare in any actual way to nuclear chaos?
Smells—the very word! Pungent fritters or autumn gusts or locker rooms.
Nothing's less decorous for polite discussion, unless it were perhaps taste—
taste of lime meringue or skunk cabbage or dry rot. How about the touch of
steaming custard mammaries or moss or silk or spikes piercing your palm?
Now, taste and touch and smell do not form bases for fine arts. Who
meanwhile would accuse any non-vocal noise of specific obscenities? Hearing, of all the senses, is subtlest, the most provocative, yet music alone
cannot *describe*, much less *be*, that which is provocative.
Nothing is as it only seems, though we do precondition ourselves. A rose is
not a rose, yet that syllable is lovely, and a rose by any other name would
smell less sweet. All's in a name.
Repulsive racket of children's voices. Children should be neither seen nor
heard. I do not like children. They need not be comprehended, nor from
their mouths do words of wisdom flow. Yet I am not jealous of them as once
was so. And I do love animals.

Animals and JH, Interviews and Evil
A diet of meat seems ever more repellent, and the "seemingness" began
well before the acquisition of Wallace, our flawless feisty feline now thirteen
years of age, although the fact of Wallace does reinforce and redefine all taste.
Before adolescence practical zoology in all its boy-like foci—collecting
snakes, breeding birds—was a prime concern, but with the advent of
puberty the whole squirming mass was sold to Vauhan's Seed Store for
sixteen dollars, enough to buy the score and records of *Le Sacre* at Lyon &
Healy six blocks away on Van Buren Street. Not until age forty-nine, with
the advent of Wallace, did I again become preoccupied with the rights of
beasts.
Last week at the fishmonger's a very large gent was pricing live lobsters.
The salesgirl plunked the anxious creatures upon the zinc while he ap-
praisingly declared, "My family's all my size, and we like good eating." This,
in front of the lobster. That he should devour his *semblable!* Twenty years
ago at Bill & Edward's lobsters were fixed for guests during cocktails. The
hosts, misinformed on the fixing, didn't dunk the crustaceans in boiling
water, but turned the caldron up slowly while the animals squeaked and
clawed the lid.
As we age, our bodies take on facets of the other sex, just as our minds
incline from left or right toward the middle of the road. If for my art I shed

maleness at fourteen, then today I grow more masculine (ah, dear me) while shuddering at the notion of broiling steaks.

I ache to communicate more "meaningfully" with Wallace, but he's been a cat an awfully long time. Maybe that's meaning enough. Wallace and I sometimes try to match wits, but I've been a man (am I a man?) for as long as he's been a cat. Together on this stage we're separated by a billion years.

Do I use my occasional exasperation with JH as a lash against myself? Can I not well afford a "duty" toward him in exchange for what he lends me with his perpetually sly *aperçus*, as active an education as Marie Laure once offered? While swearing not to let his misery drag me down, have I not truly the time to spare?

Our lives, even when we're one day old, are what we're living now. There is no future ever.

Evening picnic at Jetties Beach. Before we sup (but we have forgotten the mustard, forgotten the coffee thermos, indeed forgotten all staples) JH tests his new kite. Slowly he unwinds the long slack cord, fifty feet, a hundred feet, two hundred, until the thing floats high in the darkening sky. A flock of seagulls swoops past and one of their number is caught in the string, jerking and falling fast. The others withdraw shrieking to the beach where they alight and sit like a chorus.

JH is marvelous with animals (is that the word? he's comprehending, treats them as peers). Gradually, gradually, seeing that the great entangled gull now struggles in water and may drown in panic, he rewinds the cord, wading through the shallow surf toward the bird even while easing the bird out of the deep toward him, tensing the cord, talking and talking and talking so softly. Like Androcles with the lion JH tends the nearly inextricably snared wing and legs, cajoling, soothing, fanning, releasing, and the bird knows a friend when he sees one and does not lash back with his beak, except lightly by reflex, unhurting. The snarls unwound, JH plucks the creature from the sea, carries it ashore like an offering, releases it. The gull stands poised, hops a few paces, then flies low over the sand toward his brethren. They all take off and fade into the night.

Loeb or Leopold—which one charmed the wingèd beasts? Orioles alit on his shoulders, whispered into his ear. Cocteau's Segramor spoke the language of the birds, and they answered. "What are they saying? Oh tell us, Segramor, do." "I'm out of practice. Let me try to listen. Wait. They are saying—pay, pay, pay, must pay, must pay, pay . . ."

A happy family is rare and singular, but unhappy families are all unhappy in the same way, unless the unhappy family happens to be yours. Misery blurs identity.

Write of how JH writhes still in the platitudinous mysteries of romantic love. The one but powerful tiding at turning fifty-five is the new talent for avoiding such useless tortures. Or is it that I'm able to avoid them precisely through the example of JH?

Ain't got no one to be unfaithful to.

They have seen more of death than of life, these five-year-olds floating in the China Sea, like Apollinaire's *Bluet* . . .

Rosalyn Tureck has this month been a neighbor across the island at Quidnet. I accepted her dinner invitation on the condition that she garnish this with a private concert.

I arranged myself carefully among the rather tough cushions of an antique pink sofa, and she began to play. It was the same dusky hour as JH's adventure with the kite last year. Although the closed windows in Rosalyn's vast "piano room" are, like most windows, three feet up from the floor on the inside, on the outside they're flush with the lawn. The music, which I'd never heard, or even heard of (Bach's D-minor keyboard version of his A-minor violin sonata), was unutterably touching, and while it unwound the semi-wild fauna of Nantucket fluttered or scurried over the grass toward the glass panes and gazed through the sunset into my features. The sound, like all controlled perfection (is perfection by definition controlled?), seemed inscrutably tragic (generally I'm not given, when speaking of music, to metaphoric adjectives) and all the more satisfyingly so in that the ravens and rabbits conspired contingently to found a Peaceable Kingdom, choreographing a composition beyond their earshot. The sonata was followed by a Chopinesque adagio again from a fiddle suite) and by two sinfonias. When Rosalyn had finished the mourning doves were lowing and the sky was filled with stars.

She feigned to comprehend when I declared that, because my first exposures to Bach coincided with my first exposures to the blues, those baroque harmonic sevenths formed by the characteristic contrapuntal sequences resemble the canvases upon which Billie Holiday etched her plaints. Put another way, music smells good or bad according to its setting (those Renoirs in the Polignac music room did distract, though not necessarily "wrongly," from the formal sounds at hand, and a celestial cavatina turns hellish when you have a hangover), and Bach beneath Tureck's hand changed meaning in the very process of unfurling last night as civilized background to the animal kingdom.

Her forte is precision, and, in a sense, that's all that counts. One is never uneasy. She never travels with the score: her fingertips house ten lilliputian brains with their own infallible memories.

Alone in Nantucket. When JH leaves the lights go quite literally out. Here, when winter dusk sets in at three o'clock, he places candles throughout the house and an old-fashioned lemon-peel glow, more leveling, more unifying than death, warms us as one. Then in the flickering we forget for a while the rending disputes and sit down to a night of television.

The past year's been one of emerging from my massive depression only to witness JH sink even more deeply into his own (what used to be called) nervous breakdown, as into a leftover soup, for melancholy is catching. (Though by being passed on it is sometimes eliminated.) At least he has the gift of tears and vomit. On schedule he can weep or puke, which I cannot. I can write music, which is a kind of vomit, though it brings no relief. Yes, it does.

Over and beyond a scientific interest, does an entomologist develop or inherently possess a sympathetic, a "human," rapport with insects similar to the sentiments of a zoologist with apes, or, indeed, to the affections of any pet owner?

Despite the ever cooler afternoons the hydrangea in the front yard blooms greener and greener, sheltering (among a million more microscopic invertebrates) a lost mantis all foamy white and sea-colored and shivering crippled on a leaf. Did it or did it not feel differently about me from the way it might about some other person, as I aided it, examined it at point-blank range, purred to it about its pair of dear eyes that turned from right to left? Insects do make choices.

Perfect weather, and yes, alone: you've gone to the city. After these good eleven years you are still never easy to speak with, yet you keep things stirred up, and thus one feels a continual need to talk. There seems to be a crisis, not once a month but each single day. If I've not felt it so much lately it's because I see you provoke it with K. Still, your knack for rocking the boat stems of course from steering away from an "inner sanctum." If only, if only.

If only writing could get rid of it. Instead, writing locks it in.

Bees. When we returned after a season's absence a swarm throbbed on the south eave of the house, at once motionless and speedy, like a flying saucer. A neighbor said it'd been there for days. One hour later the bees vanished. Two days later they came back—or ten thousand like them. I was alone in the kitchen as the faint all-encompassing whir began. Gradually the entire lawn grew inhabited, then the house was surrounded, encased in a transluscent nacreous tent of yellow aspic, while the drone persisted, meaningless and purposeful like an Ashbery verse with a life of its own . . . Suddenly they evaporated. Oh, a few—maybe two dozen—hovered around the north roof, but for all practical purposes they'd gone. (In the basement three stray fighters buzzed frantically as the sun set, but quieted with the dark; and when my eyes panned in so close as to perhaps momentarily join their frame of reference the dying beauties came together, rubbed antlers, then ceased breathing utterly.)

Illusion. Those sentinels at the north eaves have remained. Indeed, they work for the cluster now ensconced in the house's framework. By the time the exterminator arrived you could feel them beating like red hot snowflakes against the warming parlor wall. The exterminator sprayed some cursory droplets under the eaves, said he'd be back next week if we needed him.

But the bees have moved in. Their intelligence lives in this home with us like Hitchcock's birds. It's midnight, I've taken a Valium. Are they in conference? Their pale angry roar continues, although the encyclopedia says they sleep quietly at night.

Next day, silence. The wall is cool. The bees have disappeared without a trace.

*

Interview appeared in today's *Times*. Wallace was twice mentioned, but remains unflappable. Not that he's so conceited he takes glory for granted, but too conceited to get outside himself and realize he's famous. Wallace asleep at the foot of the bed and I up here on the pillow, dreaming our separate dreams which, no matter how mad and fanciful we grow, we'll never comprehend. A queen may look at a cat, but never be a cat.

Misquoted as saying: "I love fame, and I love glory." The nouns are synonyms and I'm not redundant in interviews. Yes, I favor the shred of recognition that's mine, but do not love power. Self-involvement precludes manipulation of others. The fame I love is the fame of others.

If corporeally we are what we eat, stylistically we are what our interviewers make us. Interviews become our public passports.

Socrates: the first interviewer. Insofar as those *entretiens* were really *interrogatoires* drawing forth answers from a subject, the subject—the interviewee—revealed himself. But he revealed himself to himself and in toto, not to the public and in part. Modern interviews are about trivial aspects of a person (hobbies, horrors, habits), for how can a non-verbal artist of value utter valuable verbs about what makes him valuable? The interviewer makes of the subject what he chooses to make.

I've been interviewed on precisely the same matters and for the same length of time by three strangers in one day, revealed three different selves, given contradictory replies, according to how smart or nice I found the questioners, and according to the kind of journal they represented.

As there are no true villains in opera (melody representing evil by its nature renders evil extenuating and villainy vulnerable), neither are there true heroes in interviews. Because a hero is not self-defined, not what he says he is, not how his interloctor illustrates him; his identity is what the general consciousness decides.

The high point of Britten's *Billy Budd* is, of course, Claggart's soliloquy, for, despite Auden's "Evil is unspectacular and always human," Claggart's need to stain Billy's goodness turns to spectacle and is hardly human. Is Claggart evil? Oh yes. Though unlike the biggest wicked stars of history he does not ignore his wickedness. If Nero, for example, thought himself a do-gooder, Claggart wept for what he called his "depravity" and, like Carmen, choreographed his own suicide in the shape of murder. For each man gets killed by the thing he loves.

All those I know who are getting on resent mostly the awesome irreversibility of death. Is it so awesome? Irreversible how?

JH on Judas. Judas as fall guy. Judas himself was a preordained Act of God: he acted despite himself in fulfillment of ancient prophecy. By moving according to the Lord's will, though this brought eternal and universal damnation, he is a greater martyr than Peter or Paul who so soon sat at God's right hand. Let Judas now be also canonized.

People marvel at how certain geniuses (they always cite Wagner) can be so evil yet write great music. Is it not more marvelous that certain geniuses (let's cite Strauss) can be so colorless yet write great music? Artists are artistic only when they're being artists. Otherwise they're like you and me—if slightly more so. They're like anyone, but no one's like them.

Is it true you're anti-Semitic?
Not at all. I love Arabs. Like most people, I've been telling lies so long I now think they're true.
Such as?
How would I know?
Is a bird in the bush worth two in the hand?
Don't belittle the sweetest of solitary pastimes.
Describe Ravel's *Forlane*.
Beauty limps. A crippled butterfly. Here the maxim's literal. Like any vital art this ensues from the happy mistake. An artist while scrupulously following rules cannot help but break them. He's clumsy. *L'erreur bien trouvée*. Artisans are not clumsy. *Forlane*'s a lame peacock. Anything worthwhile's a lame peacock—although a lame peacock itself is not particularly worthwhile.
Have you seen Joan's new baby boy yet?
Yes, ah, that pearly pear-like fontanel! Those flirtatious unfocused leers! The flawless nostrils! Such innocent guile! And strands of down! (like the pair of curling swirls on my nape which Claude while owning me would liken to the diagram in his nursery primer of the Loire merging with the Gironde). And what's to become of the child? He'll grow up, have erections and die.
And are you anti-gay?
Good God, yes.

Night after wakeful night, slashes in the ice of sleep overflow with thoughts of dying. Across the street at 4 A.M. behind those shutters on the second floor shadowed by shuddering elms there drowses deeply some open-mouthed fool. Yet the longed-for sleep is not a rehearsal of death, as some contend, but life at its most active richest.
To be beside yourself is wrong, is bad for you. To be *outside* yourself is good, insofar as it (like suspended animation which, though you have cancer or a broken heart) stops pain during the so-called Creative Act—though when it evolves through alcohol, that too is bad. Tonight, beside myself, I drew closer to drinking (so as to get outside myself) than I have in years, but didn't.
Epigraph for a memoir: *Le beau temps où j'étais si malheureuse.*
—Madame de Staël

On awakening in the night: That truth, *the* truth, such thick wet rightness, where flown? Can truth so rapidly like a shattered dram of scent have dissipated? Was it actually there?
The small sad need of wanting to be loved.

JH after a year makes scant progress. To understand that one cannot

understand is as near as one can get: a glass fence rises between. In my
maddest hangovers I always retained a sense of the future, even in suicide,
but JH views the world quite literally as through a glass darkly. How cannot
I bleed for his bleeding, impotent to help? Who will claim that they who only
stand and wait are less battered than the actors in the fray?

Scant progress, but progress still . . . Alone and sour, and time passes so
fast, so slowly. It's terribly late. Day after day of losing contact, of seeing our
decade retreat like a galaxy, of the resultant gulf. Hopeless though it be, one
part of it is not wholly disagreeable.

Visit from John Myers. Talk turns to money, and to the artist's notorious
humiliation in procuring any. He recalls for us John Latouche's anecdote of
thirty years ago. Always skilled in rich dowagers, Latouche had an appointment with one he'd never met, in order to solicit funds for a show. The
butler, explaining that Madame would be in shortly, bade the guest take a
chair, and withdrew. Latouche was aware of a squeaking crunch. He had sat
heavily upon a Pekingese and killed it. Immediate reaction: There goes the
money! What to do? Opening a window, he flung the beast to the street.
What would you have done?

Did he get the funds? Yes, he did.

Thirteen months, and a leaden sadness has settled over JH and me, an
estranging deterioration that sometimes seems beyond repair. Yet the
strangeness of his strife seems ever less strange, snared as he is by chivalric
infatuation, and it hurts. His tears and vomit, which spew forth in lieu of ire
and fury, spew not from a congenital unnamed seat but from quickly trace-
able altercations with K:

Once I wrote: "*L'homme moyen sensuel* is by definition less human than the
'achiever,' if by human we define the logic which differentiates man from
other mammals. Sex has nothing to do with logic, but achievers treat sex
logically (with their restricting roles) while average men treat sex sensually."
Today I would add: If intelligent people, by virtue of their preoccupations
with the workings of culture, are less "good in bed" than "real people," they
are also given to more drastic suffering about non-vital problems such as love.
JH is the most intelligent person I know, and a friend without whom I could
not go on. Still, our headiest of frequent disputes center on the irrational, and
he will reproach an interviewer for stating that Wallace is my cat when in fact
Wallace is his.

Reincarnation is called another go at it. But afterlife is a mere question of
imagination. Why not a try as an amoeba on Arcturus? Even that, being
conceivable, is too near. Then why not an hour as an alligator in the eleventh
century? As the opposite sex for a day or two? As your twin for a minute?
Perhaps if we could be our own selves as we were yesterday, or even as we
were a second ago, the experience would become more than we could bear.

For months there's been a flutter in the wall, nocturnal, more irregular and
forceful than the bees two years ago. Gnawing termites? Scurry of rat paws?

If as t'is said a cat's mere presence discourages rodents, then we have no
rodents, or Wallace (admittedly quite deaf now at thirteen) is not a cat. But
yesterday morning on finding the stovetop strewn with what resembled
caraway seeds, we finally decided, against our will, to set a trap (Against our
will, for who are we to contrive the eradication of fellow mammals?) Last
evening, not thirty minutes after placing the bait, there sounded the terrible
snap. We paused long, fearful of what we'd find: sprayed blood? splayed
bones yet still gasping? Together we went, and there sure enough was a
mouse, limply dead. JH assured me it was killed before it knew what hit it—
even before savoring the exquisite fatal Brie. The mouse was not of urban
hue (not solid gray—indeed, like our mouse-colored Wallace, the royal Russian blue), but a clean golden fauve merging into sugary white on the belly,
and with wide-open garnet eyes. We put it down the toilet but it wouldn't
flush, kept belching back to haunt us like the corpse in *Purple Noon*. So we
sealed it in plastic and flung it to the garbage, and wondered when its nest of
starving offspring would start the rot and stink. The episode undid me, no
less than the morning *Times*'s detailing tortures in far-off Persia, or the far-off
boatloads of Vietnamese. I went to bed.

During the chaotic-seeming composites of dream after dream (which in
fact are sanity-pure, including surely the dreams of the insane) there was a
melding revivification of Vietnam and Persia, and of the mouse. If this
morning I invoke the limitations of John Donne—since all men *are* islands
who forever and vainly seek to play kneesies beneath the surface—I'd rather
commit suicide than have it proved I'd ever been willfully physically cruel. I
say physically, because all is fair in the "mental" game of broken hearts, nor
is the will ever brought into play where love's concerned, love thriving as it
does beyond the frontiers of time as in an ice-cold bubble where we breathe
forever and don't grow old.

As far as anyone is ever cured, JH is. As far as any other can judge such
things. The two-year stress, fanned by my own surrender to allergies (I've
been taking shots just twenty-four months now and am doing better, thanks),
has abated, due as much to illness running its course as to a fortieth birthday.
He functions. What more can one note about any friend? It's feasible to
resume the *égoïsme à deux*—the mutual solitude—as the French name
marriage.

He functions too as translator of animals, being himself a thoroughbred,
with psyche tuned to sea urchins no less than to bank clerks, exasperating
bank clerks. My own loneliness has not in a decade been linked to the waiting
for a silent phone to sound. Nor am I ever lonelier than when the phone is
sounding. Question of priorities. The solitude of work, during which all
priorities (happiness, death, taxes) are suspended, resembles like love that
cold bubble.

Last night JH pointed out that Harold Schonberg, when dealing with low
culture like chess or like mystery novels (which as Newgate Callendar he
reviews for the Sunday *Times*), is succinct and fair and at home and wise.
With high culture like musical performance (much less musical composition)
he's coarse and dull.

The rare moments critics turn toward me they're at a loss because I haven't told them what to say. A Rochberg positing his pastiches as the True Way, or a Carter explicating his concerto à la Beethoven's Fourth as though here were a novel notion, lend reviewers a hatrack. But I, just nothing but incurable charm and no exegeses, preen unheeded in the gloom, ah me.

At The Brotherhood, Nantucket's one bistro which in the subzero evening stays open late, for the first time I sit, stilly with JH, and watch the scene where everyone knows everyone but no one knows me, yet *I* know "everyone"! Except that I know only peers, and grow invisible to the young, other than those (few) who know *of* me but are either too intimidated or too pushy. Less lonely-making's when I'm all by myself, even late at night in Nantucket with wolves howling as I scramble eggs and think on work to be done, then do it, and look forward to midnight television.

Being Alone

The cliché that clichés are cliché only because their truth is self-evident would seem self-evident. Yet from birth we're taught that things are not as simple as they seem. The wise man's work is to undo complications: things *are* simple, truth blazes ("brightness falls from the air"), and the obvious way to prevent wars is not to fight. Thus, when I proclaim that I am never less alone than when I'm by myself, and am met with a glazed stare, the stare is from one who abhors a vacuum—the look of nature. But I'm complicating matters.

Comfortable rainy darkness has for days fit over the city like a mammoth tea cozy or winding sheet so that the lights of spring gleam unperceived. Earlier this evening, on my way to dine at Mother and Father's, I stepped into Julius's Bar, as very occasionally I do, for a mug of soda. Standing there among the stricken I gape through the window at the drizzling golden streetlamps, and at the women over there in Djuna's Bookshop thumbing magazines. This bistro itself is unchanged from when we drank here, merry and bloody and hot, thirty summers ago: same careful dust, same wobbly stools, same hearty smell of ale and hamburger, same drowsy jukebox emitting heart-piercing sevenths. Except tonight I am dead sober, there are no "possibilities," I know nobody and nobody knows me, and, like a Jean Rhys heroine, I feel lonely in a not unpleasant way. The sea-green reflections from the mirror in my soda seem somehow sadder than any Irish keening. But at least there are no carnal emanations, so after ten minutes I flee.

With pleasure am reading *Walden* finally after three decades of urging from Mother. Less disturbed than amused by a fallacy which jumps from every page, like McLuhan writing that writing is obsolete. If all is vanity, and the amassing of worldly goods and the longing for great place and posterity are demeaning, so too is the need to document one's vanity. Art's the biggest vanity: the assumption that one's view of peace or fright or beauty is permanently communicable. I keep a diary about the uselessness of keeping a diary, but the desire is strong and I am vain. Nor am I counter vanity. And the old man for whom nothing counted but *les merveilleux nuages* is recalled only because Baudelaire solidified him.

*

Sunlight rushes through the house like wind. Yellow brooks defy gravity flowing up the stairs and over the ceiling. Rooms glimmer with optimism. What joy to get out of bed on such mornings. Yet by midafternoon the pall's begun, and when night falls now by five o'clock the stultifying loneliness has retaken hold. Little reason to go on. The reason for the lack of reason is no longer on my list.

Walk careless and lively over the room through sunlight—blood of the day—soaking profligate into rugs. Then dissolve in wonderment that this too ends in death. Sly Death, coming on little cat feet, fooling all of the people all of the time, arranging for man—Earth's one rational beast—irrationally to persist in hoping for a life after You. On the other hand, if the world after ten millenniums finally concedes to equality of the sexes then anything is possible, even life after death.

The priest was speaking of an acolyte: "He is morbidly devout, and so fundamentalist as to shame a Baptist. Yet he is literal paradoxically. After the first communion he remarked, 'It tastes just like wine.' And the angelus sounds like a dinner bell." Then the priest walked off, bald pate gleaming like a raw steak in the sunrise.

The Holy Church forever spells out food and drink.

Suppose that, shortly after you've swallowed your LSD, God does in fact descend in a flying saucer for all the world to behold.

If, as is now suspected, trillions of lifeless galaxies will be forever turning up, why does this leave us feeling lonely, we who despise our neighbors? Astronomer Bernard Lovell declares chillingly (warningly?) that Earthlings are unique, the expansion rate of the cosmos having had to be just so, right after that Big Bang. "If the rate had been less by an almost insignificant amount in the first second, then the universe would have collapsed long before any biological evolution could have taken place. Conversely, if the rate had been marginally greater, then the expansion would have reached such magnitudes that no gravitationally bound systems (that is, galaxies and stars) could have formed." There appear also to be, beyond "us," super-universes and an ever vaster chain of Big Bangs eternally.

Now, if there is no consciousness outside ourselves, no witness of these stellar procedures, then (except to us) does the universe exist? or did we literally invent it all, including the facts of life? JH: the theory of Does-a-falling-tree-make-a-noise-if-nobody's-there-to-hear-it is puzzling only because of hazy terms. If sound means displacement of air then of course the tree makes a noise, but if sound is what's received through the aural sense then of course the tree makes no noise.

Suppose the universe is as it is, but that for some reason we are all asleep—unconscious. Does the universe then exist?

Although the dentist appointment was for two, at one-thirty I was still garbed in only a towel when the doorbell rang, and suddenly Sergeant David Durk, who lives downstairs, stood before me. Did I know anyone who might (he wanted to know) take over his lease, since he and his family are moving away forever? I explained that I had to dress for the dentist at two, but would think about it. Yet he lingered. Was it that he was too filled with his fame to spot the incongruity of a naked composer and a holstered cop in stalemated converse about real estate? Two cultured adults who speak good English but with nothing in common. It's not that Babel was polyglot but that values were dispersed. People of different tongues and classes can be in close accord, while peers feud.

Rushing to the bathroom I grabbed the first book that came to hand, which turned out to be *The Age of Innocence*. There I read again those masterful (hmmm . . . *mistressful* isn't quite the word either) last paragraphs where Archer withdraws from a longed-for reunion "lest that last shadow of reality should lose its edge"—remembering when I'd first read them a quarter-century ago. It would have been an autumn afternoon (like today in Nantucket, warm and russet) on a café terrace, Rue Galilée, and I closed the book, moved, and filled with a Paris evoked by Wharton some thirty years earlier, fictional even then, and so real.

We have the choice, the passing choice, of returning and ruining, or of refraining and keeping. If we keep too long the living person in our heart (imagining that person in a firelit room across the ocean), that person will die. Which is the case with my Paris now. I can go back and rekindle in that same café the rekindling that fired me twenty-five years ago as I evoked Archer rekindling his past. But I cannot close the book—that physically same book—and rise to keep my date with Marie Laure (who was tolerant of lateness only when the need of a book retained her date), because Marie Laure lies underground. Yet, maybe fortunately, for me the power of places has always been stronger than the power of persons.

The older I get the aloner I feel. (But one can grow only so old.) The solitude, classically divorced from company or place, is hinged to a knowledge, recognized even by children, that we rise to heaven unaided. *"Car le joli printemps / C'est le temps d'une aiguille,"* sang Fombeure through Poulenc's lips. Our springtime's but a point, a needle point, in time, but rich and poor can pass with equal ease, though forever single file, through the needle's eye. (I never knew whether that needle's eye was the same as Gide's *Porte étroite*—the "straight gate" to paradise?—mentioned by Saint Matthew.) Those hundreds who perished "simultaneously" at Guyana really died, as the clock ticks, separately.

Rationalizing. Contemporaries say I undersell myself when discouraging attempts (what attempts?) on my revirginated heart. Yet to realize there'll be no more lustful love seems by the light of day, if not of night, a productive time-saver. If it's fear of rejection, let it be known that at the height of whatever I once had (maybe today I'm at some similar, or different, height) I was no less—in my demure and vicious loveliness—no less shy.

To sit now in Piazza Navona or at the Flore how could I not suspect your motives and look the other way (turn the other cheek)? But I do take pleasure in your company? Who takes pleasure in the reality of whom? Even once when describing P. I longed for him to leave so as to savor missing him.

*

Long weekend in Philadelphia to supervise the concert of my music at Curtis in whose hallowed halls I'd not set foot for 144 seasons.

Tea chez Henry McIlhenny with Stephen Spender. We talk of Saul Bellow. I mention that Bellow is, well, a bit too heterosexual for me, if you know what I mean. Spender answers: "Yes, Bellow does treat women horribly, doesn't he!"—then goes on to equate male homosexuality with the feminine side of man's nature. Stephen being Stephen, this is surely not stupidity so much as academic hypocrisy.

Yet you *can* turn back the clock and recall cleanly as a photo each minute of a finite past. How *déjà vu* like old movies our hours are numbered even as we enjoy them heedlessly. To relive a great love—*quelle horreur*. Only the smoky smell of erstwhile roses makes a useful difference.

And you *can* go home again. Write of PQ's visit wherein the dread gave way to sympathy, though the fact that friendship can withstand decades of separation, while cheering, limns the notion of death more sharply than if there were no returns. Is a reunion really a return?

Twenty years last summer since PQ approached along Cannes's Croisette and asked, *"Vous êtes en vacances?"* Thirteen years since we met, in Marseilles. And now, better (not worse) than my memory, he's come at fifty-one for his first excursion (professional, for ecology in Saint Louis) to an America which had never appealed to him as an idea. I see the city through his eyes, and oh, our natives are plain. The golden youth from the United States, for whom the Frenchman, licking his chops, lay in ambush during every holiday of the early postwar years, has vanished. Search amid the millions, day after sodden day, in the subway or Sardi's, for one beguiling face, and search in vain. Why? PQ says it's urban living. (In his Marseilles apparently beauty still reigns, as here, empty-headed, in California.) JH says it's the achiever complex indigenous to Manhattan. Or is it from that lack of physical narcissism that comes from money? Unlike Romans, Americans don't need to be beautiful.

Americans, wrote Tennessee Williams in 1949, suffer from "a misconception of what it means to be . . . any kind of creative artist. They feel it is something to adopt *in the place of* actual living" (Windham letters, footnote, p. 307). Could not the reverse be posited? The act of making art *is* the artist's actual living, and the humdrum needs of life are a by-product of that art. The best artists, by and large, lead what outsiders would find dull lives; those whose "actual living" is overly gaudy just haven't the time for art, even when such living forms the art's very material.

Reperusing with distaste the transcribed conversation taped years ago for the Dance Collection of the Library of Performing Arts. What disparity in meaning between the spoken and the written word! Transcriptions of this sort in their "spontaneity" are less true than the "artifice" of the pen. All that I utter, in an urge to be clever and valid, turns thin and dull, except for one phrase about the aloneness of Martha Graham. Greatness has no playmates. Creative artists are no more lonely than real people, but to get work done they obviously need to be alone more than salesmen or bankers. Even love is expensive for an artist: the time love takes is thrilling, but not instructive—not even for writing about love. Greatness has no playmates, that is true. Alas, it's also true that the dispenser of tenth-rate art must dispense with playmates.

Martha is the only giant I can think of who has never been denied by her successors. She has authored perhaps 150 ballets, most of them with original scores. Yet with one or two exceptions she has caused no topnotch music to exist. Neither, except for Vivian Fine on one occasion, has Martha used music by women. Nor have I noticed that women composers among themselves are magnanimous. They are more anxious to be taken seriously by men than by their sisters.

Insomnia, colored not by private anxieties but cluttered by passing concerns. TV dominates. Julia Child mixed with Guyana horrors churning with oil prices climbing. Cut to Melville's *Pierre*, uncomfortably verbose. Back to the screen. Anxious to hear (see) Tashi play Takemitsu's new *Quatrain* on WNET but not wanting to miss Stockard Channing on "Rock Hour" scheduled simultaneously, I switch from channel to channel. "Rock Hour" is *no less good* than the Takemitsu, which is merely six sound-effects in search of a coherer. Insomnia.

Ruth Kligman, ever avid for the full life, exclaims: "I've found the most divine pill. It puts you to sleep for only fifteen minutes, and you wake up thoroughly refreshed so that you can *live* and be *conscious* and *savor experiences* and . . ."

Jane Frielicher: "I have trouble just staying awake for fifteen minutes."

We who are to be destroyed are first made sane by our Lord.

Did I still keep a diary 'twould not serve to reveal secret sex and cake recipes. The disease and dying of dear friends ever more preoccupy us all, and wonder at the cheerlessness we come to.

Is my entire *oeuvre* an *oeuvre?* In that case I do not repeat myself, since each piece is part of a continuing whole. (And although such stuff as dreams are made on generally turns out to be sheer twaddle in the morning, my sleeping hours, unlike Ruth Kligman's, feel no less urgent than the waking.)

Tonight while reworking a choral version of Hardy's *The Oxen* composed twenty-four years ago (around the time I was reading Wharton), I feel for the thousandth time how time freezes during focus on the act. Musically the inspirational shove seems identical: I may have more or less energy (more technique, less facility), but the expressive line's the same, and also the special piquant secondal harmonic clots that make me wince nicely while imagining that I and only I have ever thought up such combinations. But further still, in this icy today on America's Seventieth Street, I find my very body resurrounded by those vases of vastly odoriferous tuberoses which graced the Noailles salon where once I labored on that evening of June 21, 1954. It is enough to pore over the Métro map of Paris to be transported there, back through the ether and years, smells above all. That is one way to learn a city, through odors, as through cruising parks and pissotières, the hard-boiled egg stench, the rotten seaweed stench, the dimple on the ruddy chin of that policeman, the etc. Why must we move through time, since time, whatever it is, says the same thing perpetually?

Occasionally a stranger in the mail attests to how much my music has meant to him. Why does this trouble me? Why am I made anxious and not elated at seeing my books in a store, name in a program? (Vicious letters or negative reviews are no more terrible than pleasant ones.) Because the damage is done, the work is removed and leading its own life, influencing (or not) the unknown quantities while the maker could be dead, left with my own vile body.

People are always asking, "How do you remember all that stuff? Me, I forget things as soon as they happen." But why live if that which occurs makes no impression, can't be used, even the endless boredom? Why live if only to forget having lived? This said, my notorious total recall is abetted by date books and diaries, and by recalling the months, and divisions thereof, of returns to America, of an affair with a certain person, of the impulse for a certain piece. To live is to improvise variations on our own theme, yet those improvisations are not random but (unbeknownst to us at the moment) formal and collective. How does one manage *not* to have total recall? of this unique rhubarb tart, that red-hot torso, these November leaves, all the wars, those dying friends?

Other people are always saying, "How can you live in the past?" But the present *is* the past (as Marcel was hardly the first to show), and the older we grow the more past we have. Our shriveling future may be all that we make of it, but so is our past which changes perspective with each new dawn. Life is awfully nice, yes, and keeps getting nicer, but never nice enough, surely not enough to have been born for. And is life short? To die at seventy-five will mean that eight thousand nights stretch on ahead. How to fill them? By using them through what's been learned so far? Now, on the contrary, could it be that the past grows smaller, like a blood-flavored popsicle on which we gnaw self-cannibalistically, and when it's melted utterly, we. . . ? Owls and tigers commence their flights and prowls at dusk, and thus might symbolize Death were it not that they too, God's creatures, prey upon their own pasts, their shrinking pasts. Endless, the future? Certainly not, since by definition the future does not exist.

Still other people ask what my parents think about my prose writings. Father, always a logician, recalls my childhood's unscholarly recalcitrance and reads me with a "Gosh, I don't remember ever telling Ned that," and is proud. Mother, never a "Ballet Mother," resisted for years treating me as special. Today about my music she unqualifiedly defends me. About the prose (which renders one more vulnerable than does music) she hopes only that I'll not relate things that might later make me sad, or friendless, or get me in trouble.

1977–79

TWO

PEOPLE

WOMEN IN MUSIC

In the ten minutes which I've been warned not to exceed let me read four statements, each a variation on the theme at hand, and each a theme in itself to be varied in due course.

1) *Women and the Arts in the 1920s: Paris and New York.* The emphasis on music is weaker than on the other arts of that epoch for two reasons. First, France has never been a musical country. She *has* produced great composers and performers; but the French public, expert at looking and tasting and dressing, is unviable where listening is concerned. From a practical standpoint the French musician is not a prophet in his land, chauvinist though that land may be.

Second, and more important: Rhythms of evolution in the various arts don't synchronize, and music usually drags behind the rest, recapitulating phylogeny, so to speak. The millenniums are sprinkled with the names of women in politics and literature, and the centuries have seen women in painting and science. But music, although probably the oldest art, is nevertheless the youngest, being the last to flower as personal expression; the composer as individual is very recent, for men as for women. Thus the 1920s can claim no musical equivalent of a Djuna Barnes as American-in-Paris, nor of an Elinor Wylie as American-in-New York. There was, however, a Parisian in Paris, eventually to become a Parisian in America. So far as musical pedagogy is concerned—and by extension musical creation—she is the most influential person who ever lived.

Nadia Boulanger, who turned ninety last year, came from a highly musical family, and won a Prix de Rome at twenty. Her younger sister Lili, also a composer, was more creatively gifted, according to Nadia who was the girl's only mentor. When Lili died in 1918 the grief-stricken Nadia forsook all thought of her own composition, and devoted the rest of her life to promoting Lili's posthumous work by helping other composers to realize themselves.

Before 1920 American musicians went always to Germany for their postgraduate grand tour. But when the young Aaron Copland in 1921 wandered into Boulanger's harmony class at Fontainebleau and was overwhelmed at the woman's ability to bring her dull subject to life, he opened the trend toward France which continued for half a century. No composer

123

during that period was untouched, at least indirectly, by Nadia Boulanger: American music gained its identity through her indelible aegis.

(Worth noting: Because women have traditionally not been teachers of composition, Boulanger's listing in the Conservatoire catalogue remains: Professor of Accompaniment.)

2) Throughout the world music's creative pulse is at present less stimulated than that of movies or books. But it does throb along and perhaps beats most healthily in the United States. If I were forced to name the six best living American composers, three of them would be women: Barbara Kolb, Lucia Dlugoszewski, Louise Talma. Their ages are thirty-eight, fifty and seventy-one, and each is single. Indeed, for what it's worth, most female composers of the past eighty years have remained unmarried.

And most of those to whom I have mentioned this symposium have been less than thrilled. The sole realm of productivity which cannot be accurately located, generalized or defined even by Shakespeare, Freud or Webster's Dictionary is the artist's realm. And the sole human endeavor which does not somehow replicate itself—such as making bread, making money, making wise remarks or making babies—is the work of art. No sooner do we define the true artist's behavior than another true artist misbehaves. No sooner do we conveniently frame one artwork than a second artwork overflows its borders. We cannot therefore speak of Women Composers, but of each woman as she appears, since each one, through her work which is final and unique, provides her own definition.

3) Being a composer I naturally stress the creative aspect of my art, although music, like theater and dance (though unlike painting and poems), divides neatly into making and doing which are often remote from each other.

Women as performers have done quite well over the past few hundred years. In France during the teens of this century women come preeminently to mind as interpreters of Debussy and Ravel: not only singers like Mary Garden, Jane Bathori and Madeleine Grey, but pianists like Marguerite Long and violinists like Hélène Jourdan-Morhange. Even as patrons women seemed more in evidence than men: Misia Sert, for instance, or the Princess de Polignac, not to mention Ida Rubinstein who commissioned what turned out to be many a musical masterpiece, or even the Bostonian, Mrs. Richard J. Hall, who premiered Debussy's Saxophone *Rapsodie* back in 1895. But these people had vanished by 1919, and a new crop did not sprout until the thirties. The twenties were not rich in either sex for performers. As for women composers, France produced only two in the twenties—Marcelle de Manziarly and Germaine Tailleferre, both first-rate and thriving today—and America only one, the late Ruth Crawford, a real innovator of sorts, but whose sounds turned more pedestrian with the political overlay of the next decade. (Crawford, incidentally, was the mother of folk singer Pete Seeger.)

How have they been treated? Twenty-four years ago I wrote: "Hairdressers, harpists and cooks. Most are women, but the best are men. Women contend they have never been given a chance, but chances are taken, not given." Would I hold to this today? Probably not, on the general scene, but on the rarefied stage of the artist there is no rule beyond Everyone for Himself. All composers of all sexes are less discriminated against than merely ignored, for they are expendable. Performing musicians, on the other hand, are an investment; and since female singers, like actresses (as opposed to female painters, like cellists), are needed *as females*, they can demand and get equal pay.

4) Pensées and queries.

Why have there been so few women composers? English critic Cecil Sharp once gallantly explained that music—the very muse of music—being feminine, she needed a man to manipulate her.

"All artists," said Picasso, "are half man and half woman, and the woman is insufferable."

If we all, as some Gay Libbers profess, contain within us a man, a woman and a child, how then distinguish between men, women and children? If the obvious reply is that all contains all, but not in equal parts, the next question becomes: what is the difference in kind between the womanly part of a woman and the womanly part of a man? An artwork could be defined as the result of a marriage of true minds; the minds are within one individual, and so is the marriage, which, before being consummated, causes many a beautiful dish to be broken.

Could a case be made that even the greatest women have never given way to the same vast flights of fancy as men? Even the Grand Failure seems a male prerogative, except for maybe Gertrude Stein. Is it conceivable that a work of art is the result of the effort of a single person to produce offspring—the self-pollinating hermaphrodite giving birth?

In 1970 during the most fiery moment of the so-called Woman's Revolution I was stunned when my friend Robin Morgan turned on me with the words: "Stick to men poets. Sylvia Plath belongs to our sisters." As though poetry belonged to anyone, even the poet, once it's written! Still, maybe Robin had a point. If I feel no more need for Plath it's precisely because she *was* a woman and I am not, not even metaphorically. Not that a composer need feel, or even respect, a poem in order to set it well. And masterpieces which thrill are more impossible to musicalize than lesser verses that ring a bell. The question of which composers select which poets to set to music, and of how they set them when selected, is endlessly engrossing. A woman's setting of Plath might not be better than mine, but it will be different, not only because she's another person, but because she's female. How to prove the difference? Is there more difference between a man and a woman than between one good composer and another good composer?

Mendelssohn's sister Fanny composed. Mendelssohn advised her against turning professional, but did anonymously include some of her songs in a published collection of his own pieces. Queen Victoria sang. She once programmed a song from the Mendelssohn collection. When the composer discovered that the song was Fanny's, he felt duty-bound to admit this to his sister and to the Queen.

Collections are mischievous when it comes to art, which is why art never flourishes at the start of a revolution, for art is not community but the lonely voice. Finally there is no women's art, but art by a woman. Is it not possible that what one sometimes senses as mediocrity pervasive in all expression since the war stems from our emphasis on who produces rather than on what is produced—the who being collections instead of single souls?

April 6, 1978

MISIA

Misia! A solo noun, long favored as badge by so many iron-willed professional French females, from Réjane to Régine. If she was not in fact French, still less a professional, her will grew stronger than mere iron, tempered though it was with gold.

Misia! One name. But beneath the silk hiss of those syllables lurked as many Misias as there were geniuses to depict her. Renoir painted seven portraits; Lautrec portrayed her too, as did Vuillard to sublimate a lifelong unrequited love. She was godmother to Picasso's first child. Cocteau said: "She has a talent for walking, laughing, putting one in one's place, handling a fan, getting into a carriage, designing a diadem." If Gide never took to her ("she plays the piano in an 'artistic' manner . . . which I dislike so much . . . more suitable for displaying the temperament of the performer than the quality of the piece"), Mallarmé gifted her annually with *pâté de foie gras* and homegrown poems (all now lost, alas, except for one quatrain inscribed on a Japanese fan, with her name misspelled "Missia," which indicates that the French did not pronounce the single "s" as a "z"). Stravinsky: "I embrace you thousands and thousands of times very warmly." Satie: "Dear Madame, are you not a magician?" (Though when she committed the cardinal sin of interfering with his creative activities, Satie announced: "Misia is a lovely cat—so hide your fish.") Saint-John Perse: "Dear friend whom I love, you are there, who come from no place on earth." Reverdy: "Dear Misia, I curse the obstacles that separate me from you. You are a piece of my life. A blue piece . . ." (She herself claimed, "I've had only husbands, never lovers," and passed Reverdy on to her closest friend, Chanel, "who had only lovers, never husbands.")

Misia! She was the clay from which Proust fashioned the egret-coiffed Princesse Yourbeletieff as well as the less glorious but more powerful and crassly cultured Madame Verdurin, the wise and wealthy bourgeoise who, though sometimes a false friend, was ever a true art lover. (The present writer's dearest companion during the 1950s, the late Marie Laure de Noailles—herself granddaughter of Proust's model for the Princess de Guermantes—although probably more "creative" and surely as rich, molded her style around Misia: a day never passed, or a night, without Marie Laure remarking on how Misia did, or would have done, this or that.)

Yet who indeed was Misia, that such noble swains commended her? The
answer is found in a book which tells all (but not more than) you will ever
need to know about Madame Misia Godebska Natanson Edwards Sert who,
though still largely unknown to Americans, was the single most influential
dilettante in European art during the first three decades of this century.

Born of a wealthy Polish sculptor in 1872, Misia Godebska was one year
older than Colette, though she always posed as ten years younger, having
with her own hand counterfeited her passport. Raised in Belgium in a milieu
of privilege—she was never to know any other—Misia imposed her independence at fourteen by running off to London where she lived friendless for
several months. Returning to Paris she became a star student of Gabriel
Fauré; though she remained an amateur all her life, her piano skill was
praised by everyone from Liszt to Eddy Duchin. At fifteen (or was she really
twenty-five?) her entire dowry went into a trousseau for the wedding with
Thadée Natanson, distinguished founder and editor of La Revue Blanche,
graciously mentioned in the Goncourt Journal as "a real nest of Yids." Sloe-
eyed and moon-faced, creamy-skinned and statuesque, effusively intelligent
and passively carnal (though apparently, despite the scandal of three eventual
divorces, a mostly faithful spouse), Misia now began a career modeling for
fledgling masters and became, as drawn by Bonnard, her husband's first
cover girl. But the magazine's every policy was also in her hands; although
she was not an intellectual, Misia's instincts were nonetheless sound in matters literary. As a salonnière and co-editor she took full advantage of her
access to the leading minds and talents of the Belle Époque. Natanson was to
offer her the most blissful and purposefully elegant period of her existence.
The nineties were halcyon years of exploration, of a honeymoon in art, above
all of acceptance—and gold is a grand entrée.
    The century ended with a loss of her innocence, through new gains of
gold.
    Alfred Edwards, vastly moneyed as publisher of Le Matin, vastly manip-
ulatory and vastly vulgar (a coprophiliac to boot), decided, with the masochism typical of sadists, that he loved Misia Natanson and would die unless he
had her. He persuaded his own wife to try to persuade Misia to become his
mistress. When Misia refused, he divorced his wife, and coerced Natanson,
whom he had meanwhile bankrupted, into selling him Misia. Thus she
emerged all-powerful among the richest women in France and "began to feel
the troubling, the almost sexual stir of worldly ambition." (In 1908 Natanson
showed the world his version of the marriage breakup in a lesbian melodrama, Le Foyer, revived as recently as 1938 by Max Reinhardt.) The next
years meant renouncing her own work on La Revue Blanche, but they did
bring the friendship of such valiant workers as Valéry, Ravel, Arnold Bennett, who would join the Edwardses on the yacht Aimée to cruise through the
canals of Europe. With all her intense desirability, Misia was no exception to
the unspoken truth that history's greatest femmes fatales are never so much
"good in bed" as stylish hostesses and shrewd accomplices. But the years also
brought a heavy dose of fin-de-siècle ennui aggravated by Alfred's abject
jealousy which, not unpredictably, dissolved into indifference when he fell in

love with a scheming young actress. In her anguish Misia was not above
abetting her husband's infidelities, like the wife before her. But this union too
collapsed after four years, leaving Misia aggrieved, alone, thirty-six and well-
off.

Being well-off was no hindrance to her rapports with Serge Diaghilev.
From the minute she introduced herself merely by approaching his table at
Prunier in 1908 until his death twenty years later, she was "the only woman"
for the great impresario as well as his chief confidante. Their affinity arose
from the Slavic temperament that mutually possessed them. Both were born
in Saint Petersburg within a week of each other, both took luxury for granted
and neither was overburdened with scruples. "When the history of homosexuality is written," the biographers tell us, "Diaghilev will be seen as one of its
liberators. After all, only a few years earlier Oscar Wilde had been im-
prisoned for the 'crime' that Diaghilev displayed with so little concern. And
in her way Misia was one of the most visibly liberated of women. . . .
Neither was particularly gifted sexually, and both found sublimation in
controlling their friends and lovers by other means. . . . They adored gossip
and had talents for intrigue. . . . Their reading days were over (Diaghilev
was seldom seen to open a book), yet both were exceedingly rich in that
singular commodity called taste."

That singular commodity should be qualified as taste-that-only-money-
can-buy. Paradoxically, Misia's next and final husband, the Spanish painter
José-Maria Sert, amassed a fortune by producing murals of a cheapness-that-
only-money-can-buy. Still, he became the sole true love of Misia's existence,
making her for a very long time supremely happy. Ultimately he too succumbed to "another woman," the exquisitely unstable teenaged Princess
Roussy Mdivani, whom Misia also adored. Even after the divorce the three
for a while lived uneasily à trois. When Roussy died, Sert said to Misia, "If
you had really loved me, you would not have let me go." But in public affairs
he was a *mensch*, using his considerable influence during World War II to
protect French Jews, among them Colette's husband, Maurice Goudeket. At
his death in 1945, Misia, who survived him by four years, wrote: "With him,
all reason to live ceased for me."

Her last years were poignant. As early as 1927 she and Diaghilev, blasé in
their fifties, began to suspect with some justification that art had been better
in the old days; they referred to the efforts of their new protégés as "*des petites
crottes adorables*" ("delightful dung"). As an arbiter of taste Misia was growing
out of fashion, her eyesight was failing, so was her budget. Relying ever
more heavily on morphine (less to ease pain than boredom), she was finally
arrested as a common junkie and never recovered from the trauma. When she
died at seventy-seven, it was Coco Chanel ("still trying to wrest the crown
from Misia, unaware that it was no longer there") who prepared the corpse in
Sert's canopied bed before allowing selected mourners, among them Paul
Claudel, into the chamber. Today Misia lies near Mallarmé's grave in the
small cemetery of Valvins overlooking the Seine.

A necrophilic glamour exudes from these pages as they draw to their close
and toward our present, as though the co-authors (who in their early research

enjoyed the hospitality of the mightiest personages in Paris except precisely the one under investigation) were themselves falling in love with their heroine—she to whom they accredit, willy-nilly, the love of all who saw her. Bewitched by a woman they never met, they are nonetheless able to project onto the reader their narcissistic fascination. Consider these writers, who are, from one standpoint, as intriguing as their subject.

If Robert Fizdale and Arthur Gold did not exist they would have to be invented to write this book. Immediately after the Second World War they became more than merely the best two-piano team: they commissioned what turned out to be the best in their medium's repertory from composers as diverse as Boulez and Bowles, Poulenc and Cage. Except for Rostropovich, who single-handedly caused to exist the bulk of today's cello literature, no other living performers have served contemporary music more than Fizdale and Gold.

Private Maecenases like this pair are not often bred in the United States where foundations (sometimes) take care of subsidies. Although by birth Chicagoans and by address Manhattanites, they have ever eschewed the cozy American need for specialization. If they resemble Misia Sert not only as keyboard artists (though surely more capable) and as purveyors of new music, they are equally un-American in their wishes both to interrelate the various arts and to hobnob with artists themselves: they are snobs in the true sense of the word (which derives from *c'est noble*). Like Misia they have always moved in the ballet world, mainly that of Balanchine by whom their advice is heeded as it has been heeded by many a worthy poet and painter. Gourmet cooks, they have during recent years tended the food column in *Vogue*. Fizdale and Gold have been everywhere, known everyone, impelled like many another Francophiliac American of their generation (they're in their late fifties) by a yearning for a time they never knew—yet almost knew. After deciding against a book about Erik Satie, they have finally gathered the just rewards of their labors in the *haut monde* into the present biography.

Roughly half is taken verbatim from documents: Misia's *Memoir* dictated to her amanuensis, Boulos, and published posthumously in 1952; letters, principally from Satie, Stravinsky and Cocteau but also from Bonnard, Bakst and others; vivid phrases from other people's books. More unusual—and which lends the last pages a touching authenticity—is the fortuitous discovery of a cache of memorabilia from one Paul Uldace: Boulos's own unpublished diary; still other notes from Ravel, Colette and Vuillard; and a revealing chapter on Madame Chanel by Misia herself, originally excised from the *Memoir*. (Chanel had vetoed the essay, saying that she planned her own memoir, to which Misia retorted: "It exists already in your account books.")

The other half is so shamelessly padded with *Redbook*-ish conjecture as to be useless except as a novel. Unlike a Steegmuller or a Painter who in their exemplary studies of Cocteau and Proust confected high literature by seamlessly weaving verifiable quotes into every paragraph, Fizdale and Gold rely dangerously on their own fancy. ("Shivering with fear and delight, Misia would hold tight to her brothers' hands when they took her down to explore the huge vaulted cellars." "Often, turning from the piano, she would watch the poet sailing on the pewter-colored Seine in the calm splendor of early evening.")

I, for one, am not convinced that Misia's celebrated taste—if that word means discernment—isn't better termed flair. Did she not, after all, on commissioning a set of murals from Bonnard, take shears to them so that they would fit her walls? (Reproached for lack of respect, she replied, "I don't respect art, I love it.") And was she not miffed by her friend Debussy's dislike of her friend Stravinsky's *Sacre* on the spurious grounds that: "Every time I hear Debussy's *La Mer* I cannot help picking out the five or six passages which are almost identical with passages in the *Sacre*"?

Is it perhaps nit-picking to say that the authors meaninglessly label Debussy's *Jeux* a "cubist" masterpiece? Or that they regularly misspell Lanthelme (the sapphic demimondaine for whom Edwards divorced Misia, and who at twenty-four fell from the *Aimée*'s deck and drowned in the Rhine)? Or that they seem to ignore, when calling Misia a *donneuse*, that to the French the word means stool pigeon more strongly than it means benefactress? Or that in contending that Misia's "speech was salted with irony and peppered with four-letter words," they mean the three- or five- or six-letter words to which French smut is uniquely restricted? Or that they fall into the well-known trap of crediting Cocteau, and not Péguy, with the quip "One must know how to go too far"?

More serious is the esthetic misreading, not to mention the continual belittling, of Cocteau. "That overlay of mockery that was [his] own cynical, slightly sinister veneer," is far off the mark of one who, though sophisticated, was as vulnerable as an infant, and whose "veneer"—and core as well—pleaded loudly for love. "A little behind the avant-garde but ahead of society, Cocteau in the twenties was the epitome of the advanced artist as homosexual hero." But the avant-garde is never homosexual per se; even if it were, Cocteau was never (at least not in his public works, not even indirectly) a homosexual hero, as Gide was. "Cynical" is Fizdale and Gold's word too for Marie Laure in their editorial about "her willingness to collaborate with the Germans" (a slander first uttered in Kenneth Clark's autobiography, and here repeated), adding gratuitously that she was "brilliant, talented, and perverse [being] after all a descendant of the Marquis de Sade." If they are inexact where one's friends are concerned, how can one trust them with strangers?

Yet the weakness of any book about Misia lies not in literary quality or even in mislaid truth (this book, which will doubtless be the last word on the subject, is as good as Misia deserves), but in the fact that she was everything except the real thing. Like, say, the Gerald Murphys or Natalie Barney, she became a self-promoting promoter. Because she was really just a hanger-on, to solve the mystery of what made her tick is only superficially necessary. Still, unlike the Murphys, Misia hung on in the most vital way: she sponsored art by paying for it.

The strength of any book about Misia lies in showing how she openly responded to the principle, so rarely grasped by Americans, that artists are finally less in need of understanding than they are of ready cash.

December 1979

REMEMBERING JANET

Nine years ago in Paris I made this entry in my journal:

9 October (Thursday)
Where now's the best pastry shop in our neighborhood? Chez Vaudron, à la Fourche, corner of the Avenues Clichy and Saint-Ouen, used to sell us warm flaky orange-custard tarts with real orange slices baked into them. Last week on discovering Vaudron's replaced by a hardware store, I was ready to take the first plane out of France. I would have, too, if a month ago I hadn't already made a date to dine tonight with Janet Flanner.

The idea of the meal was a strenuous expression of pleasure from Janet for my having turned nine portions of her "Letters from Paris," as they appeared in *The New Yorker*, into a piece for chorus and orchestra, at the Koussevitzky Foundation's behest in 1966. The published score has just appeared in a handsome edition, and I brought extra copies for Janet. "Nobody's ever done that to me before," she said, examining the musical notes printed above her dismantled text, as the taxi transported us from her hotel in Place Vendôme to a restaurant in Place des Victoires.

Three hours were passed over a shrimp bisque, soles meunières, and a kilo of raspberries in thick cream, a long time considering we took no wine. Tonight as always Janet churned midwestern reticence into continental clarity. Circumspect in writing, she is outspoken in talk. As always she asked after my "dear Quaker parents," not failing to add, "what on earth did they feel about that pornographic diary?" And she examined me reproachfully through her monocle, resembling a hip and handsome Amazon disguised as George Washington playing Greek tragedy.

No one—certainly no one reviewing the Paris peace talks—reveals the French political scene to the United States more lucidly than Janet Flanner; she is at home, articulate and organized within this subject as she is within the visual arts. About current American writing she seems less informed, while her report on matters musical has dwindled to nothing. She explains: "My active musical knowledge ceased with a recognition of Debussy's whole-tone scale back in the teens of this century when I permanently quit the ugliness of the Middle West for the beauty of this geography. I'd *like* to write about music, because God knows I have trouble sometimes finding material for the Paris letter. But I don't feel secure about it anymore, now that Doda Conrad and Noel Murphy aren't around to go to concerts with. Am I missing much? It seems to me that France lacks all distinction since de Gaulle."

If she ignores the names of music critics here, she appears equally unconcerned with local society as Society, but adores gossip about the artistic rich. Her personal milieu, I gather, revolves more around the American expatriates of then and now, like Natalie Barney or Bettina Bergery or James Jones.

She hailed the waiter. I protested. "You can't pay, dear Janet. I'm a gentleman." "So am I," she answered.

As she had promised me a catalogue on Napoleon, I accompanied her back to the Ritz where, since the demise of the Continentale last spring, she now inhabits a single room on the fifth floor overhanging the garden of the famous bar, with a treetop view of the obelisk on the left, and on the right the Église de l'Assomption's dome. It is a late October midnight, but a hyacinthine breeze enters the balcony window and ruffles for an instant the aquamarine nightgown which, earlier in the evening, a chambermaid had laid out on the narrow Spartan bed. "I'll probably die here," said Janet without passion, but with the straightforward poignance of one born in 1892.

The Ritz lobby contains a passageway one block long and two yards wide, bordered by mirrors and by several hundred display cases filled with luxury products representing the world's best stores. It is empty and haunted now, at 1 A.M., as I pass through it and onto the rue Cambon where, in 1936, I spent a fortnight with my parents and sister Rosemary at the Hôtel de Castille which still stands there, unchanged.

Those ruminations date from 1969. Reading them now, one might ask: How well did Ned and Janet know each other? If "to know well" means intensity rather than habit, then we were heartily acquainted. But the acquaintance jelled, as so often happens among diasporics who eventually discover they've shared similar paths, only after we'd both resumed residence in New York. Although each of us was an Indiana-born expatriate Francophile Quaker, a sheer difference in years (she was Christ's age when I was born) precluded our meeting in her heyday as a crime reporter for *Vanity Fair*. And during my own Paris years—the decade starting in 1949—our paths seldom crossed: we were, so to speak, attending different classes at the same school. Finally, of course, I knew Janet mainly through her work (the only way anyone knows any artist), and I like to think that's how she best knew me.

She never however heard the music which most obviously united us, the aforementioned "Letters From Paris." She had planned to attend the most recent performance, earlier this month at the Library of Congress where an exhibit of her papers was simultaneously displayed. But she died. It was our dear friend Robert Phelps who had originally compiled the snippets of Flanneriana which I set to music, and it was Robert Phelps who phoned to say that Janet had painlessly passed away, on route to Lenox Hill Hospital—and not in her room at the Ritz.

Yet for all one knows, she may have thought herself in Paris. Her last years to outsiders seemed fuzzy. Janet Flanner had once been married (for a "brief, leafless moment," as Frank O'Hara wrote) to a man whose name she pretended to forget, but the final third of her life was spent mostly with the erstwhile actress, Natalia Danese Murray, who ran Rizzoli's Bookstore, and it was at Natalia's that I last saw her. To be with her there then was to be on the side of the angels. Since she spoke as she wrote, in cleanly parsed phrases, it was less embarrassing than thrilling to watch her slightly miss the point, to hear her uttering epigrams that made no concrete sense, to see her shake a reprimanding finger that always made us feel we'd been lax with homework, though we were never quite sure, following her now-illogical logic, what that homework was supposed to be. She grew deaf, lost the thread, thought she was in another place and time, yet persevered, for she loved talk. And considering the dimension she lent to talk, her conversation, at present so steeped in visible nostalgia, was worth a thousand klatches of the usual mental stalwarts.

"Writing fiction is not my gift. Writing is but not writing fiction." This seems all too true, after a perusal of her 1926 novel, *The Cubicle City*. (Interestingly, Janet's younger sister, Hildegarde, was, and is, a poet of quality, whose most famous sequence, *The Quaker Sonnets*, has often been reprinted—in anthologies of Women Writers, needless to say.) Janet was a reporter. She wrote about what she, or what other people, saw, not what she thought about what she saw.

She may never have had her own ideas, but her glory lay in translating the ideas of others. This she did in a rare and elegant English—really an American dialect—as colorfully cultured as it was wittily sparse, derived from her being an Indianapolis offshoot replanted in Paris. If an author like Julien Green wrote an Americanistic French by dint of forever depicting puritan frustrations in the mother tongue of Baudelaire, conversely Flanner (like Gertrude Stein or Virgil Thomson) composed French in American, her brittle commonplaces set like Fabergé opals in Vermont maple. The stylistic contrast between France and the United States is essentially temperamental: we Americans mean what we say and plod on to make our point; *they* don't necessarily mean what they say (they play the devil's advocate with word games), but they do say what they mean, and say it economically: the French have a word for it—*le mot juste*. The right word does not always come easily. For Janet as for many artists true ease was hard. During whole weekends, surrounded by dictionaries, she would seek, in as few words as possible, for the benefit of her *New Yorker* readers, to describe, say, a Miró retrospective by paraphrasing (encapsulating, as we Americans now lugubriously put it) the exhibit's catalogue raisonné. Her own retrospective—a half-century of articles, essays, fiction and commentary, mainly on every aspect, literary, political and sentimental, of the city of Paris—was entirely in print, to her great joy, when she died on November 7 at the age of eighty-six.

That the Pulitzer Prize, founded originally to glorify the craft of journalism, was never bestowed upon Janet Flanner, speaks more loudly for it than for her. Because she was the most eloquent American journalist of the twentieth century.

November 24, 1978

COSIMA WAGNER'S DIARIES

"I tend almost to prefer doing without to enjoying. . . . It is after all my
duty to keep him in good cheer. . . . In the morning I could tell R. that I had
slept well and—had dreamed of Bismarck. . . . He continues to insist that
the emancipation of the Jews has stifled all German impulses. . . . I find
myself thinking of R.'s words, 'Art is perhaps a great crime'; and certainly
those can be accounted happy who, like animals, know nothing of it, though
this sort of happiness seems to me like eternal darkness. . . . Glorious moonlight. Sleepless night. I shall go mad. How to get possession of the children
without leaving R.? . . . We poor women who can only love, well may we be
pitied when we divine the genius's secret!"

Such grotesque musings may not be literature, but they do add up to what
the Fench colloquially call *littérature*—a lot of talk. French, actually, was the
birthright tongue of Franz Liszt's illegitimate daughter who in 1868 at the age
of thirty-two, fled the bed and board of conductor Hans von Bülow to live
forevermore with her own illegitimate children and their father, the greatest
musician of his day, fifty-five-year-old Richard Wagner. German, however,
was the language of Cosima's diary, fluent if inexpert, begun New Year's
Day in 1869, and finished one million words later, in 1883, the night Wagner
died.

I say "musings" advisedly, for one need remember that the feature of
journals—a literary form used almost solely by the French—is on-the-spot
reaction, an author's truth as he feels it, not as he felt it. If that truth is no
more "truthful" for being in the first person, it does contain the defining trait
of immediacy as opposed to memory. The immediacy here is "grotesque"
because of disparate juxtapositions, and because, gifted with hindsight, we
know what the writer does not yet know: that despite her current bourgeois
humility Cosima must evolve into a monster goddess whose emotional ideologies will be codified by Hitler. These ideologies (casually anti-Semitic,
anti-French, anti-Jesuit, and hysterically pro-Wagner, pro-German, pro-
war), blended with non-sequitur-ial reportage on her own manic-depression
and family illnesses and details of endless high-culture tête-à-têtes, were

recorded daily in twenty-one beribboned notebooks which for a century have
been the musical world's best known unknown documents. Under legal
wraps since 1911, subject to litigation rising from the spiteful testament of
Eva Chamberlain (first of Cosima's offspring by Wagner), these tomes are
now partially available in the canny translation of Geoffrey Skelton.

Like a massive letter, or a series of fragmented aide-mémoires (many sentences lack verbs) for future biographers, the diary offers itself as an apology
by Cosima to her two elder children—legitimate, by Bülow—for living with
a man she variously calls The Friend, Him, R., sometimes even "my dear
Wagner," and who is for her no less than God or Beethoven. Her purpose, in
full accordance with God's, was to commemorate their mutual existence.
Like Persian kings whose every sigh was noted by court scribes, all aspects of
Wagner's daily life are detailed—except of course the one which most counts:
how his music was made. We are left, then, with Cosima's meanderings. The
very first entry states the recurrent themes that set off the taste and tempo of
the vast account: "his essay on the Jews," "how a woman should approach
philosophy through a man," the insomnia or nightmares, the schizophrenia
or physical ailments of the whole family and especially of Cosima herself.
Though she died only in 1930 at ninety-two she seemed during her years
with the master to be forever taking to her bed (were people in fact sicker
then, or just differently diagnosed, than we?). Yet consider her routine: She
supervises three meals a day *en famille* (though never mentioning the menu,
except obliquely: "Coffee with Prof. Nietzsche; unfortunately he vexes R.
very much with an oath he has sworn not to eat meat, but only vegetables. R.
considers this nonsense, arrogance as well, and when the Prof. says it is
morally important not to eat animals, etc., R. replies that our whole existence
is a compromise, which we can only expiate by producing some good."). She
systematically reads aloud with Wagner: Homer at breakfast, Calderón at
noon and after tea her beloved Shakespeare; yet despite this diet, and despite
her illicit, even scandalous, comportment, she retains the stuffy *pudeur* of one
who lives with God. (On sharing Aristophanes: "I suspect R. has to skip
many things in order to be able to read these plays to me.") She raises four
children, tends servants, writes countless long letters, entertains fans and
discourages interlopers, supervises contracts and translations and advises her
mate on the shape of his works, "inks in" his orchestration, takes daily strolls
with him followed by dictation for his autobiography, meanwhile feeling
victimized by the world's opinion, anxious about the whimsicality of King
Ludwig's allowance, and guilty about wanting a divorce from Bülow. All this
and the diary too, which retains its fever of hero-worship, plus modest
touches of self-worship, for she tirelessly records R.'s praise of her beauty,
her sexuality, and her power—stronger than even King Ludwig's—for in-
spiring his masterpieces. The best of Cosima's often intelligent and sometimes piercing commentary on literature and on music (though not on
painting) arises from quotes of R.W. which are seldom relieved by levity and
never by humor. A reminder that German jokes are no laughing matter: "R.
very charming, helping out with witticisms: 'I wish I had your eyebrows,' he
says to my father, which makes us laugh a lot."

Her driving need to serve a great man is occasionally relaxed, only to be turned on again. "A good night, dreamed of distant travels with R., I showed him some Raphael drawings, met George Sand who reproached me for my deeds, I listen to her humbly and say merely that what I did was grave but in my heart is not evil." Awake, would it not have been rather Cosima who reproaches Sand for her deeds? If marriageless love and bastard children were, among the well-off and artistic, no more and no less reprehensible then than now, surely such erring could be sanctioned in Cosima's eye only by service to genius. The emancipated Sand was no sister, and French to boot. Wagner is known to have loved *Carmen*, but Cosima's only comment is that they saw it together, "after which I went to the artists' reception. Much tastelessness."

Quotidian minutiae are superseded by tantalizing quotes emerging like wise uncertain whales every few pages, then sinking back into the sea of words, words, ere a concerned reader in the guise of Cosima can answer back. "Repetition!" exclaims the composer to his now-divorced new spouse. "In that one sees the utter difference between music and poetry. A motive can be repeated because it is a personality and not just a speech. In poetry, on the other hand, repetition is ridiculous, unless it is a refrain and is intended to have a musical effect." Yes, but repetition in music is seldom literal, especially in *your* music, Herr Wagner. Shifting harmony, change of key, alterations of instrumentation lend new meanings to the selfsame tune, while poetry, though it can be said to have tune, lacks harmony, just as music lacks rhyme. Thus, repetition requires separate dictionary definitions as regards these two arts. When Cosima herself asks, "What is the point of genius, when after centuries it can command no respect?", we long to retort: All art is eventually manipulated, only genius withstands the manipulation—even *your* manipulation, Frau Wagner.

As one advances through this horizonless terrain the Wagners grow less affable with their unctuous bigotry and self-satisfaction. The diary palls. For despite the fifteen years during which she hardly left her husband's side, and despite this consecration to his immortality, Cosima's book is finally about herself, the rantings of a "real" person. An essence is necessarily absent. No one has ever written of the so-called creative act in a way which *makes a difference*, because no one knows—not Freud, nor God, nor Wagner himself—what makes greatness in the great.

November 5, 1978

BOULANGER AS TEACHER

Am I the only living expatriate American composer who never studied with Nadia Boulanger? Certainly she was a friend during my decade in France that began in 1949; she did perform my music and helped with money, meals, prizes, and with advice on the good life and concern for the bad. Yet if she often inspected my work ("too many notes" was her Tallulah-voiced admonishment—the best three-word criticism anyone can offer a composer), Boulanger never really gave me lessons. She weighed the pros and cons but concluded that at twenty-four I was now formed—her nudging could only falsify what she termed my *nature bête*. When I evaluate how memorably much I gained from Mademoiselle, as she was called, in our rare hours together, compare those hours to the years granted some other musician, then multiply that musician by thousands, it is easy to see her as the most influential teacher since Socrates. I caught in microcosm, with neither envy nor love but with respect and awe, what the devotees absorbed in depth.

Maybe long before knowing her I had gleaned as much as was needed from Nadia Boulanger. I had, after all, studied with Aaron Copland and Virgil Thomson, her first overseas prodigies from the early 1920s who, thanks to a rigorous French training, had become our quintessentially American composers. But there were not only composers. After World War II, which Nadia sweated out in the United States (though she never mastered English: like many a fine musician she had no ear for foreign tongues), all of one's older colleagues, singers and dancers and drummers and managers, seemed to have collided with her. Myth credits every American town with two things: a ten-cent store and a Boulanger student. Even before the war, as a teenager, I had been imbued with her version of Monteverdi's madrigals on the one record which, still today, I would take to a desert island.

Through osmosis I knew what the mentor was made of, even to her appearance (thin bow ties, hair in a bun, pince-nez and sensible shoes, the long black dress), her technical proficiency (chilling to Americans whose homegrown training remains comparatively lax), her personal theatrics (tears on cue at mention of the dead sister Lili), her miscrediting of famous friends (Radiguet, not Cocteau, put forth the notion that a true artist has his own voice and cannot copy, so he has only to copy to prove his originality). I

138

knew everything except the essence: that her singular dynamism was determined less by undeniable gift than by intensity of attention; by upbringing she was herself a composer, as she felt every musician—at least by upbringing—should be. Yet with all her flair for unmasking the most recalcitrant student's real nature, "anyone who allowed her in any piece to tell him what to do next" (the words are Thomson's) "would see that piece ruined before his eyes by the application of routine recipes and of bromides from standard repertory. The student who sought his remedies at home, alone, would grow in stature."

How had Mademoiselle herself grown in stature?

Nadia Boulanger, who died a mere three years ago at ninety-two, was born of a venerable father (Ernest Boulanger, already twelve when Beethoven died in 1827, became a noted composer and professor at the Paris Conservatoire) and a glamorous mother, the young Russian princess Raissa Mitchesky. Boulanger *père* instilled in his daughter the assumption that music was a more urgently natural part of life than literature or even sex. Her mother stressed the moral obligation to do better, always better, and dominated Nadia with a Spartan charm. After her husband's death she shared her daughter's bedroom until she herself died in 1935, long after Nadia had become a world figure. At ten the girl entered the Conservatoire where for a decade she won first prizes in harmony, counterpoint, fugue, organ, *accompagnement* (a term covering all aspects of score reading), and studied composition with Gabriel Fauré. In 1908 she was granted Second Grand Prix de Rome for her cantata, *La Sirène*. The First Grand Prix came five years later to Nadia's fragile younger sister, Lili, the first woman ever to be so honored. Meanwhile Nadia entertained a very public rapport, which may or may not have been platonic, with Raoul Pugno, a famous and fat pianist old enough to be—who in a sense was—her father. With him she not only gave concert tours but co-composed an opera, never produced, on a libretto by d'Annunzio. From 1908 to 1918 she taught harmony at the Conservatoire. (But not until 1948 would she be named full professor, that position in France being thought unsuited to a woman, even though she was that country's most sought-after pedagogue.) But with the deaths in 1914 of Pugno and in 1918 of Lili, Nadia Boulanger stopped composing to become a full-time teacher and occasional performer.

When the American Conservatory at Fontainebleau was founded in 1921 Nadia was its chief draw which she remained, except for the war years, every summer for the rest of her life. Tours of the United States resulted in her becoming the first woman to conduct the Boston Symphony and then the New York Philharmonic. The list of her students at home and abroad is vast. Not only composers such as Louise Talma, Roy Harris, Walter Piston, Elliott Carter, David Diamond and Theodore Chanler, to mention only Americans, but interpreters like Lipatti, Menuhin, Gendron, Ferrier, and later Noël Lee, Nell Tangeman, Jean-Pierre Marty and Jay Gottlieb would never have been quite as they are without Nadia's guidance.

Second only to Bach in the Boulanger pantheon came her friend Igor Stravinsky, who habitually supplied his new manuscripts for her perusal. Stravinsky could do no wrong. Indeed, after his espousal of post-Schoenbergian methods, Nadia, who despised serial music, attempted to find some truth in his erring. In the autumn of 1964 I visited Mademoiselle Boulanger just after her return from Berlin where she had heard Stravinsky's newest excursion into twelve-tone terrain, *Abraham and Isaac*. Asked how long the piece lasted, she replied, "Does one speak of temporal data where Stravinsky is concerned?" I later understood: the piece, thirteen minutes by the clock, seemed like a numbing hour.

All her life she was newsworthy even to Philistines, an enigma even to intimates. Nadia's fame lay in her femaleness, thus in her firstness. She excelled at what no other woman ever had, musical pedagogy at its highest, but she also gave up what no woman ever had, a composing career. Was this sacrifice, as she later so hotly claimed, because her compositions were "useless," or because she wished to cede the field to her dead sister? She was never an outright feminist, always giving the benefit of the doubt to her male students while overtaxing the females; yet she was acquisitive of the females even to ostracizing them should they contemplate marriage. Her old-maid aspect notwithstanding, Nadia was a creature of high temperament. The open infatuations with old Raoul Pugno, later with young Igor Markevitch, now seem rife with pre-Freudian innocence, as do intimations of latent lesbianism. She visibly preferred men because they were not in competition with her, that is, with Lili, for beside Lili there was no room for other female composers. Nadia's uniqueness (unlike, for example, teacher Martha Graham's) was that she not only dominated what had hitherto been a solely male domain—the instruction of young composers—but in so doing had quenched, once and for all, her creative fires. Dare I suggest that the renunciation was itself a creative coup? That her own music was in fact "useless"?

Malleable toward her musical past, how rigidly Nadia Boulanger held to the social givens of her aristocratic forebears! If there was a contradiction between the anti-Semitism stylish since the early nineteenth century and the acceptance of homosexuality in upper Paris echelons, it was lost on Nadia. That a good many of her pupils were Jewish was a condition she overlooked only when they were gifted or rich, whereas homosexuality was "bad" only if it interfered with work.

Nadia early showed a knack for manipulating the well-placed and the well-off. From her youthful feud with Fauré through her elbow-rubbing with Valéry and Gide to her very funeral at Trinité where Grace Kelly and her husband recited the Our Father from the front row, Nadia's society outside school was of the most *choyé*, and even in school she never turned down a wealthy applicant no matter how untalented. To us Americans this knack seems overweening in a True Artist: if, say, Elliott Carter hires a press agent, do we not feel he should be above all that? But "all that" has always been grist to the survival of European artists. Boulanger's cajolings were strictly at the service of those artists. Deeply royalist, deeply Catholic, she was a snob in that word's oldest sense—*c'est noble*—and her noble amateurs sometimes produced pure gold. Listen again to soprano Comtesse de Polignac's rendition of *Amor* among those Monteverdi madrigals.

She was indefatigable: her first lesson of the day might be taught at 7 A.M., her last at midnight, meals absorbed with phone crooked under her chin.

Music came before all else, certainly before gastronomy or love, and she demanded no less of each student. In the final years, sightless, toothless, half-deaf, hands curled with arthritis, she kept at the routine. Leonard Bernstein, perhaps the last person to speak with Nadia Boulanger, found her nearly comatose in the Fontainebleau hospital. He asked if she heard music in her head, and if so, what music. After a long, long silence, in her marvelous husky baritone she answered from afar: "A music with neither beginning nor end."

She thrived on publicity, yes, but mistrusted the printed word. Good teaching lies in leading a student to culture and making him think. This transfer of knowledge is a contagious enthusiasm. Nadia's contagious enthusiasms grew to be rote. From year to year, student to student, she reiterated the same examples, raised her eyes toward heaven at the same phrase in a Bach aria, allowed those same eyes to flow with public tears at the annual "reliving" of Lili's obsequy, summoned the same bon mots of Péguy at the same magic moment of Stravinsky's Mass. Such repetitions, though dangerous for a creator, are pollen for a pedagogue: the identical strong story is ever fruitful since meaning bends with each listener. Still, Nadia's ambivalence had always forbidden her to grant taped interviews, to publish her speeches or to encourage a biography. Tapes trapped contradictions as well as repetitions, publication glorified writer above text and memoirs meant death. Nadia felt her life *as an event* was boring; her energies aimed strictly toward education of others and the *tone* of such energies by definition could not be notated.

Two decades ago, however, she did a dazzling series of TV broadcasts; some years later, anxious about Lili's posterity as about her own, she finally accorded Léonie Rosenstiel access to previously unavailable papers, thus making this American researcher the sole official chronicler of Nadia Boulanger. Alas, though Dr. Rosenstiel is authorized she is not quite an author.

Reading the present book, I read another half as long and twice as vital, being transcripts (untranslated) of those programs in which Nadia's voice throbs with wisdom and warmth on the very page. I was simultaneously confronted by two Boulangers—three, if my private souvenirs are worthy— and realized once again that a model can count for less than her various painters. Rosenstiel, who prefers to speak in place of Nadia, is a thesis-writer trying for style, a style that is often grudging as though she disliked her subject. Information, as a documentary mass, is the book's main and irreplaceable asset.

When the information is a gradual building of needed facts, as in the tense telling of the 1908 Prix de Rome competition, from Nadia's entry to her final high placement accompanied by the revulsions of misogynist Saint-Saëns and the ecstasies of the suffragist press, we root for the heroine. When we learn that at their first meeting in 1910 Stravinsky replies to Nadia's congratulations on his *Firebird* with: "That's not very important. What is, is that my name becomes a household word," we smile at the comeuppance of the no-nonsense demoiselle, knowing that she too will soon seek to debunk the still-held notion of the artist-as-decoration. And when Nadia on her twenty-fifth birthday, still single thanks to her enslavement as family breadwinner, becomes eligible to join the St. Catherine's fete for unmarried girls, join them she does in her starched lace headdress, declaring that "when a woman wants to fulfill her true rôle of mother and spouse it is impossible for her also to fulfill her rôle as artist, writer or musician," and we cringe at the conflicts she will suffer for the next six decades. Still, since scarcely a month of those six decades is unaccounted for, nor any viewpoint, especially an unpleasant one, unrecorded, we grow weary of the dogged inventory, the graceless anglicizing, the unverified quotes, the cold redundancies which could be cut by a quarter with no loss of content.

Long before those decades closed, Nadia grew out of fashion. In 1946, returning to Paris after a six-year stay in the United States, she found Pierre Boulez's clique booing Stravinsky; as Stravinsky's staunchest appendage the outmoded Nadia also came under fire. As recently as 1972 Boulez recalled with customary charity: "After the war, Messiaen and Leibowitz were the important figures and no one had any use for Boulanger." Like Boulanger, Boulez in his early years was a prophet mainly in foreign lands. Unlike her he returned in triumph to France where to this day, for better or worse, he reigns supreme.

As influence waned, honors accumulated. By 1977 her mesmerism had deteriorated into dogmatism, but international admirers kept up the fan club: Pompidou pinned on her the highest of his government's civilian awards, that of the grand officier of the Légion d'honneur, and the little square at 36 Rue Ballu where she had lived and taught since 1904 was renamed Place Lili Boulanger.

Nadia Boulanger is mainly remembered as a mentor of composers, although she was the guiding light for every breed of musician, not least of all the female musician, and her public career as organist, conductor, musicologist, lecturer, and even for a time as newspaper critic, was unprecedented. Yet were she judged today solely by what "her composers" composed while studying with her, her ratings might fall. For every Copland she championed were now-forgotten geniuses. Most of her Americans, owing her their strong sense of form, came home to bigger things. Of her French stable, only Jean Françaix, whom she seems to have cut from whole cloth, still prevails at eighty. As for Lili, it could be argued she is less a force than a symbol. But where are those wondrous others? Like her mezzo-forte performing style, Nadia's taste was, finally, diatonic and bland à la Fauré. How heretical might she find the vastly chromatic late works of her Elliott Carter, of Ross Lee Finney, of Copland himself? But the planet continues to turn. If Nadia Boulanger did not change the planet's shape, she shaped some who did.

Was her emphasis on technique only one of many "techniques"? Do the French with their machine-gun–solfège accuracy necessarily produce better musicians than the more flaccidly reared Americans? At least Nadia knew that to be moved without métier is insufficient, while with métier inspiration falls into place. Her "contagious enthusiasm" was no tacit encouragement for grooving, but a demonstration that structure, art's sovereign ingredient, need not be always dull, and that to write down your dreams you must be wide awake.

1982

THOMSON AS TEACHER

Composers become composers not because they take lessons, but because they beg, borrow and steal. Yet if I can credit one mentor in the scary musical marketplace of Manhattan, he is Virgil Thomson.

Long before we met I observed him on a roundtable as the other panelists struggled to define music. They were about to fall back on Shakespeare's "concord of sweet sounds" when Thomson yelled: "Boy, was he wrong! You might as well call art a juxtaposition of pretty colors, or poems a succession of lovely words. What is music? It's what musicians do." That settled that. His unsentimental summation was the first professional remark I'd ever heard— music is what musicians do—and I soon saw this in practice. At eighteen I quit the Curtis Institute to study orchestration with Virgil Thomson, and paid for the lessons by copying his manuscripts.

Yale campus is perhaps not tactful ground on which to declare that academic instruction of the so-called creative arts, notably musical composition, is an inexistent process. Good teaching, the imparting of extant knowledge, is a healthy contagion which leads students to rich mineral waters and makes them drink; but no teacher can cause a piece of music to be, he can only criticize it after it exists; if he is a composer he can teach only by himself being—by allowing himself passively to be imitated.

During the months I worked with Virgil I learned more than during years in the world's major conservatories. In mastering the art of calligraphy a young musician becomes accountable for every note, for the need for clarity on the page (because music, before it can be heard, must be visibly communicable), and the good copyist eventually knows the score better than the author of the score. Meanwhile orchestration, unlike composition, is the study of specific balances, a craft available to anyone. Virgil, in laying before me the principles of this craft, explained once, and only once, the sonic results of every physical combination of instruments. Between lessons, while I copied in his dining room, I overheard Virgil at his own work, at the piano, talking to friends or dictating by phone his Sunday article to a secretary at the *Herald Tribune*. Overhearing is itself an indelible instruction, and Virgil is nothing if not lucid: I can recall today as on a record each word he spoke thirty-five years ago.

His lucidity is due no less to an innate clarity of mind than to a voicing of that mind through an ideal language of economy: he speaks French in English. Since he knows what he's talking about and doesn't waste words, merely to be in his presence is to learn. And merely to think about him is to risk being influenced, as these pale phrases attest, for no one out-Virgils Virgil.

His music resembles, more demonstrably than with any composer I know, himself. It is impatiently terse, strong but free of fat or padding, sensuous without self-indulgence, and we absorb it like a cold acid which bathes a core of hot beauty. His music is also very, very witty—if that adjective makes sense when applied to non-vocal works. Thomson's art is generous by its very frugality—we recall it accurately forever.

If in texture Virgil Thomson—the *fact* of him—is American as apple pie, in "message" he is French as *tarte tatin*, because he is not a specialist. During the decades of our friendship (sometimes warm, sometimes cool) I have never thought of him as less than this century's most readable musicologist and most persuasive American opera-maker. Like all artists he is able to do what cannot be done. Through his prose he convincingly evokes the sound of new musical pieces, while through his musical pieces he evokes the visual spectacle of all our pasts.

March 1979

MESSIAEN AND CARTER
ON THEIR BIRTHDAYS

Are they suddenly both seventy? If time flies while art stands still, never was the paradox more positive. Though fruitful years may still attend them, their catalogues are history now, open to flows of reinterpretation—as opposed to mere misinterpretation. I love the music of each one, with a need met by quite separate responses. Thus on this anniversary how can I compare them so much as contrast them: they have little in common beyond a grandeur joined to the special madness that forms greatness, which is always incomparable. (By greatness I mean unique, extreme, persuasive and permanent daring—the risk that counts.)

Olivier Messiaen's music at first sounds thick, many notes being interchangeable; but inside each fat chord lurks a lean tune longing to get out, and which eventually triumphs. Elliott Carter's music at first sounds sparse, every note seeming irreversible; then each tight bar reveals a chain reaction of meanings, and though the whole satisfies, no single solution prevails. Or doesn't art deal in solutions?

I, an American, find Messiaen's art as quintessentially French as Colette's in that it is intelligent without being intellectual, nostalgic yet never sentimental, sensual though not lubricious. It depicts children at play in the bourgeois nursery, gods at work on a crystal rainbow, birds at song in the forests of the night. It springs from the composer's own set of contradictions (which he may or may not be aware of), and sometimes presents new ones of its own. The Frenchness emerges from a sense of *mesure:* when the blinding colors are turned down, an economy of means grows visible. What Messiaen's fans most relish are his unabashed melody, his *bal musette* harmony and his counterpoint which consists of masses moving against each other, each mass of a different tactile substance. If his rhythms look complicated on the page, they are carnal, therefore simple, to the ear, and carnality is the final proof of any artistic pudding. His "modernity" comes from colorations which he calls integral but which we hear as ornamental: the trills of the Blue Rock Thrush, the Ivesian complication of making many plain things happen at one time, and above all, the orchestration that to eye and ear becomes, with its choirs of multiple brass and metallic batteries, glamorous like a giant gold nun whose frantic tranquil voice mounts toward heaven. Messiaen's pieces are mostly long, but only because they are actually assemblages of smaller works, the largest of which are caused to move forward not through organic growth but through literal repetition.

Literal repetition is shunned like the plague by Elliott Carter. It would make a neat balance to say that *his* art is hypertypically American, like—like whose? like the Wallace Stevens he so often quotes?—by embodying certain traits; but I too am American, so find it harder than with Messiaen to objectify such traits. Surely Carter's music is intellectual as well as intelligent. Yet if words like *sensual* and *nostalgic* don't quickly come to mind, neither do verbatim versions of mankind or angels or the songs of the wild. His music doesn't purport to represent anything beyond itself, his narrative translates only as metaphor—as events happening to instruments, not to humans. Carter projects necessity. Not the diffuse necessity of didactic wisdom but the clean-cut urgency of an epileptic fit. Art is never random, and Carter's glory dwells in the knack for inscribing productive tantrums with such accuracy that after the third or the nineteenth hearing the notes fall as logically as the arrangement of animals in The Peaceable Kingdom.

The most apparent, if least significant, contrast between these composers is in their work schedules. Although born within twelve hours of each other, one bloomed well before the other. Messiaen's identity, musical and philosophical, was as recognizable at twenty as it is today. Had he ceased to exist in 1940 he would still have bequeathed those several works by which he remains best known. Meanwhile, it was not until 1946 with his Piano Sonata that Elliott Carter is generally agreed to have turned into Elliott Carter. Around that time (half his life ago!) I first met him in New York. We've known each other long, if not closely, having tread opposite sides of the same path. I was drawn to the conciseness of French impressionism, while Elliott, despite a Paris education, was formally Germanic. Then as now he could be called the last Great Master—the only composer after Bartók able to make a convincing Big Statement in the non-vocal areas, particularly in the otherwise defunct string quartet. (If the highest-valued gestures of the serious music world since 1914 have been stage works for the human voice, it is notable that Carter, no more than Messiaen, has never written an opera.) Physically, this forbidding master houses a marvelously mannered little boy with the vast cultural scope one usually finds in only continental thoroughbreds. Although he is incapable of small talk, humor nonetheless lies behind that sly Burgess Meredith glance. By extension humor must be tangled somewhere within the Gordian knot of his tones, though I've never located it—assuming that such a thing can be pinned down in music.

Humor, being the ability to see three sides of one coin, is actually less frivolous than is devotion. Now, Messiaen's music is devotional. Thus his art, like that of any genius with a one-track mind (even a comic like Chaplin), lacks humor, which is replaced by ecstasy which the composer calls joy. This joy is virtuosic, hence public, yet simultaneously private, being discourse between himself and the Almighty. But the joy must ultimately turn impersonal, like Gregorian chant, which, not officially meant for an audience, is better overheard than heard.

May it not seem chauvinist to suggest that the artist Helen Frost-Jones and the pianist Yvonne Loriod, while in no sense accountable for the nature, are indispensable to the breadth of their husbands' *oeuvres*. For thirty-five years Helen's canny comments at intermissions, not to mention her apparent service as buffer betwixt Elliott and crass practicalities, have been as solid a presence in the musical world as her own sculptures in the world of the eye. Yvonne's extravagant pianism and staunch friendliness during my first years in Morocco and France make her into a latter-day Clara Schumann. Messiaen himself I met briefly just once (and found him too to be a little boy). I did however grow up on his music, music not only gorgeous, but, well, *important*, like Carter's. That's because, in an era of what used to be named *augenmusik*, they were concerned with the ear, with sound never heard before, but whose novelty resided in order and not in chaos. In such an unbelieving age Olivier Messiaen has regiven a good name to inspiration, and Elliott Carter has regiven a good name to mastery. And so they have both given faith to us all.

Many happy returns, dear Elliott. *Et maître Olivier, je vous salue bien bas.*

October 1978

WHEN PAUL JACOBS
PLAYS DEBUSSY

I have found the ideal interpreter of my favorite composer, and the following disjointed notes spring from my joy.

As we admire a person's beauty without that person's being our type, so we can admit the greatness of music which leaves us cold. If Debussy addresses my nature more profoundly than Beethoven, then is not Debussy as important as Beethoven—despite the received idea that German music is more serious than French, and that seriousness is of itself a virtue?

If greatness is, as I believe, a matter of taste rather than a matter of fact, and if the quality of greatness belongs to interpretive as well as to creative artists (which I believe less), then Paul Jacobs, insofar as the keyboard works of Debussy are concerned, is the greatest pianist in the world today.

One definition of love might be: the need to live with. The need is no less for a work of art than for a human being.

The first art toward which I yearned—long before I yearned toward another person—was the music of Claude Debussy, and my notion of this music was both generous and proprietary. I tried to share the experience, but when the attempt was met by mockery or at best by glazed stares in gym class, I was secretly glad. Debussy, after all, was my coveted discovery. Love is blind, and stingy too. I felt guilty, to be sure. We Americans find selfishness a dire trait, as though the self were negative rather than the requisite ingredient of civilization's most selfless legacy, the masterpiece.

Yes, what we love we want to own. But if this truth bears fruit as it obtains to pets and people and paintings, it is stymied by music since music can't be tangibly possessed; and we often absorb it while sitting stoically with hundreds of others. Thus, thanks to my father and mother, I early heard the day's great pianists, Gieseking and Casadesus, play Debussy in Chicago's Orchestra Hall. Soon after, I was stealing the Debussyan discs of other greats—Godowsky, Rubinstein, even Horowitz who by some fluke had recorded one of the *Études*. These renditions for a while became the absolutes against which ensuing renditions were judged. But as I myself became a more proficient pianist I grew less satisifed with others. Not that I was so good, but good enough for my fancy to fill in an idealized version. Mother worried some about my dwelling too much on this "kind" of music, she feared I would get sick. I did get sick, of course, and remain so to this day. Debussy's piano music was the very stuff of my puberty, and I grew so intimate with its every strand that I no longer tolerated anyone else's tamperings.

This intolerance has lasted my whole life—until three years ago when Paul Jacobs's recording of the Debussy *Préludes* fell into my hands. So thrillingly did the pianist's least nuance synchronize with my very bloodstream that I felt Paul Jacobs deserved not only a barrel of rubies but a letter of praise from beyond the tomb of that enigmatic poet who, despite his evanescent tunes, was patriotically solid enough at the end of his life to sign himself always Claude de France.

Yet Claude de France might well turn in his grave at the sound of Paul of America. Not that Debussy-the-composer ought have the last word on how his music should be delivered, judging by the faint records made eight decades ago by Debussy-the-pianist. Debussy's creative psychology was twentieth-century, fragmented yet succinct, impressionistic if you will; his performing style was nineteenth-century, Romantic, expressive. Misty music to sound misty must be played without mist, simply as written. Bach takes interpretation, he should be played like Debussy. But Debussy needs no interpretation, he should be played like Bach.

When Paul Jacobs plays Debussy his own identity is not immediately recognizable as it is with superstars, for he has no mannerism beyond that of his generation: no-nonsense precision. One hears Debussy, not Jacobs. If the gamut for permissible renditions of the French master is narrower than for, say, Shakespeare or even Verdi, it is not that an instrumentalist plays less of a role than a specialist at Stratford or than an opera diva; it is that, so far, there are no entrenched Debussyan traditions. (Traditions change constantly anyhow. There have already been three or four generational fashions in pianism since 1918 when Debussy died.) Almost any composer will tell you that there is no one way to interpret his notes—though he himself may be disposed to this or that style, and indeed he may be wrong; there are as many good ways of playing a piece as there are good players.

No, a performer should not stand between the music and the composer. But who is the composer? Who treads the ideal line? Paul Jacobs happens to share my metabolism, so his playing is right for me. At least his Debussy playing.

When we were schoolmates at Curtis in 1948, Eugene Istomin used to explain to Shirley Gabis and me that certain musical phrases resembled facial mannerisms. Midway through *Feux d'artifice*, for example, there is a measure wherein a sleek glissando ascends to a suave dotted rhythm. Eugene likened this measure to the way George Sanders lifts his left eyebrow. Such comradely games are hard to crash. Paul Jacobs crashes. Hear his glissando. It is George Sanders lifting an eyebrow.

Whether executing the live gold sound of *Poissons d'or*, the low camp of *Général Lavine eccentric*, or the vast sadness of *Hommage à Rameau*, Paul Jacobs understands the music, meaning that he understands it as I understand it, not necessarily as the composer did.

Unlike William Masselos or Charles Rosen or Noël Lee, American pianists who straddle indifferently the many frontiers of current sonic language, Paul Jacobs had always been to me merely a specialist within a specialty, twelve-tonish, one of Elliott Carter's official interpreters. I'd heard his Messiaen and approved, but felt unequipped to pass on his Schoenberg since that music means nothing to me. So his Debussy came as a surprise. Whether or not Jacobs, according to the grotesque teachings of his mentor Pierre Boulez, hears Debussy as a precursor of atonality, he plays Debussy according to my wavelength as profoundly tonal. None of us can ever know how even our closest friends hear music.

Since he plays with pleasure both Schoenberg and Debussy, then like all true pianists he can probably play anything, although he may not choose to. I'm curious about his Schumann.

Did you know that Serkin, during one season in the 1940s, included Ravel on his programs? It was convincing. One need not love a composer to play him to perfection. Indeed, love clouds the mind, and music is mind.

The French have less of a grasp than foreigners on their own music. Are they too ingrown? Paul Jacobs is bilingual, which the French seldom are.

The Debussy discs, all on Nonesuch, do not comprise the complete piano works, but are a fair sampling, recorded between 1976 and 1978: the twelve *Études* (curiously the only version listed in Schwann catalogue), the twenty-four *Préludes*, the *Estampes*, and the two sets of *Images*—plus a third earlier set, hitherto unpublished. Each disc is garnished with Jacobs's intelligent program notes. Since these do not hesitate to treat music literarily—something I've always shied from—let me now try the same.

Of the three innately good piano sounds, steel and gold and silver, Paul Jacobs's is silver, as befits the *Études*. Listen to the one "For Sixths": how little he nudges the page, how the notes speak for themselves through his dangerously pedaled silver bringing tears to the eyes. Or listen to the one "For opposed sonorities" whose secondary sevenths remind me of Paris before I knew Paris (Jacobs is able to make us again "pre-know" that city). Or to the one "For composite arpeggios"—which Horowitz recorded so long ago—with its abstract flirtatious goldfish splashes growing organically from low base to high treble like the Art Nouveau vines on Métro stations. Hear the daring—the "telling"—waits midway through the final *Étude* (Debussy dares, Jacobs tells!), like lonely doors upon which nobody knocks.

Among the *Préludes*. From "Footprints in the Snow" could Mahler have stolen (wild idea) that reiterated drop of a minor third for his "dying fall," or Schoenberg (wilder idea) for the second of his *Three Piano Pieces*? Have you ever heard *La fille aux cheveux de lin* (which Virgil Thomson calls "The girl with linen hair") more simply, more Frenchly, limned, as though the pianist were—who?—perhaps Millet sketching a peasant's portrait?

Not all is just so. Does not "Reflections in the water" appear too meaning-ful, too *senti*, in contrast to Leopold Godowsky's old Brunswick recording I grew up with? We're ever guided by first hearings, even when those hearings are misguided. The same holds, incidentally, for composers in relation to their own works.

The problem in discussing Paul Jacobs is that I've never reviewed an executant artist, I've always written not about players but what's played. I haven't much to say about playing, but in Paul's case I need to live with it.

Do I know Paul Jacobs? Yes and no. We went to different schools to-gether. On the face of it we would seem to have once led similar lives, both being Francophile American musicians of roughly the same age who spent the 1950s in France. There the resemblance ends. In Paris our paths seldom crossed, although I did know Paul's adored friend, the late Bernard Saby, whose painting adorns one of the Nonesuch records. My milieu was that of Les Six, highly tonal and, if you will, more Gallic than the milieu of Paul Jacobs. He was (still is) among the faithful of Boulez whose ideologies, torn shrieking from the ghost of Webern, were inherently Teutonic. He doubtless thought me artistically frivolous, while I was scared of—and on a lower level bored by—Boulezian dogma. Not till long after our repatriation did we become staunch colleagues.

In 1967 I had a piece called *Sun* premièred by the New York Philharmonic. Paul Jacobs had already been the official pianist with that group for six years. *Sun* contains a cameo keyboard role marked "Brittle and Ugly." During a rehearsal break Paul came toward me to ask if his playing was "ugly enough." We got to talking. Suddenly he fixed me with those dark crazy eyes and said, with the wistful higher-pitched inflection adapted for serious matters (De-bussy, for instance, or carnal gossip): "You know, I've come to regret never having known Nadia Boulanger. It would have been so easy in the old days. Now it's too late." I had never seen anyone perform such an honest volte-face, and I have always admired Paul for this. He is more magnanimous than I.

Our paths still don't often cross. But we do speak on the phone, usually about French concerns—a question of translation for some program note, a confirmation of some Domaine Musicale date twenty-five years ago, the death of some mutual friend—for with whom else would we speak? New York does not seethe with knowledgeable partisans of French culture.

A year or two ago I sent Paul Jacobs a fan letter about his record of the Debussy *Préludes*, not failing to mention, with what I'm told is an irritating pomposity, a few wrong notes. Then more recently, just a month ago in fact, I told him I planned to write the present essay. But it's turned into more of a valentine.

Nantucket, June 1982

THINKING OF BEN

Some of my best friends are twelve-tone composers.

That quip sounds senseless today, the Tower of Musical Babel having melted into a pillar of magnanimity, and nobody minds what dialect you sing so long as you articulate. Two generations ago, however, our land was a diatonic prairie staked out by Aaron Copland where offspring of Schoenberg, not to mention the master himself, were unfashionable. One didn't have friends in both camps.

Who were the youngish musicians still hoeing the tone row? George Perle, mainly, Lou Harrison part-time, and Milton Babbitt. Anyone else? Only Ben Weber.

I, a tonalist born, befriended them. New in New York at nineteen I wanted to learn how the world turns, and didn't yet know that to be American was to be a specialist.

Ben Weber wrote gorgeous music which was never popular. In the prewar decades he was too wild for the neoclassic establishment, while in the postwar decades he was too tame for the integral-serialist establishment. Currently as we inch toward the live-and-let-live establishment we find Ben Weber gone. Maybe it's too late to establish him: composers of serious music are seldom popular anyway, and when they give up the ghost they risk being forgotten altogether. Still, half of being an artist today lies in promotional skill (although to accept that condition is to be half an artist). Like most "passive" creators who know their worth, Ben quietly manipulated others to work for him, and he had friends from the top drawer. I still recall Seymour Barab and Shirley Gabis, when I was a student at Curtis in 1943, playing the cello music of Ben (like me, from Chicago, though I never knew him there); Eugene Istomin performing the *Bagatelles*; Patricia Neway singing the songs. Later it was Stokowski and Mitropoulos, and above all the invaluable William Masselos who, from the standpoint of living composers, was, in the forties and fifties the most important pianist in the world. And Newell Jenkins, who commissioned the haunting *Dolmen* with those disconcerting string glissandos. And the New Music Group which recorded his Second Quartet (will anyone deny the delicious outcry that opens that piece?). And Francis Thorne who helped him financially, as Alma Morgenthau (Barbara

Tuchman's mother!) once had. And Oliver Daniel who procured him performances through the American Composers Alliance, as the I.S.C.M. once
had. And the Ajemian sisters, and Frank O'Hara, and Morris Golde,
and . . . And me this morning with fingers guided by Ben's as I type these
words.

His drag numbers were droll. He did them for everyone ("even straight
friends," we marveled). At first these were hilarious, minimum décor, just
the right length, a tablecloth as "gown." Nellie Lutcher's records were the
rage, and her 78-rpms made for terse miming. But like any prima donna
without a manager, Ben couldn't gauge when enough's enough. He graduated to *The Nutcracker Suite*, and that worked. So did *The Pines of Rome*, though
less. One night we giggled apprehensively as he put on the *Symphony of Psalms*
and began to shimmy. "He sure flings camp back into Stravinsky," said Paul
Goodman, but Paul wasn't always right. Did Stravinsky ever have camp
which needed flinging back? Our smiles faded as the wonderful music took
over, and we all wished Ben would sit down. Thirty years later he had
acquired a trunkful of Brünnhilde wigs and would invite us over for whole
evenings of opera. We hated to accept.

Because of his value as a genuine artist as well as a serious artist (the two
are not the same) these paragraphs are compiled. What do I think of his
music?
Ben Weber's music was . . . (When speaking of a man's work—obviously
composed in the past while still thriving in the present, though the man
himself no longer exists—does one use *was* or *is?* Probably both, according to
the paragraph's slant, so I'll proceed as the ear dictates.) Ben Weber's music is
always beautiful.
His melodies are true airs in that they billow toward the sky. To change
the metaphor: they are serpents splaying upward, evolving into birds which
swoop ever higher, then curve back upon their many selves and ease to the
ground. Their construction is impelled by a methodic "series" that lends
them the arbitrariness of freedom. (Yes, the "row" liberates as much as it
constricts, although the virtue of liberty in art is arguable.)
His harmonies are ever lush, like Berg swathed in Scriabinese silks ambling through the garden of Roussel. Indeed, one might suspect Ben of
nudging his row so that the acrid sevenths and mellow ninths of Impressionism would fall logically upon the staff; or inversely, he restricted himself to
the twelve-tone system so as to legalize his alien corn.
His counterpoint is merely occasional and never elaborate. Like the
French, who managed without polyphony for the centuries between Couperin and Boulez, though unlike the Germans who confected the craft of
negotiating simultaneous but independently moving strands which flowed
through fugue to dodecaphonism, Ben Weber writes tunes with oompah
accompaniments.
His orchestration is exquisite. Again like the French, he uses no doublings
when plotting symphonically, but allows each instrumental choir even at its
loudest to retain purity of hue.

His rhythm, true to his chosen language, is nil—an occupational hazard. I've always maintained that strict twelve-tone music is never inherently either fast or slow, never kinetic. Without a tonal center there can be no reiteration, and without reiteration there is no sense of beat. By the same token the twelve-tone system, so useful for scenes of pain and madness, is never witty. Wit resolves tension. But where all is discord, nothing is discord, so the method precludes a contrasting relaxation for joy. Ben's meters (like Schoenberg's), though written in large primary threes and fours, can be rhythmically complex visually, but amorphous aurally. Haziness is their beauty.

His music is always beautiful, and that's its flaw. Beautiful at any given moment—but the moments don't cohere, don't contrast, don't aim toward a target. Ben's music seems vaguely compromised, as though inside that unsmiling Germanitude lurked a Frenchman itching to get out. His heart was tonal, even as his society was humorous. Still, one cannot fairly criticize a language, only the use of a language. Had Ben written diatonic music he would not have been Ben. If his dialect as it stands is not quite solid, it is honest, persuasive and indispensable.

By standards of cinema or sauna Ben was not fetching of his person. Already balding at twenty-five, his patchy roan fuzz was mostly replaced by psoriasis, and his ivorine countenance was dominated by a shapeless overred mouth. He breathed asthmatically, perspired a lot and smelled of vermouth and vanilla. Yet he had stance and variety, and could swerve through the room with the grace of a Zero Mostel. Eyes cannily burning from behind rimless glasses, he regaled you—you or just anyone: the Duchess of Malfi, the janitor's wife—with lurid tales of exploits (imaginary?) among delivery boys while you, captive listener, fell to imagining the carnal exertion of those bright lips, those arthritic limbs. The sole excercise Ben ever took, and that only during the early years, was in strolling through the aisles of Gristede's. Unlike many plain people he did not bargain with Venus through calisthenics; he beguiled by wit, chutzpah, solemnity and piano playing.

A person playing the piano, even an ugly person playing middlingly, takes on a radiance more touching than a saint's. For a rare moment the body ignores the constant mirror and, like a cat with catnip, does not pose for our approval. Have you never fallen in love with someone *while he is playing*, precisely because he is absorbed in something beyond himself, only to fall out of love when he stops? Mutation of Quasimodo to Casanova, of Jezebel to Juliet, stems from the near-sexual suspension of ego (as opposed to the conscious eschewing of ego, as with a monk's abnegation), does not last long and usually transpires during practice rather than during performance. Public performance, however transcendental, is inevitably by an individual who, despite his protestations, offers himself with the music.

Ben played like a composer, cutting through the virtuoso's screen of trills to get quick to the bone. A composer cannot practice full-time and still compose, especially one like Ben who earned his living as copyist of other composers' compositions. A composer's approach to standard classics is always bizarre, always worth attending, since he knows the moods of Mozart or Chopin—their tricks, if you will—from the inside. Composers speak together across the centuries more easily than virtuosos, precisely because they are unencumbered with what teachers call technique. Ben's version of Ravel's *Ondine*, a "technical" piece if ever there was one, thrilled us despite the splatter of notes all over the floor. His mind supplied what his fingers missed, and he was telepathic.

What did he think of my music? Since I composed "off the cuff" I felt guilty in front of those who used a system, especially in the old days when they were older than I. Systems meant schools, schools meant teachers and teachers were always correct. (I hadn't yet earned my way to the perilous conclusion: Whether it be by Palestrina or Beethoven or Satie or Bessie Smith, all composition is finally a question of making it up as you go along.) Ben was noncommittal, but took me seriously. Three decades after we met he expressed himself obliquely on my fiftieth birthday recital:

> I was very happy to be at your Sunday evening concert, and was really pleased at what I heard and the excellent professional quality of the presentations. You looked under thirty, which could not be said for many of the old friends I saw there for the first time in a long time. I didn't come backstage afterward as stairs are a real problem for me, but give you my congratulations and love now.
>
> The stairway problems in all the new concert halls seem to be convolute superior, but then it was also in the ancient amphi-theatres (worse even), though I read that they had elevators for the animals and gladiators in the Colosseum, which they could also flood for real naval demonstrations—I'd hate to be in Tully for anything like that!

A year later he bit off more than he could chew by attempting, through the telephone at his sickbed, to organize a memorial for Jean Garrigue, a memorial to feature settings of Garrigue's poetry by half a dozen composers from among friends. The project fell through. I did finish a song called *Where They Came* which, in secret, Ben orchestrated. He then copied it in his famous orthography, bound it in orange cardboard and gifted me with it when I was fifty-one. The score rests in my treasure chest. Is there a more touching commentary between musicians?

He was matter-of-fact about his sexuality—not your normal attitude during the Roosevelt years for a middle-class middle-western half-Jew, even though he moved in left-wing "bohemian" circles. Party-line artists, outcasts though they may economically be, are no more tolerant than "real people" of homosexuality which, if not exactly evil, appears frivolous.

Ben the shut-in wrote letters. When in 1974 I proudly sent him, from Yaddo, a long interview in *Gay Sunshine*, he answered (delaying as usual the comments I so yearned for):

> . . . It would be nice to be there, as it has now been seven years

since I've left NYC. The last time I was at Yaddo in 1966, was my last excursion away from my air-conditioned (fortunately) premises. It is not quite the nightmare of Henry Miller, but there are moments—like two weeks ago, when my younger dog, who weighs 45 lbs., chasing a fly, crashed through one of my living room windows. Fortunately she did not end up out on the fire-escape, or even worse, fall to the street nine floors below. As a matter of fact, she miraculously didn't even cut herself, but the damage to my nervous system was considerable, and the whole window, frame and all, had to be replaced and fortunately they did it the very same day, as the incident happened in the morning. Getting things done in this building usually requires more than pressure, but God was working for me that day in spite of Helen, and good too, as there was an hour-long cloudburst the very next day, and I would have been flooded. I don't know what happened to the fly.

I did receive this morning *Gay Sunshine*, and will go through it carefully, and of course am especially interested in your long interview—the pictures of you are well reproduced and very good I thought. . . . My general reaction to pro-gay periodicals, etc., is usually one of some boredom, as I was gay and unashamed of it at least forty years before it became a youth "thing" and stylish. It is just as much "jive" to me as heterosexuality, by and large. To make a thing of it seems asking for the madness that the gods are all too willing to bestow. . . .

The building is 418 Central Park West in which he inhabited a minute apartment, working as professional copyist during the last quarter-century of his life, after being evicted from his adored residence on West Eleventh, scene of his great cooking sprees, for, like many composers, he was obsessed with the admixture of tastes. The dog is one of two lunging likable bitches to which he was as attached as Ackerley to his Tulip. Their barking summoned the neighbors when Ben died, and their "humanitarianism" was nearly the sole companionship (except for ten thousand roaches) when Ben lived.

How often do we Animal Lovers hear, after our anecdotes of empathy, "Aren't you perhaps granting anthropomorphic values to creatures whose intent might have been quite other?" *We* are animals too—merely human rather than canine or feline or corvine. If as animals we intuit sympathetic reactions, why are we wrong and you, oh logician, right?

Chronic insomniacs know that sleepless hours are plagued less by vast anxieties than by drab minutiae—will the alarm go off? did I put the garbage out? Futility of insomnia!

Ben's insomnia, he being a nocturnal worker, was at midday. We dreaded his phone calls, his notorious droning on the state of his body, his interruption of our production schedule, the Person from Porlock moaning for help. I always said I'd call him back, and always did, but he never remembered having called first. When Ben died, a lot of us were not surprised; but along with the sense of loss came sighs of relief: no more phone calls. Of course the maddening quirks of those we love, when withdrawn forever, become dear.

Of the many composers I have known over the years, Bill Flanagan and Ben Weber are among the few who would be called friends. Bill and I were the same age and even in our forties we fraternized daily like school pals with time to kill. Ben and I met more intermittently, generally tête-à-tête over his table—he was the most meticulous cook in town. ("I considered marinating the squid in salt water, then reasoned that it had already spent a good deal of time in brine. So I soaked it in port.") If Ben and Bill didn't particularly take to each other, they had points in common beyond a casual disparity of musical speech. As first-rate minor composers both were perfectionists with an Achilles heel: Bill's superficial training precluded fluency of voice-leading, muddying sounds that wanted clarity; Ben's indulgence in stagnant color (though he was well-versed) precluded overall flow. Esthetically each ran counter to the trends of his heyday: Bill doggedly diatonic in a era of integral serialism; Ben doggedly twelve-tonish in an era of diatonicism. Both composed slowly, and, more importantly, on an intrinsically slow tempo; indeed, most of their always sweet pieces would begin to end right from the beginning, and the ending, like a Mahlerian taffy, stretched out indefinitely, prolonging by languorous heartbeats an ever fainter but continually eloquent mood. And both died somehow wrongly and too soon. To assert that they did not die by their own hand is merely to say they did not lift that hand to save themselves. They were not survivors. Yet the farther their deaths recede in time, the closer their friendships grow.

Have I mentioned what a great teacher Ben Weber was? His low-paying pupils, along with his excruciatingly peaceful craft as copyist, were his sole means of income.

Have I too much stressed how boring he was? We thought that, like most hypochondriacs, he would live forever, so we twisted the telephone cord in mute hysteria during his hermetic monologues. And that beer-drinking—quarts and quarts a day, aggravating his ailments, but which he denied, even as he drank.

Have I suggested how profoundly unfrivolous he was, high camp diverging in a trice to solemnity?

Have I mentioned his singing voice? Except for Barber and Blitzstein, Ben was the only American who could do justice to his own songs. One might despair of his choice of texts for music—Rilke in German!—as though America hadn't ample versifiers to go against, and thereby reinforce, his improvisational textures. But Ben wasn't very American—whatever that means—nor very theatrical.

The lack of theatricality identifies him. The unapologetic explicitness about his sexual tastes to any and all seemed low-key and not even courageous simply because he found homosexuality natural and useful and no cause for dissembling. His—how to term it?—his conventionally atonal palette lacked giddy colors simply because he found mild colors more challenging.

An ironic misprint appeared in the headline of the *New York Times* obituary on May 12, 1979: BEN WEBER, 62, TONAL COMPOSER. If ever composer were *not* tonal, it was Ben. Yet Ben was implicitly ruled by—lured by—tonality, so the divine justice of the *Times* had the last word.

Dreams, like kaleidoscope patterns, cannot be passed intact between people. Indeed, our own childhoods—*pace* Proust—will never be recaptured by our present selves without shattering and repositioning their glimmering fragments into new puzzles, like crests of sunlit waves which instantly melt back into shade. Everything exists while simultaneously ceasing to exist, so that "meaning," even to itself, alters continually.

Yet what else have we except art and bullets? Well, some try to communicate through what they call love, others through mutual nostalgia. These few hundred words have briefly served, for one person in one frame of mind on one autumn morning, to call back a lost friend and introduce him to you.

Nantucket, October 1980

TESTIMONY

THE MEMOIRS OF DMITRI
SHOSTAKOVICH

Musical interpreters are often as proficient, as dynamically telling, during adolescence as they will ever become. True, the passing years just might firm up their informative powers (though time can also narrow perception and taste, and "say nothing but I told you so"), but those years will never reinforce their initial clout; precocity corresponds exactly to the period of highest sexual potency. To the musical creator, however, precocity is not brought to bear. If as it pertains to the crafting of sound precocity means more than a display of mere potential, then Mozart himself was not precocious.

Communicable composition, as distinct from performance of that composition, doesn't put forth early bloomers. Nineteenth-century France spawned no Rimbaud of Music. In our era there is only one contender: he stems not from Paris (city also of Lautréamont, Radiguet and Françoise Sagan), nor yet from the United States as we ever-young Americans would love to assume, but from, of all places, Leningrad. When Dmitri Shostakovich unveiled his First Symphony at nineteen (the age at which Rimbaud ceased writing forever), the world recognized it as the solidest symphony since Mahler. The fame that overnight lit up the young Russian burned bright and bitter for the rest of his years. By 1936 the shy thirty-year-old, rude and unglamorous, had produced such a controversial output that he represented The Political Artist par excellence: as such, he was the best-known musician on Earth. Admired by left and right alike throughout the West, at home he became a golden whipping boy. His early works being at once introverted and "ironic," this pawn was forever nagged to change his tune. Thus the middle period (on the whole less vital), dictated by current needs, seems in retrospect more descriptive of clear-cut activities like ploughing and war. The final works, when reputation and even safety seemed hardly to matter anymore, were what amateurs call "profound" (although from the standpoint of sheer structure and velocity of inspiration he never surpassed that First Symphony) because they supposedly mirrored darkness, depression and death. All these pieces were widely heard in his homeland, programming of contemporary music, for whatever it's worth, being more the rule in the USSR than in America. Since the pieces, in turn, were rewarded in the governmental press by blessings from Stalin or scourgings from his henchmen, Shostakovich shone ever in the public eye more for what his music was said to say than for what it did say. Outsiders, while reading of the trammeling purges bestowed as an "example" on Shostakovich, nonetheless grew accustomed to his regular shipment of symphonies which were always up for grabs by international orchestras—rather undifferentiated symphonies with their expert orchestration, their vast, sad largos and "satanic" scherzos. And outsiders grew accustomed to the man's never changing physiognomy: the sober prodigy with cowlick and spectacles.

These, then, are the credentials and springboard for the present book, a book that could not with impunity have appeared during the author's life, which ended (of natural causes) in 1975. Not a book, really; closer to an unabated wail emitted over the composer's three last illness-stricken years at the urging of a young amanuensis, Solomon Volkov, who smuggled his shorthand notes out of Russia in 1976.

How ironic that this panorama of long suppression in the past should emerge at this special season of the present, a season not only of spasmodic Soviet defections but of the cancellation of the Moscow State Symphony's American tour under Shostakovich's son, Maksim! That child is scarce in these painful pages, as are details of the late composer's early schooling ("The most uninteresting part of a musician's biography is his childhood. All those preludes are the same, and the reader hurries on to the fugue"), his taste in food, his love affairs, if any, and three marriages. For the terms of the book's dictation were that it be "memoirs of others," and "others" means those who tend the professional shop.

"Looking back I see nothing but ruins." The composer claims scant sympathy for most of his peers, starting with Prokofiev who, with the author, was always the Soviet composer most in view. "He never did learn how to orchestrate properly." (On Scriabin too: "He knew as much about orchestration as a pig about oranges." Throughout the book he equates the craft of scoring with the art of composition.) Opposition is par for the course, of course, since these two men were flip sides of one coin, like Debussy and Ravel. Yet the fifteen years that separated their birthdays were, shall we say, vastly narrow, like the Straits of Gibraltar, flowing between the wane of Diaghilev and the rise of Stalin. It was not so much Prokofiev's lack of talent as his lack of skill that riled the younger man. Craft is all; inspiration shifts for itself. (To a student who couldn't find a theme for his second movement: "You shouldn't be looking for a theme, you should be writing the second movement.")

Secure as a much-performed artist Shostakovich was not obliged to pander, and thus could voice publicly what for other composers is a hate that dare not speak its name. "I loathe Toscanini. Such sadists always have fans and followers, and sincere ones at that. Conductors are too often conceited

tyrants. In my youth I had to fight fierce battles with them, battles for my
music and for my dignity." For Stalin he took the same tone—Stalin, under
whose regime Shostakovich's spirit was early broken, never to mend. By the
1930s music was already defined as whatever the Teacher and Master (as
Stalin was called) could leave the concert whistling. "Tyrants like to present
themselves as patrons of the arts . . . but tyrants understand nothing about
art . . . because tyranny is a perversion." By this definition Toscanini too
would be a false musician. We in the West know that, socially and historically, art experts, like artists themselves, are no better than they should be:
look at the Pharaohs and Borgias, Wagner and Freud, dare one speak of the
living? Even Mayakovsky was a bastard, according to Shostakovich who
revered the poet, thus flawing his own premise. Indeed, like his command-
ers, he sets up straw horses (apparently real to him) assigning programmatic,
even moral, qualities to his own music, then scoffs at those who don't spot
these qualities. For us to whom art is not primarily education, Shostakovich,
with all his frowned-upon "dissonance," would seem to agree (though not in
kind) with his persecutors about extramusical content. "My symphonies are
tombstones. The Seventh . . . cannot be seen as a reaction to Hitler's attack. . . . I wanted to write about my contemporaries who spared neither
strength nor life in the name of Victory Over the Enemy. . . . The Eighth
Quartet was also assigned to the department of 'exposing fascism.' You have
to be deaf to do that: the Eighth is autobiographical."

His music is more sophisticated than his ideas about music. And yet (craft
again!) he was practical-minded. "When I hear that a composer has eleven
versions of one symphony, I think involuntarily, How many new works
could he have composed in that time?" He himself wrote quickly, in one
draft, without revisions, away from the keyboard. Beyond these facts he
speaks little of his working methods. But his disdain for any composer who
works at the piano would seem to leave, among others, Stravinsky (who
believed in constant contact with *la matière sonore*) out in the cold.

Elsewhere he states: "Stravinsky may be the most brilliant composer of the
twentieth century, but he always spoke only for himself, whereas Mussorgsky spoke for himself and for his country"—and Shostakovich identified
with Mussorgsky even to dreaming he *was* Mussorgsky. Yet the country was
not a consistent devotee of Shostakovich, who was a devoted nationalist,
though anti-regime, and saw himself throughout his life as a condemned
hostage. Any artist who has longed to lash back at his critics will sympathize
with Shostakovich's frustation, since criticism in Russia—criticism both of
and by the artist—was a matter of life and death. "Critics counted what
percentage of my symphonies were in a major key and what percentage were
in a minor key. It deprived me of the will to compose." "To be able to grieve
is also a right, but it's not granted to everyone, or always." He notes ironically that the war years were productive for the arts. "Before the war everyone was alone in his sorrow," but now: "You could finally talk to people. . . .
In other countries war probably interferes with the arts. But in Russia—for
tragic reasons—there was a flowering."

Except for Benjamin Britten, Shostakovich had no friendly contact with
foreigners. He demolishes such eminent deluded do-gooders as Wendell

Willkie: "Asked about the second front [Willkie] replied, 'Shostakovich is a great composer,' thinking he was a deft politician, but not considering the repercussions for me, a living human being. . . . Stalin's envy of someone else's fame might sound crazy . . . but a new success meant a new coffin nail." Or Malraux: "Has anyone ever asked André Malraux why he glorified the construction of the White Sea Canal, where thousands of people perished? No, no one has." Or Paul Robeson: "It's much easier to believe what you see, and you always see what you want to see." Or Bernard Shaw: "'You won't frighten me with the word dictator,' claimed Shaw. 'I've never been fed anywhere as well as in Moscow.' Why should Shaw be frightened? There weren't any dictators in England. But several million peasants died of starvation then. Meanwhile people are delighted by Shaw's wit and courage." Or Romain Rolland: "I get particularly nauseated when some of these famous humanists praise my music." Or Henry Wallace: "He was touched by the Kolyma camp's director's love of music. And he wanted to be President of the United States. . . . All of these people were lying to the world."

Was Shostakovich more lenient with the intellectuals of Russia? To him, Stanislavsky was an old-fashioned naïve joke. The director "understood nothing about what they call 'surrounding reality'" (i.e., the new "communal living"). "Poor Lenin was saddened by music—a telling fact." It is a moot point whether Shostakovich, in believing that "art destroys silence" to become "an active force," is any more right-minded than his persecutors in their demand that art incite action to become propaganda for soldering separate wills. A Westerner (including the Westernized Stravinsky) would argue that the two beliefs are one, and such a belief is incorrect: art changes no one. But according to Shostakovich, music is an active force in the Russian tradition; thus his Thirteenth Symphony is a setting of poems by Yevtushenko, *Babi Yar*, as a statement that "in our day and age, any person with pretensions of decency cannot be anti-Semitic." But he later cooled toward the poet. Toward Solzhenitsyn he was ambivalent, feeling that the author was creating an image of "luminary" for himself, aspiring to be a new Russian saint.

Except for Stalin, the pillorying of whom occupies perhaps a fifth of these pages, most of the persons named above have been mere walk-ons. Long, long chunks of monologue are consecrated to Glazunov, Shostakovich's beloved teacher revealed as a genius of sorts, a continual tippler and finally a disillusioned exile; to Gogol and Chekhov and Borodin; to the eccentric religious pianist, unknown to us, Maria Yudina; to the theater of Meyerhold to which the composer was attached in his youth; to the charismatic Anna Akhmatova, one of the few Russian poets of the last century who, like Pasternak, managed to survive the purges. (Shostakovich was bewitched by her—although "she didn't understand how music was connected to the word"—possibly because "We don't have feminism in Russia now, we simply have energetic women.")

These major portraits, however, are overdrawn and frightfully redundant. Which brings up the chief fault (a huge one) of this book. The editor, Solomon Volkov, has not seen how to tread that fine line between the literal and the literary. Despite his attested organization the result is a mess—albeit a thrilling mess: a horse's mouth speaks home truths about conditions only dimly perceived hitherto by Americans, but truths unplotted and verbose. The voice of Shostakovich, while cultured and canny (and readably translated by Antonina Bouis), is not that of a poet but of an artisan, hesitant, defensive, humorless. Still, it releases its self-justification like a river of tears, dammed up for decades, now free to flow. And the voice rings true; Shostakovich knows who he is. The residue for the reader when he puts down this book lies not in the musical aperçus nor in the trenchant peripheral biographies, but in the almost unendurable melancholy of this vastly appreciated man. "I had thought I would find distraction," he concludes, "reminiscing about my friends . . . but even this undertaking has turned out to be a sad one. . . . All I saw was corpses. . . . I've been berated all my life for pessimism, [but] a healthy attitude can be had only toward a healthy reality." One would like to hope that this is a half-truth, that a healthy attitude can be had also toward an unhealthy reality.

October 1979

BOULEZ

Seven years: the classical crucial span; a lucky number; the age of reason beyond which a priest cannot convert a Protestant; the length of the itch, of Hans Castorp's stay in the Magic Mountain, of the Egyptian plagues, and of passionate pleasure before the colors dim. Seven years: that is how long it takes for human bodies to replace their every cell. And that is how long I have been away from Paris.

If the Île-de-France, where my burning youth once lived and loved, no longer knows me, do I then, by definition, still know her? Seven years are dangerous. They can breed anxiety, yes, but also a vast indifference. There were long months since 1973 when France seemed an inactive absence, but a single hour could evoke a presence so acute that reality—indeed Being itself—became "that which was." What then could be more natural than the wish to return (before it's too late) for the first time with JH? But to find myself here with him is to exist in a time warp (Donald Windham: "Everywhere the impossible is happening: two things, the rain and the landscape, are occupying the same place at the same time"), like placing a bell jar over a cyclone. Yet JH is probably seeing the city less through my eyes than I am now seeing it through his. Once I could have wished that he too be reborn here.

Today that wish embarrasses me. So little, in seven years, crosses cultural frontiers, least of all between France and the United States. What each so takes for granted, the other ignores. They still quote Gide and pen hit plays about Joan of Arc, but draw a blank when you bring up Women's Lib or S&M, John Cheever or even Aaron Copland.

The sole American that virtually all the French admire is Richard Nixon, a man whom *we* all find, to say the least, out of style. Which partly explains the continuing local popularity of their most official living musician.

If Russia had Stalin and Germany had Hitler, France still has Pierre Boulez.

When he quit his post as conductor of the New York Philharmonic a few years back Boulez's image faded from our consciousness, and with it the old-fashioned notion of the avant-garde. If older American composers felt somehow released, younger ones with their "new" C-major chutzpah couldn't have cared less. Boulez having radically constipated music for three decades, there was a breeze of good riddance in the air—Frenchman go home!

He did go home. Today as director of the sumptuously subsidized Institut de Recherche et de Coordination Acoustique/Musique, a.k.a. IRCAM, Boulez is finally a prophet in his own land, though to what a powerful extent I had not realized until now.

The French do prefer talking about music to hearing it. Nevertheless JH and I are unprepared tonight, at our very first IRCAM program, for five-sixths *causerie* and one-sixth concert. Pierre Boulez's verbal presentation of the Debussy *Études*, of which we'd expected twelve, leaves room for but two, and those ejected by a mirthless young pianist—one Alain Neveux—wetly and inexact, sexless and without rhythm. The new Théâtre d'Orsay is jammed with a rapt crowd alert to each syllable.

The format of this Debussy-Varèse evening (we escape at the entr'acte, thus missing *Intégrales*) is the women's-club art-appreciation lecture. But first Jean-Louis Barrault, who owns the premises, squires the musician stage-center, then delivers a high-pitched preface, very touching with *tutoiements* and invoking Rimbaud again as he did twenty-six years ago when offering the Marigny Theater for the famous Domaine Musicale series: *Il faut être absolument moderne*. When Barrault withdraws, Pierre Boulez stands alone, except for Neveux nervously attending at the keyboard behind him.

Boulez tells us that for a composer material and invention are one, that matter dictates notes which inexorably define shape. Because the *matière* of Debussy's twelve *Études* was so unprecedented, when it *did* manage to explode from the mind it brought those "breakthrough" Debussyan forms that we know. *(Do* we know? Only three of the *Études* are formally eccentric; the other nine are built on that simplest of devices, literal repetition, and are original not for their shape but for their quality.)

Boulez bids Monsieur Neveux play the opening bars of the Étude-in-Fourths. Is not that jarring E-natural in measure eight a veering from the key center? we are asked. (I hear it as a mere lowered seventh, as a "blue" note, and indeed the whole lush piece as a jazz improvisation.) Neveux now sounds the closing page on which the separation of two-part chords is explained as a wrenching toward Schoenberg whose explorations in Vienna at this time—1915—were already more "sophisticated" than Debussy's.

Well, if Boulez's premise—reiterated for eighty minutes—is that all roads lead to dodecaphonism, and that in Debussy's case only death caused a detour, I'll wager that as strong an argument could be advanced for De-bussy's music as profoundly tonal even at its most extreme—which to my battered ears is never extreme. Debussy and Schoenberg have nothing in common. If they knew each other's work they would not have liked or "needed" it. I can't prove this, nor can Boulez prove the contrary. Should one begrudge him his dogma? Certainly, when one observes him still, as thirty years ago, brandishing that dogma like gospel which when refuted means banishment. Because in Paris there exists no prestigious outlet save IRCAM for living composers, and because the brainwashed critics are on the side of the state which finances IRCAM. The Rimbaud quote, which is forever invoked by poets with an ax to grind, is taken by Boulez to mean *Écoutez votre siècle*, his slogan for the IRCAM brochure. And who would quarrel with such a slogan, were not *votre siècle* better translated as *"my* century": the Music of Today means the music of Boulez's restricted coterie, nor except for Ives and Carter and Cage are any Americans known.

"His ideas are so unstartling," says JH in the Quai Voltaire bistro where we will linger, even after intermission, to savor our strawberry tarts with *cafés frappés*, "and strangely listless for one with such a big clique. He never emits any scent of his own sweaty affection for the music. And is it on purpose that the pianist is so lousy?" (I recall Boulez's recording of *Pelléas* ten years ago: nary a Frenchman in the cast, a trembling Tower of Babel emerging from a stable orchestra.) "If Boulanger taught a love for music, Boulez preaches the technique of it," continues JH, gulping his coffee with annoyance, but also with relief to be out of the concert, since he has a date in the far-off 15th arrondissement. "He uses Debussy to illustrate his speech rather than his speech to illustrate Debussy, performing an autopsy rather than describing a birth of affect. Is it their Frenchness that makes this audience take music as a problem rather than as a satisfaction? Are solutions paradoxically more important (easier) than enjoyment, even difficult enjoyment?"

Left alone in the bistro, I think this over. A solution in music, after the fact, must of necessity deductively pursue (retrieve) the problem. Now, that problem lived solely inside the composer's head. Boulez assumes, not historically but personally, that Debussy's problem lay in how to "deal with" tonality. *"Mais non, Madame, la peinture est plus bête que cela,"* retorted Degas to a dilettante ingratiator blasting her pale fire. All great art is dumb, inviolable to the theorizing madmen banging their heads against—strewing their brains upon—the pristine marble.

Boulez did make one fresh quip. In admitting that the sense of the eleventh Étude's title—*Pour les arpèges composés*—seemed elusive, he allowed that it might mean, in a poetic inversion, just what it said: *Composés pour les arpèges.* (In that case, shouldn't *composé* be in the singular?) I first learned that very Étude through the old Horowitz recording, of which one replaying would have been lesson enough for tonight.

Equating him with Stalin seems too grandiose. Boulez is the Woody Allen of Paris. He coddles a semi-informed public by spelling out ordinary ideas about extraordinary subjects. Their fans are no less flattered when Woody plays Freud for chuckles than when Boulez plays Webern for frowns. Yet Woody does intend gravity 'neath the frivolity, while chez Boulez one seeks vainly for frivolity 'neath the gravity. When all is serious, nothing's serious. So taken from one angle Boulez is wholly superficial.

With Ethel de Croisset to another IRCAM concert, this time without speeches, but with in attendance the widows Pompidou and Malraux, quick to promote Today in place of Yesterday. Boulez conducts the current version of his *Éclat/Multiple* which, heard with no hype, sounds simply in the continuing flow of Impressionism: "Reflections in the Water" watered down.

Ethel, although a fellow American, does live in Paris and is no less anxious than the other widows to appear up to date. So afterward we go backstage. But I have relinquished Frenchness and have a mind of my own. How, after all these years, could I even begin to remake the scene in this regime? It all looks so menacing, yet miniature, and long ago.

The maestro greets us with mechanical words and a cold eye.

The original ending to *The Birds* (deemed too depressing by Hitchcock's angels) shows the maimed survivors of an avian-beleaguered town in California as they near the promised land of San Francisco. Kindled with hope, they peer through field glasses, only to see the Golden Gate Bridge, covered with the killer birds!

Is there more to this virulence than meets the ear? Can my disapproval, like that of a mere Music Lover rather than of a fellow composer, be quieted by turning the other cheek? or is there too much at stake? My own music has always been—shall we say—accessible; I've never forsaken my conscience by constructing in the mode of the moment. Now that the American mode of the moment is accessibility, erstwhile hellions like Del Tredici and Rochberg are lauded for returning to the tonal corral, while I, never a prodigal son, am shunned for having written such music before it was stylish. That the European mode meanwhile should remain dissonant-saturation-Bouleziana is for me nonetheless more irksome than the success of my landsmen. Overreaction?

What did I use to think of the Frenchman?

I did not know who he was before I landed in Paris in May 1949, but everyone talked of him there. That autumn (I don't recall exactly how it was arranged) he came to play his Second Sonata on our Steinway at 53 Rue de la Harpe. With him were Bernard Saby and another man. Jean-Claude Maurice served drinks. I tried to ask about Honegger, but Boulez was not buying that, and after a minimum of small talk he sat down to play, with Maro Ajemian (in a ruby-silk dress with flared hips) turning pages. During the music Shirley called me into the bathroom where the hard sounds were making her literally ill. Immediately after the performance Boulez and entourage departed, leaving us unnerved. He was one of the few people I'd ever met—Auden and Stravinsky were others—who truly intimidated me: he so clearly knew who he was. (Shortly after this, by coincidence, I enjoyed a blurry weekend *amourette* with Saby, a hard-drinking, slightly mad and sensually likable blondish painter of gentle abstractions. Two decades later Saby died ambiguously, broiled by the icy light of a one-track-minded captor.)

Well, I have certainly thought more about Boulez, over the years, than he of me, judging from old diaries. In reperusing them I discover that, since 1950, I've written about two dozen entries on the man. They come to about twelve typed sheets. But since my published prose comes to nearly 2,500 pages, and since those pages are just a sideline to my gainful employment of writing music, I daresay I've had more in mind than Pierre Boulez over the past thirty years. Yet he has been a force to me, as to so many others. The very energy required to deny him is in a sense to accept him. Here are a few samples:

(1967) . . . America's cultural isolation from Europe during the 1940s gave rise to a maturing indigenous music. But by 1950 our effervescence began to flatten when we realized that no one abroad cared much. Europe, after all, was also reawakening after two numb decades—but reawakening into the past, namely into the dodecaphonic system which in America had atrophied, and in Germany had been mislaid by the war. This device (no, not a device but a way of thinking, a philosophy) was being revitalized not in Vienna where it had all begun, but in Paris, of all places. By 1950 Boulez had single-handedly cleared the path and set the tone that music would follow for the next decade throughout the world. And America took the cue, allowing her new-found freedom to dissolve into what ultimately became the bandwagon of International Academicism. . . . France has never been musical, despite appearances, though she was always a center for painting. Always, that is, until Rauschenberg acquired the laurel crown in 1961. Which left Paris with little international prestige, her composers having long since emigrated to Germany, yes, Germany.

(29 March, 1969) Virgil Thomson last night gave a *dîner à huit couverts*, four men and four women, all French-speaking, for Pierre Boulez, whose sister, a Madame Chapelier, has appeared in America for the first time. I sat between her and Louise Varèse. Virgil and Pierre presided at the table ends, and across from us beamed Natalie Nabokov and Maurice Grosser.

One may try to gossip with, or sometimes about, Pierre Boulez, but it isn't easy even for prevaricators: he's all business with a smile. The few times we've socialized have been strained. For me music can't be talked, only played; my conversation centers on particulars, usually human. Boulez being all generality, even around laymen like last night with whom he talks grape cultivation or family trees, I resolved not to speak unless spoken to, nor to pose any question if I didn't care about the answer. Result: three exchanges in four hours. 1) *Comment allez-vous?*, 2) *Veuillez passer le beurre, cher ami?*, 3) *Eh bien, bonsoir, monsieur.*

But Virgil went all out with bisques, off-season fruits, and Château d'Yquem served in crystal goblets whose stems represent naked females raising their arms. I found myself talking psychedelics, as I have before, with Madame Varèse (who pretends to know nothing of music, but did translate Michaux's book on mescaline), and geography with the sister whose affability flowed counter to her brother's—her cordiality invites contact, his discourages contact. Virgil was determined to learn what the child Pierre was like; that would have interested me too. But we never found out.

After the meal, when we adjourned to the parlor with the arrival of all the Sylvia Marlowes, I kept a physical distance.

Virgil this morning on the phone: "You and Pierre reminded us of Gertrude and James Joyce, revolving like planets at opposite ends of the salon." (Which one is Joyce?)

(1972) Great events do not impel great works, but they do alter method and certainly attitude. When his son died George Rochberg is said to have reassessed and found wanting the principles by which he composed.

In the light of Paul Goodman's death, an article by Boulez in Sunday's *Times* falls like a shadow of lead. The dead parent, humid with inspiration, puts into relief the dustiness of the surviving parent. Then too, now that Boulez is no longer handsome, his ideas are no longer blinding; it is clear where his followers faulted by taking him *au pied de la lettre*. If this reads like a superficial appraisal, influences of art *are* superficial, a dime a dozen, though they can sometimes be put to good use. Socrates' carnality was more than just intelligence.

(1973) If melodic meant poetic license—the stretching of a word beyond normal spoken length, and thus beyond comprehension—then a Boulez would be more melodic than Poulenc. The latter may well be the most sung French composer of the past fifty years, but (or rather, because) his word settings are more verbal than vocal.

(1975) Boulez has been for thirty years not the *enfant terrible* but the intellectual conscience of music. His early works were eerily reasonable in their avoidance of easy sensuality, and his creative influence was nothing if not a triumph of style over content. He did not flirt with the ear, and it was with the eye that we examined, on paper, the labyrinth of his processes, processes worked out for piano solo or for instruments of one family where color mixtures could not take precedence over profile. How radiantly simple, how expressive, how even gentle his new music seems. Of course, we're conditioned by knowing his old music. But he's no longer redoubtable; his reason now lies in his lack of reason—in his stress on sonority right in the tradition of French impressionists. His new piece, *Éclat*—sparkle, burst, flare, chic—is all that. Boulez here uses instruments for their own sexy sake, choices not of logician but of alchemist. Splinters of brass and copper fly from mandolin and cimbalom, and resolve themselves in our ear as perfect gold. But don't tell *him* that.

(1976, on being quizzed by the *Times* after receiving the Pulitzer) *You claim, Mr. Rorem, there is no more Establishment. Where do you fit into the spectrum of your musical peers?* . . . You'd have to ask the peers. Or rather, objective bystanders. Some of those so-called peers have no use for me, although I admire them, while others seem perversely overrated. One can't know what people say behind one's back, but by and large composers' opinions about each others' work are no longer voiced *ex cathedra* from rival camps. Rather than belittle each others' dialects, they concentrate on how the dialects are phrased. There are exceptions. If a Boulez, for instance, does not take seriously a certain sort of tonal melodism, I myself am incapable of digging electronics or aleatorics. Anyway, I've never run with the pack, composing according to fashion: I've always been a lone wolf, composing according to need. The Red Queen said you've got to run fast to stay in one place. I stayed in one place. Now it's clear I've run fast.

Nantucket, June 1980
Well, I do have a built-in revulsion for serial music, all of it, and feel, or

used to feel, threatened by the very fact of it—and so by Boulez—as though I'd been forever missing the point of something that finally had no point.

Why doesn't Ned stop flailing with windmills and tend his own garden? This attitudinizing grows vainer than trying to place a last word with professional critics.

Yes, yes, I agree. Though is there such a place as one's own garden? Our posies assume a wan or vital patina according to exterior lighting, and who knows, maybe even Boulez's upcoming roses will reflect a distant glow from my own. But yes, yes, you're right.

All the same, these paragraphs have eased my soul, so that now, if you'll excuse me, I can go back to work with a clearer head.

1980

COCTEAU AND MUSIC

"Why do you write plays, the novelist asks me. Why do you write novels, the playwright asks me. Why do you make films, the poet asks me. Why do you draw, the critic asks me. Why do you write, the artist asks me. Yes, why, I ask myself. Doubtless so that my seed will be sown where it may. I know little enough of the spirit that is in me, but it is not a tender one. It cares nothing for sickness, nothing for fatigue. It profits by my talents. It seeks to give form to the trumpets . . ."

Form to the trumpets. What a well-found phrase—and somehow a trifle sad. Form was an element which Jean Cocteau innately contained, but the trumpets themselves (though he ran, as he liked to say, "faster than beauty") were beyond his grasp. Elsewhere he states:

"It is rarely admitted that one can be a poet and a painter, that one can change branches on the same tree. I just heard Charles Chaplin say on Radio Nice that he liked living in France because a man like me could create a poem, a novel, a ballet, sets, costumes, plays, films, a chapel, without being asked to justify his activities, and without having to specialize. . . . Free, that is the word. I am free—insofar as the night self that rules me warrants. For, alas, I long to be a composer, and what Beethoven in a letter to his publisher about *Fidelio* calls 'the science of art' prevents me."

✳

Unlike specialized America where a podiatrist for the left foot refers you to an assistant if your right foot ails, Europe has ever been a land of general practitioners, and this is no more evident than in the arts. Yet even among the grandest Mediterranean G.P.s, from Leonardo to Sacha Guitry, none has included musical composition among his accomplishments. Across the channel I do count three: Gerard Manley Hopkins, although his efforts seemed dull and primitive; Noël Coward, although—proud of his inability to read notes—he improvised to a stenographer; and Charlie Chaplin—so adored by Cocteau—although his forays appear restricted to *Limelight*. (Ezra Pound, after his anglicization, did compose a full-length opera on Villon, original musically but too coarse technically to be practicable.) In France, however, where composers have sometimes been professional writers, no professional writer has ever composed, not even that most famous of all *bricoleurs*, Jean Cocteau.

If the one craft that he did not claim to profess was music, he did bemoan the deficiency, contrary to many a fine littérateur who "does without" without apology. Other fine ones, meanwhile, have countered their inability to write music by writing about music. None, at least in his fiction, has succeeded (if art about art can ever succeed) as convincingly as our better critics; they leave their musical readers smiling uncomfortably. Proust is an *amateur de luxe*; Mann, a conscientious researcher; Rolland, a romanticizer. Auden, Pound, Gide, and even Shaw, when writing on realities of the musical world, still write as tourists, from the outside; beneath their subtle grandeur they say no more than any well-trained sophomore.

France has never been musical, despite appearances. Which is to say that while producing her share of good composers plus a number of great performers—performers unable, however, to interpret their composers as well as foreigners do—she has never produced a viable public for these musicians. Indeed, music was officially banned (along with homosexuality!) by Breton's surrealists. If the seven lively arts in the countries of our earth can be distinguished as either aural or visual (and they can: no fine art except cooking and sex is dedicated to the sense of taste, touch and smell), the French have always been leaders in the visual. Is it glib to add that the French like to talk about music more than they like to listen to it?

Jean Cocteau, aware of and hurt by these generalities, had two trump cards which the others lacked. Music continually colored his prose and poems, but they inevitably reflected situations rather than constructions, social rapport with makers and their audiences rather than the "creative process." He did not write *about* music but *around* it, and was careful to subtitle *Le Coq et l'Arlequin* as *"Notes autour de la musique."* Also, more than any writer who ever lived, Cocteau worked *with* musicians; but for him a great deal of worthwhile music would not have come to be. In collaboration as in commentary he was canny: hot in the public fray, he remained cool in the joint harness. Whether his prewritten verse was being molded to song or whether he was concocting words expressly to be sung he left decisions about singability to the composer, he did not (like Auden) try to aid the composer with "musical" words. Similarly with non-verbal ballet scenarios or with movies and plays needing background music, timing and genre were the composer's decisions. Surely the sharpest lesson Cocteau learned from Diaghilev was that mixed media, to jell and endure, must be of autonomous components. Which is why *Petrushka* and *Tricorne* are inherited by us through their independent ingredients, why Cocteau's texts and Auric's music and Picasso's sets can stand alone, and why no ballet from any country during the past quarter-century has willed us a score of quality.

Is it not less astonishing that Beethoven composed while deaf than that he composed great music while deaf? Is it not less astonishing that dolphins talk than that what they utter is worth heeding? Is it not less astonishing that Cocteau now walks with the other immortal multi-talents than that he should have outstripped them by absorbing the alien art of music into his practice? None of his colleagues, *pace Persephone*, wrote memorable *livrets*.

*

"When I admire a painter, people tell me, 'Yes, but that's not painting.'

When I admire a composer, people tell me, 'Yes, but that's not music.' When I admire a playwright, people tell me, 'Yes, but that's not theater.' When I admire an athlete, people tell me, 'Yes, but that's not boxing,' and so on. Then I would ask, 'But what is it?' My interlocutor hesitated, eyes fixed in space, and murmured: 'I don't know . . . it's something else.' I have finally realized that this *something else* is, after all, the best definition of poetry."

Nicely contrived, but contrived all the same, since he avoids the sequence "When I admire a poet, people tell me, 'Yes, but that's not poetry.'" Still, we know what he means; and what he termed poetry covers everything he touched—including poetry. Had he (as he put it) "unravelled his words" onto a musical staff, would his Nocturnes have fallen into the same cover-all category?

✳

The two artists Cocteau most frequently cites in conversation—the two he is most anxious to let you know he knows—are neither of them poets. Picasso and Stravinsky.

What did Stravinsky teach him? Sobriety, says Jean. "At nineteen, flattered and fêted, I had become ridiculous and squandering, a chatterbox taking my own banter for eloquence and my wastefulness for prodigality." His meeting with the Russian composer seems, remarkably, to have been his first brush with someone who took his own work seriously. Cocteau determined to emulate the master of *Le Sacre*. The master, on his side, found the younger man's attraction to his ballet to be mainly in the scandal. Indeed, the impulse behind Cocteau's emulation, *Parade*, surely lay more in provocation than in expression. As late as 1963, a few weeks before his death, Cocteau was still declaring: "Stravinsky says, 'One must turn the pillow when it becomes warm.' You have to find a fresh place on the pillow. I often change my means of expression to let the vehicle rest, or it clogs . . ." He seems to have forever missed the *musical* point of Stravinsky. He wrote:

"I have often heard *Le Sacre* without the dances. I would like to see it with the dances. In my memory, impulse and method balanced each other in the choreography, as in the orchestra. The defect consisted in the parallelism of music and movement, in their lack of interplay, of counterpoint. Here we had the proof that the same chord, often repeated, is less fatiguing to the ear than the frequent repetition of a single gesture to the eye. People laugh at a monotony of automatons rather than at a breakdown of attitudes, and at the breakdown of attitudes rather than at the polyphony from the pit."

Yes, but is the same chord really the same chord, since each repetition occurs within a constantly shifting asymmetrical rhythm, and the chord's "meaning" shifts accordingly? And is the polyphony really polyphony, since Stravinsky was not a polyphonist? Yet Cocteau is right to intuit (as I believe he is doing) the ambiguity, if not the outright failure, of *Sacre* as a spectacle. Of course, the final reason that *Sacre* has never worked as a ballet—and I say this with the hindsight unavailable to Cocteau—is that its choreographers take it at face value. Choreography, which explains music on the music's terms, asks for trouble. Dance must go against.

Now he hits the nail on the head: "Stravinsky does not yield to the danger of autointoxication, of making himself beautiful or ugly. He transforms raw power, devising for its use apparatus ranging from factory to flashlight. . . . He composes, dresses, talks the way he pleases. When he plays the piano, he and the piano fit: one object; when he conducts the *Octet*, he turns his astronomer's back on us to solve this magnificent instrumental problem with silver figures."

Oedipus Rex, a "visual" oratorio which became their birthday gift to Diaghilev in 1927, was the sole collaboration of Cocteau and Stravinsky. It was also Cocteau's second of three treatments of the legend (*Oedipe* and *The Infernal Machine* were the others), and his most significant foray in tandem with a musician.

∗

". . . music distracts us less from a spectacle than a spectacle keeps us from hearing . . ."

∗

An artist is never wrong—at least never so long as the essays of his artistry are concerned, if he is a "true" artist and if the particular essay catches fire (for not every essay, even from a genius, lives and breathes). By the same token an artist is never right. Right how? Who are we to deem that the added shadow, the substituted semiquaver, the omitted clause on the last page, makes all the difference? Right and wrong are moral concepts, and art aims elsewhere.

This notion, worded more wittily, might be worthy of Jean Cocteau, who well knew in his secret heart—which was none too secret—that what he touched did not always turn to gold. (To Julien Green, before sketching his portrait: "My hand's not wingèd every day.") One generation's sweetness turns sour in the next; Hindemith and Hahn have faded today, Creston and Crumb will fade tomorrow. Cocteau was wrong about Satie, or right for the wrong reasons.

∗

Like other great poets who by definition have a way with the written verb—that is, an ear for what is seen—Cocteau paradoxically had not the gift of tongues. Many French of his time and class, according to whether they had nannies as children or according to which way they thought the war would swing, knew a bit of English or German, but Cocteau had none of either, nor was he embarrassed by the lack. The same with musicians. It does not follow that those with a "musical ear" have the knack for a foreign language. Some of our best composers just don't get the hang of it, while many a fool speaks many a language with unaccented fluency, and with the same foolishness in each.

Contrary to the universal claim about the universal language, music crosses frontiers with less ease than books or pictures; and music seems to be the art least appreciated by other artists. The two-piano team Fizdale and Gold recall Cocteau asking them to record the background for a film he was planning in 1949: they would improvise jazz variations on "Japanese Sandman"—or rather one endless variation that would serve as soundtrack for the entire movie. Reluctantly they confessed that they had no gift for jazz. "But you're Americans, aren't you?" was Cocteau's thunderstruck reply. Yet if he had neither an ear nor an eye for music, he did have a nose for it, and that nose was infallible for how music could decorate his own art. The score that ultimately garnished the movie in question, *Les Enfants terribles*, was the Four-piano Concerto of Bach-Vivaldi, the first use of Baroque incidental music in films, and hauntingly right. This was the only Cocteau film (actually directed by Melville) not to use a score by Georges Auric. As for the conception in 1928 of the novel *Les Enfants terribles*, the author says it was written in seventeen days without an erasure, "under the obsession of the song 'Make Believe,' from *Show Boat*; if you like this book, buy the record of the song, and then reread it with the volume turned up high."

✻

When I finally removed from Paris to New York, certain people asked, "How well did you really know all those dead French people?" I noted: *To know well* means an exchange between two participants of permanent portions of themselves. In the five or six meals I had with Cocteau, or fewer with Éluard, in certain street encounters with green-eyed strangers who took me by the hand to painful hotels, in chance tearful meetings with Tchelitchew or a hilarious single supper with Latouche, I felt a contact, a generosity, a participation, a heat, a curiosity, an indelibility which permit me to say I knew and know and will always know them well. Meanwhile I'm indifferent to some people I've seen daily for twenty years; they offer neither growth nor anecdote. *To know* has to do with intensity, not habit.

Looking back, I see that the young American artist in long-term French residence during the 1950s was rare, and that the fact of such an artist was anathema to the insulated French, even to Jean Cocteau who prided himself on catholicity. Thus I see too that their interest in me lay mainly in my interest in them.

Despite a notoriously accurate memory I can't remember how many times I was in the private presence of Jean Cocteau. (We wrote letters until he died, but I do know that we never met again after 1957 when we chatted beside the fireplace at Dugardin's party for the Poulenc opera in June.) Is this due to his so frequent bows? to his tutoyéing of whole audiences which necessarily included me? or to what many termed his enchantment, which wasn't enchantment but largesse? (Genêt: "He does not 'charm,' he is charmed. He is not a wizard, he is bewitched . . .") Cocteau was among the handful of giants—Nadia Boulanger, Frank O'Hara, Noël Coward were others—who, when with you, whatever the circumstances, behaved as though you were the one person alive. Such behavior is so special that we recall it as a magic virtue.

Did he know my music? Although he designed two covers for my songs, he never, to my knowledge, heard anything beyond a ballet I played for him in Grasse during the early spring of 1952. This *audition* was touching to Jean in two ways. First, it took place chez Marie Laure's mother, Marie Thérèse Bischoffsheim, later the spouse of Francis de Croisset, librettist for the operettas of Reynaldo Hahn who, in turn, had been the composer for Cocteau's theater debut, *Le Dieu Bleu*, just forty years ago that April. Second, my ballet was on the scenario drawn by Jean Marais from *Dorian Gray*, mounted the following month in Barcelona, with sets and costumes by Marais who also mimed the role of the progressively decaying portrait. (My score today lies in the bottom of a trunk where it shall forever remain.)

*

During our first meeting, in the red apartment of Rue Montpensier, he maneuvered the conversation around music. "Music's not just in the concert hall. That workman out there—he's whistling the start of *Sacre*." The workman was in fact whistling *La Vie en rose*, but since that tune devolves from *Sacre*, the point was proved.

Was his speaking voice musical? Was Bernhardt's golden? Esthetics change each generation, as do musical trends and even sexual appeal. Contrapuntal and harmonic periods alternate, are seldom simultaneous; plump is in when thin is out; elocutionary elegance is ridiculed by hipsters. Yet who recalls exactly? It's not the contradiction between many people's reports, as with Rashomon, but one's own reaction at different stages. His speech (like Bernhardt's, as discs indicate) was high-pitched, nasal, machine-gun fast, stemming so far as I can judge from upper-class, fin-de-siècle timbres, and emphasizing, like many of the class, male and female, an anglicized non-guttural *r*. (Interestingly, with American speech it is also the *r* which dates and classifies, being dropped where most needed, added where nonexistent. "Amnesia is easier," uttered by a George Plimpton or a John F. Kennedy or a William Buckley, becomes "Amnesiar is easiah," and sounds to bourgeois ears like the faraway nuances of the heterosexual sissy.)

*

Dinesen once pictured an influential poet as he stands on a bridge preparing his suicide, when along comes a sycophant who begins to ape his gestures. "Ah, must even my dying gasp become the *dernier cri!*"

Yet who bequeathes what? Cocteau declared in my presence—at Robert de Saint-Jean's on May 15, 1952, at around 1:30 P.M., to be exact—that it was in Péguy that he found the phrase: "We must know how to go too far."

His star became for Marie Laure de Noailles a leaf, for Louise de Vilmorin a clover, and hundreds of students learned that to be a poet meant merely to have a signature. For me the star becomes here an asterisk betwixt aphoristic paragraphs, since to write of Cocteau is to write like Cocteau.

Stars between paragraphs, but no longer in my eyes. Jean Cocteau was one of the four or five driving forces of my youth (Virgil Thomson was another, my parents, Paul Goodman, the ghost of Ravel), from the moment David Sachs lent me *Les Enfants* in 1938. Since then I have often changed my mind, never my taste. I reappraise Cocteau today in a harder light, discovering that *his* taste, specifically in music, was sometimes mediocre, while my mind about it had never been made up. The harder light is nonetheless a light of love.

*

When people ask if I ever met Les Six I always enjoy answering, "Yes, I knew all five of them." It was they whom Cocteau lists in these alexandrines:

Auric, Milhaud, Poulenc, Tailleferre, Honegger,
J'ai mis votre bouquet dans l'eau d'un même vase . . .

The vase was a ballet, *Les Mariés de la Tour Eiffel*, to which they all contributed music. The overture and ritornellos dealing with the comings and goings of certain characters were by Georges Auric. Francis Poulenc composed "The General's Discourse" as well as an episode, "The Bathing Belle of Trouville," and Germaine Tailleferre, "The Quadrille of the Telegrams." Darius Milhaud wrote a giddily violent fugue pastiche called "Massacre at the Wedding" (on one of the platforms of the Eiffel Tower), and Arthur Honegger, the "Funeral March of the General." The sixth composer, Louis Durey, had already withdrawn from the band (but their title stuck) when all this was premiered in 1921 by the Swedish Ballet at the Théâtre des Champs-Élysées.

Thirty-two years later, on November 4, 1953, Jean Cocteau stood up before a capacity crowd in the same theater to evoke the remote and golden twenties of *Le Groupe des Six* which he took credit for having formulated. That autumn evening in Paris now also seems golden and remote, falling as it does midpoint between the period and place evoked, and the period and place I write these words, in Nantucket, October 1981. What I once retained of the occasion were clarity and wisdom, and how satisfied I was as a young American to be seated with Marie Laure in a loge among these "names" with whom I was on cordial terms. (Honegger had taught me during a Fulbright season at the École Normale in 1951–52; Poulenc, whom I'd met on arrival in 1949 through his biographer, Henri Hell, was, remotely yet gently, mentor and model; Georges and Nora Auric were daily friends during the long summer months in Hyères; while Darius and Madeleine Milhaud, whom I was to know better in California during the next decade, were already staunch acquaintances.) Now to reexperience that speech is to hear it as deliciously specious and—would he agree?—*démodé*.

I am aware of the dangers in what we find outmoded. All art is locatable, for all art dates from the moment it is made, the good as well as the bad. The *Pietà* and *Sacre* date well, the *Gleaners* and *Scarf Dance* date cloyingly. Who knows but what, in the shade of millenniums rather than of mere centuries, Beethoven himself might not appear "all that good"? Aspects of collaborative ventures can date at different speeds, as a good old movie whose background music, once so stimulating, now seems to stifle the action. (Witness the ever vivid Bette Davis in, for example, *The Letter*, hampered by Max Steiner's preemptive leitmotivs.) Even one's own vantage is slippery. I used to dislike cats; now I love cats and am suspicious of anyone who dislikes them. If notions I once penned about Cocteau now make me cringe, surely my words about him today will soon be dated too. . . . Meanwhile, before that capacity crowd:

". . . the privilege of the group called *Groupe des Six* was that it was a grouping less of an esthetic than of a friendly nature. No shadow ever troubled our mutual understanding. This came about because our understanding was based more on feelings than on opinions. If there was a certain general tendency, it might have been toward rescuing the melodic line, a bit drowned by harmonic masterpieces. Each worked in his manner, no one had edicts to obey. Six artists liked one another, and in me they found a seventh. And there's the entire doctrine of the group. . . ."

So far so good, as a clean statement of purpose. However:

". . . It is only fitting to salute Erik Satie. He was not one of the Group, but his melodic line, so pure, so reserved, so noble, was always our school . . ."

Time has proved Satie to be small potatoes. But we must earn the right to declare him overrated, as well as to declare him a master. *Socrate* is among the timeless monuments, and the only important work of Satie. Yet ask any Satilophile or -phobe, as they sound off about *Mercure* or *Parade* or the aimless piano solos, how well they know *Socrate*, and they will adapt a vacant stare. Cocteau's overcompensation on behalf of Satie was his vacant stare: he didn't know *Socrate*.

". . . *The Rite of Spring* set up against our young shrubs the strength of a growing tree, and we should have had to admit that we were beaten, had not Stravinsky, sometime later, come over to our methods, and had not the influence of Erik Satie become mysteriously perceptible in his work . . ."

To claim that Stravinsky had "come over" to Cocteau's methods, and had been "mysteriously" influenced by Satie, is not only to rewrite history, but to demean both Stravinsky and Les Six, each one of whom had his own identity. As for Satie, he is perhaps the one composer who ever composed who does not "date," his work lying—"mysteriously"—outside time (ask an unalerted listener to situate *Socrate*, and he will answer: ancient Greece, Gregorian Italy, a Beatles background), while Stravinsky's music is nothing if not the very definition of its age.

". . . The young musicians of 1953 therefore owe it to themselves to contradict a new kind of counter-charm. It is understandable that they take their stand on Schoenberg and find in him an arm against works which fear his science of numbers . . ."

This is a layman's aside, compatible with the moment. Earlier that year at the Théâtre Marigny there took place the first of Boulez's celebrated Domaine Musicale concerts, sponsored by Barrault who, in introducing the series, bent Rimbaud's *Il faut être absolument moderne* to suit his *à la page* purposes. Except for Stravinsky's *Renard*, mimed as a refreshing dessert by Barrault himself, the program was strictly German: a grandiloquent Stockhausen, the woolliest Henze and other deadly serious serial excursions. Wild applause. Cocteau, perplexed, approving the music but not the reaction, exclaimed: "But why do they react that way?" "How would you have them react, cher maître?" "Why, they should be booing—*mais qu'ils huassent!*" Again, as I see it now, he was right, but for the wrong reason.

". . . Our group had its flower in a woman, a girl, a musician. Strange as it may seem (since every woman is sensitive and good at figures), although there are many composers with feminine souls—Chopin remains the best example—there is, so to speak, no real woman composer. I salute Germaine Tailleferre as a charming exception. . . ."

Well, Shakespeare too uttered things about women we now find naïve and brutal. The so-called feminine soul—so unpopular a current concept—has never been defined. Yet Cocteau would almost certainly have defined himself as a feminine soul although, notwithstanding his famous compassion and longing to be loved, he was—so popular a current concept—a sexist. The

eloquent lines from *Démarche d'un Poète* to the effect that the greatest art
triumphs over our intelligence when sexuality speaks, and if "this moral
erection does not occur, the pleasure a work of art affords is of a merely
Platonic or intellectual order and without the slightest elective value"—these
lines, though narrowly true, cannot pertain to a *woman's* appreciation of art.
Yes, Cocteau does allow that "one might say of a work of art: 'I've got it
under my skin,' as a man will say of a woman, or a woman of a man," yet he
does not add: Or a man of a man, or a woman of a woman. And we poor
musicians sigh when he omits us from "those persons whom the least comma
in a sentence, the lightest touch of a paintbrush, the merest indentation of a
sculptor's finger will put in a state where a higher sexuality prevails." What
about the slightest inflection of a sonic sequence, like the *petite phrase* in
Vinteuil's sonata? But Cocteau only writes about music when he is writing
about music; as with most authors, even in France, music is not part of his
general frame of reference.

". . . We were all insufferable—and we were right to be, for only the
spirit of contradiction saves one from routinism. . . ."

✱

Movies: an individual screen for a crowd. Television: a crowd of screens
for individuals.

If the art of film is that which, without mishap, can be transferred between
these mediums, Cocteau was among the few practitioners. It could be argued
that he was the most influential filmmaker who ever lived, and that by
extension the music for his films was the right music even though it now
seems wrong.

✱

"Is technique, as Wilde claimed, merely individuality?" asks Jean. "The
film technicians for *Beauty and the Beast* praised my 'technique.' I have no such
thing. Because there is no such thing. No doubt we call technique that
moment-to-moment balance the mind instinctively achieves in order to keep
from breaking its neck. All of which is summarized by Picasso's great remark: 'One's métier is what cannot be learned.'"

But technique *can* be learned in music. It's not for nothing that virtuosos
practice hours a day (partly, of course, like the Red Queen, to keep what
they've got, and partly to be able to master new repertory), or that experienced composers apply what they extract from the reading of new works
toward the honing of still newer works. I contend that I can teach *anyone*—
anyone with basic musical know-how—to compose a perfect song, that is, a
song impeccable in shape and flow and arch, and in comprehensible and
properly "expressive" setting of words. Whether that song takes on a life of
its own, or even lives at all, is however, not within my power, nor my
pupil's, nor Cocteau's, nor Picasso's.

✱

The superimposition of music on a movie is the final process in moviemaking and can be realized only after the cutting is finished, when the film is, as
they say, in the can. Then, in the recording studio, after a rehearsal, a run-
through and a preliminary taping of the composer's fresh score, the instrumentalists lay down their instruments and they, along with the director,

angels, tough producers and unmusical yes-men, raise their heads toward a screen upon which a rough cut of the film is projected simultaneously with a playback of the score. And all the spectators then decide whether the music "works," while the composer twiddles his thumbs. On the day that the music for *Beauty and the Beast* was recorded, Cocteau wrote:

". . . And now the silence, then the three white flashes which announce the image, then the image and the wonder of that synchronization which is not a synchronization, since Auric avoids it, at my request, and since it must not occur save by the grace of God . . ."

Here is the precise reverse of the method in Hollywood where soundtracks of, say, Aaron Copland (the American who most mirrors France's Auric in that he has composed our most distinguished movie music) must coincide to the split second with the image *before a single note is scored*.

". . . This new universe disturbs and enthralls me. I had composed my own music without realizing it, and the waves of sound from the orchestra contradict that music. Gradually Auric's score contradicts that discomfort. My music gives way to his. This music weds the film, impregnates it, exalts it, completes it . . ."

Yet Auric himself once told me that in scoring *Blood of a Poet* he produced what is commonly known as love music for love scenes, game music for game scenes, funeral music for funeral scenes. Cocteau had the bright idea of replacing the love music with the funeral, game music with love, funeral with game. And it worked—like prosciutto and melon. Since music's power lies in an absence of literary significance, and since this power dominates all mediums it contacts, any music may persuasively accompany any image or story while inevitably dictating the *tone* of the joint effort. Music's hidden force can rescue a mediocre scene or ruin an excellent one. As to which method, Coctelian freedom or Californian trammeling, is the better method, who can judge? If music can wreck the best-laid schemes, *Of Mice and Men* today is most remembered for Copland's poignantly cohering sounds, while *Beauty and the Beast*, at least to one hearer, is hampered by the insistent Heavenly Voices intruding on each frame like treacle on rubies. If I was entranced thirty-five years ago by the mixture of media, now the film and its music have both dated, one well and one badly, while *Blood of a Poet* remains the greatest wedding on film of film and music.

✳

Although the Parisian musical esthetic of the 1920s—skimming away Teutonic fat and keeping "deep meaning" to a minimum—infiltrated the United States, initially through Copland, and flourished for two decades, literary influence, specifically Cocteau's, on major figures of the next generations (with the possible exception of Paul Goodman) has been nil. It is of course through movies that Cocteau has changed forever the world's outlook, despite his name's being a cipher to American youth. With this in mind, see what the American composer Elliott Carter (b. 1908), who, although Boulanger-educated and a Proustophile, is hardly a *prince frivole* (indeed, his working system grazes the Germanic), has to say about his own First String Quartet, written in 1950:

". . . The general plan was suggested by Jean Cocteau's film *Le Sang d'un poète*, in which the entire dream-like action is framed by an interrupted slow-motion shot of a tall brick chimney in an empty lot being dynamited. Just as the chimney begins to fall apart, the shot is broken off and the entire movie follows, after which the shot is resumed at the point it left off, showing its disintegration in mid-air, and closing the film with its collapse on the ground. A similar interrupted continuity is employed in this quartet's starting with a cadenza for cello alone that is continued by the first violin alone at the very end. On one level, I interpret Cocteau's idea (and my own) as establishing the difference between external time (measured by the falling chimney, or the cadenza) and internal dream time (the main body of the work)—the dream time lasting but a moment of external time but from the dreamer's point of view, a long stretch. In the *First Quartet*, the opening cadenza also acts as an introduction to the rest, and when it reappears at the end, it forms the last variation in a set of variations. Not only is the plan like that of many 'circular' works of modern literature, but . . ."

Note that no word is said of the music—of Auric's original music—in *Blood of a Poet*. Cocteau's influence on Carter has been visual, not aural. Obviously the quartet could never replace and function as Auric's score, which was an embellishment of the film, for that would be like coincidental readings of Euripides' *Hippolytus* and Racine's *Phèdre*.

✻

As with *Blood of a Poet*, so with at least one ballet: regulate *"Le synchronisme accidentel."* Going on the correct principle that any music will fit logically with any visual, while dictating the tone—indeed, altering the very sense— of the visual, he brought to fruition a venture in which his co-workers' intentions were turned inside out. In 1946 the dancers for *The Young Man and Death* were rehearsed on jazz rhythms. When the choreography was complete, it was found to last seventeen minutes, and some "real" music of that length was needed. The overture to *The Magic Flute* being prohibitively expensive, Bach's Passacaglia was substituted on opening night. Immediately the seventeen-minute Passacaglia came to sound inevitable.

What Roland Petit had permitted for *The Young Man* was vetoed four years later by Lifar for *Phèdre*. Cocteau's "chance synchronization" might have provided a more amusing choreography than Lifar's breast-beaten notions, though even Garbo (whom Cocteau originally sought for the role) could not have overshadowed the mature Toumanova who, garbed in Cocteau's thirty-foot-wide crimson shoulder pads, paced the stage like a nineteenth-century tragedienne trapped inside a puma. And Georges Auric's score is his most "significant," outside the movies.

✻

Did he know about music technically? Auric claims that Cocteau could pick out any tune with one finger, provided the tune were in F-major.

✻

My first week in Paris, spring of 1949, I saw a newsreel of him waving at the camera, then turning his back and blending into the horizon. A voice-over said: "Cocteau renounces public life." Puzzled by the image of a man *in the act of not being a celebrity*, I had yet to read his myriad denials of fame, his upcoming *Journal of an Unknown Person* which restates: "Public life disguises and protects my secret creative life. . . . To be up-to-date is to be quickly out-of-date. . . . The poet must remain invisible. Etc. . . ." I could never swallow these contradictions of fact, not recognizing that they were precisely what made Cocteau Cocteau."

✳

"A dreamer is always a bad poet," he wrote in 1921, and: *"Pelléas* is another example of music to be listened to with one's face in one's hands. All music to be listened to through the hands is suspect." Forty years later, in 1962, he did manage the direction, sets, and costumes for a production of *Pelléas et Méli-sande,* yet he always preferred Maeterlinck's play to the music.

At a rehearsal of *Parade* Ravel told Cocteau that he did not understand music that was not "bathed in any sonorous fluid." Cocteau adopted an anti-Ravel stance in the early days of Les Six but conciliated in 1930.

What Ravel and Debussy thought of Cocteau's *oeuvre,* if they knew it, is unrecorded. Satie was their common point. (I have not here quoted Satie, "Ravel refuses the Legion of Honor but all of his music accepts it," nor Cocteau's rejoinder, "It's not enough to refuse, one must not have deserved it," because the quips are too famous to need repetition.)

✳

Marie Laure offered her ballroom in December of 1932 for *le tout Paris* to attend a preview of two new works by refugee Kurt Weill: *Der Jasager* and "the Paris version" of *Mahagonny,* conducted by Maurice Abravanel and featuring Weill's wife, Lotte Lenya. Six months later *The Seven Deadly Sins* was performed in Paris, after which Weill faded from fashion, except for Cocteau. The two plotted an opera about Faust, of which nothing remains (but a couple of pages of music and thirteen letters from the poet), possibly because Weill felt he could never compete with his mentor Busoni's *Doktor Faust,* or because Cocteau momentarily sensed that the transposition of ro-mantic legends, like that of Greek myths, inevitably lacks the power of the original—although he went on to film *The Eternal Return* and *Orpheus.* I did hear Cocteau describe, many years later, his mini-Faust: "The doddering doctor sells his soul to the devil, becomes a handsome young man, presents himself to Marguerite who merely says, 'I'm sorry, sir, but I prefer older men.'"

One remnant remains of the Weill-Cocteau friendship. Lenya recalls: "Kurt and I were invited to dine at Cocteau's one evening [in 1933]. Cocteau tried to speak a few sentences in German. Kurt expressed surprise, and asked Cocteau if he really spoke German. Cocteau answered, 'Yes—all nouns!' He then excused himself, went into another room, returned a few minutes later with a sheet of paper. On it were the first lines of *Es regnet* [It's raining]. Kurt encouraged him to finish the poem, which Cocteau eventually did. Kurt corrected some of the grammar-school errors and set it to music." The result-ing song is not vintage Weill, nor is the text more than a miniature rehash of *The Human Voice.*

✳

His only other musical intercourse with a German was still less forthcom-ing, if more ambitious. Paul Hindemith wished for Cocteau to write him a libretto. The poet in 1952 was planning the decoration of the Villefranche

Chapel of Saint-Pierre, and was rereading the Apocalypse and the Book of Saint John. From this he drew his *Sept dialogues avec le Seigneur inconnu qui est en nous* which, in turn, he adapted as an opera text of high seriousness, finishing it on September 5. Hindemith, whose musical style had never been known for its wit, had nonetheless thought of Cocteau as a humorist, and was counting on a comic libretto. Thus the poet was frustrated until a decade later when young Yves Claoué (son of the noted "esthetic surgeon" who reshaped the nose of Juliette Greco) took the book, rebaptized *Patmos*, and made it into an opera which was premièred in the chapel of Versailles whose sainted arches presumably shook at the mention of the great whore of Babylon who figures in the work.

This was not the first of Cocteau's musical texts to go a-begging. With Radiguet in 1920 he had prepared a libretto on *Paul et Virginie* for Satie, who spoke warmly of the music he was composing for it, although no one ever saw the score. After Satie's death Cocteau proposed the book to Poulenc who extracted one poem by Radiguet, then passed it on to Sauguet who extracted a *Chanson de marin*, then gave it to Nicolas Nabokov, who gave it to Valentine Hugo, who lost it.

✳

No song settings of Cocteau's verse are stunningly worthwhile, not even those *Cocardes* which inspired in 1919 the young Poulenc, our century's greatest song writer. I'm not sure why. The reason has nothing to do with whether the words were expressly made to be set (as with Weill) or already existed when the composer came upon them (as with Poulenc). The libretto for the opera *Antigone* was confected for Honegger while that of *La voix humaine* existed in its final shape thirty-five years before Poulenc musicalized it, and both works are surely stunningly worthwhile. The best songs on Cocteau words are the vulgarest. Listen to Poulenc's 1918 pop ditty, *Toréador*, if you can find it—it is seldom listed among his works; or to *Mes soeurs, n'aimez pas les marins* with music by (I think) Paul Fort, a melancholy *scena* recorded by the *diseuse* Marianne Oswald around 1940, and which I have never come across again in any form.

Most of *Les Six* wrote Cocteau songs while young, not later. For the record, one of my first good songs, written at twenty in 1944, was on this quatrain called *De Don Juan*:

> En Espagne on orne les rues
> Avec les loges d'opéra
> Quelle est cette belle inconnue?
> C'est la mort, Don Juan l'aura.

If any composer is today searching for appropriate verse of Cocteau, let him look at the hitherto unpublished love lyrics in Jean Marais's autobiography, *Histoires de ma vie*. They are of great truth and beauty.

✳

There are as many Cocteaus as there are biographers of him. If in our country he has now grown remote, in the late 1960s he was subject to a critical rush: Robert Phelps, Francis Steegmuller, Stephen Koch, Frederick Brown, Margaret Crosland, Paul Horgan, Elizabeth Sprigge, all had their say, short or long, and each presented a different character. As I remarked of Satie—one must earn the right to disapprove—so with Cocteau, and the hostility or veneration of certain portrayals seemed at times no less lazy than adroit.

Not that my own scattered notes have sprung from discipline, for I have not a scholarly bent. As cordially as possible I have collected a garland of special reactions to the musical side of the poet who, more than most jacks-of-all-trades, combined the sublimely right with the unutterably trashy. If he didn't "know" anything about music, he was a shrewd layman who somehow belonged to the world of sound—*il appartenait à l'univers orphique*, said Sauguet. And if—like a song composer (a Schubert or a Fauré) for whom poetry is a means to an end—Cocteau used music as a cloak, a source, a detachable skin, a gloss, who dares say he used it wrongly?

He didn't pretend to know more than he knew, didn't talk music in musicians' jargon, and thank God for that. But he did use musical references. (On the first day's rushes of *Beauty and the Beast* he wrote: ". . . Faults don't matter, they afford a certain relief. It was like *looking* at Mozart's music, in which the slightest detail, any four notes, can be isolated and whose movement *as a whole* is so admirable.") And he did put to wondrous use the "accidental synchronizing" which I, as a composer, find more sensible than the fussy solderings of "musical" filmmakers with a dangerous little learning who feel that music has literal meaning. (On the last day's rushes: ". . . Today is the day for the music. I have refused to hear what Auric has composed, wanting to receive the shock of it without preparation. A long habit of working together gives me complete confidence in him. . . .")

His ideas for musical subjects inevitably stemmed from those of other people, like Shakespeare and Sophocles, just as Shakespeare stems from Sophocles and Sophocles from Homer and Homer from . . . It works both ways. If Camus's *Malentendu* seems too close for comfort to Cocteau's *Pauvre Matelot* (a gloomy tale culled, so he says, from the *faits divers*), who will disagree with Gide's defense of *his* culling the *faits divers:* "I cannot understand how the merit of a work of art can be diminished through its being based on reality"?

Reality, on his best days, was changed by Jean Cocteau into a permanent and contagious magic that his musical collaborators sometimes caught and communicated intact to a world of listeners.

October–November 1981

Vera Stravinsky's and Robert Craft's
STRAVINSKY: IN PICTURES AND DOCUMENTS

The preface to this gorgeous scrapbook proposes that the next century will replace "Wagnerian" with "Stravinskyan" as adjectival modifier for "ego." Indeed, the ensuing gargantuan "portrait of the man and the musician" flows easily in the wake of Cosima Wagner's recently published diary about her spouse, except that the Stravinsky book is less quotidian reportage than luxuriant retrospect and is not really authored by his widow. Vera de Bosset, painter and actress, couturière and intellectual, handsome charmer and faithful wife (". . . the wife they all loved/Not Helen, the other . . ." sang Mandelstam), shares billing with Robert Craft, Stravinsky's longtime intimate colleague. But Craft, who defines the volume as a reflection of "this author's [not "these authors'"] feelings about Stravinsky seven years after his death," is clearly the mastermind. Of Stravinsky's ego, however, there is aplenty, though of a non-Wagnerian brand; to think oneself God would have been for the orthodox Russian artist the ultimate sacrilege. He knew his worth, with panache and clarity, as did the world in whose eyes he represented the last genius. The notion of Great Man—that Beethovenian individual blessed, or maybe cursed, by the fates—is no longer current now that Stravinsky, along with Picasso and Mann and Disney, is gone; that any grandiose living artist—Borges, Bergman, Boulez—would receive so ornate a tombstone seems unthinkable.

Igor Stravinsky was famous from the start, not just because he was great (so was Webern) but because he was public. He was public thanks to his special scope, a scope imposed by Diaghilev, the first high-class purveyor worldwide of collective art. Stravinsky continues to fire both public and private imaginations because he succeeded in rendering theater music serious—music, that is, other than opera. One example of such music, *Le Sacre du Printemps*, has become the single (non-vocal) entity unanimously deemed the musical masterpiece of our century: indeed, more than *Guernica* or *The*

Golden Bowl or the Seagram Building, *Sacre* is *the* artwork against which our international culture is judged. Anything, even a laundry list, by the maker of such a work is of curiosity value, and *Stravinsky in Pictures and Documents* more than fills the bill.

The pictures are mostly little-known Kodak shots introducing us into the parlors and cafés and onto the beaches and stages of yore with the awe of utter reality. Here sit Debussy, a bourgeois faun, and Rimsky-Korsakov with cigarette, and Ravel with his mother, all with the same breathing aliveness as Nijinsky, variously in straw hat and derby, dapper and vulnerable, palpable yet vanished. Color plates feature Benois's fire-breathing devils on the curtain for *Petrushka* (not less beautiful than Picasso's famous curtain for Satie's *Parade)*, Roerich's hallucinatory study for the *Sacre*, paintings by Stravinsky himself and close-ups of his manuscripts flyspecked with rainbow inks, bright sketches in logbooks or programs, and razor-sharp photos of the gondola-borne procession of final rites through the canals of Venice. The documents are mostly letters to and from Stravinsky, or press clippings, diaries and reviews from hundreds of sources all radically screened. The format is coffee-table—the book weighs more than my cat—with white margins accounting for a third of the bulk. The bulk of that bulk is Craft's connecting commentary, biographical (including anecdotes from his own journal) juxtaposed with analytical (including comparison of various drafts of musical works), a happier, if looser, scheme than the habitual separation of a man's music from his "real life."

If Cosima revealed more than we finally care to know about Wagner except what he liked to eat, Craft tells us not only about Stravinsky's diet (generally rich and alcoholized) and his habit of munching charcoal as an anti-flatulent before drinking champagne, but also about his fanatical order (the collecting tendencies of a nesting magpie), olfactory preferences (leather, coffee), his sexual utopia (mammary), his hypochondria (to counteract which he kept himself in muscular trim), and his extramarital dalliances (seemingly minimal, but counting Chanel).

"To speak of my own music is more difficult for me than to write it." Difficult or not, Stravinsky covered thousands of pages, and was quoted in nearly as many interviews, with words on matters mostly professional. Craft cites the master copiously, not always to their mutual advantage. If the most famous remark ("Music is incapable of expressing anything") scarce bears repeating, Stravinsky's apposite literariness becomes at once too lean and too rich to quote *hors contexte*. But he could also be smug ("What the public likes in Brahms is the sentiment. What I like has another, architectonic basis"); self-contradictory, in the light of his frequent revamping of folk tunes ("Popular music has nothing to gain by being taken out of its frame"); and superficially deep in striking balances that would seem to be, but are not, mutually exclusive ("Romantic music was a product of sentiment and imagination; my music is a product of motion and rhythm"). Stravinsky could even be banal, honoring Chopin less than "the great Liszt whose immense talent . . . is often underrated," when in fact Liszt is merely the rich man's Chopin. And he could be plain wrong as when referring to Chopin's formal and through-

written Nocturnes as "formless fragments." Craft claims that the "sum of the
parts is less than the whole, a casual remark by the man casting more light
than pages of biographers' details," and to demonstrate he quotes the man, as
though *ex cathedra:* "It is impossible for the brain to follow the ear and the eye
at the same time." Were this epigram true, would it not challenge the very
meaning of Craft's occupation as conductor? Craft's own logic is challenged
when he claims on one page that "Stravinsky . . . does not believe that . . .
external influences have any effect on his composition," and on another that
"his music was influenced to an unprecedented extent by the circumstances
of his life."

Not that Craft finds Stravinsky forever irreproachable, at least not extra-
musically. The composer's inexplicable callousness toward his first wife is
unrelentingly detailed. And an appendix called "Stravinsky's Politics" reveals a fascist bent, mainly toward Mussolini; also in 1933 he hesitates to sign
a petition on behalf of musicians being driven from their posts in the Reich
because he felt cautious about Germany. ("Also, I do not know the position-
ing of my name on the list and do not want to be next to such trash as
Milhaud.") Nor did he seem abashed by Diaghilev's outspoken anti-Semitism, toward Koussevitzky among others.

Any good portrait mirrors the portraitist. Ten years ago I wrote, "Robert
Craft has squatter's rights on public property." Today, as this book indicates, he still holds down his claim—albeit with an Achilles heel. The longest entry to deal uninterruptedly with any one subject (longer than the
consecutive discussion of *Petrushka*, or even *Le Sacre*, or of the composer's
rapports with Debussy or Ravel) is the twenty-four pages of small type,
almost a self-parody, discrediting *And Music at the Close*, a memoir by
Stravinsky's one-time booking agent, Lillian Libman. To be a solitary keeper
of the flame is one thing; when the flame turns to conflagration it's every man
for himself to respond as he feels to the dazzling warmth, the blistering
growth, and Libman surely has as much right as Craft to publish her
souvenirs.

Too much here, too little there. Of Pierre Boulez, for instance, there is
virtually nothing, though the prime-moving Frenchman, presumably close to
Stravinsky's heart, wrote a long-ago exegesis on *Le Sacre* no less original than
one by a certain Allen Forte whom Craft chooses to extol at length.

Of the nearly two dozen references to Jean Cocteau listed in the index (plus
another dozen strangely unlisted), none is warm or favorable, as though the
poet, far from being a creator of stature, were a mere opportunist. May it not
sound defensive to state that, while Stravinsky himself may have earned the
right for certain sarcasms, Craft is not well placed for backstage jabs at
unverifiable motives *chez* Cocteau and André Gide (two authors whom he—
like many an "outsider"—links, although their sole common point, homosexuality, signifies no more than the [presumed] heterosexuality shared by, say,
Claudel and Sartre, or even by Craft and Stravinsky).

The single youngish current composer of any nationality whom Craft finds
worth quoting is Charles Wuorinen who in 1961 wrote to Stravinsky: "Your
recent magnificent serial compositions . . . are inspirations to all reasonable
musicians." The implication that dodecaphonism is the True Way is actually

less fallacious than the idea of a "reasonable musician."

With the notable exception of conductor Ernest Ansermet, whose critical intelligence Stravinsky respected and with whom correspondence covers a longer span than any other in the composer's life (though, as Craft pointedly notes, Ansermet's communications greatly outnumber, and are much lengthier, than Stravinsky's), performers, particularly singers, are given short shrift. Perhaps this is as it should be, the musico-literary market being glutted with print on the executional How rather than on the creational What, and the world at large having forgotten the obvious, that music originates with composers. Still, would it be superfluous in the forty-some pages devoted to Stravinsky's longest work, *The Rake's Progress*, to list the principals of this opera's 1951 première, two of whom, Jennie Tourel and Hugues Cuénod, were selected by the composer the following fall to "create" his new Cantata?

My irritation clothes admiration, seeing how much this book's strength lies in Craft's weakness—an inability to cope with certain viewpoints not his own. But all biographers are biased. Robert Craft, more skilled with words and more educated than most, is better suited than anyone in the world to present that world with a case for Stravinsky the Man.

December 1978

STRAVINSKY AT 100

When I was twelve I heard *The Rite of Spring* and became sick—sick from the thrill of an instantaneous and permanent shift in metabolism. So this was music! A door had opened, the sun flowed in with its nourishing and mysterious gold. The occasion was a nationwide broadcast of the Philharmonic, Stravinsky conducting, which I caught in Chicago, and which (I later learned) was heard by every other twelve-year-old composer in America, with the same traumatic effect.

Before that broadcast, although I surely counted on a musical career, I loved live fauna, birds in particular, which I collected and bred and knew all about. After the broadcast, I carted four wicker cages filled with rare finches to Vaughn's Seed Store in the Loop, traded them for a few dollars, crossed the street to Lyon & Healy, bought score and disc of *The Rite of Spring*, my rite-of-passage into adolescence, and during the next four decades I never thought of animals again.

A few summers ago an interest in non-human creatures revived, along with some metabolic reshifting, when a Russian blue cat named Wallace entered my life. The passion for music, if not the need, subsided into another rite-of-passage that encouraged the rights of animals and the demystification of things artistic. That this recurrence should fall on the eve of Stravinsky's hundredth birthday lends impetus to a backward glance at our greatest composer. But before I let fly with opinions let me state where I stand.

Yes, he was our greatest composer, and his *Rite*, in turn, is so solid as to be The Absolute against which all other current art is judged. (Even movies, if you recall Pauline Kael's once touching and quickly outmoded bid to validate *Last Tango in Paris*.) Indeed, *The Rite* is a fact of life we take for granted, like Beethoven's Fifth, and seldom listen to anymore. Conditioned to a masterpiece, we digest it without question, and forget. Instinctively composers realize that the best way to keep the freshness in other people's masterpieces is to place a ban on them. But recently I decided it was my duty to buy a new score of *The Rite*, the one from Lyon & Healy having long since turned to dust. If the formidable pages now had the look of old friends, if the notorious "difficulties" now seemed Haydnesque, the impact remained, the ferocity and newness; and the nourishing gold was still there.

This said, do I adore Stravinsky as I adore others who are perhaps less overwhelming—Ravel, for example, or Poulenc? I am dazzled by his intelligence and scared by his force, but my heart is not melted.

Has my own work been influenced by his? Not consciously. Not, certainly, as were the works of other Americans during the pre-Craft forties at the peak of his power: Harold Shapero, Arthur Berger, Leo Smit, Irving Fine, Alexei Haieff. Yet to deny him is to admit him, to go against him is to go against the century, sheer vanity. No one has been immune.

What more is there to say of this most-written-about musician of modern times? Nobody with even a peripheral claim to culture has been without his word. Consider the gamuts: from the murder mysteries of James M. Cain or Caryle Brahms to the name-dropping souvenirs of Billy Rose or Misia Sert; from the workshop descriptions of Cocteau or Auden to the tersely technical précis of Erick White or Andrew Porter; from the deep gossip of Nicolas Nabokov or Lillian Libman to the businesslike and maybe, irrelevant analyses of Suvchinsky or Boulez. Nor was he himself without opinion, his prose serving as guide, sometimes beyond his music, to form the quite considered opinion of others.

What's left to say? Only personal reactions. Mine, now, shall come less through a reappraisal of his career than through a reassessment of my responses to that career, and I shall let the reactions emerge from a set of questions.

Why call him great if I don't adore him?

Partly because I too am brainwashed. My nature prefers minor artists to the makers of Big Statements, which is why I'm drawn to French more than to German music. But there is a more objective reason. Stravinsky is what the French call a *monstre sacré*—one whose greatness depends on chronological place.

The sacred monster is a personage who, through public exploitation of his personal accomplishment—an accomplishment always first-rate—grows so much larger than life as to seem no longer human. Generally he is a creative artist, though some performers and politicians fill the bill. He is, so to speak, a violent luxury which, because not really needed to make the world go round, concentrates no less on his product than on his persona, and peddles this persona no less to the discriminating aristocrat than to the philistine bourgeois. His heyday is the Romantic Era, starting with the Industrial Revolution when the Artist was no longer an appendage of either church or state, and ending with World War II when the notion of Masterpiece—that is, a piece by a master—began to smell unpatriotic. Thus Louis XIV or Sebastian Bach are too early to apply, the one being by definition sacred through no effort of his own, the other being a workman for God; while Frank Sinatra or Aaron Copland are too late, Frank never posing as better than he should be, and Aaron ever striving toward a democratic image (assuming that Americans, at least to other Americans, could ever qualify). And thus Beethoven, Byron, Bonaparte and Bernhardt become arch exemplars, while Picasso, Mann, Casals, de Gaulle and Stravinsky represent the last of a breed, with maybe, just maybe, our own Martha Graham surviving as an anachronism. Ironically, no birthright French composer fits the category.

Is his musical nature German or French (these constituting the sole pair of esthetics in the whole cosmos, all others—Dutch, Spanish, Siamese, etc.— being subdivisions thereof)?

His musical nature is French. Russia is French.

To be French is to stress a sense of proportion; to realize that humor and horror are not mutually exclusive; to be profound while retaining the spiritual levity required (at least in Paris) to get through life without collapsing, and to discover the profundity on the surface of things. To be French is to show three sides of a coin. French is witty, and wit, as exemplified by that most stylish of French composers, Franz Joseph Haydn, is ellipsis—knowing what to leave out. Wit depends on tonality and all French music true to the name is tonal.

To be German is to dig in rather than to spread out, to get to the heart of things, obsessively. As the saying goes, a German joke is no laughing matter. That which under other circumstances seems funny is soberly dissected, like Freud's exegesis of humor; that which at first seems funny gets drowned by the very terms that offer it, like Schoenberg's *Von Heute auf Morgen*. Serial music, especially in the theater, lends itself ideally to moods of injustice and dreamlike madness because the system depends on irresolution; but where Schoenberg uses this lugubrious language for his "comic" opera, pure stultification ensues.

A case could be made, though I shan't make it, that Schoenberg's science, like Freud's, while being irreversibly branded on the globe, can now be viewed as a blind alley. Freud entered a cave which expanded toward ever deeper shadows rather than narrowing toward a ray of light. Schoenberg, in "emancipating" dissonance, ultimately justified flaccidity. Dissonance by definition resolves, otherwise it is not dissonant (dissonant to what?); but where all is dissonance nothing is dissonance—no relief, and at the same time no tension.

Though younger than Debussy, Schoenberg closed the nineteenth century while Debussy opened the twentieth. We now recognize Schoenberg's frenzy to have been not innovative but agonized. He was the last Romantic, Debussy the first Modern.

Stravinsky, as Debussy's foremost heir, traced modernism along a diatonic course. Everyone knows that he abhorred Meaning in music, let alone deep meaning, but few stress his C-major frivolity, even silliness. Stravinsky was grandly aware of the importance of unimportance.

Yet if at his most serious he doesn't scratch my heart as do Poulenc and Ravel, is this because of the Russian side of his gallicism? Peter Yates wrote: "His religious music remains, in the Catholic tradition, objective—celebration, ritual, lamentation, narrative; it does not question in the German style, like Schoenberg's, the religious ultimate of nature and relationship of man and God." Not that Ravel (who never wrote religious music) or Poulenc (whose heaven was on his sleeve) tried to be deep thinkers like Schoenberg, or were less crystalline or, indeed, less "French" than Stravinsky; but their sounds concern warm specifics while his are cool and general.

Is he harmonist or contrapuntist?

Harmonist, in the tradition of France. He wrote a fugue or two (so did Ravel), notably the one which forms the second movement of *Symphony of Psalms*, but we don't recall it as a fugue. Indeed, do we even recall it compared to that piece's celebrated opening sound—one of the composer's two most famous chords? This eight-voice E-minor triad is the essence of verticality, and while born for the orchestra was clearly concocted at the keyboard, so symmetrically does it fall beneath the two hands.

"Dance of the Adolescents" from *The Rite of Spring* contains Stravinsky's other famous chord, also in eight voices, a chord which more than any other represents The Sacre Sound. The Sacre Sound devolves not from the scoring of the chord (string double-stops eccentrically punctuated by horns), nor yet from its daring reiteration (280 times in the first seventy measures), but from the vertical clash between the four top and four bottom parts which we used to hear, at the very least, as bitonality. Today we hear it as an unresolved E-flat dominant seventh over a lowered submediant triad, both having the potent potential for resolving to an A-flat tonic.

Polyphony was Schoenberg's nature, as it must be for those who conceive by tone-row, but harmony was Stravinsky's, even when, late in life, he too composed according to a series. His music is always heard as tonal (of course, I hear everything as tonal, including Boulez and Babbitt—it's my conditioning—and I contend that everyone, including Babbitt and Boulez, hears everything as tonal), even when apparently sewn with independent threads. By extension, his music is heard harmonically: the entrances of voices on the first pages of *The Rite* to the eye may look like horizontal waves but to the ear they freeze into chunks.

What about his tunes, his rhythm, his color?

His melodic sense, even in vocal music, had an instrumental tang aimed like Beethoven's or Debussy's toward the reiterated slogan rather than, like Chopin's or Ravel's, toward the long arching line. Motives, not cantilena. The motives are contagious, being oft repeated. And they are repeated unaltered—that is Stravinsky's signature, a signature adapted to the various periods of his career. (Viz., the obstinate trumpet solos in "The Doll's Scene" of *Petrushka*, in *The Nightingale*, in *The Soldier's Story*, in *Agon*.) Peter Yates said: "A well-conceived conventional theme plus some related episodic material can suffice for a large fugue. It is not the subject but what happens along the way that makes the difference between talent and art. Not the melody of a tone-row but its organic shape in consideration of all that can grow from it. . . ." This is misleading. Bach's great fugues are great from the outset; the themes are rich in themselves, like Stravinsky's themes to which often nothing "happens along the way." Meanwhile, the "melody of a tone-row" is never a question (rows are frequently presented vertically). Though Stravinsky's melodies are not songlike, they are usually stated, as songs are, with simple support, and Yates is right here: "Seldom in his compositions are more than two things happening simultaneously [as though he] overcompensated for German expressivity."

Ask anyone what single component most defines Stravinsky and he will answer rhythm. The rhythm in turn is characterized, like our jazz but unlike anything European, by metrical precision—by a persistent motoric beat that does not get faster or slower according to shades of dynamic, or according to non-symmetrical continually changing time signatures. Thirty-five years ago Virgil Thomson, in discussing the rarity of the non-accelerating crescendo in European musical execution, told us: "Of the three most famous crescendos in modern music not one is both tonally continuous and rhythmically steady. Strauss's *Elektra* is tonally continuous, rising in waves from beginning to end; but it presupposes no exact metrics. Stravinsky's "Dance of the Adolescents" and Ravel's *Boléro* do presuppose a metrically strict rendering, but they are not tonally steady crescendos. They are as neatly terraced as any Bach organ fugue." (Thomson could have included an even more famous crescendo, Berg's B-flat-unison interlude in *Wozzeck* which, though European, is surely both tonally continuous and rhythmically steady.) Stravinsky's fast music is intrinsically fast, not slow music played fast. If twelve-tone music is never kinetically fast, despite florid figurations, that is because a sense of speed comes through ostinato, and ostinato is by its nature repetitious, which serial composition is not allowed to be.

His color comes through using the ordinary extrordinarily, like the aforementioned E-minor triad from *Symphony of Psalms*. His orchestration is recognizable as French by its avoidance of doublings, recognizable as Stravinsky by its assignment of the least obvious instruments to given phrases. (For an example of the no-doubling, see any tutti passage in *The Rite*. For an example of the least obvious instrument, see the renowned bassoon solo which opens the same work.) The economics of his orchestration altered with the world's economics, since no one after World War I could afford the mammoth Mahlerian agglomerations, but the principles of his orchestration remained fixed.

The great composers are usually, but not always, fluent and convincing with every variable of music: chords, lines, beats, tunes, hues; and in the several mediums: chamber, opera, symphony, songs. But if the great Stravinsky was, in an age of musical specialists, a general practitioner like Britten, were not Chopin and Schubert, though perhaps no less great, specialists in an age of jacks-of-all-trades?

How was he as a word setter?

His editor confided that when the manuscript for *Three Songs from William Shakespeare* was submitted for engraving, it was necessary to tell Stravinsky that two verses were missing from the opening sonnet. The mortified master asked that the score be returned and that the affair remain secret. The restitution of the forgotten lines appears in the printed version of this song, a version which nevertheless contains what I deem a worse misdemeanor (though sanctioned by many): repeating words at whim.

Does not a song composer who repeats phrases not repeated in the poem he is setting threaten that poem's integrity? Is he not rewriting the poem—a rewrite which, if read aloud without music, he would reject for its now unbalanced meters, false echoes, too obvious redundancies? If he justifies such additions as needs—a reflective rhythm here, an aural rhyme there—why not by the same token justify omissions? (How many songwriters have not, like Stravinsky, inadvertently left out great swatches of poetry, phrases swept away by the first élan of inspiration, only to discover sheepishly when copying the finished piece that a crucial predicate has vanished!) Suppose he even takes a poem wherein the poet does repeat a word ("Nevermore, nevermore"), but consciously opts, for whatever reason, *not* to mime the verbal clause with his musical clause. Is this option less legitimate than the other? It would seem so. One just doesn't delete lines from Shakespeare, so it should follow that all poets need protection. Poets may well claim that the songwriter makes them say twice what was meant to be said only once (Valéry: "Hearing verse set to music is like looking at a painting through a stained glass window"), or that he forces them to say what they never meant to say. Since the setting of a poem to music is necessarily a distorting of that poem, even when the sequence of words remains intact, whoever disturbs the sequence adds insult to injury; he is not serving poetry but allowing poetry to serve him. I'm referring, of course, to a modern composer's use of a poem sufficient unto itself and by a poet with a sense of style—a poem being the most economical, the most compressed of literary forms; I'm not referring to madrigals of yore whose authors and composers were often the same person—Dowland, Campion—confecting words especially to be repeated in the manner of folksong, randomly. Now, a composer can have his cake and eat it. There is almost no example of a musician's mangling of verse which could not be recomposed generally by using melisma, so that the poem reverts to its "pure" state while the vocal line retains its identical curve.

That off my chest, let me say that Stravinsky was a marvelous composer for the voice. The marvel had nothing to do with proper word-setting, i.e., concern for parsing, declamation, quantities, considerations aimed toward comprehensibility of a sung text. In a text sound more than sense absorbed him, which is why he was happiest and most convincing in Latin. Since no one knows how that language was spoken he is free to let accents fall where they may. From the start of *Oedipus Rex*, for instance, the hero's name is thrice intoned, each time with a new stress. In *The Wedding* the whining grace notes of the bride, the harrumphing swoops of the male guests, the ritual chanting and the moaning yelps, all these are novel sounds to vocal literature, apposite and exciting, indifferent to prosodic rules. By treating larynxes like woodwinds, even as he revolutionized orchestration by treating woodwinds like strings, Stravinsky deconventionalized common practice.

Then why do I decry his misbegotten Shakespeare Songs? Partly because they are in my native tongue so I hear too clearly where he errs. But also because at the time of these songs his erring was changing focus. The year 1951 unveiled his longest theater work by far, and his most bloodless. *The Rake's Progress* was his first foray into English, and verbal intelligibility seems now to have been his aim. To join the world's best poet with the world's best composer was a coup only in theory; in fact, poets do not the best librettists make, and Auden, despite his campy couplets, his in-jokes and Dickensian nouns, was too respectful of his collaborator—worse, he succumbed to the amateur practice of combining words that are "helpful" to the composer. Stravinsky, for his part, awash in this jargon, despite a few touching airs and some unexpected colors, produced a tired pastiche with such inadvertently burlesque word-stresses that each character seems to sing with a Russian accent. Undaunted, he immediately composed three more works in English (including a setting of Dylan Thomas's *Do Not Go Gentle*, the sole poem of Thomas that musicians seem to have heard of), ever striving to be "correct."

Most of Europe's masterworks have been for human voice. Exceptions are notably from the nineteenth century which, notwithstanding Wagner and Schubert and the Italians, was an instrumental age. Beethoven and Chopin are not primarily remembered for songs and choruses and operas, nor are Brahms, Schumann, Tchaikovsky. In our time Stravinsky too is an exception, in the light of Ravel and Schoenberg, Berg and Britten. He is the only great composer in history whose greatest works are for dancers.

What of his notorious utterance, fifty years after the fact: "Music is incapable of expressing anything at all"?

Music is the hardest art to speak of because music has no meaning to speak of. Yet we all speak of it, and none more eloquently than composers themselves, especially Stravinsky. Like the *Pietà*, or, indeed, like *The Rite of Spring*, Stravinsky's quips have entered public consciousness. But quips aren't holy writ.

Of course music expresses something, but the "something" cannot be verbalized, that's why it's music. If the arts could express each other then we'd need only one. (One wonders how the canny Stravinsky could approve Goethe's canard: architecture is frozen music.) Mendelssohn was more to the point: "Thoughts which are expressed to me by music are not too indefinite to be put into words, but on the contrary, too definite."

Was he original?

By original, people really mean innovative, placing a high price on this Hollywoodian virtue. Yet the most remarkable innovators have never been the finest composers, because innovation and composition are separate professions and no one has time to excel in both. The big artist steals the raw novelties of the little artist, then cooks them with his own spices. The question composers hear most often, and the one they most often avoid, is: "Who are your influences?" (implying: "How original are you?"). The question is normal to outsiders who are convinced, quite rightly, that nothing comes of nothing, but who are unable to see, as they can with painters and poets, the thread that sews yesterday to today. Composers see all too easily the thread; knowing whom they've robbed, their singularity—their private stamp—lies in the act of breathing the special life into silent models, and they aren't about to tell you who lies beneath the disguise.

Despite this theory Stravinsky's reputation seems secure as both innovator and genius. He himself was always quick to promote his loves through pastiche (notably of Pergolesi and Tchaikovsky in *Pulcinella* and *The Fairy's Kiss*) while belittling the procedure in others (notably Poulenc, whom he credited with giving plagiarism a new meaning). Yet the road from pastiche to paraphrase is short. If *The Rite of Spring* sprang in its unique glory full-blown from its creator's head, no one ever points out Stravinsky's shameless borrowings:

Is not the extended strident solo piano clattering above nervous strings in the first movement of his *Symphony in Three Movements*, written in 1943, too close for comfort to Bartók's extended strident solo piano clattering above nervous strings in the second movement of his *Music for Strings, Percussion and Celesta*, composed six years earlier?

What of the famous *Petrushka* texture, recognizable in a split second? Would these close-harmony roulades for a pair of clarinets have been scored that way in 1910, had not Ravel in 1908 invented an identical scoring in *Rapsodie Espagnole*?

More disconcerting are the three samples of parallel octaves meandering over forty years from Mussorgsky's *Sans Soleil* through Debussy's *Nuages* to Stravinsky's *Rossignol* prelude, the last named making no pretense of camouflage.

Getting us before we get him, Stravinsky acknowledges his debt to Verdi during the making of *Oedipus Rex*, though despite his E-flat tenor air in Latin being frankly a variation on Verdi's E-flat tenor air in Latin from the *Requiem*, who would mistake the one author for the other?

But would the rhythm beneath Jocasta's harangue, also from *Oedipus Rex*, have come off quite as it does had Bartók not written his first quartet in 1908?

And did not Satie's simple but singular ostinato, of three longs and a short, in *Socrate*, anticipate Stravinsky's *Tango*?

Did I know him?

I don't know. I do know that I was thrice in his presence.

In 1944 Alexei Haieff asked several of us to meet Stravinsky for tea at Kyriena Siloti's. Did we shake hands? I can't recall, too many people, the room was dark, I said nothing. Stravinsky withdrew early, just as Aaron Copland was arriving. I do remember that Aaron found this relay perfectly appropriate—one good deed deserves another.

That same year I attended a rehearsal in a radio studio of *Persephone*, Stravinsky conducting, with Madeleine Milhaud as Speakerine. We did not truly meet then either; but that was the first of many times that I would be charmed by the aspect of Stravinsky on the podium, his small dancer's frame, lilting and sexual, wordlessly describing the definitive performance. ("I conduct," he told Gregg Smith, "so as to learn my own music.")

In 1954 I was forbidden entrance to the Rome Opera at the same time as Stravinsky for not being in formal attire. Next day the occurrence had become a *cause célèbre* with my name linked to the maestro's in newspapers throughout the world. So much for reflected glory.

How bodes the Met's triple bill?

Well, there is only one genuine opera, *The Nightingale*. The oratorio, *Oedipus Rex*, is strongly visual, however, and as a sung work its inclusion is plausible. But to mount *The Rite of Spring*, a ballet, and an unsuccessful one, is vanity.

A word on each work:

We talk about a creator's "periods," although composers have them less noticeably than other artists. But with Stravinsky the stylistic plateaux are as neatly definable as those of Picasso or of Henry James; and within one of his pieces, *The Nightingale*, his personal phylogeny is ontologically recapitulated. Composed over many years, it reflects three manners: impressionist amorphism, post-*Rite* exoticism and a foretaste of the belt-tightening 1920s which in turn anticipates the so-called neoclassicism of the 1930s. The Prelude is dispensable, not because it is unoriginal, but because its not very interesting material is never "brought back" during the course of the three-act spectacle. The piece should begin straight off with the gorgeous Fisherman's song, which is the opera's binding force. Heard not once but four times over the course of the work, this extended Gershwinesque blues is among the few cantilenas Stravinsky ever penned. Yet it is not a "vocal" melody: the text could be any text, stretched over a pre-written tune. As with Poulenc's *Dialogues* wherein the best music—the Latin choruses—is extrinsic to the Bernanos script, here the best music—the Fisherman's plaint—is adornment to the Andersen tale.

A 1952 French production of *Oedipus Rex* reunited Cocteau and Stravinsky after many years. Cocteau not only declaimed the Speaker's role, he refashioned the twelve-foot puppets of Remo Bufano. I recall him before the dress rehearsal happily hammering at the props, Paris stagehand unions being more lax than ours. But Cocteau was in that year out of favor with the fickle French. (Although we ourselves have placed them there, we can grow to resent and thence to crush theatrical idols for their stance upon the pedestal. If this has not been the case for such moral irreproachables as Shaw or O'Neill or Arthur Miller, it has been the case for Wilde and Williams and Jean Cocteau.) At the gala the elderly perfumed public, laced with Camus-oriented youth chained to an outmoded ritual, jeered each appearance of Cocteau until he raised a famous hand to stop the orchestra. "If you don't respect me and my work," he pleaded, "at least respect Stravinsky who is a great composer." The hall grew still, the music started up, Cocteau sat down again on the little stool at the edge of the stage, motionless and crestfallen. Nobody missed the irony when he pronounced the final lines—the very lines Stravinsky had discounted as superfluous—when the King finds himself snared in his own trap: "He falls. He falls from high. . . . Farewell, poor Oedipus, we loved you." As for the score, the starkly iterated inexorable triplet pulse like a column supporting the male chorus is a monument of musical terror among other monuments. Yet the terror of Sophocles (as is ever the case with updated Greek tragedies) resounds more purposefully than the contributions of either Cocteau or Stravinsky.

As Sophocles to adapters, so *The Rite* to choreographers. This ballet is forever undanceable partly because the story is taken at face value, but mainly because the score smashes all contenders. True, Paul Taylor, avoiding the risky "pagan" tone of every version since 1912, did make a go of it; and he did ape Nijinsky's knock-kneed profiles. But Taylor's success owes much to the four-hand reduction: the black-and-white keyboard offsets the black-and-white comic-strip yarn in the black-and-white modernistic décor;

and the Nijinsky stance is brash allusion, not sober homage. However, the music's glamour rests in orchestral color; were Taylor dumb enough to use the full score, his *Rite* would turn from comic-spooky to monotono-silly. (Disney's Technicolor version wasn't bad. He inclined, as they say out there, to Mickey-Mouse the music, but he, if anyone, had the right.)

Just as Satie's *Parade* is too weak for a viable ballet, Stravinsky's *Rite* is too strong. Even if the latter *were* viable, why it, and not another large vocal work like *The Wedding* to round out the trilogy? Since *The Wedding* happens to have been composed as a ballet, a *sung* ballet, the Met could have had it both ways.

For the sake of a point I have, like dozens of musicologists, weighed Stravinsky against Schoenberg. The point was that, despite what even the man himself contended, Stravinskyan flavor relies on a core of constant tonality permitting a colossal scope. The scope nonetheless has frontiers—not defects, but self-imposed limitations. From the bittersweet violence of the big ballets to the luxuriant chutzpah of the two-piano pieces, Stravinsky is powerful and profound, sparse and playful, indeed everything we connect with great masters, except pessimistic. The music is simply never depressing like, say, Bartók's *Bluebeard*, Berg's *Lulu* or Schoenberg's almost anything. On the other hand are those composers, with all their might, ever witty? It could be argued that wit, like charm, must reside in all genius (why, even Beethoven had charm!), or conversely that all genius must house a certain morosity. How pursue a matter so clearly of taste? Which brings back my gambit of French versus German esthetic.

Stravinsky's glibness was grave. His varied career produced few weak works. He robbed many a nest along the way, but some Borgesian alchemy arranged for each egg to hatch out another Igor—and that includes his accounts of *The Volga Boatmen*, *The Star-Spangled Banner* and *Happy Birthday to You*. So happy birthday to you, dear centenarian maestro, for whom only the world's end will prevent ten thousand more.

Nantucket, August 1981

AN AUDEN

My friend Frank O'Hara once recalled showing his verse to Wystan Auden. Said the master: "You've got to be an Auden to get away with lines like that." An Auden! the younger poet marveled, taking in the prune-like lips dribbling vodka onto a sweater unchanged for weeks, the tobacco-stained thumbs and the urine-stained pants, the seedy carpet slippers (which because of chronic corns Auden wore everywhere, to the drugstore as to the opera), the whole pontifical form slumped like a mummy in a gutted sofa whose dust beclouded a setting no less gorgeous than the Collyer brothers'. This portrait of the artist as an old mentor, corroborated by all who met him, is but the rough side of the canvas, for Auden was the most disciplined, the smoothest and maybe the greatest English-language poet of our time; O'Hara had seen him as he saw others:

> . . . I imagine you before my eyes
> Flushed with the wine I order and my wit.

A product of industrial England—he was born in York in 1907—Auden might nonetheless be placed intellectually somewhere between Jean Cocteau, eighteen years his senior from a country he avoided, and Paul Goodman, five years his junior from a country he adopted.

Like Goodman, Auden was a clearheaded formalist in a distressingly unhygienic body, a rude bully who was momentarily kind, profoundly homosexual but a champion of the family as stabilizing unit. (When Cyril Connolly learned that Auden, who adored anagrams, had turned T. S. Eliot into "toilets," Connolly turned Wystan Auden into "a nasty unwed." Yet Auden's wedding in 1935 to Thomas Mann's daughter was legal and lifelong, though of strictly political convenience—they never lived together. But his thirty-year union with Chester Kallman was, at least on Auden's side, modeled on bourgeois values. After Erika Mann died in 1970, and Chester was far away, Auden proposed to other women, including Hannah Arendt, to her purported embarrassment.) Both Auden and Goodman reveled in music but played the piano thumpingly, confusing love for ability; expert at hearing others, they couldn't hear themselves. Both were professional and caring teachers, periodically looked upon as arbiters, wielding no less influence

200

through sociological belief (Auden liberal-conservative, Goodman regi-
mented-anarchist) than through verse forms. Yet both were finally forsaken
by the young; while planning to live until eighty, each died in his sixties of
overwork and disenchantment at having evolved into the obsolete species of
Educated Poet.

   Like Cocteau, Auden was an aphorist who monopolized conversation with
quips that brooked no argument. Cocteau too, vastly "official" in his waning
years, had been spurned by the very generations whose style he had shaped,
and he died, successful and sad, in a mist of self-quotation. When Auden had
become a monument he welcomed the interviewers he had shunned for
years, but spoke to them solely in epigrammatic non sequiturs. ("As a poet,
my only duty is to defend the language from corruption. . . . History would
be no different if literature had never existed; nothing I wrote against Hitler
prevented one Jew from being killed. . . . I live by my watch. I wouldn't
know to be hungry if I didn't have my watch. . . . Italian is the most beautiful language to write in, but terribly hard for writers because you can't tell
when you've written nonsense. In English you know right away. . . . I don't
go along with the generation gap. We're all contemporaries, anyone walking
the earth at this moment. There's a certain difference in memories, that's
all. . . . Art is our chief means of breaking bread with the dead—you can
still enjoy the *Iliad*. . . . I like to fancy that had I taken the Anglican Holy
Orders, I might now be a Bishop.") Like Cocteau, Auden was a jack-of-all-
trades, authoring not only haiku but very long poems, plays, librettos, screen
scenarios, translations from many a language popular and obscure, and the
most original essays of our century on subjects far from his "specialty." Like
Cocteau, Auden was also a professional actor and a social star, but while both
were wildly candid in the parlor they were circumspect in print: when their
respective forays into so-called pornography, *Le livre blanc* and *The Platonic
Blow*, were stolen and published, they were nervous. Because Cocteau's
musicality was less proprietary (music was the one art he did not presume to
practice), his collaboration with musicians was more expert: he did not, as
did Goodman and Auden, concoct "settable lyrics," but left musical decisions to the composers. Nor did he fall into the fatal trap of the others who,
during later years, revised early poems, making changes for change's sake,
always to the disadvantage of the original. To Cocteau revision was a moral
error; the old poet is not the same person as the young poet although they
bear the same name.

   Auden's thoughts on Goodman aren't recorded. But as early as 1929 he
asked himself, "Do I want poetry in a play, or is Cocteau right: 'There is a
poetry in the theater, but not of it'?" Neither he nor Goodman ever created
for the stage with the inborn panache of Jean Cocteau, probably because, too
literarily convinced of what theater *ought* to be, they grew hamstrung before
the fact. Auden did translate two plays by Cocteau, of whom he wrote: "The
lasting feeling that his work leaves is one of happiness; not, of course, in the
sense that it excludes suffering, but because, in it, nothing is rejected, re-
sented, or regretted." That is the only good word he ever had for any
Frenchman of any period. He loathed France, the French and, as he termed
it, Frog culture.

✳

The foregoing play of comparisons could seem extravagant but for the lingering influence of Humphrey Carpenter's definitive thesis, of which each infectious page echoes the games of the protagonist, forever sizing up society and art through contrast and metaphor, and emphasizing that the best reviews are made from quotes. The very fact of the new book is itself an exercise in contradiction, Auden having claimed that "the biography of an artist, if his life as a man was sufficiently interesting, is permissible, provided that the biographer and his readers realize that such an account throws no light whatsoever upon the artist's work." He did add that "more often than most people realize his works may throw light upon his life"—this, despite earlier admonishments that his letters be burned. Such admonishments, of course, always mean "Don't burn my letters." So he had his cake—for posterity to eat. Now Carpenter has made an elaborate icing to Charles Osborne's memoir of 1979 (most of the anecdotes are identical, but the tone is less chatty, the narrative more thorough), serving also as complement to Edward Mendelson's historical interpretation of the poet's work up to 1939, *Early Auden*.

The youngest of three sons, Auden grew up in a secure and musical milieu, behaving ever afterward like a precocious favored child. His lapse at fifteen from the Anglican church ("people only love God when no one else will love them") coincided with a growing homosexual awareness, which in turn concurred with his emergence as a poet. The emergence came in a flash, fired by the offhand question of a chum at Gresham's boarding school:

> Kicking a little stone, he turned to me
> And said, 'Tell me, do you write poetry?'
> I never had, and said so, but I knew
> That very moment what I wished to do.

Until "that very moment" he was pondering a future as a mining engineer, and until he died he remained less drawn to the Mediterranean décor that was his eventual home than to the northern melancholy of factory neighborhoods which shaded so much of his work. As to stylistic landscape, he underwent the necessary influences—Frost, Hardy, Dickinson, Owen, de la Mare, Riding, Eliot—but achieved his own mature voice quite early. "An incurable classic," he labeled himself, and like a true classic—Ravel, for example—he can't be relocated by "periods": he sprang full-blown from the head of his muse, his coolly intelligent timbre altering little with the decades. Since the French are nothing if not also coolly intelligent (what did he think of Ravel?), Auden's Francophobia seems to have stemmed mainly from revolt against the Francophilic generation immediately preceding him. But he was also anti-Romantic, notwithstanding an abiding attraction to Freud (nothing if not Romantic), and given to psychoanalytic quips, both toward his own guilt about feeling guilty ("And that Miss Number in the corner/Playing hard to get;/Oh I'm happy I'm not happy,/Make me good Lord, but not yet"), and toward the psychosexuality of others, e.g., "Ackerley did not belong to either of the two commonest classes of homosexuals, neither to the 'orals' (among whom Auden placed himself) "who play son-and/or-Mother, nor to the anals who play Wife-and/or-husband . . ." Indeed, in the interests of high camp he often replaced "I" with "Mother," either to set matters straight (from the audience to a lecturer on Debussy: "Take it from Mother, *Pelléas* is shit!"), or to jar an over-solemn subjectivity ("Mother wandered lonely as a cloud").

At Oxford, despite doing badly on exams ("There is nothing a would-be poet knows he has to know"), he was already the famous leader of a gang that included Isherwood and Spender. To the latter he wrote: "My dominant faculties are intellect and intuition, my weak ones feeling and sensation. This means I have to approach life via the former; I must have knowledge and a great deal of it before I can feel anything."

"Feelings" began to turn up, along with a knack for suppressing them, in Berlin where the newly graduated Auden plowed the terrain before Isherwood made it notorious. There the poet became dazzled by one John Layard, a sort of precursor to J. D. Laing, and by his own notions of psychosomaticism which seemed to cover anything. "Rheumatism is simply a refusal to bend the joints, and therefore an indication of excessive obstinacy. Abnormal tallness such as Stephen Spender's is an attempt to reach heaven. Cancer and homosexuality are caused by the frustration of the wish to have a child."

Returning from Germany to Larchfield Academy in Scotland, later to Downs School at Colwall, he was, in the guise of schoolmaster, about to spend the most contented five years of his life. As eccentric ham and practical joker, as one who talked to all people on his own terms and not theirs, he was a born instructor. Like Kenneth Koch today, Auden showed schoolchildren that "poetry" was no more and no less than "memorable speech. We shall do poetry a great disservice if we confine it only to the major experiences of life. . . . Poetry is no better and no worse than human nature." Teaching also afforded him the leisure for book reviewing and essay writing ("It's awfully important that writers aren't afraid to write badly. . . . The moment you're afraid of writing badly . . . then you'll never write anything good"), for he hadn't previously developed a prose style. As for poems, his first collection was published in 1930 by T. S. Eliot at Faber & Faber which remained his English outlet until the end.

By 1932 his Communist sympathies allowed him to declare that "unless the Christian denies the value of any Government whatsoever, he must admit . . . the necessity for violence, and judge the means by the end," a viewpoint he would refute. Later he would refer to "the intellectual Communism" of his youth as "old-fashioned social climbing," though he was never embarrassed that his poems of the earlier period preached ideas to which he did not readily subscribe, for in poetry "all facts and beliefs cease to be true or false and become interesting possibilities."

In 1935 he switched careers dramatically, becoming scenarist for Government documentary films in which he collaborated regularly with Benjamin Britten, his first real work with a musician. Yet he was always a bit lofty about movies, and interrupted the work to co-write three plays with Isherwood, and to travel in Iceland, land of his forefathers, from where the news about Spain brought him back to the "real" world.

Before leaving for Spain, where he felt duty called, he wrote the best known and last of the lyrics whose subject is no longer explicitly homosexual, but on the impermanence of all interpersonal rapports: "Lay your sleeping head, my love/Human on my faithless arm." The Barcelona of 1937, with its open Communism, elated him less than the closed churches depressed him; how could his "side" stop people from doing what they liked, "even if it is something silly like going to church?"

The next year he traveled with Isherwood to China as professional correspondent, and, as with Iceland, made a book from it, *Journey to a War*. The two men returned to London by way of America where they were wined on red carpets, provided with "blond boys," and offered high fees (by British standards) for their writings. Neither of them put it immediately into words, but each one planned in his heart to emigrate, and they accordingly did the following January on the eve of World War II. The poet Richard Eberhart announced prophetically: "Auden's coming to America may prove as significant as Eliot's leaving it."

So much for the first half of the poet's life.

America offered Glory and Great Love. Glory, of course, had strings attached. "One makes more money by lecturing on poetry than by writing it." And there is evidence that had he bent to the Swedish Academy's demand that he retract remarks to the effect that Dag Hammarskjöld took himself for God, he would not have had to say stoically in 1964, and every year thereafter: "Well, there goes the Nobel Prize." It might be argued too that there was a decline in the energy, the *necessity*, of the later poems. Auden did have a trump card denied most poets, his prose, which increasingly and dazzlingly took over.

The Great Love also had drawbacks. Chester Kallman, a quick-minded student ("far cleverer than I"), a poet, very blond, son of an immigrant Latvian Jewish dentist ("It is in you, a Jew, that I, a Gentile, inheriting an O-so-genteel anti-Semitism, have found my happiness'), age eighteen, appeared at a time when Auden, at thirty-two, was fed up with one-night stands. If the older man enjoyed the Socratic role, he in turn learned from Chester who was a marvelous cook (though sloppy to a fault), a connoisseur of camp (everyone was "Miss this" or "Miss that") and, most importantly, a devotee of Bel Canto which Auden adopted completely ("No gentleman can fail to admire Bellini") along with Chester's aversion to Brahms. Chester meanwhile took on Auden's most dubious points, but his loud, drunkish opinions lacked authority because he lacked Auden's supporting gifts. Arrogance without talent is galling, but when certain friends recoiled from Chester—among them the gentle Britten, and even Auden's father—Auden credited their dislike to anti-Semitism and dropped them. Chester was cavalier with Auden as well, calling him "Miss Master," and, more gravely, halting permanently their sexual relationship while flaunting his own promiscuity. Their "marriage" was ultimately founded on the sympathy of mutual work which they accomplished while cohabiting, for better or worse, for three decades. One cannot know to what extent Auden's librettos, assuming he would have written any, might have been different had he worked them out with someone else—with Isherwood, for instance, who is unmusical, and so would not have let his text adapt an untheatrical preciosity due to "musical considerations." Nor can one know to what extent the librettos themselves might not be largely the work of Chester. Auden had answered Stravinsky's invitation to write the book for *The Rake's Progress* with: "I need hardly say that the chance of working with you is the greatest honour of my life." The work itself, while surely honorable, is hardly the greatest effort of either man (though it's Stravinsky's longest by far); but the real collaboration was between Chester and Auden, which Stravinsky used as a *fait accompli*. The fact remains that innumerable operatic adaptations of classics, plus four major operas—one by Stravinsky, two by Henze, one by Nabokov (none of whom had English as a mother tongue)—would never have existed, whatever their worth, were it not for the Kallman-Auden union. When Auden died, Chester survived him by little more than a year, stating that "my criterion is gone."

The remaining chronology is divided by Carpenter among six subjects:
Conversion. In 1940, aghast at what he perceived, in the Allies as in the Axis, to be "this denial of every humanistic value," he returned to the church. Long after the war when Auden, declaring himself an "old hand at this sort of thing," agreed to write a text for Stravinsky's elegy to Kennedy's memory, the composer said to Robert Craft: "Wystan is wholly indifferent to J.F.K.; what he cares about is form. And it is the same with his religion. What his intellect and gifts require of Christianity is its form—even, to go further, its uniform." Another musician, Marc Blitzstein, remarked: "Wystan doesn't love God, he's just attracted to him." Such *bon mots* in retrospect seem more glib than the poet. Auden had immersed himself in Kierkegaard ("the individual must either abandon himself to despair or throw himself on the mercy of God") who influenced his epic *New Year Letter* ("versified metaphysical argument is very difficult"). In the face of England's annoyance with his defection in time of war—Harold Nicolson called him "a disgrace to poetry"—Auden felt that "aloneness is man's real condition. . . . At least I know what I am trying to do, which most American writers do not, which is to live deliberately without roots." Those "American writers" with whom he lived, literally under one roof on Middagh Street in Brooklyn, were Gypsy Rose Lee and Golo Mann, Paul Bowles and Jane Bowles, Carson McCullers and George Davis, and also his countrymen Benjamin Britten and Peter Pears. Auden played Mother Superior to the motley household, presiding at meals and ordering punctuality, but kept private his weekly excursions to the Episcopalian Mass.
Crisis. Another motive for the return to God was his breakdown at discovering that Chester had taken another lover, a person whom he seriously planned to murder. The situation was aggravated when Chester's affair withered into a series of casual adventures which were to endure forever after. "His promiscuity is harder to take," Auden confided, "because it fills one with jealousy and anxiety for his spiritual welfare while a genuine love fills one with jealousy and respect."

> If equal affection cannot be,
> Let the more loving one be me.

. . . and he survived, as he always had and would, through routine: "The surest way to discipline passion is to discipline time."

Teacher Again. Routine, no matter how innovative his curriculum, is the teacher's sine qua non, and Auden relished his 1941–42 stint at Ann Arbor. He refused courses in so-called Creative Writing and modern poetry—"Poets who teach should keep as far as possible from their own field of work"— launching instead a syllabus ranging from Aeschylus to librettos, and forbidding his class to take notes, since "one person cannot really commmunicate anything specific to another." As usual, he arose each dawn to pursue work on *A Christmas Oratorio* as a memorial to his mother, the only work in which he used Christianity as a direct subject, for "culture is one of Caesar's things." In 1943–44 he taught at Swarthmore; in 1945 returned to Germany as a Bombing Research Analyst; in 1946 became at last an American citizen, went briefly to Bennington, had an affair with his secretary (female), spent a long season on Fire Island (". . . where nothing is wicked/But to be sorry or sick"), visited Tanglewood to hear Britten's *Peter Grimes* which left him lukewarm, and with whose composer he had a permanent falling out due partly to the failure of their operetta, *Paul Bunyan;* then moved back to Manhattan, living this time at 7 Cornelia Street where, when Spender once tried to let in some daylight, the curtains fell down ("You idiot! In any case there's no daylight in New York"). In 1947 *The Age of Anxiety* won the Pulitzer Prize. Auden was indifferent to the Bernstein-Robbins ballet composed on this long poem, but was overwhelmed when Stravinsky, the same year, approached him for a libretto. Thus began a permanent change of inventive focus, and the first of his long chain of co-billings with Chester.

Ischia. The 1950s saw Auden ever less in the United States. The decade began with *The Rake's Progress* Venetian première. Despite its success, Stravinsky never worked with Auden again (possibly because Auden announced far and wide that Britten, who had seen the score, liked everything except the music). Auden and Chester summered in Ischia now, and commuted to their new and final American apartment on Saint Mark's Place in New York. The Latin sunshine, some say, contributed to Auden's premature and bizarre wrinkling ("my face looks like a wedding-cake left out in the rain"). After a Residency at Oxford, he finally removed his summer abode, in 1957, to Kirchstetten. To live within reach of the Austrian opera houses attracted both Chester and Auden, who also relished the prospect of a German-speaking community. Yet Auden—and here is a paradox among great artists with an "eye" for words—had scant talent for either talking or writing foreign tongues. He was deeply moved at finally owning a home of his own ("what I dared not hope for/is, in my fifties, mine"), and although he never regretted quitting the Italian island, he wrote:

> . . . though one cannot always
> Remember exactly why one has been happy
> There is no forgetting that one was.

"*A minor Atlantic Goethe.*" While working on translations of Goethe, Auden came to think of the German poet as a "dishonest old hypocrite," and yet "Great Mr. G" grew into an image of what he himself hoped to achieve at this period of his life. His enduring prolificity and fame led Chester, now middle-aged and balding, to vanish for periods into Greece to lead his own life. Auden was lonely, drank, was obsessed about money, returned to Iceland and otherwise traveled widely as lecturer, revised his old works and worked unstintingly on new ones. He and Chester continued to work together on musical projects. But by the 1960s the world saw Auden as an unquestioned Absolute, a sort of Anglo-American Aschenbach as well as a deteriorating specimen on whom liquor, cigarettes and the airless years had taken their toll.

Return to England. He remained listed in the Manhattan phone book. When an anonymous caller announced, "First we will castrate you, then we will kill you," Auden was delighted by his quick reflex: "I'm afraid you have the wrong number." Yet he was increasingly unnerved by American violence. Though far from senile, he seemed incapable of give-and-take conversation; though far from self-pitying, he feared a coronary which might leave him dead and unapprehended on the bathroom floor. He arranged, for his own safety and for reasons of nostalgia, to become writer-in-residence at his Alma Mater where he moved in 1972. The move was a mistake, the old Oxford days were gone. As irony would have it, the dreaded heart attack occurred not in Oxford but in a Viennese hotel room. By further irony, however, it was not a chambermaid but Chester himself who found the body. The body is buried in his beloved Kirchstetten, and the lane where he lived is now named Audenstrasse. On the memorial marble in Westminster Abbey are engraved these lines from his elegy on Yeats:

> In the prison of his days
> Teach the free man how to praise.

Anyone who uses the phrase Great Artist must surely thus qualify Wystan Auden. Not only is his verse as strong, original and influential as any in English since Eliot, his work has a breadth generally linked to the notion of Great. As a man of the flesh Auden was a Master, insofar as the term obtains to those Romantic creators whose personae were no less viable than God or State: he was for half a century an intimidating and coercive leader, a well-trained organizer of the intellect and, not incidentally, a maker of Master-pieces. Two shortcomings, however, denied him the wreath of what the French call Sacred Monster. First, his sense of frivolity: the public of the Great frowns upon Charm. Second, he was just too young: the period of the Masterpiece, which ran roughly from Beethoven to Proust, could in a pinch be stretched to Mann or Picasso or Stravinsky, but ours is no longer an age of worshipping individuals, when even rock superstars are promoted as being like you and me.

Humphrey Carpenter's survey is a model of scholarship. It is virtually without editorializing, and almost willfully without style, a wise choice—if indeed choice is involved—since to write with style about style is to becloud the issue. If the book lacks the color and compassion of Millicent Dillon's concurrent biography of Jane Bowles (yes, the same Jane Bowles who in the famous house on Middagh Street served briefly as Auden's stenographer), that's because Auden was not a walking wound; he kept his wound at a distance as something to write a letter to (his chronic anal fissure became the object, not the subject, of a lengthy piece—"you are taking up more of my life every day"). If on the face of it Auden seemed invulnerable, it's that like many an artist with an iron will he could hold his vulnerability in abeyance, check it at the studio door.

Carpenter's book, considering its great length, has only the minimum of redundancies, mistakes in French and juxtapositions of chronology which disorient the reader. If the book errs—and I'm of mixed feelings about this—it is that Auden's ongoing libidinous history threads the pages as prominently as does his poetry. Are documenters of heterosexual poets—of Wallace Stevens, say, or William Carlos Williams, or even the rakish Dylan Thomas—as prone to detailing not only each gloomy romance but every casual pickup? When Carpenter goes beyond this, he has a knack for entering that studio door without calling attention to himself, and of collecting what he finds on the other side. The result is a treatise that appears all that will ever be needed on the remarkable subject.

Nantucket, July 1981

COURAGEOUS COWARD

On a cool but humid evening twenty-one springs ago I met Noël Coward in Paris's Club Élysée and we spent the rest of the night together. Next morning he listened carefully to my music which, unaccountably, he termed "forbidding," although he hoped I'd make an opera from one of his plays. That afternoon he flew back to London, and I never saw him again. Yet twelve years later when I read of his death I felt deprived of a friend; and at the small memorial service to which, for some reason, I received a golden invitation, I shed the gentle tears of loss, although in that show-biz milieu I was a fish out of water. Now I have just read Noël Coward's diary which I began with the double interest of one who knew the man (would he mention me?), and one who would review his words (should I mention "us"?). It is a very long book. But I learned less about Noël Coward in these nearly seven hundred pages than during that brief encounter in 1961.

I recall a man with style, vulnerability, vast culture and, above all, with a talent for listening which only the securely famous—they are few—seem to afford. And I recall a man involved with the passion and risks of romantic love. His journals portray a person not so much of style as of manner, with few self-doubts, knowing all the answers yet closed to the crafts that do not touch him—that is, to the darker sides of painting and music. Although that person is clearly gifted in the art of friendship, especially if the friends are rich and royal and celebrated, he would seem to have no private life, no ardent attachments, no sex. In one trembling transient entry he nearly succumbs to "that old black magic," but the tune is never taken up again. Indeed, his book would be just what Coward detractors might assume— brittle, sarcastic, straining for wit, a self-parody—were it not for the charm it exudes. Charm is the identifying escape hatch and valuable it is, for charm, even less than fame, cannot be bought or faked. Charm, which is the ability to ingratiate without cloying, can be sold, however, and it was Noël Coward's chief barter.

No small part of his charm lies in his naïveté, though this greatest of all sophisticates might be stunned to hear it said. I don't mean merely that his diary shows him to be as starstruck as you and I, although stars are his sole society and he is himself one. Rather, it is his cocksureness on matters he

knows little of. It is usual for us to admire jacks-of-all-trades in all their trades
save the one we ourselves practice. Among musicians I am surely not alone to
wince when Noël Coward writes, "The music is pouring out and I can
scarcely go to the piano without a melody creeping from my fingers, usually
in keys that I am not used to and can't play in." Yet his score for *Bittersweet* is
on a par with Gershwin who is on a par with Schubert. The paradox is that,
on a ground where angels fear to tread, Noël Coward a half-century ago
composed a sheaf of torch songs and waltzes more cherished than those of
many a modern master of technique. I'll never forget Noël stating proudly
that he, like Irving Berlin, was musically unlettered, or at least unnoted,
"despite my magic tunes which now form part of the collective unconscious.
I just play them into a dictaphone and they're taken down in shorthand by a
lackey." Then: "Lenny Bernstein's one of my greatest fans, but must I take
seriously his 'serious' music?"

About serious classical music, current and of yore, Noël Coward comments with forthright innocence, as though deaf to the diatonic logic of our
most inspired composers. A few samples: "Britten's music is dull, without
melody. It has the same effect on me as a Braque painting." "I hate Mozart
and I loathed the libretto *[Così fan Tutte]*." "I have taken to cooking and
listening to Wagner, both of which frighten me to death." "[Menotti] doesn't
seem capable of writing a true melodic line. It's all bits and pieces." "Madame
von Karajan had kindly invited me to her box. [The Beethoven] was quite
lovely at moments . . . until the choral part of the Ninth, when I got the
giggles." From the mouths of babes! The giggles, in my opinion, are the
proper response to this most overrated of masterpieces. Yet the response to
the lyricism of the young German composer Hans Werner Henze is perhaps
not quite thought through: ". . . *Ondine* at Covent Garden in which Margot
was superb, Freddie Ashton's choreography brilliant and the music tuneless
and hideous." Of my music (for yes, he mentions me) Coward quaintly
declares: ". . . an evening with Ned Rorem, avant-garde American composer, amiable but a trifle too 'advanced' for me," when even the most
reactionary critics have pegged me as backward.

Of serious musical performers he speaks even more strangely. Isaac Stern
(identified in a footnote as "distinguished Russian violinist") is described as
"brilliant, but looked dreadfully funny." ". . . dear Artur Rubinstein . . .
played the Schumann Concerto with exquisite taste but he is, poor darling,
looking a bit old." "I drove with the Queen Mother and we sat together in the
first row. Rostropovich really was marvellous, thank God, otherwise there
would have been grave danger of the giggles." He did admire Maria Callas as
"one of the few really great artists that I have ever seen"—seen, not heard.
The only other inclusions in this category are Laurence Olivier, and the
author of *African Genesis*, Robert Ardrey, "the most extraordinary brain I
have ever encountered." His crush on Joan Sutherland was colored by "how
thrilling to hear that glorious voice singing my music," while the Beatles in
1965 were simply "bad-mannered little shits [about whom] it is still impossible to judge from their public performance whether they have talent or not."

If Coward's musical appraisals are the conventional ones of the ignorant
literati, they reflect but a minor part of his concerns. But since they reflect on

my major concerns I stress them, because nobody else will. As a diarist Noël Coward has every right, literary and moral, to whatever passes his fancy, even to enumerating his opinions on music and eliminating his lusts.

The distinguishing trait of a diary as opposed to a memoir is on-the-spot reaction, the writer's truth as he feels it today. The intimate journal is a format used mainly by the French, who keep it as a sideline—a book about how hard it is to write a book. Not only France's authors, from Rousseau and Baudelaire to Amiel and Green, but her other artists too, like Berlioz and Delacroix, de Gaulle and Poulenc, have made literature of their lives. The genre has never been popular with non-French continentals, and is virtually unpracticed by Americans who, with all due liberation and collective carnality, do retain a decorum toward their personal selves. (We know more about the actual life of André Gide than we do about that of John Rechy.) If the British prefer autobiography, some of them—Virginia Woolf, Harold Nicolson—have kept journals, presumably for their eyes alone.

However, *The Noël Coward Diaries*, as they are posthumously named, were clearly penned for other eyes. His final written words in 1969: "I perceive now, 31 December, that there has been no entry since 7 September. With my usual watchful eye on posterity, I can only suggest to any wretched biographer that he gets my daily engagement book and from that fills in anything he can find and good luck to him, poor bugger." The poor bugger is Graham Payn, actor and longtime intimate of Coward, aided by Sheridan Morley, author of *A Talent to Amuse*. They might well have heeded an earlier entry: "It is a truly wonderful gift, my natural and trained gift for dialogue. . . . Other people far less clever than I can often be dead right when I am wrong. . . . I will never again embark on so much as a review sketch that is not carefully and meticulously constructed beforehand." Could the writer of those phrases have wished this book to appear as it stands? Except for about a hundred central pages Coward's diary is little more than a "daily engagement book." He drops names like old Rockefeller flung dimes to the people, meager tokens, promises of nothing. On VE Day: "Lunched at the Savoy with Lorn and we rested our poor feet. My Victory article appeared in the *Daily Mail* together with the King's speech and the Prime Minister's. Visited Mum. Went to Juliet [Duff]'s to have a drink and to see Georges Auric. Stayed on to dinner with Juliet and Desmond MacCarthy and took them both to see the Stage Door Canteen. Made a brief appearance and got a terrific ovation." Seventeen years later: "I dined one night with Ginette and George Axelrod. The next night with Dick Quine, Kim Novak, Bill [Holden], George [Axelrod], and Capucine, who is a dear. The third night by myself. Heaven. And the last night with George Cukor." The identities of—though not anecdotes about—these people, and scores of others, are found in the endless footnotes which adorn every page. Jerky reading. What it adds up to can seem silly, though in deference to the author's value, one might call it profoundly shallow. Anyway, silliness is germane to the diary-as-genre; the self-congratulatory musings of an Anaïs Nin are no less cloying in their solemnity than Noël Coward's in their glee.

A diary is the only literary form without rules; like a life, a diary can be said to take shape only when it is ended—that is, when it has died. This one spans but half a life, having been started only in 1941 (Coward was born in 1899) and continuing until 1969, three years before he died of a heart attack in his Jamaican villa. The reader might bear in mind that most of the work Coward is remembered for was completed long before this diary began.

Those hundred central pages are compelling as backstage scenes composed by an authority of timing. Because he is as famous as he thinks he is, and because when he gets going about some of his famous friends (he has no others), Coward's thumbnail portraits are definitive. If as a feminist he's old-fashioned (on Vivien Leigh: ". . . enchanting women can certainly wreak havoc when they put their silly minds to it"), he's acute on the Lunts ("Lynn is mentally slow with flashes of brilliant swiftness; Alfred quick as a knife with flashes of dreadful obtuseness. They are deeply concerned with only three things—themselves, the theater—insofar as it concerns themselves— and food, good, hot food"), or on sixty-ish Clifton Webb's puerile mourning of his mother ("There is no future in the past"), on sites like Las Vegas which he loved or the Actors Studio which he loathed, or, indeed, on the demands of his immediate geography (". . . it is no use imagining I can escape the consequences of my own fame and that I am bound to be set on and exploited by people wherever I go"). As a pacifist I am personally nervous about his insights on the meaninglessness of war when they are balanced by blind patriotism—royalist to the core—and defenses of capital punishment "as a deterrent." But it's fun to hear about Marlene and Gertrude and Larry and Tallulah and Diana and Princess Margaret and Tony and Bob Hope and the Queen herself and all from the horse's mouth, and how they do adore him, and how awfully hard he works, yet travels incessantly despite his several lavish homes and his kidney stone, but his Big Opinions are generally bro- mides even on atomic energy or on the sickness of pals, although the tale of his Mum's agony and death rings true in its terse excruciation. The rapports he claims to value most, however, are those, not with, say, the difficult Claudette Colbert, but with the wise Rebecca West who did join him at a Swiss clinic where they each had the hormonal youth treatment by being injected with the liquefied organs of an unborn calf, or something of the sort.

Who is this self-confident creature with the inscrutable mien of an Oriental sage in white tie and tails, that we should devour his daily thoughts? Com- parisons are fragrant.

In 1946 he makes his sole entry on Jean Cocteau: ". . . we went to *La Belle et la Bête*, which I rechristened *La Belle et la Bêtise* on account of it being long, dull and badly constructed, but *d'un beauté* [sic] *formidable* every now and then. I wish creative artists like Jean did not consider it necessary to be 'precious,' 'amusing' and 'different.'"

Well, it takes one to know one. Probably Jean Cocteau and Noël Coward were not much interested in each other—any more than the French and English ever are—each being so quintessentially of his country. Yet they are more comparable than any two artists of different nationality in our century, and no other *bricoleur*, not even da Vinci, has ever remotely resembled them. In an age of specialists they were general practitioners excelling in every area:

poetry and playwrighting, essays and novels, moviemaking and movie acting, librettos and cabaret lyrics, oil painting and set designing. If Coward in
being a composer—and a real one—went Cocteau one better, the latter was
the more astute prosifier *about* music. Both were aphorists, and both made
their personal selves—their very bodies—into public exhibits. Coward was
Cocteau's junior by exactly ten years. Both died at seventy-three and the
deaths in each case followed shortly after the highest national homage: for
Cocteau an entrance into the Académie Française, for Coward a knighthood.

Diaghilev's notorious *Étonne-moi* which so shaped the future of Jean Cocteau could have been paralleled by an *Amuse-moi* to Noël Coward. One might
reasonably argue that Cocteau represents Coward's deeper nature; that
Orphée and *Blithe Spirit* are the somber and bright faces of the same medal;
that *Les Parents terribles* and *Private Lives* are but the sad and happy versions of
the same boulevard comedy; that their many solos for prima donnas were, so
to speak, identical twins of opposite sex; and that in short Noël was the
optimist's Jean. Both wore their charm as armor against a press which,
though benign in their dazzling childhoods, consistently massacred their
middle lives, relaxing only for the triumphant comebacks in the shadow of
death. If Noël lacked the imagination of Jean, and even the basic chic (Noël
backward—Léon—is French slang for hick), neither was he ever the anxious
sycophant that Jean could sometimes be. Cocteau's movies aimed higher and
endured longer, while Coward's plays seem to have more staying power.

Cocteau's influential antecedents were on the whole inferior to him, and he
worshipped them. (Montesquiou and Rostand *fils*, for example, were precious hacks.) Coward, on the other hand, descends from the great Oscar
Wilde through Somerset Maugham. But Wilde for Coward "was one of the
silliest, most conceited and unattractive characters that ever existed." While
Maugham as a serious novelist embodied, in his own words, the best of the
second-rate, Coward as a giddy dramatist was the best of the first-rate.
Coward himself claims the nineteenth-century playwright Clyde Fitch, of all
people, as predecessor. "His writing is undoubtedly trivial," Coward tells us,
"and his view of life largely circumscribed by the times in which he lived, but
they are full of entertainment value, well made and every now and then
witty. . . . Of course he was decried by the critics; anyone so immediately
successful would be. There is a certain analogy between him and me, I think,
except that my scope is wider and I think and hope that I have a little more
depth, even in my comedies. In those days, of course, the theater was still a
place of entertainment and not a platform for propaganda and orgies of racial
self-pity." Yes, Coward was revolted by all the angry young men; yes, he
was elitist ("I have no real rapport with the 'workers'," he noted in 1942, "in
fact I actively detest them *en masse*"); and yes, he was obsessed and devastated
by reviewers who, despite his continued popular success, treated him as an
anachronism after the war. "It is foolish for a writer constantly to decry the
critics," he observed in 1964 for the thousandth time; "it is also foolish for the
critics so constantly to decry anyone who writes as well as I do."

If I am ambivalent about him, seemingly unable to react except through
my own piecemeal diary-like paragraphs, it's that I am ambivalent about

myself. During my Chicago infancy Noël Coward was an idol, but he was not *my* idol; I never felt his spell as I did the vastly grander Cocteau's, and was repelled as much as attracted by his oeuvre. Like Auden—who in 1926 was busy writing "unreal" plays and put down Noël Coward's realistic drama by asking "Is it like this/In Death's other kingdom?"—I seemed vaguely trapped in my generation, gazing at the indolent wit of the irretrievable past while simultaneously focusing only dimly on the dutiful violence ahead. I craved both luxury and sparsity in art, and Noël was only luxury. No ambivalence about Coward himself, though. Unlike the greatest artists who are a sum of contradictions, sacred and profane, he was just what he seemed—his life and his art were one.

Uneasy as I was made by the superficiality of his book, I, who am morbidity incarnate and who also keep a diary, was nonetheless elated by his ability ever to rise above adversity, mainly by sheer conceit. Courageous Coward! (Some readers act annoyed at this conceit, as though the childlike honesty of it were not endemic to every creator, good and bad.) He had a lot of fun being Noël Coward, and I'm envious. When I asked him, on that evening so many years ago, what he thought the ideal life was, he answered simply, "Mine."

Nantucket, September 1982

SHAW:

THE GREAT COMPOSERS

All composers are verbally literate but few authors are musically literate, and those few who nicely write about music write as lovers more than as connoisseurs. Nietzsche, Gide and Pound did speak with learning on compositional processes, but the learning—come to by years of hit or miss, then proferred in hushed tones—could have been garnered in a week of applied counterpoint. Forster, Proust and Huxley wove musical phraseology into their fiction's fabric, always colorful and sometimes even wise, though with the shading and wisdom of precocious amateurs. If Thomas Mann with his *Doctor Faustus* was so professionally accurate in technical excesses of method that he created the first make-believe composer who did not make real composers wince, that method's actual begetter, Arnold Schoenberg, sued Mann for plagiarism—and won.

The only pro author whose lay comments on music cannot somehow be laughed off seems to be Bernard Shaw; even *his* enthusiasts emerge mainly from beyond the fringe. When Eric Bentley, prefacing an early collection, cites Auden—"Shaw is probably the best music critic who ever lived"—we hear one non-musician vouching for a second non-musician about a third. Now, if composers have not always been fine critics (Schumann, Wagner, Debussy), the finest critics have always been composers (Berlioz, Tovey, Thomson). Still, in perception and style, not to mention girth (six fat books), Shaw in his time, as an educated layman, became more clear-minded a muckraker than any, and his credentials were good.

His sister had a beautiful voice, though "her very facility," wrote the younger brother, "prevented her from becoming a serious artist." But their mother was an established opera singer, and her Dublin household for many years contained one George Vandaleur Lee, a successful manager who rehearsed performances in the parlor, immersing the young Shaw in the backstage ambience he adored. An ungainly executant, Shaw nonetheless learned, in those pre-phonograph days, to sight-read scores well enough to gain vast practical, theoretical and historical know-how. In 1876, at age twenty in London, with Mr. Lee's help the penniless young man became a ghost music critic—or "musical critic," as they qualified the job in Victorian jargon—for *The Hornet*. Eventually he served as regular reviewer on *The Star* and *The World* between 1888 and 1894, working under the pseudonym of Corno di Bassetto. He produced a book, *The Perfect Wagnerite*, and dozens of occasional articles on music almost until he died in 1950. A few years before that final event Shaw reminisced on his Irish youth versus his English fashionability. "To this day I look to the provincial and the amateur for honesty and genuine fecundity in art." That dangerous motto determined the tone of his critical writing.

Now Louis Crompton, Professor of English (another non-musician) at the University of Nebraska, has expertly assembled a huge wreath of Shavian musicana curving around a central theme, Shaw's view of greatness, and held together by choices which focus more on what is played than on who plays it. Readers are thus deflected from Shaw's privileged vantage on performance— on the now irretrievable pulses and pauses and pastels of a Calvé or Richter or Eames—and guided toward compositional values which they can perceive on equal footing: Shaw's veneration of Wagner, contempt of Gounod, ignorance of Fauré, laceration of Liszt, indulgence of Elgar. If some who know him solely as dramatist and social reformer are jolted to learn that Shaw was a canny (and paid) commentator on his earliest love, for others who are not really so old, yet who could have spoken with him, the jolt comes in realizing that calendrically Shaw was closer to Chopin than to us. Suspending disbelief we watch him flog many a still-breathing nineteenth-century horse.

Like any caring thinker he clung to tight biases, and like every viable inventor he structured his *trouvailles* on eccentricity. His biases were Bach, Handel, Mozart, Beethoven and especially Wagner whose life overlapped his own by twenty-six years, and whose "truth" he took as yardstick by which to size up all music. His eccentricity lay in the promoting of currently vanished ciphers like Hermann Goetz ("the only real symphonist since Beethoven") at the expense of Schubert ("a more exasperatingly brainless composition was never put on paper"), Brahms ("nothing more than a sentimental voluptuary") or Tchaikovsky ("no distinction, no originality, no feeling for the solo instrument, nothing to rouse the attention or occupy the memory"), and in raising Wagner to the skies.

To doubt Wagner's genius is to provoke a tantrum chez Shaw. He is at his literary best with artists he loves but does not forcibly idolize (Beethoven, for example, whose "diagnostic is his power of unsettling us"), or with charting aspects of the past. (On the then unadmitted decline of religious music: "One hundred and fifty years ago it was still possible for a first-rate intellect to believe that in writing for the Church its powers were enjoying their worthiest use.") Less pertinent are predictions. If England since Purcell has "been blotted out of the music-map of Europe . . . [and] what broke English music was opera," Shaw was mistaken that redemption could not come through the theater because "the Englishman is musical, but he is not operatic." Benjamin Britten, explicitly with his operas and within Shaw's lifetime, single-handedly put England back on the map. Healthy are his arguments against both dogmatist and Philistine ("learn thoroughly how to compose a fugue, and then *don't* . . . Fugues are unsaleable, a musician can make more money without them.") Healthy too are his own quasi-Philistinisms: "A successful revolutionist's first task is to shoot all revolutionists"; though Mozart was no such thing, nor even "the founder of a dynasty: in art the highest success is to be the last of your race, not the first." "Bishops are generally wrong, just as Judges are always wrong." "Justice is not the critic's business." Yet Shaw judged: "We have in Liszt's *Preludes* a far better example of appropriate form than any of the 'regularly constructed' works of Mendelssohn"; while Liszt's "devotion to serious composition seems a hopeless struggle against natural incapacity." "Schumann was greater as a musical enthusiast than as a constructive musician." "The chief glory of Victor Hugo as a stage poet was to have provided libretti for Verdi." "*La Traviata* is before its time instead of behind it—it is a much more powerful work than *Carmen*, which everybody accepts as typically modern."

Although Rossini may well be "one of the greatest masters of claptrap," Shaw elsewhere perceives the composer as truly "great in spite of himself." Meyerbeer too, "whose merits are now rarely disputed" (time passes), is given high marks, as is Grieg who, along with his singing wife, receives the only physical portrait in the book; and though Shaw claims to despise "pretty music," he is pleased by the Norwegian's small gifts, however unworthy they may be to bestow on Peer Gynt.

Although Shaw not infrequently drops a French term, correct if superfluous, into the heart of a sentence whence, like a bath crystal, it spreads out to tint the whole paragraph, the term invariably illustrates some Teutonic oeuvre. For Shaw was immune to the graces of France. Except for Offenbach's "wicked music" ("every accent in it is a snap of the fingers in the face of moral responsibility: every sparkle on its surface twits me for my teetotalism, and mocks at the early rising of which I fully intend to make a habit some day"), and, more tepidly, Gounod ("who does not express his ideas worse than Handel; but then he has fewer ideas to express"), Shaw is unreasonable and cranky with the French who "would be a very tolerable nation if only they would let art alone." He was more at ease in England, though a bit off the beam with his favorite Elgar who "could turn out Debussy and Stravinsky music by the thousand bars for fun in his spare time."

Necessarily excluded from this volume (which deals in greatness, not in performance), is a valiant side of Shaw which all "musical critics" possess: an innate cognizance of so-called popular art, and a willingness to treat it, when it so deserves, as seriously as "serious" art. His 1894 appraisal of the young Yvette Guilbert, a grand free soul of vaudeville (Parisians never use that French word, saying instead *le music hall*), in its skill at evoking exactly the sight and sound of this *artiste* in all her verve and folly, is on a lofty par with our own Virgil Thomson's limning of Edith Piaf. Less chivalrous was Shaw toward the *Requiem* of his British contemporary, Dame Ethel Smyth, perhaps the first woman composer ever to present herself as an equal to men. Yet though Shaw advances bits of sexist wit ("Miss Smyth's decoration of the mass," "the orthodoxy of the lady," "her powers of expression do not go beyond what the orchestra can do for her"), he shows himself a true feminist by declaring that "since women have succeeded conspicuously in Victor Hugo's profession, I cannot see why they should not succeed equally well in

Liszt's if they turned their attention to it." That he is proved right a century later is indisputable, though his implication was that no woman can be a Bach.

For Shaw the greatest music has, or should have, literal sense, connotations beyond itself, even moral effects, and this explains his prejudice against absolute—or what he names "decorative"—music (he accommodates Bach uneasily by calling Bach's method "unattainable"), his affinity to Wagner's lyric dramas (pacifist though he was, Shaw nevertheless championed Nazi-esque superman sentiments), and his urge to read "meaning" into abstract areas like the early movements of Beethoven's Ninth (which I, for one, find vulgar, though Shaw says "vulgarity is a necessary part of a complete author's equipment"). He posits the questionable premise that "the greatest of the great among poets, from Aeschylus to Wagner, have been poet-musicians: how then can any man disdain music or pretend to have completed his culture without it?" Well, Henry James disdained music, and so did Kafka and T. S. Eliot, yet who will define their culture as incomplete? And was Wagner a great poet?

Bernard Shaw played Pied Piper to a huge following for whom he could do no wrong, and who have kept the flame burning undisturbed. Yet if the Great Man could say of a treatise by his colleague, Sir Charles Parry, "Somebody must act as devil's advocate in his case; out of pure friendliness, therefore, let me try to find a little fault with his book," one could as quickly act the devil for Shaw. Among his lesser offenses is fuzzy grammar (clauses of Proustian size but lacking in modifiers, or antecedents, or indeed, predicates), for he was a long distance runner who wouldn't look back. Defensive sarcasm about his critical force as opposed to others' weakness draws attention to his long-winded self and away from the subject at hand. Long-winded, ah yes. In Shaw's total nonfiction output as in the present hand-picked specialties, a good half of the trees are hidden behind this cutup's forest of dead wood.

A good music critic is one who makes readers experience in sight what they may have missed last night in sound, one who brings readers to a keener viewpoint—or earpoint—on music they may already know, or wish to know. The effect is accomplished by description, not opinion. If description is accurate, opinion cannot but simmer through, and need not be strained for. Obviously the two stances can intermesh or I wouldn't be practicing what I preach, since in this article, in describing Shaw's work by letting him often speak for himself, opinion has pressured my choice of quotes. Shaw's ability to deal with his material as represented in this collection—nineteenth-century musical creators in northern Europe—may be more secure and original than I seem to allow. Insofar as Shaw himself allowed opinion to govern his hand he was tiresome and uninformative, but when his knack for description soared he was unsurpassable.

Nantucket, August 1978

THREE

THE MUSICAL VOICE

TEACHING AND PERFORMANCE

A commencement speaker is invited presumably because he knows something the listeners don't, because that something is worth knowing and because he knows how to impart the knowledge. If he happens to be a composer he is invited because of his reputation as a composer. By nature speakers are thinkers, composers are makers. A composer may be a thinker too, but that is a sideline to his function; in the ideal world he would never be called upon, as a composer, to voice an opinion.

Ought the ideal composer-as-speaker be able to tell you how to compose? Why not just play his music? since music lives or dies despite its author's blurbs.

Critics of words use words. Critics of music use words. The best comment on a work of art should be another work of art. Yet here I am this morning without music to hide behind.

Since it is hopeless to verbalize a composer's inside world, maybe some random notions touched with reminiscence about the outside world will prove useful.

Certain nightmares forever haunt musicians—like appearing naked on a stage where you are supposed to sing an opera you do not know in a voice you do not possess.

I was a student in these hallowed halls one hundred and fifty-six seasons ago. My earliest songs were written here at eighteen, the lonely age of First Times. I still remember, pungent as yesterday, the lemony fragrance of tea poured on Wednesdays by the ivory hand of Mrs. Bok (who later that year we were tutored to call Mrs. Zimbalist), and still taste the black coffee in the Crillon Tavern across the square where I lingered, hung over, late to a class for which I'd done no work. I still see those December snowflakes at the windows as I practiced Chopin for Freda Pastor, and still hear Good Humor wagons through the same windows reopened in April during Menotti's seminar, to the bemused aspect of classmates whose minds were far away.

School stresses minds, yes, but coincides with the heart expanding like a rose to the first icy-hot blasts of sex and art, and becoming prey to the fun and horror that will endure until it ceases to beat. Though I left Curtis long ago, I still feel the same queasiness about the future that you who are about to graduate must feel, and also perhaps the same enthusiasm. Meanwhile, what have I learned about music's two realest aspects, teaching and performing, as they apply to the composer?

To teach means to demonstrate before the fact. To compose means to demonstrate after the fact. Good teaching is a constructive contagion: it leads a student through college and makes him think.

Teachers know, composers know how. Teacher and composer may inhabit one body. But for the composer teaching turns to danger; after the first year he starts to believe what he says, thus to repeat himself; that is fatal for his music. Teachers, however, may repeat themselves with impunity since repetition is the crux of learning.

Some students are bored by yesterday; you can't teach a young dog old tricks. Of course, tricks are by definition new; when they're old they're rules.

A teacher takes joy in other people's self-discovery. A composer takes joy in other people's joy in *his* self-discovery—a joy edged in pain which adds to its worth like goldplate on silver.

Painters and poets are seldom asked about craft, but composers always get the question: How do you hear those notes in your head? In infancy everyone is shown how to draw and to write; even without talent we can all shape mud pies and rhyme cat with rat. Yet, while we also learn to sing, we are not shown how what we sing is made. If basic notation were taught in kindergarten, people would never maintain that composition is a mystery. Music is not mysterious, but education makes it so.

Teaching necessarily precedes learning, even when you teach yourself. Composition students don't learn by instruction but by imitation. Can composition be taught? Composition, unlike, say, orchestration, is not a practical science, so can only be judged after the fact: a composer cannot show a pupil how to get ideas, he can only show what is wrong with the ideas once they're gotten. Yet the rudiments of form are there to be taught to anyone.

Plays and books and movies and dance are mostly contemporary. The music we hear is mostly a century old. Contempt may breed contempt, but familiarity breeds only familiarity. My utopian nursery features an "appreciation" course just on today's music. Back in the eras when music was no mystery, the present alone was considered while the past had to shift for itself. Most audiences today are probably bored most of the time with most music, especially the classics, but they don't resent the classics because they are used to them and only *hear* them. Modern music impels listening, hence reaction. People hate to react. Logically the music most meaningful to people of today is music of today because it is steeped in today. Today may be hard because it is alive, and life is hard, but this hardness talks to us even when we don't like what it says, whereas the classics approach us like sleepwalkers.

Sleepwalkers are predictable, even when standing atop skyscrapers. And the risk is theirs, not ours—like a coloratura reaching for that high F in a

Rossini aria. When the coloratura comes back to earth, we clap. But is it *her* high F or Rossini's we applaud?

How can we know the dancer from the dance? By forgetting the dance, and by heeding critics for whom, as for the public, there is only a question of the dancer. New ballets are often reviewed with no mention of their music. The play's not the thing. In our universe players, not creators, are stars. The coloratura's fee for one appearance could pay for a composer to write a whole opera.

Recently, along with revolution in more urgent areas, composers of quite different aims have become live-and-let-live. They even peddle one another's wares because they are united against establishment stars who ignore them. Gone is the time when composer and executant were one. Today they seldom meet. Players face out, composers in. When occasionally they do bump against each other, fireworks ignite.

A few summers ago Barbara Kolb and I were the token composers at Marlboro, that haven for great soloists who come each year to forget their fame and to practice German chamber music together. One courtesy offered guest composers at Marlboro is a performance by the stars. The performers that Kolb had mainly known before were of that accurate rare breed of New Music Specialist funded by Paul Fromm. Here she was now, rehearsing her hard new work with General Practitioners of nineteenth-century masterpieces. "How's it going?" I asked, expecting to hear: They don't know what they're doing. "They're terrific," she answered. "They play it like music, not like Modern Music."

Appropriately, these stars treat the sounds of their time, without condescension, as all in a day's work. However, "It's O.K. for Marlboro," they say, "but real audiences don't want modern music." Although in fact, the public takes what it's given. Fire, not repertory, draws the moneyed moth. So then the soloists confess that modern music does not show them off, or that, as in the case of singers, it wrecks the instrument. But is it not their starlight which should instead show off the music? and in the case of singers, is it program or training which wrecks the instrument?

The star system is the direct cause for the stalemate in the dissemination of contemporary American music.

Yesterday on TV I saw a class of young lawyers being graduated from a Rhode Island college. The speaker italicized duty, saying: "What for your clients is a once-in-a-lifetime emergency, for you will be a daily occurrence." The newscaster then added: "Most of these ex-students will spend the next year looking in vain for jobs."

Is their plight easier than ours? In this, the most civilized land on the planet where more and more young adults can neither read nor write, good music floats like a rarefied breeze, not so much unappreciated as unheard. But while the lawyer (if he finds a job) must deal with passing trouble, the musician (job or no job) will deal with lasting beauty, and that is a large consolation.

Let me recapitulate and add a coda to these scattered paragraphs.

The art of words and the art of notes answer to separate calls; for if the various arts could express each other we would need only one. Were a composer able to say what it means to compose, he would not need to compose.

Thus I have wished to speak to you socially, yet with an ax to grind. To justify the grinding, I hoped first to show that you and I are much alike, with the crucial difference that I have a longer past, and have used that past exclusively to discover how one American composer ticks. I have learned that true musicians need not be well-rounded if they have viewpoint, but that musicians whose viewpoint does not first focus on the composer put the cart before the horse. Insofar as we are all musicians we are fellows, vaguely strange to outsiders. Yet as fellows we split into categories, makers and doers, working at cross-purposes.

These cross-purposes start in grammar school, grow through college, and spread out across the careers of concertizers whose obsession with the classics leaves their creative colleagues out in the rain.

To go forth as a serious artist, even for the highly successful, means to go into a world which largely doesn't care. Hence it is imperative that *we* care, since our rewards are less from Mammon, or even God, than from ourselves. If, as Wilde claimed, "All art is quite useless," music is the most useless because, unlike a painting, it cannot be owned as an investment. If, as Auden claimed, "Poetry makes nothing happen," music makes less than nothing happen because, unlike words, it has no propaganda value. But these claims are economic and do not concern the spirit.

The spirit in other arts is fed by the new. We speak of the plays of Chekhov, or even of O'Neill, as revivals, yet would never refer to, say, Beethoven's Ninth as a revival, so regularly drenched are we in its comfortable sounds.

The saying that "Those who can, do; those who can't, teach" is belied by the Curtis faculty where teachers and doers are one. You are the harvest of that faculty, which includes me—a composer. As a composer let me say:

To you instrumentalists who are about to become professional chamber players, soloists, even stars: emphasize the present, and the past will fall into place. To you who will go into orchestras: tell your conductor (if you dare) to promote the living and to let the dead fall where they may. To you who are vocalists: do not sing in languages you cannot speak, but copy your foreign colleagues by learning your own language first; the catalogue in English is vast and valuable. To you who will be teachers: help your students to be kind to live music by befriending live composers. And to you live composers: good luck. Because our culture will finally be judged not by performers but by what they perform. For that culture to survive we do not need the past so much as we need each other.

May 14, 1982

THE AMERICAN ART SONG

What, you may well ask, is an art song? I myself had composed dozens before ever hearing the term, and suddenly realized—like the Molière character who learns he's been speaking prose all his life—how clever I'd been. Yet then as now I mistrusted the term, found it pompous, never used it. For "art song" is not a description but an opinion, defensively American, coined to distinguish the genre—in kind if not in quality—from "pop song."

The genre may be defined as the musical setting of a lyric poem for one voice with piano accompaniment. The setting is by a specific American composer as opposed to anonymous or collective authorship; is self-contained as opposed, say, to an aria, which is part of a whole; and is strictly as opposed to approximately notated like so-called popular songs (even such sturdy hits as Gershwin's or Sondheim's), which can be rendered by any voice in any arrangement at any speed. "Art song" is our answer to the German *Lied* or to the French *mélodie*, which implies a through-written recital song as distinct from a *chanson*. But the distinction is fading between recital songs and those performed elsewhere: "good song" and "bad song" are logically the clearest distinguishing terms. This brief essay will refer simply to "song," assuming that readers now recognize the species.

I showed those first songs of mine to Virgil Thomson, that best of all possible songsmiths, with whom in 1944 I was studying in New York. All he said was, "Janet Fairbank would love them," and picked up the phone.

She lived on the then uniquely tree-lined, almost rural, block of Fifty-fifth between Lexington and Park. The tone of that street is as vanished today as the viewpoint evinced in the soprano's apartment. Janet Fairbank, a plain but stylish and well-off Wisconsin "bachelor girl" (as she called herself), chose to inhabit a two-room walk-up with a hot plate and an upright, and to spend all her money on "modern music." If her voice, though firm, was neither agile nor very pleasing, it did possess a more infecting theatricality than many another non-voiced specialist since. Again, unlike the others, she neither deluded herself about her voice nor thought of herself as performing a service to American song. Without sanctimony, she performed from sheer affection, mildly astonished at the small but solid public she drew to her annual concert

225

of always new songs. Also, she had no competition. Oh, there *was* a host of
terrific professionals around: Priscilla Gillette, Mina Hager, Romolo di Spirito, Alice Howland, William Horne, William Haines, Naomi Farr, Lys Bert,
Ethel Luening (wife of composer Otto Luening), and of course Mack Harrell,
Povla Frijsh, Nell Tangeman and Jennie Tourel. But theirs was a generalized
vocabulary of the unhackneyed, whereas Fairbank had a specific monopoly
on current Americana.

From floor to ceiling her rooms burst with manuscripts begged from or
offered by live composers. For twelve months, replacing her regular accompanist Henry Jackson, I served as her rehearsal pianist, daily sorting through
this virgin morass.

We worked hard on new songs by William Ames, Ernest Bacon and
Harold Brown (whose mysterious "Alisoun" seems now to be lost); on Paul
Bowles's "David" and Theodore Chanler's "Doves." Henry Cowell, whom
one doesn't think of as writing songs, gave Janet a "Toccanta" with a flute
obbligato and also "The Donkey." David Diamond's "Brigid's Song" and
"David Mourns for Absalom" (to name but two masterpieces from the perhaps eight-score by this man) turned up and were memorized, as were settings by John Duke, Norman Dello Joio and especially Celius Dougherty,
who cracked the dangerous secret for the perfect encore by musicalizing the
dictionary definition of Love. Where has John Edmunds gone? He is not so
much underrated as unknown, yet at least half his four hundred songs (like
many a song composer he tends to be only a song composer) are program-
mable. Consider "The Cherry Tree," "The Isle" or his Purcell realizations.
Edmunds rates a plaque for his lifelong proselytizing on behalf of Song in
English. Lou Harrison concocted just for Janet his rousing "Sanctus," which,
in the words of Virgil Thomson, "opened up the gates of heaven and brought
down the house," while Quincy Porter offered her his prize "Music When
Soft Voices Die." Still more songs came from Normand Lockwood and John
Lessard, from Douglas Moore (svelte versions of Donne sonnets), and from
the very young Charles Naginski, whose career ended before it began when
he drowned in the Tanglewood lake. If Paul Nordoff's "Lacrima Cristi" was
a gem flawed only by a mawkish text, texts chosen by Daniel Pinkham erred
not. Janet liked to use Pinkham's version of the anonymous "Faucon" to open
a group with three other settings of the same stanzas (by Edmunds, Ramiro
Cortes and me).

Fairbank publicly performed all these songs (of which the manuscripts
now lie in Chicago's Newberry Library) in Carnegie Recital Hall or in the
old Times Hall on West Forty-fifth. More important, nearly all were
printed, under her aegis, by Richard Dana's Music Press. Songs being an
even less marketable commodity than squid eggs or poetry, it is creditable
that these publications, later sold to Mercury and eventually passed on to
Presser, remain to this day in stock, many bearing an inscription to their
Onlie Begetter.

For Janet *was* American Song, to a point where *Time* magazine itself finally
reviewed her, stressing the point that she was not crazy ("No nut stunt for
Janet"). Surely her sense of responsibility to her vocation acted as a revivify-
ing serum. At forty-four, stricken with Hodgkin's disease, she had already

crossed the deadline set by doctors. She did not, however, survive to witness her certain mark of permanence, the lovely brown-and-green Music Press editions.

I recall the afternoon in October 1947: Doorbell and phone rang simultaneously. A messenger delivered the thrilling complimentary copies of my first published song, "The Lordly Hudson" on Paul Goodman's poem, dedicated to Janet Fairbank. On the wire Eva Gauthier was saying that Janet had died that morning.

Next day, like the consolatory angel, Goodman came bearing a poem that begins:

The end of music is still silence,
the end of desire is still sleep.

Eva Gauthier, she of the blue hair and endless supply of satin hats, inhabited a tiny flat in the now defunct Hotel Woodward on East Fifty-third, with an upright Knabe, ten crates of scores and a yapping Pekingese. Mme. Gauthier was four feet ten inches worth of experienced opinion, always precise, sometimes precisely wrong. Was she already seventy when I began playing for her coaching sessions in 1947? Certainly she was from an era of inexpert sight-readers—from when prima donnas did not decipher. Debussy had taught her Yniold in *Pelléas et Mélisande* by rote, she claimed. She also claimed intimacy with Ravel and Gershwin, showing us her programs devoted exclusively to this pair. During those programs she changed garb with each group, involving vast swatches of stuff from Java, where for years she had lived with an importer husband. Her tendency to the graphic, or to getting things slightly off center, titillated those youngsters who came to her after the war. To a young tenor after singing Fauré's "Prison": "Keep in mind that this poem was conceived by Verlaine in jail where he was put for cutting off Van Gogh's ear." To another tenor excusing his high A's because of a cold: "Be glad you don't have to hit them during your period, with blood seeping onto the stage." To me, about to accompany her in the demonstration of a scene from *Pelléas*: "Skip the rests, it's mood that counts."

But what a fantastic teacher, if "teacher" means one whose enthusiasm is transferable—who leads horses to water and makes them drink. Gauthier's enthusiasm was for the *intelligence* of music, and though she couldn't read music she could talk it.

What students sought from Pierre Bernac in Paris and from Maggie Teyte in London—French repertory from someone who knew the words—they could find from the Canadian Gauthier in New York, plus the bonus of native literature. The songs Fairbank discovered in the early forties, Gauthier was now teaching in the late forties; so far as she was concerned those songs were *faits accomplis*, normal and needed as Schubert. After her death Jennie Tourel remained the only active singer in New York (the musical center of the world!) equipped to coach Franco-American repertory. Today, no one.

What literary sources most attracted American composers during the thirties and forties? Usually not American ones. Except for Cummings, whom virtually everyone was setting, and of course Whitman, the poets came mainly from the British Isles and from the past: from the England of dark ballads, Chaucer, and also, naturally, Shakespeare, Donne, Herrick and Blake. A great deal of Yeats and Joyce (though copyright permissions weren't always granted) and vast portions of the King James Bible. Even so quintessential an American as Copland went to the Old Testament for his largest choral work and to Arthur Waley for his earliest song. Except for Chanler's Father Feeney, Thomson's Gertrude Stein and my own Paul Goodman, none of our composers had their "house" writer as Schumann had Heine or Poulenc had Éluard. Thus when Paul Bowles around 1949 published his *Blue Mountain Ballads* based on poems by a man of the hour, Tennessee Williams, the effect seemed at once eccentric and awfully fresh. But it hardly set a trend.

Serious composers have always set words from the past far more than words by their contemporaries. This is no less true of Brahms and Beethoven with the Corinthians and Goethe than of Palestrina and Machaut with their liturgy. Boulez has used Mallarmé more than he has used Char. Britten used Michelangelo, miracle plays, Rimbaud, Tennyson, Hardy and Donne far more than he used Auden. I don't speak of opera texts, though these too, throughout history, have usually been *about* the past.

No conclusion may be drawn, still less a rule, though two points are worth noting. First, insofar as a composer uses a contemporaneous text, the two aspects of that eternal bastard known as Song merge and, pushed to the extreme, become pop, wherein words and sound are one. This is the case with the Bowles *Ballads*, which verge on blues. And it explains the hip fan's confusion defending the propagandistic power of rock music when he means rock words.

Second, poets who write lyrics (that is, words to be set to music rather than words in the abstract) tend to lose their identity as poets. As for poets who versify *about* music, the most abstruse and up-to-date of them (Ashbery, O'Hara) are likely to laud the least abstruse and most *démodé* composers (Sibelius, Rachmaninoff), the very composers with whom, ideally, they should have collaborated. The best collaboration is between conservative and avant-garde, but when two artists of the same persuasion work together the result is redundant.

Philip Miller's charming article "The American Art Song from 1900 to 1940" [the program notes for New World Records NW 247: *When I Have Sung My Songs*] tells us that vocal stars of the first quarter-century regularly performed and recorded, with relish and without question, the songs of American composers, which were conscientiously stocked in music stores throughout the country. Not only nationals like Louise Homer, Edward Johnson and Nordica but Europeans who scarcely knew English, like Schumann-Heink, believing strongly in what they were singing, promoted songs by Watts, Nevin, Cadman, Damrosch—enough for these composers to make good money.

The quality of American song, of course, mellowed considerably after this period and by 1950 had turned to pure gold. We composers were not yet clearly aware that the normal display for such gold, the song recital, was already a losing proposition. Nor was pocket money any longer fair exchange. It would not occur to a singer, not even to Janet Fairbank, to pay for a song. Song was for love. So we continued to bring live nosegays to ghostly stars, courting a moribund breed. We were (to switch images) like young mothers lactating for their dead offspring.

Miller suggests that this cul-de-sac was partly made by composers themselves, for whom a "traditionally melodic line became exceptional." It was more likely a question of finance. Recitals no longer paid off. If in Fairbank's decade there were still a number of genuine concertizers who could fill a hall, by 1955 those singers who attracted the public to a vocal-piano affair did so solely on their operatic fame, and generally sang more arias than songs. By 1959 there existed not one American singer—not one!—who was first and foremost a recitalist; we could afford no equivalent of Souzay, Schwarzkopf, Fischer-Dieskau. That year, when William Flanagan and I launched our series, Music for the Voice by Americans, we had trouble finding student singers who knew that songs were not arias. Although busy earning a living as they could, through opera, those few pros who *knew* (Patricia Neway, Donald Gramm, Phyllis Curtin, Regina Sarfaty) were only too glad to donate their services, for recitals were now luxury items. The handful of composers still writing songs were the same as two decades earlier, if they were still alive. Younger composers (with exceptions like Richard Cumming, Richard Hundley, John Gruen) were either trying to make it in opera, after Menotti's example, or were writing strictly instrumental pieces. More than ever American vocal training stressed opera to the exclusion of any other music, since only in opera might fame come.

Our singers now learn every language except their own. In this country of specialists, the one area of general practice is vocal literature. In Europe, where general practice prevails, a singer nonetheless masters his native language first; our students prefer singing badly in languages they don't comprehend to singing well in their own. Their excuse, and the excuse of their brainwashed teachers, is that English is ungrateful—but that's only because, understanding English, they see the pitfalls more clearly. The only thing bad about English as a vocal medium is bad English.

If there exist, shall we say, eight major composers in America today, four are women. This was hardly the ratio a generation ago, especially among songwriters. Not that good women composers weren't around. But song as a medium ironically carried a feministic stigma—the perfume of Ladies' Music—to which the emerging female artist was allergic. I do seem to recall a few settings by Vivian Fine, Dika Newlin, Peggy Glanville-Hicks (on poems of Paul Bowles) and Miriam Gideon (although her famous *Hound of Heaven*, because of its length, its oboe and its string trio, is not formally a song), but otherwise no one special.

Women, however, uniquely dominated the promotional areas of new music between the wars. If Fairbank and Gauthier, far more than any men, were the chief performer and chief professor of American song, five others of their sex loomed large: Claire Reis and Louise Varèse as organizers of the League of Composers and the American chapter of the ISCM; Minna Lederman as founder of the review *Modern Music;* Alma Morgenthau as publisher of, among other editions, a famous song volume (and as partial subsidizer of such musicians as song-composer Howard Swanson and conductor Dimitri Mitropoulos); and Yvonne de Casa Fuerte, who, as Parisian member of this sorority, brought her supportive know-how overseas along with her violin— for she was and remains an active artist. (Need it be noted that the primary value of these women, including Louise Varèse, lay not in their capacity as wives?)

By 1960, then, song recitals were mere adornments of the past. But song itself underwent a revival. Though government was not yet attentive, glimmers of subsidy elsewhere, personal and public, began to demonstrate an awareness that composers, even song composers, had to eat. On the one hand was a woman—another woman. On the other, a foundation.

The gifts and interests of Alice Esty, a soprano of style and means if not especially of temperament, were designed to delight a small milieu with similar interests and gifts. Since 1954, under the watchful eye of her more than competent Svengali, pianist David Stimer, Esty performed yearly for an invited audience, then recorded on a private label programs of those twentieth-century songs, French and American, that most pleased her. Five years later, having exhausted that repertory while befriending many who had created that repertory, she began a commissioning campaign.

She started by approaching Francis Poulenc, who immediately composed his now classic cycle *Le Travail du Peintre,* of which Esty sang the first performance in March 1959. From 1959 to 1968 she solicited, paid for (music *and* poetry, as the case arose) and premièred major cycles by these Europeans: Marcel Delannoy, Germaine Tailleferre, Henri Sauguet, Darius Milhaud, Henk Badings, Gunnar Bucht, Alexander Goehr. She did as much for Americans. Since it's safe to say that none of their songs would have existed without Esty; since many of the songs, although of high order, are yet unpublished; since they all fit this article's definition of "song" (a genre that will possibly be composed less and less as composers more and more continue to weave the voice—when they weave it at all—instrumentally into their ensemble fabrics); and since the list is nowhere on record, it is worth publishing the details. Between 1960 and 1969 Alice Esty commissioned and premièred in Carnegie Recital Hall the following American cycles:

Eight Poems of Theodore Roethke	Ned Rorem	April 3, 1960
Songs for Alice Esty (Kenneth Koch) (published as "Mostly About Love")	Virgil Thomson	April 3, 1960
Roman Suite (Tennessee Williams)	Paul Bowles	March 13, 1961
From Marion's Book (Cummings)	Marc Blitzstein	March 13, 1961
The Ways (Pauline Hanson)	Ben Weber	March 29, 1962
Symptoms of Love (Robert Graves)	Quincy Porter	March 29, 1961
Greetings from the Château (James Schuyler)	John Gruen	April 11, 1963

Song of Jephthah's Daughter
  (Robert Hillyer)   Daniel Pinkham   April 22, 1965
Anima (from *Piers Ploughman*
  by William Langland, 1377)   Charles Jones   May 21, 1969

In addition, for a commemoration on January 13, 1964, of Poulenc's death, Esty commissioned these international composers (plus a number of poets, including, in my case, Frank O'Hara): Badings, Lennox Berkeley, Henri Dutilleux, Frank Martin, Milhaud, Vittorio Rieti, Rorem, Manuel Rosenthal, Sauguet, Tailleferre, Thomson and Ben Weber.

For the record, Carolyn Reyer, a mezzo with a similar mission, was nationally active during the sixties, promoting particularly the new songs of Diamond, Robert Baksa and the present writer.

Meanwhile the Ford Foundation, during two briefly enterprising seasons, caused to be born a series of song collections. The gimmick was to select upcoming vocalists, who in turn selected composers. Thus Betty Allen chose Thomson, who tailored his *Praises and Prayers* to her talents. Donald Gramm had Richard Cumming do likewise with *We Happy Few*. I wrote *Poems of Love and the Rain* for Regina Sarfaty. (The pervious season voice-and-orchestra works were made for Phyllis Curtin by Carlisle Floyd and for Adele Addison by Lukas Foss.)

What to add? There are omissions of many names crucial to the epoch: Sam Raphling, Randall Thompson, Irving Fine; or Everett Helm and William Bergsma, both of whose sonic ideas about E. E. Cummings were winning indeed; or Vincent Persichetti, whose *Harmonium* on Wallace Stevens poems is, so far as sheer proportion goes, a national monument; John La Montaine, whose songs are mostly with orchestra; Jack Beeson and Robert Ward, whose careers as opera men have overshadowed their youthful songwriting. I have detailed little about quality, and not played much favoritism. (Opinions about Blitzstein's *From Marion's Book*, for example, or about the whole field of William Flanagan's efforts I've expressed elsewhere.)

I have not brought up twelve-tone songsters because, except for Ben Weber, there were none. Nor have I brought up the ever intriguing subject of what type of creative nature turns to song. Modern Germany and Italy, with all their grand vocal fertility, never birthed, as France and England did (at least one apiece, with Poulenc and Britten), the hybrid equally adept at song and opera. (Indeed, modern Italy has produced no song at all, while the songs of Richard Strauss form a race apart.) But the hybrid has been spawned successfully in the United States with at least Barber and Thomson. Also, all our opera composers, including Menotti, have written decent songs, and all our song composers, including Chanler, have written decent operas.

The past fifteen years have seen a new crop of American singer—not properly a recital singer—skilled to deal with current vocal concepts. These concepts stress words as sound no less than as sense, and inevitably enmesh the voice in a jungle of instrumental hues. The parent work is Boulez's *Le Marteau sans Maître* (1954), and the spin-off interpreter in America is Bethany

Beardslee, who could always do anything, as can Julius Eastman, Cathy Berberian, Jan DeGaetani and Phyllis Bryn-Julson. The new pieces are not songs, because they do not restrict themselves to piano and lyric poem. They are shows—narrational, terrifically up to date, yet still using texts from another time and place, like George Crumb with Lorca, David Del Tredici with Lewis Carroll, or, from abroad, Peter Maxwell Davies's Mad King and Henze's Runaway Slave. (Curiously, no English-speaking composer has yet concocted a theater piece with just piano, as Debussy and Poulenc did long decades ago, with *La Boîte à Joujoux* and *Babar*.) But these paragraphs were not meant to evaluate the present decade.

I have not named singers from the thirties because I don't know who they were (it would be nice to learn who first sang Citkowitz and Copland). The thirties were a bit before my time. The fifties took me away from the home-land. To justify its focus this paper, rather than claiming to be research, should be subtitled "A Personal Survey." A more experienced documenter, like Philip Miller, or a composer with different connections, like Elliott Carter, might have painted quite another picture. But the ensuing nutshell critiques of the seven composers may add resonance to the tone of a bygone era.

Theodore Chanler   *(1902–61)*

They remain arguments endlessly open: whether in opera good librettos can be sustained by mediocre music, and whether good music can overcome mediocre librettos. Song literature is clearer cut. No bad setting of good poetry is a staple, though good settings of bad poetry are common fodder. Observe the works of Chanler.

Theodore Chanler's songs, that part of the already small oeuvre for which he is most admired, number fewer than thirty. Of these, half are based on more or less acceptable verse by standard authors including Blake. The other half are on the smarmy simplistic musings of a poetaster called Father Leonard Feeney. Yet each song is flawless on its own terms, and, like the sighs of inspired innocents, each rings true.

What do they have that allures both listener and singer, that gives them—like all-time pop favorites with forgettable lyrics—their staying power? The answer is tune. The greatest songwriters always seem to share not so much a generalized gift for melody (Wagner, Verdi and Puccini weren't songwriters, after all) as a gift for economy, the ability to impose the inevitable minimum of notes unapologetically on a group of words and to make the group speak, or rather sing, independent of accompaniment. Parenthetically, another common point among composers who are primarily songwriters (*primarily*—not Mussorgsky, say, or Debussy) is that they never innovate in any formal sense. The genre of song as defined earlier cannot lend itself to tampering and still retain its identity as a tune-over-figuration. When far-out John Cage writes a straight song like "The Wonderful Widow of Seventeen Springs" he shows us his "conservative" side, while far-out Milton Babbitt's *Philomel* becomes what can no longer be termed "song."

Chanler's genius of brevity was extreme. No one in history, not Dowland or Satie or Webern, ever more convincingly carried a hearer from doubt through heartbreak to resolution in a span of five bars. Look at his "Anne Poverty." If Duparc gained Parnassus on a lifetime output of just thirteen songs (though Baudelaire's words did help), Chanler might make it merely on his delicious *Eight Epitaphs*—nine, if you count the "Four Husbands" unearthed by Phyllis Curtin—which all together last under ten minutes.

The spirited "Thomas Logge" is the fourth of the *Epitaphs*, each of which is a thumbnail sketch of an English eccentric memorialized by poet Walter de la Mare (1873–1956) during a stroll through an eighteenth-century churchyard. Chanler composed these in 1935.

Ten years later he composed *The Children*, a cycle of nine songs on words of Leonard Feeney. Included here are the title song, an attractive ditty of the kind kids invent while skipping rope; "Once upon a Time," another childlike air, using words so mindless that only an adult could have penned them, skillfully set off against a (difficult) curving Schumannesque keyboard rôle; "The Rose," homespun philosophy of the don't-make-waves brand popular during the war as heard through the irresistibly lush harmonies once known as Ladies' Music, wherein the voice is doubled throughout by the piano; and "Moo Is a Cow," a successful trick in that the accompaniment manages constantly to Mickey-Mouse the words without once forsaking its independent energy. (The vocal line of this last song provides, in small notes, an optional obbligato—if this is not a contradiction in terms—whereby it becomes a duet in undifferentiated counterpoint. For no apparent reason, beyond the not insignificant one of charm, the song can thus be performed by two singers at once or, as in the present mechanical case, by one singer in harmony with himself.)

Archibald MacLeish provided the poem for the sad and lilting "These, My Ophelia." Don't the music, with its continually shifting beats, and the words, with their intimations of mortality, bear a spiritual resemblance to Paul Bowles's "Once a Lady Was Here"?

Paul Bowles   *(b. 1910)*

Composer-authors have always existed, but their prose careers invariably reflect their music careers. They are critics or librettists or autobiographers. Has there ever been a novelist-composer, equally adept and reputed in both fields, until Paul Bowles?

American by birth and training, having apprenticed with Thomson and Copland, Bowles is Eurafrican by preference, having spent half his life in France and Morocco. His professional life has also been sliced cleanly in two, with no seeming relation between the pieces.

During the WPA and World War II years Bowles was hyperactive as a practical composer, furnishing music to some two dozen plays and to documentary movies. Less practically, he wrote chamber works for lush combos (winds with gongs, keyboards, maracas, milk bottles); a haunting *zarzuela*, *The Wind Remains;* and above all, songs of all sorts, some to be heard in plays by Shakespeare and Saroyan, others strictly in recital by four (black) sopranos with two pianos, on prose by James Schuyler. Despite the occasionally morose texts of Lorca or Saint-John Perse, all of Bowles's music is optimistic. It pretends to no more than it says, and what it says affects the body more than the mind. It stems from blues and hot jazz, is entirely in small forms (even the opera—*Denmark Vesey*—is a series of set numbers), contains no polyphony (songs seldom do) and often is very fast. Bowles's musical metabolism is indeed so spirited that one might say his lentos are like prestos slowed down, just as, for instance, Fauré's prestos are really lentos speeded up.

In 1946 the death of Gertrude Stein, whom Bowles adored but who did not adore Bowles's literary efforts, was rumored to be a liberation for the young writer. That year Bowles became an author, stopped composing and left America for good. Since then he has accepted a few musical commissions and returned briefly to see them through, but for all intents and purposes a new career began. He has now published fifteen books, most of them fiction, nothing on music, everything on pessimism.

Paul Bowles might appear schizophrenic, his pair of métiers being so unrelated, did not all real artists demonstrably speak two dialects, their lifeworks being neatly divided into hard and easy, light and dark, church and state, whatever. It's just that Bowles's dialects are uttered through separate mediums. Which one is sacred and which profane is for you to decide.

The words for "Song of an Old Woman" (1942) were written, when she was very young, by the composer's late wife, Jane Bowles. She may not have been much of a poet, but there are those who class her among the most touching and original novella writers of our time. I remember when Povla Frijsh, no longer young, bravely programmed this song on her penultimate farewell recital. Swathed in parrot-green velours from toe to throat, she struck an exhausted pose, one hand on the piano at which was seated—was it George Reeves?—who began the corny theme as the mood indicates, like a hack in a Weimar bar. And Frijsh forgot! Ah, but forgetting with her was a rehearsed affair: the memory slip as a fine art. Anxious to prove that her artistry was both musical *and* literary—that she could think as well as sing in eleven languages—she would make last-minute substitutions for the written word, "mute" for "dumb," "*triste*" for "*pauvre*," "*sorriso*" for "*allegro*," etc. In this case "shame" was sung in place of "fear," with the quick change (to honor rhyme) of "blame" for "hear." The poem wasn't too damaged.

The verses for "Once a Lady Was Here" (1946) are by the composer himself, who, like Jane Bowles, is better at prose. Still, they fit the music's passive evocation, like the nostalgia of a saxophone played under water ten miles away ten years ago.

John Duke (b. 1899)

Any singer will tell you that one of the chief problems—and pleasures—of the trade is what they call program building. It is not enough to have the world's most beautiful voice, for without presence beauty palls. Presence comes from drama, drama from contrast, and contrast from construction. Of course beauty is no hindrance and, coupled with intellect, can afford risks. But the monochrome all-Schubert or all-Wolf evening of a Lehmann or a Schwarzkopf, who made each song a world, is not managed by just anyone.

Americans of the 1940s especially felt that variety was spice, at least in song programs, which included four or more languages. On the rare occasion one of these languages was their own, the so-called English group (including Americans tacked on at the end) was a devitaminized compost, no more than one goody by each composer, all humoristic. Leave the audience feeling good! Such reasoning along with a dearth of local goods both first-rate and rousing, led to the eschewing, at least by standard recitalists, of cultured repertory (by Ives, for example, or even Ornstein) and to the selecting of encores from only the inevitable Zuccas or La Forges or Worths, or older favorites by Foster, Cadman, sometimes Kern, or even Negro spirituals tossed off with a croon by snow-white contraltos.

The crying need for "closing songs" of high quality was partly filled by Celius Dougherty (who as a longtime professional accompanist "knew theater") and John Duke. Nothing is as mercurial as humor in instrumental music; such humor as can be conclusively located in music is always in vocal works, humor (as distinct from wit) being a literary concept. Most jokes can't be sprung twice, even garbed in pretty tunes. His three songs based on the American-as-apple-pie meters of Edwin Arlington Robinson, which are superior diction lessons, are exceptions. May John Duke not feel patronized to find them defined as anecdotes that bear retelling!

Israel Citkowitz (1909–74)

Within that microcosm known as Composers' Composers dwells a still rarer race called Song Composers' Song Composers. No one in the outside world ever hears about them, but to themselves they are sacred monsters. In the 1930s, whenever new songs were discussed by those few who cared, people always brought up Israel Citkowitz. "He's really the one who first turned American song into a serious affair," they would claim, and they claim it still. So again I hopefully pick up that Rimbaudesque musician's complete works, consisting uniquely of his settings of James Joyce's "Chamber Music," and again lay them down with the uncomfortable feeling of Why the fuss? Of all our underrated composers Citkowitz is the most overrated.

His sheaf of songs dates from 1930. He never published anything before, and never composed anything after, although he led a life of variety and culture. The variety resided in travel between countries and marriages, between money and no money, and between the responsibilities of an actual father and those of a father image. Culture resided in the latter role. Citkowitz was a warm, protective person, a born esthete. Continental in style if not in fact, caring for art with a hot contagion. He was an experienced piano teacher of nonpro pianists: music-loving actors and doctors, other piano teachers, pianists' children and composers suddenly required to play their own songs. As the subtlest species of dilettante, Citkowitz surely realized, on some level, his compositional limitations, but he never spoke of them.

If in later life he became a sort of idol of amateurs, his first champions were known professionals like Theodore Chanler and especially Aaron Copland, who saw to the printing of the Joyce songs in the now legendary *Cos Cob Song Book*. Musically Citkowitz reflected both these men, but in a paler light.

He and Chanler resembled each other in that their songs, while linear rather than chordal, are paradoxically harmonic rather than contrapuntal, with vocal parts that bend around sparse rolling ostinatos. But they differed where it most counts. Citkowitz may have had better taste in poets, he had no gift for tune.

Listen to "Strings in the Earth and Air." Here the debt to Copland is most obvious; indeed, played in slow motion, the languorous merging of Lydian and Dorian modes becomes a paraphrase of Copland's *Music for the Theater*, but without a firm line to bind the colors. The melody is mere harmonic fill, as though some hack had sung the first notes to fall on his tongue. Again, in "When the Shy Star," the voice improvises with unneeded notes all doubled in the harmonic thicket. In the third song there is little differentiation between the roles of voice and keyboard: without vocal interference the piano provides a pleasant scherzo. "Bid Adieu" does have tune, however, harmless tune, but why the overlong noodling interlude, the functionless change of meter? At least the tessitura is logical, by contrast with the range of the other songs, particularly the fifth, "My Love Is in a Light Attire," which shifts from too low to too high and back. Given the easy diatonicism of the language these shifts seem less contrived than inexpert.

Not that naïveté isn't nice sometimes. Indeed, the ingenuous effect is the be-all of much of what Citkowitz emulates, not just in the Americans mentioned but in the *petits maîtres* of Paris—Couperin, Gounod, Beydts. *Mais n'est pas innocent qui veut.* What works for others fails for Israel Citkowitz. His artlessness lacks art.

Roger Sessions (b. 1896)

Walter Piston once exclaimed to a pupil who brought in a word setting, "Anything but that!" Songs, he felt, were beyond his ken; he could neither write nor judge them. Still, there *are* principles by which one can assess, if not necessarily feel, a song. More subjectively, the arch and flow of much of Piston's own instrumental output could be described as "vocal."

Roger Sessions's vocal output conversely could be described as instrumental. If of the seven composers featured here Sessions has emerged as the most "advanced," he is also the least singerly. I write this advisedly, aware of his blazing Theocritus *Idylls*, his elephantine *Montezuma*. Conventions of opera and concert aria are nonetheless not automatically transferable to song, the burden of the former being theatricality and of the latter lyricism. And one era's practices cannot be transcribed to another. The Purcell-Handel conceit of reiterating verbal passages—"Alleluia," "Shake the clouds from out the sky," "Gloria," "Would I might die"—that by their origin were comprehensible more as music than as poetry is questionable today except as pastiche, even when dealing with old texts, certainly with new. Thus when Sessions takes the brief, self-contained "On the Beach at Fontana" and stammers half-verses with no clear musical or poetic justification ("A senile sea numbers each single Slime silvered stone, each slime silvered stone . . .," "I wrap him warm And touch his trembling fineboned shoulder, his trembling fineboned shoulder . . ."), the result is queasy.

Viewed from outside, song is silly. To superimpose pitches onto prewritten words for tenors in fancy clothes but without formal ceremony to emit for a silent public: that is sillier still, particularly to any poets involved. Art is silly, and so finally is life, even death. Good song convinces us that what is silly is not silly. Arbitrary repetition of words from a famous poem does not solve the problem. How agonizing to realize that Sessions, with a bit of melismatic coaxing, could have left his vocal line intact, and also the poem of Joyce.

Yet Sessions's song, with its keening tune over the piano's lonely breeze, is persuasive, and vocally it must be rewarding to perform.

Aaron Copland   *(b. 1900)*

Four-fifths of Copland's wide and varied catalogue is instrumental, composed over a half-century period. The other fifth, the vocal music, was composed mostly during a single five-year span in mid-career: *In the Beginning* (1948), *Poems of Emily Dickinson* (1951) and *The Tender Land* (1953). To be sure, he wrote other choruses in the forties, a school opera in the thirties and isolated songs in the twenties. But after 1954 nothing for voice.

Not that Copland hasn't always "used" song. His instrumental works, programmatic and otherwise, have forever been strewn with undisguised American folk and hymn tunes, as Charles Ives, Virgil Thomson and Roy Harris strewed before him.

Copland may not think of himself as fundamentally a composer for the voice, yet (unlike Piston) he would clearly like to leave his mark on every musical category. Indeed, except for solo double-reeds and solo lower strings, he has already contributed to as many standard combinations as Hindemith. It is tempting to wonder whether Copland's writing of, say, the Dickinson songs was an intellectual decision. Did he coolly list what precisely had hitherto been wanting in American song—a major cycle, a highly disjunct yet tonal vocal line, an individual piano part—and then proceed to fill the gap? Whatever the case, and perhaps *because* of their composer's objectivity, the songs are exemplary, fun to sing, inspired-sounding, very serious, very popular.

It's often said that Aaron Copland, while speaking one language, willfully creates in two separate dialects, the "uncompromising" and the "accessible." If this is true then his vocal music, all of it, falls into the second category. All, that is, except his very first song, "Song," dating from 1927. It bears no touch of the novice. It is a suave and model exercise.

See how the whole is exposed in the first two measures, how the singer's line follows like melted speech the curve of E. E. Cummings's stanza, how that line (always the same five intervals—the five that Copland will use again, decades later, in "I Heard an Organ") winds purposefully upward so that the climactic verb "turn" will coincide with its needed high A, how the second climax, not quite so grand but a bit quicker, comes on "kiss," then subsides into the past where "were" is attacked alone, to be rejoined hurriedly by the piano, which is allowed to die with the voice. The piano meanwhile has supported the voice throughout while retaining a semi-independence, conducting, so to speak, a little affair of its own without which this song—any song—might as well be a cappella. For an accompaniment must be just that, a sustenance, a friendly rival, a fresh dimension, not (as in the Citkowitz songs) a twin.

"Song" would seem to contain the entire future Copland in miniature, the likable and the severe, the expert and the sensualist whose rich but lean chords combine with the graciously craggy melody that has become the master's trademark. "Song" contains all this, but without the breath of life.

Samuel Barber   (1910–81)

Barber is our sole songwriter who in the old days seemed always to have access to "real" singers. Avoiding the non-voiced specialists with lunatic reputations, he understandably favored divas with big gorgeous sounds. He did write *Monks and Raisins* for Frijsh (who could deny her?) and *Mélodies Passagères* for Bernac (whose link with Poulenc had grand cachet), but they were European. One thinks of Barber mainly as the composer of *Knoxville: Summer of 1915* and *Nuvoletta* for established star Eleanor Steber and of *Hermit Songs* and *Prayers of Kierkegaard* for upcoming star Leontyne Price. Sadly, it was not to songs but to stars that the public was drawn, and without arias even stars were not certain magnets. If foreign composer-singer tandems like Poulenc & Bernac or Britten & Pears once had box office in the United States, the famous homeboy, without an orchestra behind his soloist, did not. When Barber & Price were offered as a package during the early 1950s they had too few takers to continue.

Inside all composers lurks a prima donna longing to get out, yet they are famed for their frightful voices. Sometimes, as with Marc Blitzstein, a composer's wheezy soundbox works to his advantage, particularly when his songs are talky show tunes with "personality." (Indeed, during the long run of *Threepenny Opera* the continual turnover of performers hired seemed to be based on how much they sounded like Blitzstein.) Mostly, though, singing composers sabotage themselves. Two exceptions: Reynaldo Hahn, whose recording of *Chansons Grises* shows a clean, affecting tenor enough removed from his original inspiration to render it without self-indulgence; and Samuel Barber, whose recording of *Dover Beach* reveals a true baritone of professional class. Barber, in fact, minored in voice at Curtis and, being Louise Homer's nephew, frequented a milieu where the human instrument was a practical, not a theoretic, matter.

Today still, at parties, if pressed Barber will accompany himself—though never in his own music—in some dear bonbon of yore, "Pale Hands" being a favorite. Yet what he mocks is precisely what he once most felt, for his own student efforts are close to Carrie Jacobs Bond. Which explains their continuing popularity on safe recitals. Despite his very stylish choice of authors (Prokosch, Hopkins, Lorca, Rilke, Horan), his early songs lack profile. Consider his setting, from 1939, of the rather nondescript verses of James Agee (whose prose six years later would serve as text for Barber's masterly *Knoxville*). It is neither the simple tune nor the primary harmonies of "Sure on This Shining Night" that render it bland (the Bowles and Chanler pieces are no more "advanced"), but the ear searches in vain for a personal signature. The piano may echo snatches of Canteloube's *Auvergne* orchestrations, much admired in those days, but the music could have been written by anyone.

I would not presume such harshness were not Barber an American glory. His instrumental music dating from this period, his operas, ballets, concertos and above all his song cycles during the following three decades are from the pen of a musician who, so far as elegance is concerned, stands alone.

New York, 1977

MORE NOTES ON SONG

"There's two things a singer can't buy, beg or steal, and that no teacher, coach or conductor can give him. One is his voice, the other is the language that was born in his mouth." So penned James M. Cain, of all people, forty-five years ago in *Serenade* (wrongly called by some "the first gay detective novel"). As a composer of songs often built on American poetry I have a stake in the "things a singer can't buy," since we are what we sing and we sing what we are. Yet I have never heard the matter better stated than by Cain, certainly never by professionals presumably more qualified than he.

Europe seethes with general practitioners in everything but vocal repertory. America seethes with specialists in everything but vocal repertory. German, Italian, French, even British singers are weaned in their native tongue, sometimes to the exclusion of other tongues. American singers are weaned to sing badly in tongues they cannot speak, usually to the exclusion of their own tongue which, when they do sing it, sounds incomprehensible with the rolled *r*'s and dragged-out vowels of continental elocution. We Americans, still at this late date, suffer from an inferiority complex about matters cultural, while holding to the notion that size is value. Regarding musical performance we still cower in Europe's shadow. So, having decided that our language is unviable in serious song recitals, we rationalize that, in any case, opera's where it's at.

Three facts:

The only thing musically bad about English is bad English. (Who belittles the settings of Purcell and Dowland and Britten and Berkeley? of Billings and Griffes and Thomson and Bowles?)

Of the ten million American vocalists born each year (and who will never learn English), none will make it to the Met.

If no major orchestra in America today is headed by an American, neither is any American singer today fundamentally a recitalist.

The reality of English diction nonetheless exists, is even imparted (among others by Madeleine Marshall at Juilliard, by Dorothy Uris free-lance). Yet when I ask singers with marvelous diction—all three of them—what their secret is, they don't start talking vocables and triphthongs. "I try to render

240

the poetry," says Phyllis Curtin, "and to sing what I know about, just as I prefer to speak only when I know what I'm saying." "I must take the beauty of my voice for granted," says Donald Gramm. "If I'm not impelled to prove I'm a great baritone by swallowing consonants, I am free to think about the lyrics. I pronounce them as I would read them." (Who is the third singer? I want to keep my friends.)

The fact that American singers *comprehend* their native tongue inhibits them. To stand before an audience and enunciate great verse, especially verse revested and inflected with formally curving sounds, is so very self-revealing, so thrillingly excruciating, so ecstatic and so silly, that the only protection is bad diction. Which is why singers not born to our language (Crespin, for instance, in Poulenc's *Dialogues*) might well sing English more cleanly than we do. And which is why American singers of Latin or Jewish extraction, reared on the two coasts within extrovert and tactile milieus, sing better—more intelligently and more "emotionally," if not more mellifluously—than midwestern Wasps. I speak of soloists only. Choral singing is nowhere in the world more perfect, surely not in New York where union fees prohibit ample rehearsal, than by the golden-haired slave labor of Protestant colleges in upper Minnesota.

It turns out that American instrumentalists are also specialists, judging by the audience last night at Bert Lucarelli's oboe recital. I recognized not one face. Flutist Paul Dunkel with whom I sat (we were two coppers in a panful of garnets—is that the image?) said he felt out of place among this swarm of oboe students. Waiting in line to pick up my ticket I had overheard an exchange between two post-adolescent females:

"I went to this opera down at NYU by Ned Rorem. *Miss Julie.*"

"Oh. How was it? His songs are okay."

"Well, some of it was God-awful, and some was okay. The oboe player was okay."

Dear Andrew:

Your intelligent essay on Barber's opera contained an arguable clause about a subject close to my heart:

. . . the publisher who, in the blunt modern manner, has tied together the tails of eighth and shorter notes, as if voices were no more than wordless instruments. This procedure regularly prompts singers toward metrical delivery rather than an eloquent utterance . . .

Assuming that singers learn by note rather than rote, i.e., by themselves rather than with coaches, and that even when a phrase is memorized and "in the voice" they'll retain that phrase (as many good musicians do) through the mind's eye rather than as a series of sounds, you'd still be hard put to prove that their interpretation depends on how that phrase first looked on the page. Do we never hear metrical delivery from one who learns from old unbeamed "vocal" editions, or eloquent utterance from another who learns the same music from an updated "instrumental" edition?

Can a mere listener know that the "home" note value of, say, a Chopin scherzo is a quarter, rather than the psychologically faster eighth or sixteenth? Can he know that the "home" note of a Haydn largo is actually a sixteenth rather than the psychologically slower quarter or half? Sure, the appearance of the music necessarily affects the performer's learning, but the public ear can't vouch for it. At least my ear can't. After a lifetime of pondering the pros and cons of notation (first as a student, then as paid copyist, finally as composer), and of hearing new music and later studying the scores of that music, I am continually excited at how different the notes can look from how they sounded. Especially notes for vocal music.

Vocal music in growing more complex has tended to be written instrumentally, beginning with Berg and early Messiaen. Today, with the notable exception of Britten and of certain elderly conservatives, all composers beam rather than syllabify their vocal lines (or they'll use both methods, like Boulez in *Le marteau*), although much of the time there's no choice since vocal lines are now so often melismatic rather than recitative. (But when they *are* recitative, a metrical delivery would seem implicit, not because of the looks of the notes but because of the sense of the words.)

Publishers, at least in America, are of two minds about all this. Singers themselves don't seem to care—they don't even think much about it. What singers perhaps lose at first sight in word sense, they gain in rhythmic clarity. But anyway, as we all know, singers (including the most intelligent ones) more than any other performers tend, no matter what the "school" of music they're singing, to veer from the score once they've learned it. Which is why I'd love you to show me just one singer who, due to publication "in the blunt modern manner," is regularly prompted to metrical delivery when metrical delivery is not called for by the composer.

Warmly,
Ned

Singers always refer to their instrument as "the voice"—never as "my voice"—as though it were disembodied and kept in a case like a violin. Yet violinists say "my violin," not "the violin."

Complete run-through of Joyce Mathis's upcoming program, including my *Women's Voices*, for a dozen guests in a private hall. Joyce's vocal coach, Cornelius Reid, does not remain for my songs. That a reputable voice teacher should depart, for whatever reason, before the unveiling of a new cycle is no less insulting to that cycle's composer than to all writers of songs today, and underlines once again the indifference to contemporary American vocal music. (21 October 1976).

✳

What is the purpose of composing? If I were horribly incarcerated, would I emerge to continue writing exquisite songs? The question's fair, though what composer could answer? Music is never journalism (it may not even be reaction), whereas all writing, even the obscurest verse, is in a sense reporting.

If music makes us see more clearly, who yet can explain? If a life could be saved by the banishment of the very music through which we "see clearly," would we . . .? The question's unfair, since the situation's unreal.

One difference between poetry and music is that while verse can be scanned and explicated a score can only be scanned. Mallarmé notwithstanding—"Poetry's not about ideas, it's about words"—words do stand for other things, are symbolic if you will (the word "metaphor" is a symbol for metaphor), and aren't in themselves emotions but represent emotions. Like abstract painting—defensively named abstract precisely because it is not abstract and never will be—a poem calls forth personal representations of the words it contains. Music, meanwhile, is itself the emotion (the idea): it represents nothing beyond itself. And so music cannot be intellectualized.

Mr. Rorem, what do the words to this song mean?
They mean whatever my music tells you they mean. What else can I tell you in words?

I am fond of insisting that anyone can be taught to write a perfect song. It's a fact: for musical composition is a craft—as well as an art, whatever that means. Yes, anyone can be taught to write a perfect song, but no one, not even Schubert, knows how to lend that song a living pulse and inject it with flowing blood.

Performers, especially performers of instruments like the organ (though not singers, strangely) which have wide coloristic options, often ask what sounds I had in mind. I don't compose with sounds but with pitch relations and melodic flow in mind. When I orchestrate, of course, I choose colors (sounds) carefully. The choice is self-explanatory; and, naturally, orchestration is not composition.

She speaks well and wisely, but understands nothing—not even what she says. (One of the phrases I first taught myself in Italian was: *Io parlo benissimo ma non capisco niente.*)

Music, in contrast to pictures or words, does not deal in facts, that is, in associations which by their nature concern the past. Yet music is associative. Of what? Music is the sole art which evokes nostalgia for the future.

Back from a strenuous twenty-four hours at Yale where Phyllis Curtin sang another impeccable recital. I sat next to her daughter, Claudia Madeleine (named for Muzio and Milhaud), age thirteen, and wondered at her reactions to the diva there on the stage, swathed in silver and false lashes, intoning with all the artifice of nature the verses of Vilmorin and Verlaine,

244 N E D R O R E M

frustrated and grown-up. *My* mother never did things like that. My case is the reverse: people wonder at the parent's reaction to a child who persists in writing music.

Jane Austen in *Pride and Prejudice:* "For I consider music as a very innocent diversion, and perfectly compatible with the profession of clergyman."

"A high [female] voice has long been a potent symbol of eroticism in opera, and that symbolism has carried over into popular music," claims John Rockwell in today's *Times* (4 March 1979). But he forces the claim to his purpose, for facts are contrary. A high female voice has long been the symbol of purity in opera: sopranos are heroines, heroines are virgins. It is the contralto voice that has long symbolized eroticism, sex being evil and mezzos being villains. Ditto in pop music. Examine such thin, flutey-sounding voices as Helen Morgan's, or even Billie Holiday's, and you'll discover that their tessitura is largely below middle-C. Billie's range was the same as Marian Anderson's. Dietrich, Greta Keller, Juliette Greco were baritones. And Libby Holman was a bass. Surely they were what Hollywood called "other women," while Jane Powell and Kathryn Grayson, toeing the high wire over the staff, represented the untouchable girl you might someday marry.

How do you choose poems for setting to music?

Formerly by what's called inspiration, the yen for self-expression that has nothing to do with talent. Today I choose them according to pre-set requirements. My approach—fast or slow, soft or loud—to a given poem varies according to whom I'm musicalizing it for, and to whether it's to be one of a sequence or standing alone. Yes, I am drawn to poetry which, as we Quakers say, speaks to my condition; and whatever my songs may be worth, I've never used a bad poem. But my *kind* of good poem may not be your kind, sonically speaking—or singing. I concede the greatness of much poetry that has no need to be put to music, at least not by me.

Usable qualities are prescribed as much by sequence as by inspiration. (If we did not assume the true worth of an artist's inspiration we wouldn't be concerned in the first place.) Otherwise stated: art is the communicable ordering of your bright ideas. My essay, *Notes on Death*, was originally narrational, glued together by characters speaking paragraphs. By cutting and reshifting, but by leaving unaltered all that was salvaged, I fooled editor Nan Talese into accepting the new version which she no longer recognized. Similarly, when I compose a so-called cycle (has anyone ever defined that term?) the order of songs is not necessarily determined until the writing is done. I may even add a quick waltz here, a moody one there not because the verse decrees the tempo, but because the theatricality of the whole requires contrast. Poems work at any speed, or fail at any speed.

Do you set your own words to music?

As an author I'm a polemical diarist who wants to set matters straight. But I can't set them straight to music, for I am not a poet. My poetry is my music. If I could write the kind of poem that I like to set to music, I wouldn't need to set it to music. Indeed, I would no longer be a composer but a poet.

Poetry isn't life, it's poetry, a distillation. Life has alternatives, dead ends. A poem is invariable, being the only possible arrangement of the words it contains. How insolent therefore that a composer should "enhance" those words with music. How much more insolent—since in any case he will break the metrical spine—that he should change the order of, or even repeat, certain words. Yet even Britten (why "even" Britten? is he God?) repeats words, and unimportant words at that. Britten does this no doubt in the tradition, and according to the ancient conceit, of Handel, who, however, repeated *important* words: *Alleluia, sing.* Britten is wrong. A composer who solves the problem of his song by altering the verse does not solve the problem of his song, insofar as song is the setting of a poem.

What about revision?
Here is an absolute rule: Changes, after a certain period—let's say one year—are never for the better. When in *The Lordly Hudson,* two decades after it was written, Paul Goodman amended "Be quiet, heart!" to "Be quiet, Paul!", he took the verse away from us and back to himself. Why not simply write a new poem? Myself, I revise as I go along, never retrospectively. I resist making changes in my early works, because another person wrote those early works.
Those of my own songs that run most often through my head are those which, for one reason or another, remain in manuscript and have never been heard. Some date from childhood. Suppose I were to prepare them for publication? Would I, in the process, "improve" on them?

What do I retain of the visit to Phyllis Curtin last month at Yale where we performed, in honor of Virgil, a sheaf of his dearest songs? I retain the frightening fact of the quads where a thousand tawny graduates sunned while disco music was systematically aimed into the air from dormitory windows for the throbbing delectation of all. When I remarked on this—and not just to the music department—the reaction was: don't make waves.
To be captive audience to any preemptive sounds (even, surely, to the sound of your own music) is to be tortured. If our greatest university allows the students to make the rules, what of the others?

Dear Andrew:
To your presumably rhetorical question, "Is there any bad Elliott Carter?", the answer is Yes—namely the two recent vocal works, *Syringa* on John Ashbery's words, and *A Mirror on Which to Dwell* on Elizabeth Bishop's, both failures because they neither heighten, add new dimension to, nor even illustrate the verse.
Never mind that, to my certain knowledge, at least one of the poets despaired of the music, or that at least one of the singers despised the voice line. Songs, after all, no longer belong to their composers, much less to their poets, once they are finished; and a performer's opinion finally has little to do with how convincingly, or even correctly, he performs those songs. No, the Bishop cycle fails because the vocal arch, being continually disjunct, grows

undifferentiated from song to song; because the orchestration, being superfluous ("all those cluttered instruments"), grows merely fussy where a clean piano would have sufficed; and mostly because what is sung never represents what is read. *Insomnia*, for instance, never seeks the bluesy lilt, and thus the acrid humor, of the stanzas, while the setting of *O Breath* descends to the amateurish duplication of words or syllables which the poet felt the need to state only once. As for the Ashbery rendition, it fails for the same reasons, and because the composer, lacking the courage of his American poet's convictions, dazzles and distracts us with a substructure in Greek.

Although I agree with the contention in your very next sentence that "Rochberg writes music whose appeal is to closed, unadventurous minds . . . and could become fodder for the New Right: Down with progressive thought!", your implication that Carter can do no wrong strikes me as irresponsible—indeed, as fodder for the Old Left—for surely you'll agree that there is even bad Beethoven.

I say this, who have elsewhere and often written of the unique power and grandeur of Elliott Carter's instrumental masterpieces.

Fondly,
Ned

(1977) Beverly Wolff surprisingly will give her very first solo New York recital in Town Hall on December 6 (Mother's eightieth birthday, as it happens). The whole second half will be my songs. I learn this by hearsay, not by Beverly, for she assumes the songs to be part of "the literature" and thus need no special pleading. Very flattering to the composer. Meanwhile her manager phones, unbeknownst to Beverly, wondering if perchance I have an as-yet-unsung goody that she might add, or could I maybe accompany her—anything to get a crowd. But that wouldn't get a crowd. Nor do composers have unsung songs that are worth the singing. I admire Beverly for feeling the music is music, not a device to attract critics.

Thrill of misunderstanding. Summer 1954, Hyères. Having just finished with pleasure Buzzati's *Le Désert des Tartares*, I suggest, before retiring, to Denise Bourdet that she take the novel to bed with her. Next morning Denise tells of her disappointment on opening the book to find the title was not (as she had understood from my slurred speech) *Le désir d'être en retard*.

The symphony, being the closed sonata form, is the strictest of musical shapes. (A fugue is not a form but a device.) The diary, being open-ended, is the freest of literary shapes.

Songs are my hobby. I believe only in hobbies. I have no profession—except piano playing. I abhor Major Statements, and so, in America, must perish.

Have you never considered fiction?

Fiction? Like James M. Cain? These notes are my fiction.

September 1980

FAURÉ'S SONGS

Asked how fast a song of his should go, Fauré replied: "When the singer is bad—very fast." The quip sounds glib. But remember, composers do have fewer preconceptions about their songs than about their sonatas; song is subject to legitimate distortion by virtue of a singer's range and sex. On a more personal level, and surely unbeknownst to Fauré, the quip suggests a shady truth: maybe his songs are all intrinsically slow. Music necessarily reflects the humor of its composers. Those of broad scope, like Chopin and Strauss, are choleric-melancholics capable of both the inherently fast and the inherently slow. Narrower sanguinaries like Rossini or Scarlatti conceive only allegros (their slow pieces being really fast pieces played slow), while phlegmatics like Delius and Fauré are men whose fast pieces are really slow pieces played fast.

Or so I always believed.

Already at twenty, confusing love with knowledge, I cast myself as an American authority on French Song. Ravel and Poulenc sat at the top of the ladder, Debussy and Duparc on middle rungs, and at the bottom, with Gounod, crouched Fauré. Those dozen Fauré chestnuts that I knew ("Prison," "Au cimetière," "Le Secret," etc.) seemed mere bloodless models for Poulenc's vital copies. During the next decades my closed mind gave the composer nary a thought.

Now two recorded sets of Fauré's "Complete Songs," both from France, have come out in the United States in honor of the fiftieth anniversary (three years late) of Fauré's death. Having listened to all 104 songs twice through, with a blush of surprise I realize what I've been missing.

Yes, he does compose basically slow music. Even in *La bonne chanson* with its busy piano, the voice never patters à la Poulenc, but moves at the "sensible" speed of conversation. Within the slowness is not much variety—little rhythmic invention, no contrapuntal curiosity. Nor is Fauré tunefully spacious. His famed graceful vocal lines are graceful by dint of exquisite prosody, pregnant pauses, "telling" twists of phrase. They do not soar in the Puccinian sense, are not obviously virtuosic, do not "show off" the voice. The French for song is *mélodie* (a tune is an *air*). But song writers, unlike

opera writers, seldom compose a sweeping melody, in the English sense of
that word. Poems can't sweep; only prose, bolstered by orchestras, can.

Being decorated emissions of the verse he admired, Fauré's songs are
exclusively declamatory, one note to a syllable. And they lack guts.

Then why can one listen, hour after hour to song after song, without
indigestion but with quickening delight? For the reason that one can stroll
through room after room of Renoirs with a growing sense of welcome. Hunger, as the French say, comes in eating, and familiarity breeds not contempt
but more familiarity. Fauré's uniqueness, like Renoir's, lies in the flawless-
ness of his jewels which, though they resemble each other, are each self-
contained. Perfection may be a minor virtue (greatness always walks with a
limp), but virtue it remains. Fauré is a harmonist. Though he was known as a
tunesmith, his craft shows less in tune itself than in chords rising from
below, like sap through a lily's stem, to color the pitch or figure, and by
extension the word, thereby changing, or at least heightening, the poem's
meaning.

If modernism in music means an elusive tonal core, then Fauré could be no
less modern than his pupil Ravel, and far more modern than his descendant
Poulenc (who professed an allergy to Fauré, doubtless because he owed him
so much) or to such continuing Parisian song writers as Sauguet and Damase.
Yet many of Fauré's most "elusive" songs are already a century old. Not that
he was ever atonal, but Fauré did anticipate the fondness chez Olivier
Messiaen and Benjamin Britten for Wagnerian chains of endlessly resolving
augmented fourths. Try out on some unalerted friend the Passacaglia from
Britten's Peter Grimes, Messiaen's "Danse du bébé Pilule" and these samples
from Fauré: measures 11–19 of "L'aube blanche," measures 16–19 of "O
mort, poussière d'étoiles," or similar sequences in "Dans la nymphée," "Dans
la forêt de septembre," "Le Don silencieux." Then ask the friend who wrote
what.

But there was also Fauré's oh-so-tonal use of lowered sevenths in a manner
then known, five thousand kilometers away in Dixieland, as blue. Already in
the Requiem the theme bends jazzily at letter E. Listen now to the words sons
and tout in "Soir." Or to sages and pâles in "Reflets dans l'eau." Or to the
whole last stanza of "En prière." Did Fauré hear those notes as we, geared by
intervening decades of pop, hear them?

The world's best song composers of the past always majored in poetry
either contemporary or of the preceding generation. Invariably though, they
ventured toward, even dwelt long among, more distant poets: Debussy with
d'Orléans, Ravel and Poulenc with Ronsard. Fauré is the only prolific song
composer I can think of whose texts, with one brief exception (Molière), are
drawn exclusively from his own century. The statistic is noble, the details
plebeian.

People always ask if second-rate poems can make first-rate songs. Yes, but
only if the composer thinks the poems are first-rate. Fauré was known to be
cultured and up-to-date, frequenting both Mallarmé's "Tuesdays" and Robert de Montesquiou (Proust's Charlus) who showed him Verlaine's verse. Yet
the composer never set Mallarmé, and, except for Verlaine, the great poetry

he did use fell flat. As experienced through Fauré, Hugo seems too weak and Baudelaire too strong. Unlike Debussy, Fauré is not devious, he says what he says. He preferred now-dim poetasters such as Prudhomme (Nobel laureate though he was), Bussine, Samain, Mendès, and also one Louis Pommey, official supplier of verse to soprano-composer Pauline Viardot, mistress to Turgenev and first big-time performer of Fauré's songs. Their paraphernalia was quaint: endless perfumes, dreams, girls, sighs, sorrow, dead leaves, living waters, tears, roses, moons and dawns and graveyards. But Fauré's staunch conviction, through his convincing gifts, convinces us.

The first and much better of the "Complete Songs" is a two-volume set (four discs) issued by the Connoisseur Society of Pathé Marconi. It features baritone Gérard Souzay, soprano Elly Ameling, with Dalton Baldwin as accompanist.

"Accompanist" has servile overtones. I prefer simply pianist. Still, if accompanist may obtain to pianist *and* singer (who accompany each other through an adventure wherein their instruments mesh), then Dalton Baldwin is the best since Gerald Moore. He can play. He is not self-effacing. In those many moments where the piano is in fact an accompaniment—a strumming, an ostinato, a flow—Baldwin becomes more than mere support: he is the velvet upon which rubies are offered, the landscape against which portraits are sketched. Fauré, however, was the first *mélodiste* to give the keyboard an identity. Even in such young songs as "Claire de lune" or "Nocturne" the vocal lines seem afterthoughts imposed on a self-styled piano solo, while in the icy *Chanson d'Ève* voice and piano form complements of independent counterpoint—the closest Fauré, or indeed any Frenchman of the period, came to straight polyphony. When Dalton Baldwin pedals with an Achilles' heel, it is precisely during these rare linear sections (viz., inexpert twos-against-threes in "Comme rayonne"). He is otherwise accurate, economical, generous, tasteful without passivity and (especially with Souzay, his daily collaborator for twenty-five years) persuasively inevitable—assets which make him, although he is American, ever so French, at least on the surface.

French too, although she is Dutch, is Elly Ameling, at least on the surface, with her neat-tailored non-vibrato concepts. The sound is sapphirine, all notes (except an unstable middle-C) being more gleamingly focused than any light soprano's since Stich-Randall. Her diction is dutifully clean in French, as indeed it is in English here ("Mélisande's Song" is Fauré's one foray into English; and incidentally, in harmonic and thematic plotting, it is an *esquisse* for the later *Chanson d'Ève*). Ameling's main fault is her faultlessness. You wait in vain for a risk, an eccentricity. Listen to her bland and proper "Nell," then recall the "Nell" of Nell Tangeman or of Povla Frijsh with their hot enthusiastic swoops. Yet if Ameling's *Chanson d'Ève*, for ripeness and energy, falls short of Phyllis Curtin's (Cambridge Records, 1964) it is nevertheless there that her nubile hues glimmer most favorably. The cycle is Fauré's only extended vocal piece which does not sound better in a masculine voice. Insofar as the suite of poems is intoned by, and mirrors, what is often called Feminine Viewpoint, one might be tempted to name it Female Art, were not both composer and poet (Belgium's symbolist, Charles van Lerberghe) men.

Yet what woman composer today would select such fragile texts, or dare to concoct such scented sonorities as have come to be known, erroneously, as Ladies' Music? Other centuries, other stigmas. Fauré the man, with that Mark Twain face and irreproachable domesticity, was bourgeois to the teeth, as were all French composers (though not poets or painters) of the nineteenth century. His dialect was delicate, like Monet's or Mallarmé's, but no less manly than Berlioz's or Delacroix's, for art, though sexual, is without sex. Fauré is never ribald like Ravel and Poulenc. He is often *croyant* unlike Ravel and Debussy, but like Poulenc whose "religious" works could still be ribald.

So much for the fiction of specific sensibility in art.

In fact, the male timbre was Fauré's ruling texture. His metabolism, his heartbeat, his humor mentioned earlier are baritone by nature, that is, words sung which are slower, not faster, than words spoken. During his final years the composer adopted Charles Panzéra, to whom *L'Horizon chimérique* is dedicated, as his protégé. Panzéra in turn inaugurated the age of the French song recital, establishing a convention by which "Fauré" became synonymous with "baritone." Pierre Bernac a generation later inherited the mantle. Eventually *his* protégé, Gérard Souzay, took over. Years have passed.

That Souzay's voice is no longer young alters our pleasure no more than do evening shadows in a gorgeous oak. Among such shadows the *mélodie* comes to roost. Souzay's sound gives off an exhausted hint of nasal sadness which to me is quintessentially French. The cycle *Mirages* was composed for Madeleine Grey (still indomitable in the Rue Blanche, when last heard from), but can you imagine another voice than Souzay's inflecting those bittersweet opening bars? As the Baronne de Brimont's harmonious swan glides forth from Souzay's lips the whole land of France somehow fans out, the same way that all of America is echoed on those last discs of Billie Holiday—not through sense but through sound. Listen to the unfolding of the nine moods in *La Bonne chanson:* how the voice swerves in and out of the shade like the tinted edges of a Rouault pastel fading imperceptibly from midnight blue to cobalt to azure.

Purple metaphors do not a critic make. But just as Souzay's most singular quality—the Frenchness of his musicality—cannot be taught, neither can it be described except through comparison. His least singular quality is all too describable, if harmless. In contrast to Ameling who inclines to underdo, Souzay sometimes tries too hard. "Après un rêve" is a case: He will not let the words sing themselves, he must feel them, *interpret* them. Interpretation, of course, is the forte of Bernac who is the only reliable teacher of French song literature in the world today. But what works for the teacher may not be needed when a pupil's voice, in itself, is evocative.

Souzay commits likable word-errors here and there, substituting an *et* for an *ou*, a *quand* for a *lorsque*, a *front* for a *coeur*. (Frijsh used to do this too, accidentally on purpose maybe, to prove that her comprehension wasn't rote.)

With Ameling we have an agreeable Fauré performer, but with Souzay we have the definitive one. And with Dalton Baldwin, as equalizing force in this healthy *ménage à trois nations*, we have a magic keyboardist.

THE MÉLISANDE
NOTEBOOK

Every generation has its golden calf. Young composers in all countries, like young poets, are prone to admire, and so to being influenced by, a single recent work—though often these poets and composers (who never synchronize, so far as the texture of "trends" is concerned) are moved by opposing forces. Thus in the American fifties Ginsberg's rhapsodic *Howl*, which freed many a small Eliot from the previous decade, contrasted with Carter's formalistic quartets, which displaced the looser Coplandiana then in vogue. Thus in the Spanish twenties Falla's aristocratic Harpsichord Concerto stamped exotic classicism onto all Hispanic musicians for the next two decades, while Lorca's plebeian surrealism has yet to be superseded. And thus in France at the start of this century, when new writers and painters were dizzied by Valéry's brains and Braque's cubes, every composer in Paris staggered under the non-intellectual non-angular but leanly opulent and sensually clean impact of *Pelléas et Mélisande*.

When Debussy's magic first charmed me, musical children were still more geared to yesterday's Europeans than to current landsmen. Debussy had been dead only five years at my birth (the same span that Schumann had been dead at Debussy's birth), and his influence by 1938 washed over Illinois like LSD. Artistically he was the most important man of my childhood, hence of my life. Meantime, while my poet friends rewrote Yeats, their painter friends repainted Dali. Alas! it required a vast and real war during the next decade for America to perfect an identifiable signature. For me it was too late: I'd been branded by Paris, and brands don't rub out.· I was French in Chicago long before I went to live in France.

Great works provoke nostalgia for that which they do not contain. So sometimes does even mediocre music, music being the one art which can excite the memory to situations remote from what that actual music is speaking (or singing) about.

Along with its appeal to the more evident senses *Pelléas* is a piece that can be smelled and tasted (though probably not touched). I've known the opera all my life, mainly through score and disc, but I've seen it too, a half dozen times in as many cities. To prime the writing of these notes I attended the present Metropolitan Opera version, my first live performance in years. I was all alone, with two good seats, and the voluptuous expectation of soon being engulfed by the Europe of my young manhood.

Oh là, what melancholy joy the Met affords each time those two-ton diamond brooches rise fading toward the roof, while we all sink back into our seats as into some huge hot homemade rhubarb tart! But the expectation unexpectedly veered. The first D-minor bars did not dredge up the Café du Flore of 1949, nor Maeterlinck's nineteenth-century Jugendstil (which the French call "modern style" and we call "art nouveau"), nor yet his fictional Allemonde, but my own beloved Lake Michigan and Chicago's university campus. Just as we cannot hear, say, Frescobaldi as he heard himself, because of our conditioning by the constant crests of the waves which flowed out of him for centuries afterward (the passing sevenths and ninths and elevenths formed from baroque horizontal counterpoint, for example, still hit me vertically, even bluesily, because of the Benny Goodman records which I first learned along with Bach), neither can we hear any music except within the context of our initial exposure. The hearing also evokes extramusical thrills: the smell of grape punch at the annual gym dance while "our song" was playing. Now, I first made love while Debussy was playing, and if Mélisande's harmonies do not always today bring Mélisande to mind, they do momentarily reunite the transient with the eternal—my own lost youth with Everybody's Art.

It's my favorite opera. Yet it contains the two things I most abhor: the scrim, and the boy soprano. An audience, by the rules of the game, is plunged in darkness. To be thereupon for any length of time confronted with a stage plunged in darkness is to be cheated. Theater is make believe: real gloom cannot *represent* gloom, and scrims are the set designer's easy (I mean hard) way out. As to children who sing, I am in a class with those philistines who hooted Yniold off the stage during the dress rehearsal in 1902. Sung by a woman the part seems silly. Sung by a boy the insult of rasp is added to the injury of Yniold's music, which is second-rate and maddening.

Debussy is said to have said that he wanted to eliminate beginnings and ends, and to create a music consisting solely of middles. (Godard, asked to acknowledge the necessity for having a beginning, middle, and end in his films, replied: "Certainly, but not necessarily in that order.") But try switching scenes in *Pelléas*—and, of course, eliminating Yniold—and see how far you get. His music, all of it, was traditionally formal.

Do you believe in ghosts? or are they just a fancy form of willed coincidence? No sooner did I type that last word—*formal*—than a book fell from the shelf with a dainty crash, and, like the flask labeled "DRINK ME" in *Alice in Wonderland*, the book screamed "QUOTE ME."

Retrieving from the floor Fred Goldbeck's little volume on modern Mediterranea, called *France, Italy and Spain*, published years ago in England, I found the margins penciled with forgotten reflections. Those pertaining to the composer, who in his waning years years signed himself *Claude de France*, I herewith reveal:

Debussy is called The Emancipator of the Consonance (in reaction to German emancipation of dissonance), and from that bon mot stems much of Goldbeck's premise. I like his references to "the tradition of anti-traditionalism" in describing post-Beethovenism; and if "Beethoven's own Fate knocks at his symphony's door . . . Debussy's art owes its character to being veiled by impersonality."

Debussy: "The only rule I admit enjoins pleasing a musician's ear." Goldbeck: "He knew pretty well how not to reveal his sources," and adds that Debussy's dislike of Berlioz's music was "perhaps because he knew it through inadequate and vulgar renderings." A more likely truth: Debussy found Berlioz vulgar and inadequate.

However:

To assert continually that Debussy is anti-romantic requires an understanding of the term. Musicologically Romantic may be a distinction from Classical; to me romantic means loving, and since I first learned Debussy when I learned loving, his music still gives off a tabooed mystery and smell of physical passion which is romantic indeed.

To declare that *Mouvement* is static, sounds like a witty paradox. In fact this piece does move from one place to another both through space and through time, i.e., in and out of keys from point zero to point four-some minutes.

To call *La Mer* the North Sea is conjecture.

To call the bland Ansermet "that unsurpassed interpreter of Debussy" is to be blind in the light of Monteux.

To call Debussy a master prose writer, when in fact his prose was acid platitude, is to be blind to the light of Satie.

To wish people would stop calling Debussy an impressionist, then to state that "only a disingenuous listener would, if he had ever seen a Turner, a Renoir or a Monet, deny that *La Mer*, *Fêtes* and *Reflets dans l'eau* remind him of these painters" is careless. (The sea reminds *me* of *La Mer*, though *La Mer* never reminds me of the sea.)

To write ". . . the whole-tone scale—a scale almost as conspicuous a Debussy fingerprint as impressionism itself; metres that dispense with squareness . . ." is flat wrong. The whole-tone scale *(Voiles* notwithstanding) accounts for less than 5 percent of the composer's oeuvre. He used it sparingly, always to unique effect, as Delacroix might add a rare brushful of ochre to make a recalcitrant patch of sunlight "speak." As to dispensing with squareness, Debussy's freedom is by everyone overstressed. His forms often parse as more than square—as foursquare—and not just in those young piano suites. Consider the late "revolutionary" Études (those in thirds and in sixths, for example), honed from periods of four-measure phrases literally restated. Meanwhile, the "baroque" and "mysterious" architecture, which Goldbeck would superimpose upon the two Books of Préludes when played as a unit, is a blueprint of fantasy, appealing but invalid, like saying that a man can plot his whole life from birth.

To claim that Debussy's vocal style is "a kind of conversational psalmodiz-ing" that tells us about Pelléas and Mélisande "in the tones of a well-informed chronicler," is to hear all song in terms of aria rather than tune, and to ignore the historical fact that Debussy was involved to a point of hysteria with Maeterlinck's play. If Debussy's vocal lines are not spacious in a Puccini sense, they are always melodic, never recitative, the distinction being that melody haunts, recitative doesn't. Of course, there is no Right Way for hearing (or for listening to) music, but to experience Pelléas as the work of an uninvolved chronicler makes one curious about Goldbeck's way.

So much for ghosts.

Can anyone know how others hear?

One can detest opera yet love *Pelléas*. One can love opera yet detest *Pelléas*. And one can love both, so long as one does not search through Pelléas for mad airs and mob scenes. Yes, it is my favorite piece, but my wisest friends loathe it; wisdom does not reside in the ear, and I can only conclude that they are not hearing what I hear. For them the rôles come over as undifferenti-ated, monochrome. For me Debussy's vocality is not a series of soldered fragments but a concentrated melody (the "spun-out line" reduced to lowest terms, as opposed to Verdi's stretching of the line to highest terms, or to Webern's ultimate dismissal of such terms) which also often fulfills harmonic chores by replacing a "missing" instrument. If the score never blossoms in the usual sense, it does so in reverse, like a galaxy expanding under a microscope.

Hearing it in the inner ear as it *should* be done, how can I stand it as it *is* done? Alone at the keyboard I fabricate the greatest performances: in the flesh which I've added to the bones are embedded, like diamond shards, flecks of priceless melodic shape which have become mine alone. No living Arkel, perhaps not even Debussy himself in Heaven, will ever intone as capably as I do the inborn inevitability of certain phrases.

Such music exists only ideally, in the abstract. *Pelléas et Mélisande* is of that rare race of masterpiece which must never be performed. I can think of no non-vocal works about which this need be said, nor indeed of any non-French works.

Debussy was sometimes wrong, as is any composer, when explicating his methods. (How could he state better in words what he's clearly stated in notes?) "Symphonic development and character development can never un-fold at the same pace" is his excuse for what one commentator calls the "quasirecitative" style of the opera. But the style is not quasirecitative, and the two developments do unfold simultaneously. ". . . the action should never be halted, [so] I wanted to dispense with parasitical musical phrases. . . . Melody, if I dare say so, is antilyrical." Yet deed contradicts act. And melody is where you find it.

As it happens, the only English words which Fauré ever set to music were *Mélisande's Song*, by one J. W. Mackail, after Maeterlinck. In song texts, if Fauré used almost exclusively poets of the present, Debussy used poets of the past. Or, when Debussy used poets of the present, their subject matter was the past, especially the Dark Ages.

If the poetry of our late Frank O'Hara is now sufficiently far away to be experienced as the past, it is yet too close to be convincingly embellished by music in the present. Debussy set Baudelaire a half-century after the poet's death, and both are now remote enough for us to see (hear) them as one. O'Hara was nothing if not a poet of the present. But we are his future, unfocusing his quiet grave. The tone of the immediate past juxtaposed upon the tone of the present produces a unison just slightly out of tune. To a trained ear this is more discombobulating than a juxtaposition of centuries. The legend of Othello, adapted by Shakespeare, prosified by Boito, musicalized by Verdi, recorded by Tebaldi, reaches us with no sense of anachronism. But if we can caricature the fifties now, the sixties are still too close for comfort.

Virgil Thomson once wrote that Mélisande will do anything to avoid not being loved. "A lonely girl with a floating libido and no malice toward anyone can cause lots of trouble in a well-organized family. . . . The opera is her show, hers and the conductor's."

Thomson is right. It is no less right to claim that the opera is Golaud's show, his and the conductor's. (Within one artwork cannot two viewpoints paradoxically occupy the same space at the same time, like rain and landscape?) The drama's kernel lies in Golaud's jealousy which dictates—or rather, ignores—the comportment of his nearest and dearest. What others might say in their own defense goes unheard by Golaud, he is beyond the pale. He was a goner even before he met his bride, as he admits at the outset, likening the metaphoric loss during male menopause to the literal loss of Mélisande, who knows neither who nor where she is. Golaud's confusion, like Othello's, is a villainous weapon, razing those around him, finally himself.

No villain is all bad in opera. Iago, Claggart, Hérodiade, Sparafucile, because they sing, grow vulnerable, thus to some extent likable despite their absolute wickedness, for music is a great leveler. Of course, Golaud is not a villain—is, in fact, the play's most touching player, not merely acting but reacting, evolving and being allowed the only loud sounds. Do those reiterated anxious chords through which he pleads with a dying wife suspiciously echo Rodolfo's cry of "Mimi"? Il Tabarro may well have been cast up by La Mer, but La Bohème predated Pelléas by six years and would have been known to the Frenchman. (How wearisome to forever read of Debussy as Influence, especially to a background of Satie's Sarabandes, or even Rebikov's oozing ninths. Debussy was not cut from whole cloth, nor was he even so original. It's not that he was different than. He was better than.)

As for Debussy's opera being a conductor's show, great singers with a bad orchestra are unacceptable, whereas bona fide renditions with second-rate singers are feasible provided the orchestra excels. Witness the Boulez recording, a gargantuan symphonic canvas upon which pastel voices are permitted to limn inexpertly, though the net result comes over as faithful.

Similarly, Pelléas in translation is not a betrayal. My first hearing was in Philadelphian English, and a thrill, while all ensuing Parisian versions miscalculated perspective with histrionics and vibratos. When musical texts are so very French, perhaps they can be communicated only in English to Americans, whereas pieces in an "international" style (by Elgar, say, or Monteverdi, Massenet, Wagner) should be sung always in the original. The opposite could be posited: non-ornamental prosodic settings like Debussy's, or like Satie's *Socrate*, should never be translated, but nothing is lost when coloratura is Englished.

Maeterlinck's play is sophisticated, taken at face value rather than for symbolism. Mélisande becomes an Antonioni heroine, wealthy (as they all are) without explanation, who doesn't answer questions, and is herself not always given replies. Meanwhile the demented echoes, non sequiturs and shifting repetitions of speech sound as timeless as nursery rhymes or lovers' quarrels. Debussy responds to the text literally, even occasionally Mickey-Mousing (despite Satie's warning against letting the scenery make faces) when there is talk of fountains, sheep, death, creaking gates. Such effects are, of course, all instrumental.

Indeed, if Debussy demands the same requisites for finished performances as other opera composers—good singers, good orchestra, good blend of the two—he ideally demands more balanced proportions than, for instance, Donizetti, whose accompaniments can be so-so if the singers are sensational.

To psychoanalyze a composer according to subject matter is risky (but fun) even if the subject matter is literal—that is, extramusical—as with vocal settings, which reflect the poet's as well as the musician's preoccupations. Music's real subject, of course, is, as they say, abstract (motives, colors, dynamics, rhythms, shapes); and even if abstraction could be taken apart and psychologized, it would not be the composer's specific choice of abstraction (theme) so much as the composer's *way* with the choice which might "reveal" him or her. But if music is abstract, therapy is concrete; so if Debussy repeatedly deals in, say, water, what does that tell about Debussy, even after one discusses *how* he deals in water?

Unasked questions:

Is Pelléas gay? The sentiment and its realization were rife in the nineteenth as in every century, but the word and concept were not yet formulated by the mind doctors. Probably neither Maeterlinck nor Debussy, both bourgeois family men, were much concerned, even peripherally, with the love that dare not speak its name. Yet their unconscious slant on the hero seems . . . well, slanted. Who is the dying Marcellus for whom Pelléas would quit his own dying father? How could Pelléas help but resent everyone in the castle, most of all the new Mélisande, who keeps him from this friend, evoked anxiously, then never mentioned again? To worry the question may appear old-fashioned, yet if only one baritone could determine that, for himself, Pelléas was or was not homophilic (at least so far as Marcellus is involved), the rôle, and by extension the music for the rôle, would shed its habitual sappiness and don a carnal dimension, a fullness, a reasonableness that only Martial Singher has thus far lent to it.

Mélisande? Is she, as Mary Garden contended, Bluebeard's last spouse (". . . and I only am escaped to tell thee") wandering deranged, complete with crown, through this foreign forest? What ship brought her? the one with the *"grandes voiles"* now sailing off at full speed? Has she been weeping for a day, or a month? If for a month, what has she eaten? There is never talk of food, yet at one point we learn of famine in the land, of beggars dying in grottoes; but of this, as of Marcellus, there is no further mention, and the protagonists seem sufficiently healthy to languish only for love, nor do they trouble with government.

And where and when is Allemonde? *(Allemagne?)* In the fourth? the seventh? the eleventh century? Bluebeard, or Gilles de Raiz, was Joan of Arc's lover, but the traditional décor suggests a somberer era.

A dozen references to people's hands: by the men to Mélisande ("Donnez-moi la main"), Mélisande to herself ("On dirait que mes mains sont malades"), Golaud to Pelléas ("Donnez-moi—non, non, pas la main . . ."), but no tactile contact except with hair. Would that the audience followed suit. The final page is the most beautiful in history, yet I've never heard it live because, such hands as are not slipping on gloves while the heroine expires, are clapping as the curtain lowers.

Why do the characters say *vous* and *tu* to each other interchangeably?

The one definitive book on Debussy is, alas, the noxious tome of Lockspeiser which contains no insightful paragraphs on the composer's life (though one smarmy phrase, about the marriage to Rosalie, "this simple good and unaffected girl of the people, was the natural result of the genuinely simple and unaffected life led by Debussy during the nineties, moving among the ordinary honest folk of Paris . . .", recalls my father's quip about someone being born "of poor but dishonest parents"), nor any description of the music not pertainable to any other music (". . . this is treated so simply and beautifully it could not possibly have been done in any other way," etc.), but does offer an occasional useful quote from the composer:

> The scenic realization of a work of art, no matter how beautiful, is always contrary to the inner vision which drew it in turns from its alternatives of doubt and enthusiasm.

And, when seriously tempted to give the part of Pelléas to a woman, Debussy wrote to Messager:

> Pelléas has not the ways of making love of a hussar, and when he finally does resolve upon something his plans are so quickly checked by the sword of Golaud that the idea might be worth considering.

Worth considering, too, is the idea of "pure" sibling adoration between the two young people. The game is without end. Debussy has become history and is now open to reinterpretation as opposed to mere misinterpretation.

These random notes have sought briefly to set forth a few facts and opinions not generally bandied about in the now vast wastes of Debussyana. One shrewd reader or two, with a huff, may recognize some of these sentences as having been dug up verbatim from my other writings. Mea culpa. However, such sentences have never appeared in this sequence or context, nor, obviously, have they before been copied out by me at the age I now enjoy. Thus, like Borges's literal transcription of Cervantes, old phrases acquire new senses according to their look on the page, and to the molecules of a given decade.

December 1977

FAURÉ AND DEBUSSY

What did Gabriel Fauré, born in 1845, and Claude Debussy, seventeen years his junior, think of each other? "Never speak to me of Debussy," warned the older man. "I don't want to know there is a Debussy. If I like Debussy I can no longer like Fauré. How can I then be Fauré?" Debussy's only published reaction to the other composer is enigmatic: "We heard a Ballade by the Master of Charms, almost as lovely as pianist Madame Hasselmans herself who kept having to straighten her shoulder straps, as they fell down at every scale. I somehow associate these gestures with the music of Fauré himself. The play of fleeting curves that is the essence of his music can be compared to the movements of a beautiful woman without either suffering from the comparison."

Could their mutual wariness have been due to the singer, Emma Bardac, for whom in 1892 Fauré composed *La Bonne chanson*, and for whom ten years later Debussy left his wife? Could there have been proprietary scufflings over their attraction to the poetry of Paul Verlaine? Fauré, unlike Debussy (or for that matter unlike Ravel, Gounod, Saint-Saëns, Roussel or the Germans of the preceding generation) continually favored contemporary poets; only in the choice of Verlaine did their penchants overlap, even to frequent duplications of specific poems.

Comparisons between Fauré and Debussy are quite in keeping with the present record, although no texts are duplicated. All, however, are by Verlaine, and every song saw the light within one brief decade, *Ariettes oubliées* and *Chansons de Bilitis* being composed respectively in 1888 and 1897, and *La Bonne chanson* between 1892 and 1894. Fauré's long career encompassed Debussy's as Haydn's encompassed Mozart's and in both cases the shorter-lived artist was the more versatile. If Fauré has come to be known as something of a specialist (he published 104 songs to Debussy's 57), Debussy made magic of every medium he touched. Given these statistics, and succumbing to the idle joy of the game, which one do you feel wrote the finer songs? Such tests are doubtless unfair. More useful would be to locate these two men within the current esthetic.

Will anyone deny that Debussy and Fauré wrote the most significant songs of nineteenth-century France? But if you dare equate them to Schubert or Schumann eyebrows go up. Why is the *lied*, even to otherwise rabid Teutoniphobes, so much more beloved than the *mélodie*? As an American who does not shudder to admit a ·preference for Gallic art, I have never before faced the question, chalking it up to taste.

Probably the general bias toward German vocal music owes less to profundity than to accessibility. The best French songs, despite a reputed superficial scent, are really harder to listen to—their ingredients are more complex. This disparity in turn owes less to national bent than to historic trend.

The last century produced almost no songs of quality in England, America, Iberia and Italy; alone France and Germany nourished the form, and their great practitioners were few. The golden age of *lied* spans scarcely three decades and contains but a pair of composers, Schubert and Schumann, with Brahms carrying the torch into the next generation. The golden age of *mélodie* begins late in the century, includes but two composers, Fauré and Debussy, with Poulenc carrying the torch into our day. (Yes, yes, Germany had Beethoven and Wolf and maybe Pfitzner, France had Gounod and Ravel and maybe Duparc. But Beethoven's songs, like Ravel's, though gorgeous and unflawed, are too rare for a major category, while the other composers are of a lesser breed.) Now, Schubert and Schumann were dead when Debussy was born; in any case, his and Fauré's musical dialect stemmed from local literature more than from tunes across the Rhine. Those tunes, even at their most persuasive, had been strophic, repeated literally with each stanza, the piano a mere accompaniment without independent identity. Then as now virtually any serious concert *lied* was grasped at first hearing as easily as a folk or café refrain; it was the melodic genius of their composers rather than their freshness of form that lent German songs their staying power. In France at this period song composers—Chabrier, for example, or Saint-Saëns—were no more formally subtle; indeed, their *romances* were also of an eighteenth-century mold—couplets set to an endlessly repeated pattern, with inevitably unsynchronized lyrics. Though no more naïve than the German counterpart, the mold was far less solid, and gave forth salon ditties. By the time the *mélodie* was evolving in Paris, the grand men of *lieder* were fading away.

Mélodie (which we Americans, with our pat insecurity in matters melodious, call Art Song lest it not be taken seriously) was a new genre which took form almost single-handedly with Fauré. He let the sonic thread flow to the shape of each new stanza, tracing the vocal arch according to the words and freeing the piano from its rôle of mere support. Such an approach necessarily accommodated itself to more sophisticated poetry, though let me stress that Fauré's opting of poets was on the whole as second-rate as Schubert's. Still, it is a fallacy that mediocre verse makes the best songs: *Winterreise* is wonderful despite, not because, of Müller's bathos, and surely the beauty of Verlaine does not detract from Fauré's most thrilling settings.

The novelty of those settings rests in the telling elasticity of their declamation when sung, as opposed to the poems' versicle strictness when read. French, being the sole European tongue in which multisyllabic words have no tonic accent (that explains why the French felt the need to invent the defiantly rhythmic alexandrine), there is no single prosodically right way for musicalizing it. If Debussy stretched this elasticity still farther—and it is impossible to parse his Verlaine settings—every word remains nonetheless comprehensible, as it does also chez Fauré and Poulenc. The comprehensibility comes partly from a tradition of allowing sung poetry to unfold at the speed of spoken poetry, and partly from the eschewing of melisma; it is seldom that one hears in French (as opposed to German) song a syllable assigned to more than one note.

It is pertinent to conclude that both Fauré and Debussy (far more than their grandchild Poulenc) carried tonality to a point of ambiguity nearly a century ago. The ambiguity, dogmatized years later by Schoenberg, was thus as much a French as a German *trouvaille*. Yet it is not the harmonic vagueness of their songs which disconcerts the *lied* lover—who often as not loves Berg and Webern too—so much as the separate strands of nuance, the less obvious airs, the "decadence" of Mallarmé as contrasted with the "nobility" of Heine.

Perhaps in the final analysis one's musical disposition *is* a matter of taste.

Nantucket, November 1981

CONSIDERING CARMEN

I.

Some of my best friends are Carmens—starting with my father. When I was old enough to get around the keyboard I used to accompany him in Bizet's airs, ideal for amateur baritones. And Father chaperoned my first cultural outing, the Chicago version of *Carmen* starring one Coe Glade, with whom I fell in love.

These homey facts, waxing into a taste for mezzos, would never have struck me had not Robert Jacobson, over a soufflé at Café des Artistes, recently suggested I "do something on *Carmen*." Why me? "To avoid type casting." Indeed, I have never in print examined a pre-modern composer, one not somehow concerned with being new, with changing things through innovation more than through mere excellence. Now, since being new is strictly a hang-up of twentieth-century artists, and since I too inhabit the century, my easy task had always been to show that nothing's new. But what do I know of Bizet?

Well, I have known his opera all my life. Still that knowledge is involuntary: it's the one opera everyone knows. *Carmen*, the most popular serious piece (or the most serious popular piece) ever penned, has entered the collective unconsciousness. As it happens, my young education converged perversely—and I believe correctly—around what used to be termed Modern Music. By the onset of puberty I had memorized *Petrushka*, *Pierrot* and *Daphnis*, not to mention Carpenter's *Skyscrapers* and Schelling's *Victory Ball*, yet I wouldn't have recognized a Brahms quartet, nor even a Bach gavotte. Contempt may breed contempt, but familiarity breeds only familiarity. Except for *Carmen*, I had to get used to "classics" as others get used to "moderns."

The past is a problem still, for I never turned into an opera buff. Nor do I enjoy pure song for itself rather than for how its composer manipulates the text. Also, like most composers, I'm more involved with my own music than with other people's. (But yes, I would rather hear that music sung by dumb singers with golden echoes than by smart singers with leaden echoes.) So finally I have a narrower knowledge of opera than many an amateur. Yet what I know is my own. As for what I know about *Carmen*, no sooner had Robert Jacobson bid good-bye than associations began streaming.

✳

Northwestern, 1940. Despite Father and Coe Glade, it was less a love of voice than of verse which fired my first songs. I made a dozen settings of E. E. Cummings before comprehending that these might actually be interpreted. Then one morning, overhearing *Carmen* practiced in the next studio, I decided to ask the young mezzo to read through my efforts. That she happened to *be* a mezzo was fortuitous; although my music thus far had been intuitively concocted around my own deepish hummings—vile to some, sweet to me (inside every composer lurks a diva longing to get out)—it was a decade until I learned there were strata to voices, hierarchies and lowerarchies of vocal literature, and that all singers, like it or not, are consigned to tessiturial castes.

The reactions to hearing those early songs emoted by Frances Maralda (where is she today?) set the stage for all my future music.

Philadelphia, 1943. Muriel Smith, she of the burning eye, blue burnished hair and butterscotch skin—now brought life to my sonic skeletons, then became the first of our Curtis group to defect to big-time Manhattan as Carmen Jones. (Like Dietrich's Lola, Muriel's Carmen was more sisterly than sinister, and, sung in English, lent a likability to the role new to Americans.) She was the first ever publicly to sing my tunes, among them a Cocteau quatrain named *De Don Juan*.

Were the French deranged by Spain before Bizet? If the Gallic Iberia is forever as quixotic, at least to Spaniards, as Kafka's Amerika is to us, the teenaged Poulenc with Cocteau in 1919 gave that quixoticism the coup-degrâce in their "Chanson Hispano-Italienne" titled *Toréador*, a crazy waltz which depicts a Venetian corrida:

Belle Espagnole
Dans ta gondole
Tu caracoles
Carmencita . . .

Jennie Tourel, between rehearsals for *The Rake's Progress*, first sang me those lines at the very site of their inception, Piazza San Marco, the French notion of an elegant bullring.

Tanglewood, 1946. Before the curtain rises on the U.S. première of Britten's opera (for which the composer is present), Koussevitzky mounts the stage and begins to speak. "There is *Carmen* . . . and there is *Peter Grimes*." Carmen? Is she an absolute by which to judge Peter? True, Britten may be a finer artist than Bizet, but more than one Brittenism was previewed in Carmen's cards.

New York, 1948. So far as my own music went, Nell Tangeman's wise, lush contralto became the defining instrument. During her brief peak, from 1948 to 1954, hers was the one "real" voice doing new repertory. All I wrote then was for her, and by extension all I write now comes from what I learned with her. I think mezzo. Nell and her friend Martha Lipton were learning *Carmen* simultaneously. Martha, who focused on—and speaks still today of—the gypsy's "broad scope of honesty, playfulness and courage" went on to sing the rôle throughout the land. Nell, who preferred the rôle's violence and bitchery, never sang it publicly, although at the end of her life she was studying it in German on the off-chance of an audition in Düsseldorf. *Frei war sie geboren, und frei will sie sterben!*

Free she was not. Unlike Carmen, Nell practiced the privileges of fame without the responsibilities; overcelebrating at parties in her honor, she would skip rehearsals next day. During her heyday she presented all my vocal music as well as premières by Copland, Ives, Messiaen, Bernstein and Chanler. She was the first American to sing Jocasta's big aria under Stravinsky's direction. That's as close as she ever got to the Habañera, but it's close. Yet at the time of her suicide in 1965 no obituary appeared.

Paris, 1950. Samuel Barber arrives with violinist Charles Turner. They are preparing Barber's concerto for recording. Who is the rehearsal pianist? Why, Pierre Boulez. Barber kids the stoical Frenchman about the twelve-tone system. "Is the Habañera a row?" he asks. (He loathes the imputations of the serial elite. He persists in addressing the perplexed René Leibowitz as Mr. Ztiwobiel. "Well, if a composer can't recognize his own name in retrograde, how can his listeners be expected . . . etc.")

Hyères, 1951. Robert Veyron-Lacroix permits me to play "primo" in *Jeux d'enfants*, while there by the window, his pate turning the shade of a Café des Artistes soufflé in the Provençal sunset, Boris Kochno loudly recalls staging these goodies for Diaghilev. Boris claims to have heard Mary Garden as Carmen and found her wonderful.

Felix Borowski at Northwestern had taught us that Garden, after felling not only Mélisande, but Judith and Salome and Thaïs and Louise, met her own downfall by tackling Carmen, defeater of all her sisters. Virgil Thomson saw her too, and found her "redhaired, small, psychiatric, intelligent, basing her action on Mérimée."

Sopranos who turn mezzo, like Callas or Price, fare better at Carmen than mezzos who turn soprano, like Verrett or Horne.

Hyères, 1954. A road company, replete with Bizet's bizarre orchestra and featuring the sadly deaf Valentine Tessier in the short rich role of La Renaude, unfolds *L'Arlésienne* upon the town square. We all are dazzled, conditioned by knowing that Freud once decorticated this meridional drama to the annoyance of its author, Alphonse Daudet. Also in the cast: a donkey, rented from the Toulon slaughterhouse. After the show Marie Laure asks the manager what will happen to the animal. "*Il rentre à l'abbatoir*." So she buys the beast, which lives in her stable for the next six years, fitted with a collar of silver bells that awaken us daily as he trots forth to graze on the front lawn. He is christened Alphonse.

Besides owning a donkey named Alphonse, how does Marie Laure de Noailles—my best friend in France, but scarcely a Carmen—fit into these notes? Her maternal grandmother, Comtesse Adhéaume de Chevigné, was one of two models upon whom Proust fashioned his Princess de Guermantes. The other was Madame Émile Straus, widow of Georges Bizet.

They say that a rapport at no more than three steps remove can be construed between any two persons on earth. Our friend Nadia Boulanger—alive and well and living in Paris—is the daughter of composer Ernest Boulanger who was already twenty-three when Bizet was born in 1838.

The heirs of some who die comparatively poor and obscure grow quickly rich and chic by wearing just their names.

Other Carmens who have shaped my end? Regina Sarfaty, Elaine Bonazzi, Betty Allen, Beverly Wolff.

And now enough of shapeless reverie. How is *Carmen* shaped by the eight operatic components: chords, line, beat, tune, color, vocality (both solo and ensemble), formality (both sectional and overall) and theatrical panache?

2.

Wagner loved *Carmen*. Contrary to general thought composers are more leery than indulgent of music which resembles their own. That Bizet was once deemed a Wagnerite seems now merely funny: *Carmen* is as wholeheartedly diatonic as *Tristan* is not. The Habañera? It is chromatic only melodically. Harmonically, with those 120 measures of seesawing over a pedal-D, it is more doggedly tonal than a Clementi sonata.

Nor was the lead-motive a Bizetian need; his airs once sung stay sung. True, strands dangling from certain early statements—Micaëla's mainly—are sometimes tucked back into the formal fabric. But only the Death Tune, announced in the prelude, recurs and recurs and recurs, with that Cui-like augmented second which Frenchmen up to and through Ravel identify with sex, sex being always blamed on other countries and this interval deriving from Russia which used it to denote the wayward East.

Harmonically Bizet was not, as we say today, inventive: his chords are triadic, especially in set numbers, while diminished sevenths he employs forebodingly, according to the cliché of his day, to advance the plot. Chordal sequences, when at all tonally evasive, are so nearly always anchored to a drone that the device becomes a signature. Exceptional are the Seguidilla's precipitous modulations to the Neapolitan sixth, cribbed sixty years later by Prokofiev. And if the rare presence of secondary sevenths seems as pungent as, for example, the very cassia bloom José describes, the opening chords of the flower song could be by Fauré thirty years later, while the closing chords (as well as tune) were filched intact only fifteen years later for Tchaikovsky's *Pathétique*. So Bizet did shape the future somewhat, but through his harmonic quality, not originality.

His counterpoint was negligible like that of all French composers. God knows their schooling italicizes polyphony as much as solfège, and Bizet's fugal improvisations in the parlor were as glittering as Liszt's. But the only considerable canonic forays found in written French music are chez Franck, who was Belgian. Oh, in *Carmen* there is a psuedo-fugato to close Act I; there are many little stretti-at-the-octave descents to close smaller scenes (hear the ends of the Street Boys' first chorus, of Carmen's first exit, of the first Entr'acte, of Escamillo's first exit); there is so-called part-writing, like the heavenly choir of Cigarette Girls (seemingly voices in imitation, actually just voices in harmony). But there is no Germanic concern for independent inner lines nor Italianate concern for two or more viewpoints expressed at once. Bizet flirts with neither undifferentiated nor differentiated counterpoint (to steal Thomson's terms), the one being the same material echoing itself, as in a fugue, the other being unrelated materials simultaneously executed, as in *Lucia*'s sextet.

(A sly pedant might propose that the opening chorus, "Sur la place," was built on an inversion of the Habañera—the inversion of Stravinsky's Jocasta.)

Like a vat of sangria being brought to boil, the Gypsy Dance of Act II is as physical as the rumble from *West Side Story*. Rhythm alone explains the mounting wallop. Not rhythmic interest, however, but rhythmic *lack* of interest: hypnosis rather than psychedelia, monotony in place of variety. Bizet does step up the tempo thrice, building from a metronome 100 to 138; but the chief tactic, as with *Boléro*, lies in piling on of dynamics and weight rather than, as with *Sacre*, an increasing of metric intricacy. In song as in dance *Carmen* is straightforward; meters are never more eccentric than a square three or four, nor within the bar do there occur rhythmic enigmas, Chopinesque juxtapositions.

A steady beat makes the dance tick, but what makes it "good" is the strong line traced over the tambourines (though this line too is unchangingly reiterated). Indeed, melody, which makes all good opera good, is what makes *Carmen Carmen*. *Carmen* seethes with tune, apposite and first-rate, some of it stolen. If Prokofiev's Neapolitan mannerism stems from the Seguidilla, the Seguidilla itself stems from the orchestra of Mozart's Commendatore, while the Habañera grew from a nightclub song. (Bizet may well have made thirteen revisions for Galli-Marié, the final version of the Habañera remains so close to the original that Sebastián Yradier must live in history as its only begetter.) And as in the orchestra of Mozart's Commendatore certain of *Carmen*'s most ravishing curves unfurl without the distraction of a human voice: for instance, the thirty-eight measures of the second Entr'acte wherein single winds weave a nearly three-octave gamut like a silver snake through gold harp strings.

To object that his tunes aren't always his is to object to Shakespeare's or Beethoven's sources. It's an ungracious quip, the one about sexual prowess, "It's not what you've got but what you do with it"; yet we are now distanced enough from Bizet to hear him, not as his contemporaries heard him, for the plagiarist that he was, but for how personally he used his robbed goods.

His arias are true arias, not ditties with instruments. The difference? No aria can work on a song program (tell that to your stars) because by definition an aria leads from past to future, advancing the soloist in time and space, while a song is self-contained, sans plot, leaving the soloist where he began. Of Bizet's forty actual songs only one, *Adieux de l'hôtesse arabe*, has much profile, and many of the others seem to be extracted from unfinished stage works and garnished with fresh words after the composer's death. If Bizet did not possess the gift of song (contrary to, say, Fauré who lacked a sense of drama), his arias are nonetheless song-*like* in that they will repeat themselves literally and with identical accompaniment.

Notoriously, *Carmen*'s Paris flop killed its composer although posthumously the piece became quickly a hit from Munich to Moscow. Can one sense the causes in another time and place? "It is lovable," Nietzsche felt, because "it does not sweat. . . . Through it one almost becomes a masterpiece one's self. . . . Farewell to the damp north." And farewell to Lohengrin, he might have added, for Nietzsche loathed the Wagner he loved, and betrayed him with a Parisian. But how exact was his French?

Insofar as a person not born to a language can presume to assess a native's accent, let me state that Bizet is often prosodically illogical. French being the sole European tongue without a tonic stress (no syllable having more value than another), any sung layout of verse can be argued as correct. Yet throughout *Carmen* one senses that words have been forced onto pre-existing tunes, especially the tunes of Don José; not only at the start of the Flower Song, with *la* strong and *fleur* weak, but in more tactile talky moments where declamation should be dictated by nature. Why, for example, with the phrase "Laisse-moi te sauver" in the final dispute does José hit *te* rather than *sau* on the highest note and strongest beat?

Something's amiss with Don José. By current American standards he's a mama's boy (*un fils à papa* in French): his need to cast out both fiancée and career while reeling between mistress and mother strikes us as Freudian, while for the nineteenth century the predicament would seem more Roman than Romany (unless it were Jewish, since Halévy and not Mérimée contrived the situation). Were the tenor's lyric inspiration less grand, Americans would hear merely the bathos of this Spaniard behaving like an Italian singing in French for the sole delight of Germans.

Bizet is less expert at *le mot juste* than at *la phrase juste*. Winton Dean calls him a "master of the paragraph," meaning that "the rise and fall of the melody produced whole numbers that seem to spring forth complete from the first bar to the last." I get edgy when people start to compare the arts (architecture is frozen music, etc.), for if the muses were interchangeable we'd need just one, not nine. But if Bizet did compose paragraphs, they were stanzaic, for he was no prosifier; and though music can't rhyme it can certainly echo. Perhaps he was more a master of the sentence, or rather, of the verse. Such verse swells not through development but through repetition.

Yet through all *Carmen* flows the technical inevitability one finds in a disco palace, a linking, an overlapping of numbers granting them both independence and interdependence, and sending them all finally to flight like some doomed Greek family, heroes and jesters alike, toward a horridly needed apotheosis.

Formally the opera bites off more than it can chew, then chews it.

She's a liberated woman, she makes the rules, and like great actresses she speaks of herself in the third person, especially as she nears the end. She's a merry and obsessive lover, but a sad and gluttonous one too, and death more than lust seems her dish. At the hour of her suicide—what else can you call it?—Carmen seems fed up. Why? Music explicates where psychoanalysis fumbles. But if Mérimée's tale continually instructs us (his etching of Spanish Romany is no less morosely veridical than his Corsican Mafia in the masterpiece *Matteo Falcone*), who can deny that some pages of the opera sound silly? The males of the chorus, extrovert Latins though they be, are kidding when they ask Carmen when she'll love them (love them collectively?), whereas José, in taking her literally, shows himself crazy and provides his own doom. But Bizet was not kidding (and surely he, not his librettists, was responsible for the stretchings and ricochetings which veer toward farce) when he invites our sympathy during the Gilbert and Sullivan exchange between Micaëla and the Garde Montante. Operetta conventions of yesterday are today unwilling suspensions of disbelief, and not only poor Micaëla suffers in our eyes as she giddily parrots her would-be lover's remarks (*Sa mère, il la revoit* . . . etc.); Escamillo and Carmen too, glamorous public figures, go around saying they're in love—to just anyone.

There is little indication that Bizet and friends like Massenet or Saint-Saëns, at least in their musical speech, were out for a revolution. If things were different after *Carmen*, the difference lay in a (to us) minor French definition of what constitutes grand opera. So far as the ear is concerned, *Carmen*, while becoming the indisputably best lyric drama of its age in France, remains strictly in the tradition of opéra-comique, unaltered by Delibes or Hahn, by Poulenc or Sauguet, or by Rosenthal or Damase a century later.

Half the opera is choral.

Do the choruses, in their inevitability at scene-setting, their directness of melody, their lean virile languor and bull's-eye femininity, provide the most gorgeously inspired minutes?

Before deciding, hear again "La cloche a sonné" as the unison tenors for only twelve bars intone a series of tetrachordal arches more perfectly symmetrical than those of the Pont du Gard (no, architecture is not frozen music), and which, though they speak but once, satisfy our memory over the context of the next two hours. How almost immoral that so telling a fragment be followed by another more elegant still: unison baritones, against sixteen measures of fluxing hues among undulating cellos and near-motionless reeds, chant but two notes, over and over, only sinking ecstatically to a third as they give way to the long-awaited girls. Hear these girls now, this time in pairs, curling their vowels around each other like the very smoke they evoke, and growing, growing ever higher in the air. Oh, one could go on. Yes, the choruses do form the most beautiful moments.

Paradoxically, it is possible to conceive a *Carmen* (as opposed to a *Meistersinger* or a *Dialogues des Carmélites*) without chorus. The drama is among the few, not the many, and requires no kibitzing. Carmen's choruses are marvelous clothes on a marvelous body.

Had I never heard the orchestration but only seen it, I'd say it couldn't work. I would be wrong. The chances we are taught to avoid when scoring for voices with instruments seem not to be chances to Bizet. Balances or areas that on the page look top-heavy or empty are to the ear always right; the scoring is unstintingly crystalline.

But the scoring is not unusual. Beyond a predilection for low flutes, for solo bassoon and for crossed strings (listen to the sudden soft parentheses between which, after fifteen minutes of rattling fanfare, Escamillo emerges in the final act and,,with string quartet, speaks his piece, ominously intimate and self-contained as a black opal centered in a crown of a thousand diamonds), Bizet doesn't really run risks. The major difference between Germans and French is that in their orchestration the ones use layering while the others do not. Of course, not to double (i.e., to reinforce, for example, the strings, with one or more winds at the unison or octave) is probably in itself a risk, like any vulnerable exposure, but it does make for an air-filled luminosity in which the vocalist is not forced to scream for his life, whereas the Germans had to breed a new race of singer to withstand their triple-thick orchestration.

3.

While in Paris in 1947, enjoying some adventures in the line of duty entertainingly recounted in her current *Other People's Letters*, the Proust-ophilic historian, Mina Curtiss, coincidentally and almost by accident gained legal access to a cache of memorabilia which opened as unexpected a window onto cultural France as Watergate did onto political America. The cache was in the hands of one Magda Sibilat, the likable but unstable and none too well-informed widow of the nephew of Émile Strauss, himself heir to his second wife, Geneviève, née Halévy, daughter of *La Juive*'s composer and, by a first marriage, spouse of Georges Bizet. The memorabilia were an acre of letters—letters from Bizet to all his family, letters from Gounod and rival geniuses to Bizet, letters to Fromental Halévy from Rossini, Verdi and Berlioz, letters which had never before been seen by anyone but the correspondents themselves. Letters, said Madame de Sévigné, are the wings of friendship—a manifestation no longer extant, but still in Bizet's day so frequent as to seem no more historically useful than our telephone. Surely no such thorough documentation has come down to us from any other artist of the epoch. In her pursuit of what she calls the truth about Bizet, Curtiss spent the next decade immersed in an accurate vision of the past, and by 1958 had published what is maybe the grandest profile ever composed on a composer, *Bizet and His World*.

Consider how many volumes appear every month, how many hidden data may still be around on the Second Empire, and how famous are such men as Duparc or Chausson, Gounod or Fauré. Then realize that no books are readily available on these men, nor are there decent biographies of even Debussy or Ravel. And the past fades with each passing day. Bizet's each passing day is meanwhile revived, as through a tea-drenched madeleine, and with it a new sense of the man's musical importance, thanks to the Curtiss book. Or is it not Bizet's book? since a good fifty percent is "in his own voice," drawing verbatim from letters judiciously woven into context.

Now, this new sense of Bizet's musical importance—is it a matter of luck, of historic availability? Supposing the author had stumbled upon a store of, say, Meyerbeeriana, with Gounod in a walk-on role (as he has in the present book) and Bizet a mere cameo? Would the status of these figures be rearranged in our consciousness? Or is importance irrelevant to worth? (In a sense, because of his defining influence on Wagner, Spohr is more important than Wagner, as Rebikov is more important than Debussy.) Durability in music probably does not rely upon what is written about the music—or its composer—since the musical and the literary publics do not overlap. Mina Curtiss herself is a musician only second hand (Marc Blitzstein's aid in this case was invaluable), though she is a born snoop. Thus her useful book appears built less on a devotion to music than to research. My copy's margins are sprinkled with notes.

Bizet made a living out of dying, at least for his closest relatives, all of whom survived to enjoy his fame.

Marie Reiter, the family maid, at the end of her life in 1912 informed her grown son Jean that he was the offspring, not as was always supposed of Bizet *père*, but of Georges himself. She doubtless lied.

In musical accoutrements—sight-reading, singing, getting the point— Bizet was wildly talented. He could "do" anything. But so could many a prize Conservatoire graduate. Though his professional reputation was solid, his whole bourgeois life was passed as an overworked teacher and copyist with both social connections (all artists had those) and money problems. The woes and joys were those of today's composers: unrehearsed premières, but premières all the same, mixed reviews, jealousies. He retained boundless fidelity to those he admired, Gounod especially, and developed what looked like an American equation of failure with death.

If flop after flop is patiently chalked up by Curtiss (as by Winton Dean in his less factually documented but more musically canny biography), she is understandably defensive about her subject. The fact remains that Bizet's output was mostly mediocre. Even his best works—the young Symphony, *Jeux d'enfants*, parts of *The Pearl Fishers*—are in the salonistic genre of his period. There were no first-class gods in France then, as he semiconsciously realized; those he invoked were ever foreigners (Shakespeare, Homer, Michelangelo)—except for Meyerbeer, whom he classed with Beethoven.

There are no flukes in art. Yet *Carmen* is a fluke. Its high quality, if not its style, is incongruous in Bizet's catalogue.

Curtiss hints that when it comes time to court Geneviève Halévy there will be Jewish problems. These are not brought up again, nor is it clear on which side of the fence such problems may foment. For all her reference to the Halévy clan she never charts relationships. Here they are: Fromental Halévy (né Lévy in 1799) composed *La Juive* and ran the Paris Conservatoire. His younger brother Léon wrote librettos for him. Léon's son Ludovic was co-librettist with Meilhac of *Carmen*. Daniel Halévy, Proust's school friend, must have been the son of Ludovic (it isn't explained). But Geneviève, his aunt, was the daughter of Fromental. She did marry Georges Bizet, and they were not the ideal couple despite attempts at appearances even reinforced by Gounod in his eulogy at Georges's grave. She outlived her mate by over half a century of neurasthenic splendor.

Once I stated (and was roundly scolded) that Jews, being by origin epic improvisers, mainly in stringed instruments, can't play French music, French music being by nature concisely lyric with built-in rubati unneedful of "interpretation." How did Jews play French music when they themselves began composing it? (Bizet would have known, for in a sense, by osmosis, he composed it himself.) What was music life like among Jews in nineteenth-century France? The Dreyfus affair may well have brought to the surface an anti-Semitism in the upper classes (though as Proust himself demonstrates, to be a rich Jew in France is to be just rich. For example, the Rothschilds), but was any kind of Semitism visible in artistic classes?

Bizet is said to have said, "If they want trash I'll give them trash," and wrote the Toreador Song. Just who are "they," snug in their opera loges, crying "We want trash"? And just how is this song trashier than another?

The world knows Faust through Gounod (not Goethe) and *tauromachie* through Bizet (not Goya). Does the world know wrong? *Toreador* is a non-word, like *glissando*, good as any. We know love through Wagner.

Curtiss uses the witty locution "libretto-land," a locale dreamed up by Scribe, which Marc used to accuse me of inhabiting. But Bizet, composer of the exotic *Djamileh* (V. S. Pritchett recently wrote, apropos of George Sand, "A scene of Oriental luxury was indispensable to the Romantics: the looting of Egypt was Napoleon's great gift to literature"), kept his feet in patriotic gore and, unlike me, was no pacifist. (Were there pacifists, *proprement dits*, in France before World War I?) Yet he reminds me, in his rapports with Gounod, of myself with Virgil, from whom I learned everything, but perhaps not without taints of rivalry.

The prose and principles of all this clique—Halévy, Gounod, Massenet and Saint-Saëns—were high-flown and golden and real, yet their art somehow lacked danger and kept to a lower plane than that of their non-French predecessors—Chopin, Schumann, Wagner and Verdi. Despite salty credos their sound was saccharine, none of it so purposefully tight as Poulenc's, their logical culminator. (How do Franck and d'Indy fit in?)

In 474 pages are but two sentences of bodily portraiture, these uttered by the young librettist, Louis Gallet: "[Bizet] had a very gentle, but very acute expression behind his indispensable eyeglasses; his lips were almost continually arched in a mocking smile. He spoke quietly, in a slightly hissing voice, with that air of detachment I always noticed in him." (For the record, in his preface to *Thaïs* Gallet comes up with a snappy definition: "A lyrical poem is a work in verse handed over to a musician to convert into prose.")

The rare success of Bizet's collaboration with Daudet, claims Curtiss, was due to "the capacity both men had of translating into living theatrical expression an intuitive psychological grasp of certain facets of human passion and behavior. This gift neither artist appears to have recognized in himself."

Do artists ever seek to "recognize" such gifts within themselves? Is not theirs but to do or die, saving reason to apply toward others?

4.

What do I myself think about Bizet and his Carmen? Except that the requirements of this article have lately kept them uppermost in mind, I rarely think about them. Henceforth I shall readily admit that Carmen deserves her continuing glory: her musical worth is almost on a par with Pelléas, her narrative worth almost on a par with Aschenbach, her vocal know-how on a par with Norina.

Is *Carmen*, rather than *Fidelio* or *Lulu*, the perfect opera? Yes, because all the elements (beginning with the libretto—an improvement, at least in stage-worthiness, on Mérimée's tale-*cum*-document) are first rate: the traditional symmetries are perfect, the literal repeats are perfect, the exquisite banality is perfect. But perfection does not a chef-d'oeuvre make. Many a masterpiece is flawed, for beauty limps, and grandeur, though spectacular, can turn top-heavy.

Then is *Carmen* a chef-d'oeuvre? Yes, because the perfect elements all catch fire and gleam with life—they are, as we say, inspired, and together they jell: they have hardened into immortality.

Yet *Carmen* does not make my mouth water. (No offense, neither does Schubert.) I like everything about it except *it*. I do not object that in the final analysis the opera is really so corny and predictable, but my taste buds crave a Frenchness that did not yet exist, a longing for the almost edible sadness that resides in the sharp seventh recipes of Debussy and Ravel.

Perfection is a realistic goal, greatness is not. Greatness is an endowment—a postpartum present, if you wish—never consciously, nor even necessarily, bestowed by the maker. One can admit to the fact of, and even cheer, certain universal marvels without needing them, while in the private heart one elevates to Paradise lesser works which merely (merely?) satisfy.

To conclude these scattered notes I must choose between two lines:
Carmen is the most perfect opera ever composed, but it is far from great.
Carmen is great, but Bizet is not.

Nantucket, July 1978

NOTES ON A FRENCH BIAS

If the universe were split into but two esthetic pigeonholes, German and French, I would fall roundly into the latter. Looking back—or rather, listening back—I seem to have loved French music almost from the age of reason. This Mediterranean yearning acted as antidote to midwestern Wasphood. "Meaningful" post-classical music eluded my childhood, but I took to the glamour of so-called Impressionism as to a very, very nourishing dessert. Because I was so hooked, specifically on Debussy and Ravel, it went without saying that they were Great Art; by extension all French music was Great Music. It never occurred to me, as I drowned willingly in their golden meringue, shunning as much as manners would permit the leaden fare of standard academia, that Ravel and Debussy had predecessors and progeny and, indeed, colleagues across the border. I agreed with Busoni: "The German is sober, sentimental, and awkward—all that goes against art. The German is bourgeois; art is aristocratic."

Forty years later I still prefer sweet "aristocratic" dishes to meat and potatoes. Tastes seldom change, though mine have narrowed. My repertorial knowledge has nonetheless broadened enough to embrace some Gounod, Chausson, Chabrier and naturally Berlioz; and, beyond the Rhine, some Brahms, Schumann, Wagner and naturally Schubert. In "The Game of Two Esthetics" my body still opts for Gallic sound (what makes French music French? a sense of thrift evolved from speech? a sensuality based as much on the visual as the aural?), while my intellect admits that, at least for the nineteenth century, German is probably "greater." These passive *idées reçues*, albeit *reçues* by myself, remained long unchallenged, at least by me.

Sometimes the obvious is too obvious to mention, even by obvious fools. (When did you last hear anyone say: "Beethoven's Fifth is a great piece"?) Bright notions fade, are absorbed into mass consciousness, occasionally resurface as new coins. Thus a year or two ago while researching for an article on *Carmen*, I was suddenly stunned by a revelation of the obvious. Fool that I am, I dare to mention it: *There are no first-rate nineteenth-century French composers.* Yes, certain second-raters like Bizet may paradoxically come up with one masterpiece; but France bore no single master whose output was on a consistently serious par with a Chopin or a Schumann or even a Mendelssohn, nor yet on a par with his literary compatriots—Balzac, Baudelaire, Hugo,

273

Flaubert. (Were Franck and Berlioz perhaps first-rate? Franck was Belgian, and really awfully corny. Berlioz was German at heart, and really stuffed with sound and fury.)

Another game: Besides *Carmen*, how many first-rate pieces can you name by second-rate French composers? Begin with *Socrate* by Satie. Ironically Satilophiles, who adore his innocuities, seem generally unaware of this timeless work.

First-rate second-raters are those who aim low but hit square center. If nineteenth-century French composers may be so defined, the reason lies not in their technique which is thorough but in their *salon de thé* thematic material. Nor outside the conservatory do they pursue a contrapuntal tradition which lends so solemn an overlay to all German music since Bach.

Second-rate first-raters are those who aim high but just miss. No nineteenth-century Frenchman fits the category, but Bruckner does, and Reger, and also Hugo Wolf (in contrast to the modest but superior Fauré). So too does America's Germanish Charles Ives who lacked the know-how to grant communicable scope to his grandly true *trouvailles*. The genre is surely rarer in music than in other arts; a poet or painter, their métiers being learned in kindergarten, can hit it big by hit-or-miss, whereas the know-nothing composer is a contradiction in terms.

Today I find no reason to amend my youthful instincts. I still love French music above all, while allowing that, in the shadow of vastly richer German outpourings, there have not been, since Couperin, more than four wholly first-rate composers from France, and their music is all from the last ninety years. Debussy and Ravel (like their equally great contemporary Proust who preferred the bloodless composer, Reynaldo Hahn) created on the cusp of centuries, their best works—and hence the best music of France—having been written during the four brief decades from 1890 to 1930. The music of the late Francis Poulenc and of the still volatile Olivier Messiaen was mostly written after my consciousness was first raised, and which I took to my heart in the mid-1940s.

Music changes meaning as it recedes in time the way stars do as they approach in space. But the meaning of stars grows clearer, while that of music grows vaguer—at least the original meaning. Claude Debussy has become history. He is now open to reinterpretation as opposed to mere misinterpretation. What made him special?

Formally he was not "new," although much has been made of his longing to dispense with old forms by inventing a continuous middle without beginning or end. But except for a few songs where eccentric structure was dictated by the poetry, or in the shorter *Préludes* which are organized (like Satie's which predate them by twenty years) without "development" sections, Debussy's forms were fairly accessible. Even those late *Études*, which many call his crowning achievement, can mainly be parsed in the simplest manner, being built like so much of his early piano works on continuity through literal repetition, less "daring" than Chopin.

Melodically he was short of breath, given to evolving fragments rather than to spinning threads. (However, I do grow restless with people who adore *La Mer* but are bored by *Pelléas* because *Pelléas* "has no tunes." Why, the opera seethes with tunes, arias in microcosm with no recitatives! Listen again to just this short strophe of Arkel: *"Et depuis la mort de sa femme il est si triste d'être seul"*; or this of Geneviève: *"Je ne sais ni son âge ni qui elle est, ni d'où elle vient, et je n'ose pas l'interroger"*; or Mélisande: *"Est-ce vous, Golaud? Je ne vous reconnaisais presque plus"*—and have your memory bejeweled no less satisfyingly than by the complete-in-themselves miniatures of Schubert.)

Harmonically he derived from, consecutively, Massenet and Satie, Mussorgsky and Rebikov, the popular music of Cambodia and Spain and America, and finally from the Stravinsky he had himself so influenced.

Rhythmically he was foursquare and rather predictable.

He was special because he was better than others playing the same game. The game could be called *sound*, sound taking precedence over shape, over language. Surely, if the key word for, say, Palestrina is line, for Puccini is tune, for Bach is structure, for Prokofiev rhythm, for Berlioz energy, then for Debussy the word is sound. Surely, too, that explains his popularity as sensualist among today's young. For although sound ironically figures less than style or content in pedagogical discussions of music, it is the one ingredient to identify and distinguish this art from all others.

Never let him be defined as Impressionist, that being a term for painters who seek to avoid literal representation. When a musician tries for impressionism, he seeks to *become* literal.

Once I wrote: "Because we enjoy Ravel more than Debussy we assume he's less good than. Another generation will acknowledge Ravel as better precisely because he's more enjoyable." That generation is now, guilt about pleasure is abating and gorgeous music is no longer suspect. Do I still consider Debussy less pleasurable? In any case, people still liken the two composers whereas it's their differences that "speak," the older man being reactive, the younger man objective.

Some quick reactions to Maurice Ravel's objectivity:

In 1875 he was born (on Jane Austen's hundredth birthday) of well-off and understanding parents in the village of Ciboure near the Spanish frontier. These few facts illuminate all that he became. His art straddled the border as it straddled centuries, being in texture as opulent as a tourist's notion of Iberia, in shape as pristine as Rameau, in intent no less modern than ragas or group therapy and in subject matter mostly anti-romantic. Listen again to *Boléro*. ("It's my masterpiece," said the composer. "Unfortunately it contains no music.") French logic drenched in Basque mystery.

A nation's music resembles its language in all respects, and since French is the only European tongue with no rhythm (no tonic accent), any metricalization of a French phrase in music can be construed as correct. Lacking natural pulse, all French music becomes impressionist. French composers when they opt for rhythm exploit it squarely, like children. The spell of *Boléro* dwells in its non-variety, its contrast to Gallic speech which inherently rejects hypnosis, as opposed to American speech which like jazz is pure monotony. (Not for nothing was hypnosis first documented by a Frenchman, Charcot. Where rhythm is a stranger, rhythm is a prophet.) *Boléro* has nothing to do with French music, yet only a Frenchman could have composed it.

(What makes French music French? Practicality taking precedence over hysteria. Sadness taking precedence over anguish.)

Ravel's signatures are harmony and tune. His melodies are based on, and emerge from, chords. His identity, like Puccini's, rests in long line.

Ravel's music was famed for its exquisite taste (which no one defines), yet he claims to have been more influenced by the prose of Poe (no arbiter of taste) than by anyone's music. Taste in music—like wit in music—can be located only where texts are employed; Ravel's vocal works were never about love or religion, but rather about childlike concerns of fancy and nightmare. Children are beyond mere wit and taste.

The difference between French and German orchestration is that the latter uses doubling. Reinforcement, yes; but where in Strauss a string tune is thickened with winds or brass, in Ravel the fat is skimmed off and held in abeyance. This makes for what is known as transparent instrumentation—a sound both lush and lean. By extension the sound applies to his piano works and to songs. Sumptuous bones.

Nobody dislikes Ravel, and nobody disapproves. Can that be said of any other musician?

Poulenc's sound is, superficially, a combination of Ravel and Debussy. To say the least. He was more than merely influenced: he rifled intact the treasure of others. This was once common practice (Bach-Vivaldi), and Poulenc revived the practice, a risky one for those few minor musicians who used him as model only to discover he was no model at all. For his practice was an end, not a beginning; like all strong artists he did not open doors but closed them. Originality is a hollow virtue; everything's new under the sun. Anyone can invent a new language, but not just anyone can speak an old language freshly. Yet the premise of unoriginality must be the basis for any assessment of Poulenc's music, for everything he stole ended up sounding unmistakably like Poulenc.

His tunes, shorter than Ravel's but longer than Debussy's, are, when sung, the result of declamatory rather than of melismatic settings of words: each syllable gets a note.

His harmony? Take Chopin's dominant sevenths, Ravel's major sevenths, Fauré's plain triads, Debussy's minor ninths, Mussorgsky's augmented fourths. Filter these through Satie by way of the added sixth chords of vaudeville (which the French call Le Music Hall), blend in a pint of Couperin to a quart of Stravinsky, and you get the harmony of Poulenc.

Counterpoint is no more an ingredient of Poulenc's recipe than of any other French composer between 1850 and 1945. Only when compelled, as in unaccompanied choral works, does he concoct minor elaborations in the fifth species. But never even an abortive canon, much less a fugue. Elegant and satisfying though his polyphony be, it always serves the means to a harmonic end.

His meters are never, but never, other than in three or in four. Well, almost never.

He reinvented folk song for the concert hall. He instrumentalized the martyrdom of a nunnery in the style of Gershwin, and made you believe it.

If it could be argued that an artist is one who retrieves unbroken the fragilty of his past, or that a child is "the musician beforehand," then Poulenc, as glimpsed through the bittersweet contagion of his vocal phrases, is the child-artist incarnate.

Olivier Messiaen is the most important French composer of his generation. Born in 1908, he is seventeen years younger than Darius Milhaud, seventeen years older than Pierre Boulez, and his national contemporaries are Baudrier, Lesur and Jolivet with whom in 1935 he formed a school called *La Jeune France*.

If in the 1920s Milhaud and the *Groupe des Six* had been busy de-Germanizing their music by replacing message with means, a decade later Messiaen and the *Jeune France* were concentrating on Meaning with a capital *M*. To this day Messiaen remains the complete romantic whose involvement quite overpowers finesse of style. His message is God: not a god of convention like Bach's, but a god of private fantasies whom he celebrates as Richard Strauss celebrated Man, or as Scriabin celebrated Satan, or Debussy nature. The Roman church forms the kernel of Messiaen's being, hence of his art. It is also his worldly provider, since for all of his adult life he has been official organist at the Église de la Trinité in Paris.

His textures derive from the chromatic ecclesiasticism of Franck, his melody from the lean pantheism of Ravel. Like Franck in his time he is the best living composer for the organ, yet like Ravel, he performs his instrument clumsily. His pieces are mostly long, but only because they are actually assemblages of smaller works. The longest are sustained through hypnotic repetition (like tribal dances or Gertrude Stein) rather than through organic growth (like so-called Classical sonatas). Many are impelled by Christian epigraphs, yet their formal realizations may be planned around Hindu ragas.

His pieces finally are all copiously strewn with program notes wherein the composer describes his music devices and their results. Yet the arcane complexity of these notes, though engrossing, is ultimately too special for enjoyment of the music. They explicate a work as being the algebraically controlled aggregation of bird calls, of the Agony of Jesus, of a color alphabet wherein chords are touched with red and edged with gold, of theories on theology, and of verbal systems based on labials, etc. Since Messiaen obviously cannot live up to such prose, neither can he live it down; the thrilling pedantry renders him easy prey to pedagogues who demonstrate that his structural formulas do not carry through. (Not to mention wry cracks by professional cohorts. It was Virgil Thomson who first brought Messiaen to attention in America right after the war, by saying that France now had a new composer "who could open up the gates of heaven, and bring down the house." Stravinsky found his music "a crucifix of sugar.")

Interestingly, in Europe since Monteverdi it has always been the experimental composers who have written the operas, in America it's been the conservatives. Yet Messiaen—nothing if not avant-garde—with all his theatricality has never composed for the theater. Yet as I type these words, I learn that, at seventy-two, he has just finished a huge commission for the Paris Opéra. It is called *Saint Francis*, is scheduled for 1984 and I, for one, look more forward to it than to anything since Debussy's *Pelléas* before I first heard it forty years ago.

Nantucket, October 1980

A TRIPTYCH NOTEBOOK

Reactions to the Theater Pieces of
Ravel, Poulenc and Satie
Which the Metropolitan Opera Will Mount
in February 1981

1.

If my house were on fire and I could take only three records, they would all be *L'Enfant et les sortilèges*, the most beautiful music ever written. Yes, *Pelléas* and *Sacre* and *Wozzeck*, when I first heard them in adolescence, forever changed my state of mind. But Ravel's masterpiece changed my state of body.. It became the one work which most overtly influenced my own, and which, in some far corner of my being, I have listened to every day of my life.

I grew up among scattered parts of *L'Enfant*. As a child I owned a disc of one Piero Coppola conducting something named "Five O'Clock" from *Dream of a Naughty Boy*, a nattily scored ditty that seemed healthily catching. Years later Eva Gauthier, already seventy but retaining the vocal sassiness of a "naughty boy," used to intone that boy's diamond-clear *Toi, le coeur* against my piano background. Later still—November 20, 1946, to be exact (poet Paul Goodman's son was born that night)—Ballet Society offered Balanchine's "The Spellbound Child." That was my first complete hearing; sight obliterated sound and I was not bowled over. The next spring, however, Ernst Bour's record provoked an epidemic. We were all as bewitched as the protagonist, clutching our red-and-blue piano-vocal scores (in Catherine Wolff's bright translation) like seminarians' hymnbooks. We played that same record for each other, day after day—"we" being Bill Flanagan, Noel Farrand, David Diamond—all of us wishing we'd written the piece, for where do you go from here?

What beguiled us—the opulence? If World War I did render the vast Mahlerian palette obsolete, Ravel continued to employ the forces of Before the Deluge. *L'Enfant* dates from the lean 1920s yet the orchestra includes even the kitchen sink. In 1947 we had just come through another war; and

278

while America was emerging, for the first time ever, as a sober self-defined musical entity, here suddenly was a French work, already twenty-five years old, as lusciously carefree and timely, indeed, as *American*—with its daft blues and dizzy fox-trots—as anything *we* could think up.

The revelation of *L'Enfant* lay in spaciousness, in sovereign melody. The notion of Modern Music in the 1940s tended toward the spare; Stravinsky and Copland, out of Nadia Boulanger and Debussy, eschewed *la grande ligne* in favor of motives, figures, frugal staples. Behold Maurice Ravel's cornucopia of tunes, tunes, tunes—of song without guilt. No two measures of his hour-long piece are barren of purposeful melody. From the outset a pair of malignant oboes twines around a high-pitched double-bass as the mezzo whines: three different-colored threads braided firmly, only to loosen into the Mother's theme (that falling fourth!) which in turn swells into the Boy's sequence of shrieks—each shriek a tune, not an "effect." The shrieks then dissipate into the frightful yet protecting dream where inanimate objects like teacups and armchairs sing songs as sad and silly as those we ourselves made up in the cradle. Such logical elisions are of a born tunesmith who is also a Theater Man. Listen again as the Shepherds with their blue dog peel themselves from the nursery wallpaper in a two-part canon as touching as a Gluck ballet. Listen as the coloratura Fire, almost quenched by rippling clarinets, flows through the harp to the golden-haired Princess, and how she with her moon-colored flute becalms the recalcitrant child who then utters ("in a half-voice," the composer marks it) the famous Air which is close, but not too close for comfort, to Puccini's "Un bel dì." Listen to the Dragonfly Interlude as both choirs of unison violins weave a seamless never ending, ever shifting rainbow over a still more gorgeous new-forming melody of Frogs. Listen to the notorious Cat Duet (and invite your own cats: mine react wildly) which, though formed of screeches, is screeching to the gentlest theme of *La Valse*. And listen to the final six-part madrigal as it graduates into a curving cantilena like a caterpillar edging along a silky rope toward that pair of oboes, benign now, which have returned to say good-bye. Alone this ending, like the ending of Britten's *War Requiem* which springs from it, will have carried Maurice Ravel through the gates of Paradise.

Then there was our vision of Colette. Who was this most literate of librettists since Hofmannsthal? Why, her very stage directions could be chanted! Yet the verse was so prosy that Ravel—the first "serious" French composer ever to do so—ignored the final *e-muets* as pop singers do; how else does one deal with such bilingual madness as *Black and costaud and vrai beau gosse* which to our virgin ears sounded like "Back the custard and pray for Gus"? And that plot! about a bratty son and a dominant mother, smack out of Germany's vicious *Struwelpeter* yet indulgent of all flora and fauna and the slangy exotica of the twenties. How attuned to our Freudian forties! (I asserted that whenever Ravel set the word *Mother* to music he used a descending fourth, clearly a sexual innuendo, that skip being the inversion of a fifth, the chief interval of his most carnal work, *Daphnis et Chloé*.) Colette was not, any more than Ravel, a moralizer, much less a psychoanalyzer. She was a literal naturalist. Could she, like Gide, have known the tales of Oscar Wilde? Her *livret* resembles "The Star Child" even to the boy who speaks the language of the

280

squirrels he tortures, and even to that boy's redemption in the eyes of his mother. But Wilde goes further. Once he has turned the nasty beauty into a benevolent hero, he crowns him king: "Yet ruled he not long, so great had been his suffering, and so bitter the fire of his testing, for after the space of three years he died. And he who came after him ruled evilly." How would Colette's little monster have grown up? Like the rest of us?

Having declared Ravel a tunesmith and a Theater Man, I still can't place the genre of his *L'Enfant et les sortilèges*. A ballet with words? A danced opera? A vocal tableau? A visual cantata? The only production that ever convinced me, as a production, was Babilée's made-for-TV choreography in 1972; the filmed close-ups tellingly underlined, rather than distracted from, Colette's intimate text. I've seen the work staged many times, never happily. The sheer mechanics of gigantic bats and butterflies are mindful of the Marx Brothers in *A Night at the Opera*, making a joke out of a lament. The only medium for *L'Enfant* is the phonograph.

No ambiguity about the genre of *Les Mamelles de Tirésias*. It's the one real opera on the Met's triple bill, and eminently stageworthy. Leonard Bernstein it was who on his Tenth Street Baldwin first played me this highest piece of camp since *Così fan Tutte*. Lenny had returned from Europe in the autumn of that same fruitful 1947, with a signed copy (a signed copy? had he actually met the master?) of *Mamelles* under his arm. "Just show me the divine parts," I requested, expecting the sort of Poulenciana I already knew—vaudevillian tongue twisters and lulling caramel plaints. So Lenny turned to the group number that begins *Comme il perdait au Zanzibar*. Well, if you think Ravel's "Toi le coeur" harks back to "One Fine Day," Poulenc's big chorale is a steal from Kern's "Fish Gotta Swim." (Ten years later we would hear the same corny sequences at the tragic peak of *Dialogues des Carmélites*.) Then and there I learned that although Poulenc never penned an original note, every note became pure Poulenc through some witty alchemy. I learned too that Poulenc's so-called profane and sacred styles are really the same. (I once said this to some born-again Christian students in Hattiesburg who nodded sagely, all music being the voice of God.) And I learned that his fast music is as solid as his slow; that, unlike many a single-barreled genius, Poulenc's muse functioned on two contrasting but simultaneous metabolisms—hence the high camp, the unexpected *kind* of music disconcertingly yet successfully embellishing a given scene. Could one wish that Poulenc had, like Ravel, lived to use a book by Colette (*Chéri* perhaps) or by Flaubert (say, *Madame Bovary*), fit subjects for one who never composed about individuals so much as about situations? Or do all the French—Flaubert and Colette included—compose only about situations?

"Whenever in the midst of the worst buffoonery a phrase can effect a change in the lyric tone," said Francis Poulenc, "I have not hesitated thus to alter the character of the music, well knowing what sadness was hidden behind Apollinaire's smile. In the same way, those who know the secret meaning that Apollinaire attributed to certain words will note that when it is a question of Paris or the Seine, the music also is moved."

The best-known photograph of Guillaume Apollinaire shows an ageless, overweight, likably intelligent, dark fellow in army uniform, with a radiant smile and a bandaged head. Like many a naturalized citizen (he was born illegitimately of Polish parents in Rome in 1880), he became more French than the French, and enlisted during the 1914 war, although as an Italian citizen he could have been exempt. In March 1916 he was wounded in the scalp by a shell fragment while reading a new issue of *Mercure de France*, and two years later died from this wound, having become what he remains today: the greatest French-language poet of the twentieth century. Though it is vague whether the young Poulenc ever knew the poet, it is certain that Apollinaire never heard the thirty-five settings the composer made from his poems between 1918 and 1956. Apollinaire is the bard to whom Poulenc most often returned for inspiration. The two shared a spirit of tasteful vulgarity, a ribald poignancy stemming from an upper-class attraction to what we now call populism, a seemingly crazy extroversion invisibly checked by the reins of art. Poulenc was never the experimenter that the writer was, but he had a keener dramatic knack. How logical that when he chose to compose his first opera in 1944 (the première would come in June of 1947), Poulenc should begin by "decubistifying"—as he put it—Apollinaire's 1917 satire and by relegating the action to the happier era of 1912.

But what is *Les Mamelles* about? Apollinaire in his life seemed at once patriotic and anti-military, condescending to women and socially egalitarian (he had an affair with the same Marie Laurencin whose mauve-and-citron décors garnished Poulenc's *Les Biches* in 1924). Did he coin the term *Surrealism* —"the rational arrangement of the improbable"—to justify his ambiguous comedy which promises to be feminist, pacifist and liberal, but winds up hawkish, nationalist and reactionary? The heroine, for all her initial bull-headed glamour (will you ever forget the sheer glee of Denise Duval as, hitting her first high C, she releases from her blouse two great balloons, one blue and one red, which sail into the orchestra!), turns into a repentant 1930s Hollywood boss-lady baby-maker who again lets Men run the world.

The second time I heard *Les Mamelles* Poulenc himself sang it at the Pleyel of Alexis de Rédé, in the spring of 1951. His voice resembled his person (a cross between a cornet and a weasel) but it brought back the sound of Lenny Bernstein's, so "imprinting" is a first audition. My third hearing was finally at a full-fledged performance at the Comique; this time it was Madame Duval who sounded like Poulenc. Thus creators have the last word, for inside every composer lurks a singer longing to get out. Yet if of the hundred composers I've heard sing, only two (Reynaldo Hahn and Samuel Barber) have been able to carry a tune, their implicit voices will stamp a whole cast. Ah, you writers of song! *Vous faites des enfants, vous qui n'en faisiez guère.*

"If I'd known it was so silly I would have brought the children." Jean Cocteau loved to quote that quip, overheard at a performance of *Parade* in 1917. The safe implication lay in the naïve wisdom: Cocteau knows, and we agree, that silliness is a valid base for art, and that children are the best judges.

My own opinion is that *Parade* is silly in the worst way, that children are not the best judges, that Cocteau's motive for the scenario was superficial if not dishonest, that although Picasso's curtain is marvelous Satie's score is worthless, and that the Met missed the boat by attaching *Parade* rather than Satie's masterpiece, *Socrate*, onto this triple bill. For *Parade* is already a famous ballet—the poor man's *Petrushka* in need of no further promotion—whereas the comparatively unknown *Socrate*, with its five solo voices, is a sung spectacle legitimately allied to the Poulenc–Ravel spectacles.

As Cocteau, in 1946, manipulated, with his "accidental synchronization," the choreographer of *Le Jeune Homme et la Mort*, so, two years later, with the filming of his play *Les Parents terribles*, did he manipulate the composer, Georges Auric. Auric remembers: "I wrote a series of short pieces, and when they had been recorded, Jean himself pruned and rearranged them and decided exactly where they should fit. When I saw the final cut it was as though I myself had chosen the placement of music, so right did it seem."

Now, these happy accidents postdated *Parade* by three decades. Cocteau's earlier manipulation of—indeed, his attempt to *invent*—his distinguished collaborators, Satie and Picasso, might have been tenable had it resulted in more than mere scandal. Scandal, in and of itself, was always for Cocteau a kosher ingredient of Art; in the case of *Parade* his primary aim was to cause a stir as big as *Le Sacre*, the proof of Stravinsky's viability being in the riots he caused. *Mais n'est pas scandaleux qui veut*—true scandal doesn't come when it's called. My instinct suggests that Cocteau toyed with history as he toyed with his colleagues, by deciding ex post facto that his work had been misunderstood, since to be misunderstood is to be an artist. Actually, the audience may have seen the work for the claptrap it was, and booed from boredom.

The ballet's argument is a blueprint for Cocteau's film *Blood of a Poet*. Because the public can enjoy the barker's tease for free, they will not pay to enter the tent; yet to enter the tent is to *comprehend*, for there one joins the true heat of the artist's bloodstream. The public will never concede, content only with exteriors, so the poet dies alone.

In the long years I lived in France, adoring as I still do the multi-sided gifts of Jean Cocteau, I never understood why so many of his friends repeatedly called him a liar. Wouldn't his avowal "I am the lie which speaks the truth" preclude their need for sarcasm? Since he was the most avid public figure I've ever observed, his protestations about being a private person sounded more endearing than false. In his heart Cocteau knew what all poets know: art *is* exterior, and its meaning—whatever meaning means—is located only by academics who pry open the style.

Was he musical? Composition was the one craft he did not profess to practice, though he worked continually with musicians (from Markevitch to Marianne Oswald, Honegger to Edith Piaf) and wrote shrewdly of the art, careful always to specify that the writing was around, not about, music. Indeed, he seemed to have more of a nose than an ear for music, flairing its dramatic possibilities rather than needing it to soothe his savage breast. But he rarely missed the point of music. If, as I feel, he did overpraise Satie, at least he was in the savvy society of, among others, Milhaud and Diaghilev and Thomson. In America today Cocteau has come to be a forgotten quantity, even to moviemakers who, via Truffaut and Resnais, owe so much to the poet. Erik Satie, meanwhile, has internationally grown into a moneymaking commodity, and so has Francis Poulenc.

2.

Last April I returned to Paris for the first time in seven years. With me was JH, who did not know the city. We were lucky to have the huge apartment of Gérard Souzay, who was on tour in Japan. By coincidence this apartment is but half a block from the Place des États-Unis, my home throughout the 1950s. The wide dislocation in time superimposed on the narrow dislocation in space colored the sojourn. JH had to return to New York after a fortnight; I stayed on ten days. That fortnight was a madeleine containing the long ago, but after JH left, every pastry shop and chestnut tree began to remind me of him. Paris turned into the Chicago of my childhood. Although I was another person, surroundings seemed so indelibly the same (not, as you'd expect, smaller and smudged) as to be flat and dull; the dead were buried, and only the immediate past now seemed plaintive.

Meanwhile, knowing I'd eventually be writing this piece for *Opera News*, I visited an old acquaintance, Manuel Rosenthal, who would be conducting the triptych under consideration. And I visited an old friend, Jean-Pierre Marty, who would not be conducting the triptych. I kept some pertinent notes from which the following paragraphs are derived.

Dîner chez les Rosenthal.

The subway from Boissière (my stop) to Corvisart (the Rosenthals') is mainly above ground—or above water—and arches over poetic geography. It crosses the river by bridge (*"sous le Pont Mirabeau/coule la Seine et mes amours"* wrote Apollinaire in his most famous poem, one of the few which Poulenc did *not* set to music), and arrives on a track rising over the Boulevard de Grenelle. ("For Apollinaire and for me," said Poulenc, "the banks of this boulevard are as rare and romantic as the banks of the Ganges are for others.") One sees pots of early geraniums on ledges five feet from the train window, and behind these, lamplit kitchens with be-bibbed infants and well-bred poodles; then, between buildings, one spots the bronze dome, seemingly polished by hand, of the École Militaire, and farther still, the distant Invalides. Now we skirt the Boulevard Montparnasse so one hums, if one chooses, Poulenc's great song, *Montparnasse*, based on another Apollinaire poem. ("Let us imagine"—again Poulenc speaking—"this Montparnasse suddenly discovered by Picasso, Braque, Modigliani, Apollinaire. The more I re-read Apollinaire the more I am struck by the rôle Paris plays in his work." The poem dates from 1912, the musical setting from 1942. And now Poulenc's words, uttered in 1959, fall into the nostalgic concrete of history.) Over there, just beyond the Champs de Mars, see the Boulevard de Port-Royal named for the same convent which Poulenc would immortalize in *Dialogues des Carmélites*. An American composer may occasionally extol the sidewalks of New York, but never a singular sidewalk (not even Ives in *Ann Street*) with the detailed devotion that French rhymesters and pop singers always have, since Villon and before, evoked the neighborhoods of this city. I recall JH's remark: Paris is built for the sane, as opposed to New York built for the mad. The French do not anticipate irrationality on the subway, no graffiti or murders. Their food too is more sensible than ours, and their clothes, even their sex, and surely their music.

The Rosenthals have always inhabited Rue du Moulin des Près, a quarter-mile from the Corvisart stop, in a section of the 13th arrondissement that could as well be *en province*: cobblestones, twisting lanes, cheese markets and horsemeat stores shaded by lilac bushes already blooming thickly, hitching posts and a floral merchant from which I buy three dozen coppery jonquils. Since first I was here two decades ago, their three-story house has been revamped, now with a glassed-in *potager* where blackbirds trill louder and louder as the late northern daylight grows dimmer and dimmer. Claudine has prepared a meal (*feuilletés* of ham and mushroom, small roast chickens *en brochette*, watercress salad, a *meule* of Dutch cheese, a *macédoine* of oranges and baby strawberries, and very black *café filtre*) during which we talk politics. Like all the French they approve of Nixon, as well as of Maurice Béjart.

I had forgotten how Parisians prefer talking about music to listening to music. Manuel owns neither piano nor phonograph, so our access to the art under discussion is strictly through the massive scores laid out on the kitchen table. I've never seen the orchestration of *Les Mamelles*, but not from want of trying. As a composer who, no less than another, is anxious about the distribution of his published works, I feel uneasily vindicated in learning that even the piano-vocal score of *Mamelles* is unobtainable not only in New York but in Paris. Philistine commentary: monuments are monuments in name only.

Discussion of Boulez's Germanization of France. Manuel tells of Max Brod, years ago in Israel, describing how Kafka roared with laughter at his own prose. The Czech considered himself the Offenbach of letters, and imposed a classical distance between himself and his black comedies. Would this stance be comprehended by Boulez who, though French in his "objectivity," is German in his humor, and for whom Kafka's Jewish jokes are deadly serious? I bring up JH's theory of Parisian sanity: how no barricades are erected against the fifty-yard drop at the Trocadéro, it being assumed that citizens will not fling bottles, or even themselves, over the parapet. And I recall Cocteau describing the mirth on the set of *Frankenstein*: it did not occur to Karloff any more than to Kafka that the world would shudder at the shock of recognition.

I ask what makes French music French. "Absence of the self, of Romanticism. Debussy, who was also the greatest, was the only French Romantic since Berlioz, while Ravel was the arch-classicist."

Then why do I cry at the final choir of *L'Enfant*? "You cry at the perfection—at precisely the craftsman's ability to omit himself and to leave the path pure. Perfection is all too rare in French music, and altogether absent from German music, as well as from Debussy. Which is why a Debussy score needs a rehearsal of checks and balances in order to 'sound,' while Ravel's orchestration falls quickly into place even under a third-rate baton."

Hesitantly I agree, thinking of that heart-melting device found in French composition (and it *is* a device, not a *coup d'inspiration*), but never in German, consisting of a spare statement of purpose, often unaccompanied, followed without ado by a restatement, richly supported. Examples: the entry of the tenors in the aforementioned chorus, *Comme il perdait*, or the entry of the full strings for the last eleven measures of Ravel's *L'Enfant*. The device is nowhere in *Parade*, though God knows Satie's not German. I consider this silently, but ask aloud: Yet isn't German music, whether you need it or not, greater than French?

"*Oui, sans doute*. Perhaps not greater really, just more involving. Ravel excluded himself from his work so far as to invite Auber to complete *Daphnis* which was losing its flavor. When Auber refused, Ravel propped up Rimsky's *Scheherazade* to use as model for the grand finale. As for *L'Enfant*, much of the music existed before he began on the *livret*. Ravel reused intact his notes for an unrealized opera from long ago, *La cloche engloutie*, merely imposing Colette's text upon the pre-existing harmonies, the way Handel pieced together *Messiah*." So much for inspiration and *le grand souffle*. The public weeps as Ravel and Kafka laugh.

And Satie?

"A Racinian tragedy." (This from Madame Rosenthal, the soprano Claudine Verneuil who sang the *Chauve Souris* on the Bohr recording of *L'Enfant*.

Again I agree, but only so far as *Socrate* is concerned, and go on to explain my old notions. He was a composer's composer. More exactly, a Francophile composer's composer, meaning he never played in those waves of colorful virtuosity which attract even the most sophisticated amateur, not to mention performer. His Frenchness lay in economy and wit, often lightweight though never dull. His music, more like drawing than painting, gave, said Cocteau, more than it promised. "Satie protected his music like good wine; he never shook the bottle."

The trouble with—the *thing* about—Satie is that he really hadn't much to say musically. Those clicking typewriters don't rescue *Parade* from blandness any more than airplane propellers rescue *Ballet mécanique*. Like Antheil, Satie used noise without exploring it, whereas Poulenc with his guilloutine in *Dialogues* or Ravel with his slide-flute and cheese-grater in *L'Enfant* used noise as an integral hue. Are the Rosenthals buying all this? I ask: "Is Poulenc a French composer?"

"Ravel said that Poulenc's one gift was for inventing his own folk song, and French folk song, even those souped-up *Chansons d'Auvergne*, is as cool a glance at the growth of the soil as German folk song is tearful."

Can *L'Enfant et les sortilèges* be staged? Or do you agree with your countrymen (who still rate Disney second only to Poe) that animated cartoon is the ideal medium?

"We'll see how Dexter fares. Certainly the notorious notion of Ravel's brother Édouard, after seeing *Fantasia*, is folly. The composer himself never 'saw' an unstaged version. I conducted the very first concert presentation in December of 1937, eight hours after Ravel's death. A beautiful performance, the Salle de la Radio filled with long faces, including Stravinsky's."

"The French," claims Manuel, "swarm to a Boulez concert precisely because they are less musical than logical. Practicality is also what keeps them from spawning great music. Great art overflows—is the rational residue of madness. Insofar as the French aren't mad they aren't great artists."

Is he nettled at my talk of French sanity? Is he siding against the French? Shall I ask him those tired questions: Was Ravel Jewish? Was he homosexual? (It's assumed he couldn't have been both.) No, I'll ask him another.

Manual Rosenthal, whose initials are those of the musician about whom, as the sole surviving pupil, he personally knows more than anyone alive and whom he adores no less than I do, being equipped to answer, I feel justified in asking: Was Maurice Ravel mad?

Goûter chez Jean-Pierre.

Last Friday night Jean-Pierre Marty conducted an oratorio version of *Dialogues des Carmélites*, complete, for a big crowd at the Champs-Élysées theater. This was the first real music I've heard in a city now dominated, financially and emotionally, by the lifeless prejudices of Boulez. An English soprano, Felicity Lott, sang Blanche in imitation of, but with finer vocal cords than, Denise Duval; and Crespin, for the first time in French, played the Première Prieure, her mahogany tresses coiffed in a satin swoop over her arms dripping rubies as she persuasively moaned the sanctimonious text of the dying self-denying nun. Jean-Pierre conducted cleanly, never relaxing into the sentimental trap, not even when Crespin tried to drag him there, so alluring in this piece which, clear through, is a suite of pop songs garbed in *grand sérieux*. Twice I wept (and I never weep): during the *Ave Verum*, remembering how JH so tenderly directed it eight years ago at the Chapel of the Intercession, and during the unendurable *Salve Regina*.

Today, tea with Jean-Pierre in his ideal new flat, Rue Regrattier in the Île Saint-Louis. The ice cream he serves is the best I've ever had in this land where what Americans call French ice cream is an unknown quantity: a log of rich red cherry sherbet tasting truly of cherries. He plays the tape of "his" *Mamelles*, as conducted last year for the radio, with Ana Maria Miranda (sounding like Duval sounding like Poulenc sounding like Bernstein). The performance resembles the ice cream in being the best I've heard, and not very French.

The French aren't always the inevitable interpreters of their own music. Because they find that music crisp and dry they play it "profoundly" rather than letting it speak—or sing—for itself. Composers themselves betray themselves. (Listen to the player-piano transcriptions of Ravel performing his *Sonatine*, and hear how, in the style of Paderewski whose right hand always dragged behind his left, he willfully muddies his own clear line.) But French music *is* crisp and dry. The French raise banality, as distinct from triteness, to the level of art. The ostinato that opens *Rapsodie Espagnole* is in itself undistinguished when compared to, say, a Purcell or Britten ostinato. Insofar as Ravel employs banality as basic matter, does he dig less deep than Debussy? Debussy signed himself *musicien français* for patriotic rather than for artistic reasons, yet no one would have taken him for German. Yet he was Germaner than Ravel in that he aimed toward Meaning.

Germans are seldom banal, though they can be trite. In the *Diabelli Variations* Beethoven was consciously trite, thus not really trite so much as fruitfully banal; he was unconsciously trite in the finale of the Ninth, thus producing junk. By these terms Debussy's chief work, *Pelléas*, remains high tragedy while Ravel's *L'Enfant* remains high camp. (Not that tragedy cannot also be high camp, but only in Italy.) And by these terms Jean-Pierre Marty takes *Les Mamelles* for what it is, a pleasure, rather than the lackluster pain of the old Cluytens recording.

Jean-Pierre was a glittering, overheated teenage pianist when I first knew him as Julius Katchen's chief protégé in 1951. At that time he was also something of a composer, slight but real. As a composer he had a way with other people's music that standard virtuosos, with all their dazzling accuracy, lack: a quick cutting to the bone, without undue technique, and without undue idolatry. Today, as one of the three youngish French pianists who have turned to conducting (Pommier and Entremont are the others), Marty is the most in view, the most adept, the most attuned to his national repertory, and—precisely because he is also a composer—the most natural.

If Ravel was an undependable saboteur of his own music, Poulenc playing Poulenc has never been bettered. Poulenc also played Schubert and Schumann "with understanding." Does anyone know how Ravel played other people's music? Does anyone know, even third hand, about Satie as a performer?

"Nobody laughs in France today," says Jean-Pierre. I hear this from everyone. Indeed, the self-indulgent sense of First Times, of blasé or risky Young Love as once depicted by Juliette Greco, of red wine staining the hotel sheets, of good cheap thrills—these things have vanished. Of course, most of those I speak to are of a generation quick to explain that Young People Today have little to laugh about. As to what Y.P.T. read, I'm told they're less taken with books than with Yves Saint Laurent. Still, while allowing that high fashion and high intellect are more allied here than in America, I don't believe all I hear.

True, humor no longer has much to do with French music, and never had much to do with youth. Witty music has yet to be defined. But if the three works in question are among the wittiest ever composed, realize that Ravel and Satie were both fifty when *L'Enfant* and *Parade* were written, and Poulenc was forty-eight when he wrote *Mamelles*.

3.

When Satie died in 1925 at the age of fifty-nine, Ravel was fifty and would survive twelve more years, Poulenc was twenty-six and would live until 1963. Their views of each other were necessarily varied.

Satie: "Ravel has refused the Legion of Honor, but all his music accepts it."

Ravel: "The musician who has most influenced me is Erik Satie."

Poulenc: "I'm not worthy of Ravel's little finger."

Satie: "Little Poulenc is a playboy."

Ravel: "Poulenc is talented, let's hope he'll work."

Poulenc: "Satie's hold on me was profound and immediate, not only musically but spiritually."

Though notorious and funny, Satie's crack about Ravel is rancorous and inappropriate. Ravel was never a conformist. And his claim that Satie "influenced him" is more homage than fact. (The one work of art most crucial to Ravel's growth was not musical but literary—Poe's *Philosophy of Composition*.) Debussy, Satie's senior by four years, was the one who really showed the influence, to a point where certain works—the *Sarabande*, for instance, or *Pour l'Égyptienne*—sound like facsimiles, facsimiles which *improve* on the original. As for Poulenc's remark about Ravel, it was uttered long years after he had renounced the anti-Ravel stance stylish in the twenties. Yet Ravel's stamp, like Satie's "hold," on Poulenc was apparent from the start, as were Stravinsky's and Mussorgsky's, Chopin's and Schumann's—what composers indeed were *not* ransacked by Francis Poulenc and remodeled in his image!

Little Poulenc was a playboy undeniably, a *fils à papa* dedicating songs now to the Duchesse d'Ayen, now to the Vicomtesse de Noailles, now to Madame Cole Porter, now to the same Misia Sert who nurtured not only Ravel but Satie himself. And did not Satie compose his grand *Socrate* on command from the Princesse de Polignac? That's how things were done before today. Like Chopin's Études, *Grafin d'Agoult gewidmet*. Did Satie pooh-pooh the high company kept by Liszt, or before Liszt by Beethoven, by Haydn, Palestrina, Machaut? Yes, Poulenc did "work," as Ravel hoped he would, and, like Proust's, his milieu served as canvas.

In 1939 Virgil Thomson wrote: "Every composer's music reflects in its subject matter and in its style the source of the money the composer is living on while writing that music . . . [although] the quality of any piece of music is not a function of its author's income-source." Well, that was a generality for specialized Americans. Satie, who was poor, wrote many a merry pastiche of Chabrier waltzes. Ravel, who was bourgeois, wrote many a merry pastiche of Chabrier waltzes. Poulenc, who was rich, wrote many a merry pastiche of Chabrier waltzes.

I am a blue pencil. Breathes there a finished work of art so inviolable that I do not wish to improve it? With German works the improvement's a vast slash with no change of detail. With French works the improvement lies in minor shifts or tailorings—squeezing a word here, raising a note there—to enhance the integral elegance. No matter how right, is there any music or prose that can't be made righter—even Beethoven's, even John Simon's?

Rimsky's invaluable treatise on orchestration contains examples of only his own works, simply because he knew why he did what. Ravel always wanted to compile a treatise using examples from *his* own works which were miscalculations. He never did it—how could he have?

Ravel composed just two duds. The short song *Les grands vents d'outremer* is a blurred self-imitation. *Introduction et Allegro* (the only harp piece unanimously praised by harpists) has a good theme but an irritating development that repeats rather than evolves. Not bad—two rotten apples in a barrel of a hundred. The other ninety-eight are ripe and flawless; they could never be "improved." Perhaps the perfection stems from Ravel's so-called classicism, although I've always felt that this classicism was evoked as a red herring to contrast with Debussy's presumed freedom. (The only thing dimly classical about Ravel is the printed score, and then it's not the formality of Haydn but of Doric Greece. Eugene Istomin once pointed out that the similarity between the look of the long, loose grace notes in the first movement of Ravel's *Trio* and the sequence of fluted columns in the temple of Paestum. But does the coincidence lie in the composer, or in the engraver? Or in Eugene?) Ravel was perfect because he was a perfectionist. His music is non-Romantic and plotless; he would have thought of himself as a Modernist.

Satie composed just two pieces that were not duds: *Socrate*, and the suite of three *Gymnopédies*, inimitable, like nothing before or since. Not bad—two fresh apples in a barrel of a hundred. The other ninety-eight are underripe and flawed, too insignificant to warrant improvement. The inimitability of the two "good" pieces stems from their timelessness, an element I've heard in no other music. Particularly in the case of *Socrate* (a setting of three Dialogues of Plato) one finds a sort of removed respect, indeed, a humility, which is not an element one especially associates with genius. Yet humility is precisely the genius of *Socrate*: the words of Plato are not illustrated, not interpreted by the music: they are framed by the music, and the frame is not a period piece; rather, it is from all periods. Which is what makes the music, unlike Ravel's, so difficult to identify. Is it from modern France? Attic Greece? or from Gregorian Italy? Like Bizet with *Carmen*, Satie with *Socrate* becomes that rare example of a second-rater who produced one first-rate marvel. In all the rest of his catalogue, *Parade* included, Satie never did anything that Debussy didn't do better.

Poulenc composed duds and hits in equal measure. The utter duds are among his piano solos. Because he was a glib, a natural, keyboard technician he was inclined to pass off as finished compositions what in fact were passing improvisations, a dazzling froth floating on nothing. The demi-duds are mainly in the songs—but again, just in the piano parts which can be so much note-spinning. They are worth improving because of the vocal lines—but who dares revise the work of the newly dead? As for the hits, it is with anguish that I ask: Why must he becloud his impeccable *Ave Maria* (in the *Carmélites*) by adding useless timpani to the bass line? Why must he sully *Les Mamelles* by plagiarizing, rather than tactfully "recalling," Stravinsky in opening the second act? Why must he "end wrong" one of his most important songs, *Le Disparu*, by petering out rather than tightening up? (He never brings back the opening theme. In this kind of music—pastiche—that sounds amateurish rather than inventive.) And why did he never check the misprints which continue to infest his music, no less than they continue to infest all editions of Debussy, inexcusably, after seventy-five years?

Ravel's music offers little challenge. But, except to the Germans, challenge is hardly the sole criterion for listening. Ravel's career opens up to us in retrospect like a fan, always smooth, even-keeled, he was born mature, didn't "advance." Today one can't imagine him as revolutionary, yet *Valses Nobles* once incited catcalls. The music is both raunchy and restrained, but as smartly crafted as any in history. Ravel the man, meanwhile, seems much less intelligent—literary, intellectual—than most composers. One could liken his mind to that of a painter, were he not so fastidious. We make a fuss about the mystery of his personal life, precisely because there was no life.

Satie the man, on the other hand, like Andy Warhol, has superseded his work. (Though does Warhol hide a *Socrate* in his drawers?) Today in Paris the worst music of Satie is played continually in discos and on the radio, while his life, with its iconoclastic sarcasms, is admired, as Rimbaud's yesterday, by the young.

Poulenc the man, finally, like his music, was a sum of his obvious parts: dapper and ungainly, wicked and pious, a slipshod perfectionist. As a performer he led a very public life; as a citizen, and as a denizen of both *salon* and *bistro*, he was outspoken about his private life. But his private life was not, unlike Cocteau's, his public life.

Item: The day I left Paris I finally found a score, the only one in stock, of *Les Mamelles* at Leduc's where the salesman behaved as though I'd asked to buy the *Gioconda*. No score of *Parade* is available anywhere. If I do own the orchestra score of *L'Enfant*, it is because I made the investment thirty years ago.

Statistic: Schwann lists forty-three recordings of *Boléro* versus two of Ravel's masterpiece, *L'Enfant et les sortilèges*; six recordings of *Parade* versus one of Satie's masterpiece, *Socrate*; and no recordings at all of Poulenc's three great operas.

4.

Can music summon up remembrance of things past? "Association" strikes musical professionals as vaguely illegitimate, yet we're all prey to it. It creates its own category which resides in nostalgia, like your high-school dance band conjuring extramusical thrills. But the habitual pleasure of music is, for me, neither experiential nor intellectual, but, well, musical. Music is about nothing I know. Except Ravel's *L'Enfant*.

The all-knowing Colette, habitually a slow worker, wrote the libretto for *L'Enfant* in a week, on spec, and at the urging of a M. Rouché who wanted a fairy-tale ballet for the Opéra. Ravel was not on her mind; his name was suggested as a possible composer only after the book was a *fait accompli*. Ravel accepted. Five years went by in silence. "He allowed me no comments," wrote Colette, "no premature audition of the score. His only concern seemed to be the 'miaow duet' between the two Cats, and he asked me with great seriousness if I saw any objection to his replacing *mouâo* with *mouain*, or it may have been the other way around. . . ." Another five years passed before the première in 1925. What did she finally feel about the music? In 1950, toward the close of her life, Colette thought back: "The score of *L'Enfant et les sortilèges*—I had thoughtlessly entitled it *Divertissement pour ma fille* until the day Ravel, with icy gravity, said to me: 'But I have no daughter'—is now famous. How can I convey to you my emotion at the first throb of the tambourines accompanying the procession of shepherd boys, the moonlit dazzle of the garden, the flight of the dragonflies and the bats. . . . 'It's quite amusing, don't you think?' Ravel said. But my throat was knotted tight with tears: the animals, with swift whispering sounds scarcely distinguishable as syllables, were leaning down, in reconciliation, over the child. . . . I had not foreseen that a wave of orchestrated sound, starred with nightingales and fireflies, would raise my modest work up to such heights." Colette's reactions burn bright in the mind as I type these last sentences.

We seldom reread great books, not even those that have most moved us, although we may sometimes refer back to details within them. But great music, and often less-than-great music, we listen to dozens of times, each time re-experiencing it in toto. Obviously *War and Peace* is a longer experience, as the clock ticks, than *Saint Matthew Passion*, even to fast readers. A given time-span being inherent to music, and not to literature, we can return to the whole of a musical piece more aptly than to a book.

A few rare musical works, after a vast and violent trial period, need no reconfirmation. They are so dissolved in the bloodstream that we seldom listen to them again, although they dwell forever in some nook of the brain. We become like Beethoven who, because of his deafness, never in the realest sense *heard* the last works fomenting inside him . . . Thus it has been ages since I have sat down to savor once again the fact of *L'Enfant* for its own sonorous sake. I have just done so, score in hand. The disc was Maazel's expert, clankety-clank, unsentimental version. (Are you objecting that *L'Enfant* is not supposed to be sentimental? that a cool "removal" is exactly what distinguishes a Ravel from the hot anxiety of a Mahler? Ah, listen again to the Beasts' penultimate outcry swelling on that most dangerous of nouns, *Maman!*, as the strings overwhelm them in a sheer burst of Fannie Hurst, and tell me again it's not sentimental.)

The effect was the contrary of Proust's madeleine. I did hear Eva Gauthier singing again as though she were alive in the room; and I did see Bill and Noel and David again with tears in their eyes. Yet I found myself attending as through a glass darkly, uninvolved, in something which I had nonetheless invented, like the Chicago of my youth, each street awash in identical sunlight. Nothing's changed except myself. The change does not cover me with gooseflesh, it leaves me indifferent. Time passes (Paul Goodman's son is dead), and memory is stronger than fact.

Parade, L'Enfant et les Sortilèges, Les Mamelles de Tirésias. What a courageous bill of fare for the Met to offer! It's not a meal the French would find courageous since, being French, it's par for the course. For us the adventure lies in its being all twentieth-century.

I look forward to it as I looked forward to Paris last April. And I ask nothing better than that the experience should not obliterate so much as revitalize the past, even as Paris took on a new sense when I observed it from the vantage of another person. At their worst, Poulenc and Ravel will never bore me. If Satie turns out to be best, let me be the first to cheer.

December 1980

THIRTEEN WAYS OF LOOKING AT A CRITIC

1. Critics of words use words. Critics of music use words.

Those thirteen syllables, penned a decade ago, are as pertinent as any I can make on the matter.

If the final comment on a work of art is another work of art, might some critical prose equal, as art, the art it describes? Yes, but that very prose is independent of the art it describes.

The best critical writing is superfluous to its subject, and musical criticism is the most superfluous of all.

2. The music reviewer differs from fellow reviewers in that he deals with ephemerae, and hears mostly the past.

Concerts are one-shot deals. If a Rubinstein or a James Galway "ran" for five months, like Gielgud or Lena Horne, would they pack them in each night? Unlike the painting or movie or theater or dance critic, the music critic writes epitaphs rather than birth notices. Since what he reviews won't be repeated, how can his readers profit?

Meanwhile the fellow reviewers are immersed in new works. Oh, they do consider retrospectives of old masters like Picasso or Tennessee Williams, Balanchine or Ingmar Bergman, but they speak of "revivals" of O'Neill or of Oscar Wilde. We musicians do not speak of even a Beethoven revival since Beethoven is our rule.

The music critic is thus prey to the ennui of the Eternal Return, and to the anxiety of being unneeded. But if he cannot aspire to high art so long as he deals in other people's art, he can be a useful citizen by committing himself to the music of today and letting the chips of the past fall where they may.

3. Some of my best friends are critics; but the basic rapport with, for example, Virgil Thomson or the late William Flanagan, has always been compositional. Flanagan-as-critic was a purveyor of free tickets; Thomson-as-critic was the best in the world and hence free of rules. But that was in another time.

The New York Times's policy was to fire reporters who were found to be practicing musicians. Thomson's *Tribune* policy was to hire only practicing musicians. The *Tribune* wrote from the inside out and sometimes the writer was female. The *Times* still writes from the outside in and is represented solely by males.

Whether composers make the best music critics is debatable; but composers, even bad ones, know better than anyone how music is made—providing they have heard their works in good performances.

4. The critic as composer manqué is an old notion. The composer as critic manqué is more amusing. As one who straddles both professions I grow schizoid. But both composer and critic are different from "real" listeners. The drabbest reviewer is necessarily more responsible than the brightest Music Lover in that he must formally set—or rather, reset—the tone of a concert. When I must report on a concert, I listen differently than when I am the General Public. Indeed, I hear my own music differently according to the occasion.

As a sometime critic my duty is to every composer. As a full-time composer my duty is only to myself. In theory, all composers, even the despicable ones, are my brethren, while all critics, even the adorable ones, are my foes. I carry an enemy within me.

5. Some of my best friends are performers. But since composers and performers mostly face in opposite directions in our day, those friends are among the 5 percent who care about me and my (sometimes despicable) brethren. They are a race apart and the pariahs of critics who, merely to earn a living, are more concerned with who plays than what's played. Even the listings in their periodicals name minor performers but not major premières.

A soprano friend claims that her long career is now but a mass of yellowing newsprint. Is the critic's career more? Do not his stardom, his power, stem from a ubiquity which, like the soprano's, must continually be reaffirmed? Nothing dates like yesterday's paper.

6. 3 August 1980. Back from New Mexican glory, I open newspapers for the first time in weeks to rewitness, not unexpectedly, exhaustion, corroborated, in her already notorious dressing-down of Pauline Kael, by Renata Adler, who declares in *The New York Review of Books*: "No serious critic can devote himself frequently, exclusively, and indefinitely, to reviewing works most of which cannot bear, would be misrepresented by, review in depth." And so sometimes these reviewers theorize, as when Tom Johnson adjacently in *The Village Voice* describes in 300 words the whole history of contemporary music as a "quest for freedom," without once explaining: freedom from what? From the past? But the simplest observer knows that the most rigorous censorship has never squelched art so much as obliged artists to confect alternative molds, whereas electronic studios, while presumably supplying composers unlimited palettes, have come up with nothing very worthy. Meanwhile in the *Times*, during his second week as the world's most powerful music critic, Donal Henahan bemoans the sterile outcome of the promising sixties: "We [who is we?] continued to harbor the pitiable hope that the next turn of the cards would bring us another Bach, another Mozart, another Mahler." Why always the Germans? Why not another Debussy, or Ives, or Britten? But of course there is never "another." Artists are the only non-duplicable commodities that exist. Even in America. While Henahan extols the past as ever true and Johnson berates the past as ever false, both bark up the wrong tree in assuming that any work of art is "like" any other, even by the same artist. Now, what Renata Adler says about critics (whom she does not subsume in the artist category, though it's usually done these days) is equally applicable to artists. The latter on schedule must come up with new works, if not with new ideas, or die of hunger. It has always been so. An artist refashions the same notion over and over and disperses it always for a price. Not only Andy Warhol, Edgar Rice Burroughs, Georgia O'Keeffe and Francis Poulenc, but Braque, Tolstoy, Michelangelo and, yes (whisper the name), even Mozart. Artists have only four or five ideas in their whole lives. They spend their lives sorting out those ideas in order to make them communicable in various guises.

7. A critic must be able to tell—and then to tell you—the first-rate from the second-rate. In every field except music this question has been settled so far as the past is concerned, and concentration centers on the moment. Music critics' chief business should be the discouragement of standard master-pieces. At this point his function is moral: to warn against being beguiled by trends.

Most new music is bad, and it is the critic's duty to say so. But let him say so with sorrow, not with relish. The glee with which some of our head critics declare "I told you so" as yet another première bites the dust is no less contemptible than Casals belittling Stravinsky in order to sit on the Russian's throne. The great unwashed in heeding these spokesmen become exonerated from what should be a normal need for today's music.

8. The most honest description of the creative process is: making it up as you go along. The most honest description of the critical process is: judgment according to kinetic reaction. Neither process is casual. But for every Henahan who at least knows what he hates, there is one who is not sure of what he likes. Do we even know what we believe? If so, how to react to the belief? The not knowing has itself become in America a kind of belief. We like to talk about it more than to listen to it; it is made in order to be reviewed; it does not exist if it is not discussed.

9. Gide's quip, "Don't be too quick to understand me," obtains to us all, since we don't even understand ourselves. A composer doesn't want to be understood, he wants not to be misunderstood. Of course, Gide could also have said, "Don't be too quick to misunderstand me."

Can a living composer be a sacred cow? Can a living composer become a fallen idol? If one never sees raves for, say, Virgil Thomson's non-operatic works, neither does one see reviews that are less than deferential. Why? Meanwhile, even a Harold Schonberg gives Elliott Carter the benefit of the doubt. Why? And whatever became of the unanimous championing of George Crumb? If you explain that, well, lately Crumb hasn't written much to review, then why not review the eighty-seventh performance of an old piece, as you do with Verdi?

If critics are tastemakers, why has none blown the whistle on the concept of greatness—whatever that may be—as absolute and irreversible? Perhaps Beethoven's Ninth is trash. Perhaps even Babbitt and Sessions are antiseptic bores who, if they appeal to executants, appeal through challenge and not pleasure. (And I do allow the role of ugliness-as-pleasure in art: Mozart and Ravel, at their highest, contain ugliness. But when all is ugly, nothing is ugly.)

10. If critics applaud the emperor's new clothes along with the Philistines, some recognize the real thing when they hear it. But what critic will put his finger on the *absence* of the real thing?

Who ever questions the repertory of American song recitalists who sing in all languages but their own? More interesting, who ever remarks on how our national inferiority complex extends to those few composers who still write songs? Why are the texts of Crumb and Bowles almost all in Spanish, those of Perle and Weber almost all in German, of Harbison and Thorne in Italian, of Harrison and Glass in Esperanto and Sanskrit? Should these men claim to "feel" their music in these languages, I reply: You have no moral right to feel these languages before exploring the gnarled thrills of your native tongue, your gift, and yours alone. What a waste! Can you name one European who has forsaken his language to compose only in American?

11. The same Donal Henahan who knows what he hates has on four occasions reviewed my cycle *War Scenes* with four conflicting verdicts: memorable, bad, good, forgettable.

Have I ever learned about my own music through reviews of it? No, no more than through annotators who sometimes point out *trouvailles* I never knew were there. I've never altered a piece because of a critic. Unlike a performer, a composer is always ready: his performance is "honed," cannot be improved. A good write-up, alas, seems never to assure further performances.

Can I as a critic criticize myself as a composer? Yes, during the composing process, but no, during the performance. Unless the performance is years later . . . at which time I am no longer the composer of the piece performed.

12. Does public criticism otherwise affect me? And what do I stand to lose by voicing these opinions before critics?

Bad reviews make me feel worse than good reviews make me feel good, but no reviews are saddest. Although I've never read anything about myself that I've agreed with, or even understood, bad or good, I still prefer good to bad, since friends and foes might read it. But mainly I am ignored by the press. If the punishment for complaining is to be further ignored, I have nothing to lose.

Why be paranoid about a career that has prevailed for three decades? Yet what is there to think when, for instance, *The Village Voice* and *The New Yorker* show good will toward certain composers they disdain, listen to tapes of others whose concerts they've missed, while leaving my three decades quite unrecorded? Perhaps they have nothing to say because my work is devoid of device; expressivity in itself is not food for comment. When the fatted calf is killed for those prodigal brethren coming back to the C-major fold, no one attends me precisely because I've always been a good boy. In longing for proofs of love, I have held back, literally wept. In flailing out in prose I have shown myself naked and been answered with derision. To combat critics on their terms is a losing game. The frustration of being nonexistent keeps us awake, while they arise fresh in the day to hand out or withhold yet again their merits and demerits based on who builds a better mousetrap. The critic forever has the last word. Or as the case may be, the last silence.

13. In *Thirteen Ways of Looking at a Blackbird* Wallace Stevens wonders

> . . . which to prefer,
> The beauty of inflections
> Or the beauty of innuendoes,
> The blackbird whistling
> Or just after.

In music there is no "just after." A critic will never recapture the sound. The writings of even a Proust, a Shaw, a Tovey may be music—evocative, penetrating, ambiguous yet inevitable—but they are not *the* music. We can recall being in love but we cannot revive lovemaking except while making love. Sometimes when we finally hear the piece a critic has so wonderfully extolled we find no link. Stevens has it both ways but only within his poem, and our memory of his peom *is* the poem. Similarly, the memory and therefore the criticism of music lie only within the music.

Nantucket, July 1982

FOUR

EARLY PIECES

WRITING SONGS

Songwriting is a specialty within the general field of musical composition just as the writing of poems, novels, plays or history is a specialty in the area of literal or verbal interpretation of human experience. In emphasizing songs I will present some general principles which underlie all composition, as well as some practical problems which face the individual composer.

I have chosen songwriting to illustrate a composer's methods for several reasons. Song is one of the briefest musical forms. Its concern with words makes it less "abstract" than other music, therefore more accessible to the non-composer. In song, words are encompassed by a melodic flow of short enough duration for the good listener to feel logically how he is taken from beginning to end. The composer's decisions are fewer and clearer to the layman, and less complex than in systems of development needed for larger and purely instrumental pieces.

Problems of music-making vary from medium to medium and no two composers solve them in the same way. My purpose is not to explain how to write a *great* song; its qualities cannot be ascertained even after it exists because the essence of greatness cannot be verbalized. Nor am I concerned with questions of inspiration. A composer takes inspiration for granted and proceeds directly to perfecting his technique; a facility with his craft is ultimately second nature, so his choices are not always conscious. What I hope to show is a manner by which a song might be written from start to finish. Its future after that is speculative.

For the purpose of this examination I will narrow the definition of song as follows: *A lyric poem of moderate length set to music for single voice with piano.*

A lyric poem is an expression of its author's feelings rather than a narrative of events. A moderate length is up to five minutes. Single voice means the instrument of one human singer. And piano is the instrument with which we are all familiar.

Which comes first, chicken or egg? Words or music? In the world of jazz, lyrics are sometimes concocted specially to synchronize with music already completed. In literature of the formal vocal recital, music always comes second, being a result of the words—a wedding, so to speak, of words and music, in which neither ought dominate the other. A third element of greater magnitude is indicated. This "whole" is a piece of music integrally employing the impetus of words, and differs from a programmatic work that is meant to evoke an image or story without oral recourse.

The composer may force a lyric into the mold of a melody already existing in his notebook and which seemed to be waiting for just these words to come along. In my own working the notebook ideas later used in songs become accompaniment figures above which a tune is imposed. A composer may also have drafted tunes so embryonic they take on entirely new character when joined with words. As a rule, pianistic and vocal ingredients are conceived simultaneously. Today, especially, accompaniment is often composed as a counterpoint equal to the solo line.

The composer's initial job is to find an appropriate poem. The test of this is a poem's final enhancement by music; it is contrariwise inappropriate when both words and music add up to an issue of mutual confusion. One poem may be so intrinsically musical that a vocal setting would be superfluous. Another may be so complex that an addition of music would mystify rather than clarify its meaning.

All words of a song from lyric poetry are ideally understood in a continuing stream; making them comprehensible is the composer's (and ultimately the singer's) chief task. Some songwriters are free in reiterating words and phrases stated only once by the poet. It is uncertain whether such songwriters do this to illuminate the sense, or because they are carried away by their own music and haven't enough words to see them through. A poem *read* aloud with these gratuitous redundancies would not only sound wrong, but lose all of the author's metrical flavor.

A song is not a poem read aloud but something else entirely; music inclines to alter a poet's rhythmic subtlety, no matter the composer's will to prevent it. The sin of duplicating words at discretion is that it retards and cripples the motion intended in verse.

Sung words will almost always be slower than spoken ones, even without repetition; songs last longer than their poems. If the poet is alive he can be consulted about alterations. If he is not, it would seem the more interesting problem is that of making a poem comprehensible without resorting to facile verbal repetition. However, specialized verse forms (such as certain folk songs, nursery rhymes and jazz improvisation) can lend themselves to arbitrary inner repeating.

A sung poem should be comprehensible without amending the text if declamation and prosody are correct, the tessitura plausible, melodic rise-and-fall natural and tempo indication comfortable. You may have wondered what these words mean.

Declamation is the effective rhetorical rendition of words with regard to correct emphasis of each word as it relates—sense-wise—to the others. What is called *melodrama* is a procedure of speaking words with systematic accents against musical background. Milhaud, in his *Orestes* cycle, makes hair-raising use of melodramatic declamation: the fury mutters and spits and howls in rhythm with an all-percussion orchestra.

Prosody is the science or art of versification, the synchronizing of musical phrases with the natural movement of speech.

Tessitura refers to that part of the compass in which most of the tones of a melody lie. It should not be confused with *range*—meaning the entire possible gamut of notes a given instrument is capable of performing. A voice's most gracious tessitura is the area of its range in which it performs most graciously.

Excessive concern with these devices will sometimes produce a song so finicky that purely musical values are inhibited. Indifference to word values, using verse solely as an excuse to make music, may result in a song devoid of literary sense. A given poet's style will—where the higher art of song composition is concerned—refer significantly to the musician's treatment. There is a great gap between the inherent freedom of a folk ballad and the inflexibility of a sestina. Each composer has his approach. The poem's rightness and the success of the resulting song come only with a sense of style and taste in determining the kind of music used with the kind of poem chosen.

These are the principal rules—if you wish—that govern song composition. After a poem has been selected, the effectiveness of its union with sound will result from the composer's judgment in dealing with the words and their ideas.

At this point a digression to examine the poet's attitude about the musicalizing of his verse.

Some poets oppose the process. Tennyson complained: "These song-writers make me say twice what I have only said once." Valéry stated this same superfluity a bit more prettily: "Hearing verse set to music is like looking at a painting through a stained-glass window." But he personally despaired of poetry's future because of a greater power he felt growing in music.

Walter Pater maintained that "all art aspires to the condition of music." If he were right, poets would long to equal musicians with only verbal tools. Contrasts in language are limited compared to those available in music. Perhaps it is an issue of sour grapes; within their sphere poets surely create an entity, but some feel that the addition of music is gilding the lily.

Others just don't care. Apollinaire's writing was the source for great songs of modern France, yet he was not particularly musical. His attitude was: "If the musicians are amused, let them go ahead, I have no objections!" But he saw no relation between his words and the music.

And the late Paul Éluard was unable to recognize his own verse as realized by Poulenc. Preoccupied with the qualities of human speech, he felt vaguely betrayed by singers. "But since composers have to set something," he would say, "why not me?" He was active in the Surrealist party, which is *a priori* disinterested in music. This disinterest seems to be less the result of repugnance than a disguise of inner fear. (Kafka too was afraid of music.)

Yeats is a tempting poet for composers, but now that he is dead, music editors must apply to his widow for permission. She is said to go into a trance and consult the spirit of her husband with regard to a composer's eligibility. The ghost of Yeats has been known to relent where incompetent musicians are concerned; remarkable settings of his work, however, remain unprinted.

I believe T. S. Eliot allows certain of his poems to be used by all, others by none. Edith Sitwell favors Sir William Walton. Auden is agreeable and seems receptive to most comers; moreover, he is deeply musical. But like the observations of many who are well informed about a trade without practicing it, his suggestions tend to be impractical or pedantic.

In Old England some composers wrote lyrics for their own songs—like John Dowland and Thomas Campion. In other cases musician and poet alike were commissioned by the court. Purcell fancied the verse of his contemporary Dryden. And everyone knows Gilbert & Sullivan.

Goethe liked his poems set to music but defensively preferred lesser composers; he felt Schubert overpowered his words. Maeterlinck allowed Debussy to use his text of *Pelléas et Mélisande* as an opera, but fell asleep while hearing it.

Colette, who imagined a wonderful libretto for Ravel's *L'Enfant et les Sortilèges* (even the stage directions could be sung!) was overcome by the music: it made her text breathe and shimmer and bloom. She felt—too modestly, I believe—that her words were but a humble foundation upon which a masterpiece was constructed.

Young poets today love having their verse set. Since they have no public anyway (except each other), they hope this unification of the arts will give them prestige through reflected glory. Many are willing to write poems, or even extended librettos, without remuneration, for any composer who asks. But they are inclined to provide material so esoteric that it becomes meaningless when sung.

The modern composer understandably prefers to set poetry by his national contemporaries, but the pickings are slim. Lyric poetry is out of fashion today. As for librettos, a dramatist may have a better sense of music-theater than a poet whose product is by nature fussy, and who seems to forget that what is seen need not be sung about.

Maybe songwriters should amend their notion of what constitutes a proper poem for music-setting. Or perhaps song has grown obsolete. Not infrequently the composer will revert to the Bible, Shakespeare, or Romantic schools of the eighteenth and nineteenth centuries to search out texts for his lyrical songs.

Certain American poets, in possible revenge against songwriters, have taken to reciting their works to the accompaniment of improvised jazz. The trouble here is that the poem is an unchanging quantity while this music is never twice the same; the two elements are mutually exclusive. If the poet were consistent he would either request an unalterable backdrop for his narration, or would himself improvise verse to the spontaneous music. Of course, the latter situation would lead to incantation and hence to the Blues—back where it all started!

The Beat Generation is the first literary movement to concern itself seriously with music. But it has achieved nothing in this. The connection is merely a vague endorsement of extramusical emotions stimulated by the rhythm (or beat) of jazz, and is quite different from an organized union of words with music.

Poets are not always musical, nor even necessarily literary (poetry is about words, not ideas). They are rarely the best judges of the type of music to be used for their verse, although one finds that eminent writers are amenable to word changes a composer might wish to make, while the unestablished or mediocre will not be swerved from details of their original conception.

Songwriting is a collaborative and therefore impure expression. Collaboration implies concession, but concession is, after all, a part of adaptability which in itself is learning. In this sense the self-imposed limitation of the medium is a severe test of technique.

The songwriter writes what he hopes a singer can perform and should be willing to change notes at a singer's suggestion if given a valid reason. The professional poet too might alter a phrase if the composer's request seems rational. Lesser artists, conforming to cliché ideas of integrity, live in ivory towers. Not that a creator should not be idealistic; he can sharpen his craft by keeping an open mind to advice offered by executants who, after all, know more than he about performance. This applies both to poets in relation to composers, and to composers in relation to singing performers.

Before he begins work, a composer would do well to obtain rights for a lyric by applying either to the poet himself or to the publisher. Otherwise the music may be denied hearing and printing. Prior to the advent of copyright laws composers faced no such problem and uninhibitedly indulged their bias for the writings of contemporaries.

Although there may be a scarcity of suitable poetry, the practice of making songs from the work of living writers is desirable. Artists of today, whether they know it or not, have basically more in common with each other than they have with artists of the past. I might add that the music most comprehensible to the people of today is the music of today, because it is penetrated by today.

When he has found a poem, the composer inspects it with an eye toward determining the music's dimensions. The term *song form* is too broad for precise meaning. There are as many forms for a song as there are groups of singable, organized words. Regular lyrical systems exist, such as couplets, quatrains, sonnets, odes, hymns, roundels, even limericks, and also arbitrary sequences which poets invent and order to the nature of their mood.

None of them really fits the so-called ternary A-B-A framework which applies less to vocal than to instrumental music. Or rather, in a general way, it can apply to *all* music in that pieces have beginnings, middles, and end at a point related to the start.

The A-B-A form consists of a primary tune, a secondary tune, and repetition of the primary tune. The commonest version today, our thirty-two-measure pop song, is slightly more complicated: there the first A is repeated twice. This repetition establishes the theme, so that we feel at home with its return from the more transitory B section. Most "popular" music is built on this formula, and some of it—the show tunes of Gershwin, for instance—is unsurpassed in its way. But the music of so-called Art Song takes form from the poem itself, which is seldom versified in the primitive fashion of pop lyrics.

Whatever the poem's design, in one way or another it always dictates the shape of the song. No matter how many liberties the composer takes, it will be the poem itself which provokes these liberties. Meretricious originality is to be avoided at all cost. This might be illustrated by what Hollywood arrangers call Mickey-Mousing; for example, when a brick falls on the protagonist's foot the music goes *ouch!* A composer is not required to write a "lovely" chord on the word "love," or score a bleak low note on the word "death." He seeks to shed light on a meaning of the poem without musico-literary interpretation; he would otherwise be doing what Tennyson deplored: saying twice what the poet says once.

There is obviously no one adaptation of a poem. Different composers have put the selfsame words to different music, each with similar success, each lending both personal poignancy and impact to their understanding of the poem.

There are nevertheless valid unorthodoxies. For instance: a songwriter might have the music play against the words, just as a choreographer has his dancers move against the beat. Dancers can move with extraordinary effect in animated precision to a sustained music with an indefinite meter. The meaning of their motion is nonetheless an evocation of the music, just as in song the meaning of notes is born of words. Although music has a more primal appeal than poetry and is thereby inclined to take over a song, a composer cannot deny that it is the particular expressivity of the given words that provokes the musical mood.

Words provoke the musical mood in a number of essentially mysterious ways. It might be assumed that a song's most logical shape is that which conforms exactly to the shape of the poem. Though it cannot rhyme—as poets understand the word—musical meter can literally illustrate poetic meter: four stanzas of poetry can be imitated by four "stanzas" of identical music. The difference is in the words, which are not the same for each stanza. But a free adaptation is accomplished by ignoring given divisions of a poem and substituting others, or even fashioning a long non-repetitive melody which blends the stanzas into a single current.

On the other hand, a musician may choose free verse and subject it to rigid patterns of tonal repetition, imposing a new dimension extraneous to the music; or he may allow the free verse to carry him along according to its own rules as he himself carried the strict verse in the previous example. Whatever happens, the poem and music will always have a common superstructure.

A composer examines verses with an intention of determining what manner of music will coincide with what words in what section of the poem. He seeks highs and lows, and points of intensity toward which to direct emphasis. Most likely he will first decide upon the musical climax by looking for a group of words that sum up the poet's message, hoping among them to find one with dramatic connotation, and also a vowel that will sound good on a low or high note. Use of a note in extreme vocal registers is the commonest method for producing effective climax in song.

Particular types of voice have a particular tessitura that is more touching than others. We assume the composer is writing for a particular voice. Just as he would know that the soliloquy of a girl in love is not suitable to a bass, nor a warrior's marching tune appropriate for a typical soprano, so he would probably not arrange the most telling moment of his bass line to lie in an upper and strained tessitura, nor allow the high point of the coloratura's song to fall on middle C.

The climactic note (or phrase) of a song is one that is the result of accumulated tension; contrast is achieved by removing this note from the normal tessitura of speech.

I am not sure that high and low have our implication of tension and release in other cultures, but with Western vocal music, audiences find satisfaction in well-contrived high or low endings, soft or loud endings, endings of contrast, endings that sound difficult (even when they're not). Audiences like all endings: they feel that the virtuoso has run a risk and come out victorious. And they like to be sure when the end has come, so as to know when to clap.

It is no concession to be considerate of public appeal in a final stroke that provides extreme notes for a singer. All music must contain climax. In song it appears when a vocal line arrives at the inevitable point toward which it has been moving. Since a composer feels safer in knowing where he's going, before he begins composition he calculates this point of crisis, insuring the direction of the road which will lead him—both forward and backward—to his overall form. This overall form is what gives contour to melody.

Melody, of course, is the primary ingredient of song: simply say the word and it suggests the human voice! But what is a great melody? Can a musician learn to write one?

Great melodists are not necessarily great composers. Nor is it prerequisite of a composer to be able to make unforgettable tunes. We associate the continuous arching flow that is melody not with Beethoven, Debussy and Stravinsky, but with Tchaikovsky, Sibelius or Bellini, from whom the well-proportioned long phrase emerges painlessly. Yet the first-named are widely thought to be more "important."

A composer's inborn talent for good tunes probably determines the medium upon which he will concentrate. Those, like Beethoven, who have difficulty in evolving attractive melodic material to be developed into a work of multiple variations, are likely to center their interest in larger forms where evolution of material is of itself the keynote. Others, like Puccini, who seem disinclined to imagine tunes without words, and whose tunes are born as spacious lines all but complete in themselves, will probably concentrate on vocal mediums. Still others, like Mozart, direct their melodic gifts to every field.

There are all sorts of good melodies, ranging from a four-note motive to extended growths of inexhaustible variety and renewal, yet always related to the seed from which they flowered. These many kinds of melody share in common the gratifying proportions that provide artistic fulfillment. The components of good melody *can* be analyzed from a purely technical standpoint; hence a musician of average ability is capable of inventing one. But that special something that makes it memorable, endows it with mysterious embodiment with power to move us, begs analysis. No one, not even the composer, can tell you much about it.

I noted earlier the importance of words being understood, and proposed that only certain vowel sounds are practical in extreme registers. One vowel sound is practical when it is easier than another for the singer to produce, and so for the hearer to comprehend. For example, "i" is more comfortable high and low than "e." An intelligent composer will not choose the vowel "i" for an extreme note, without good reason, just because it's easy; nor conversely use an impossible "e" in a similar place only because the atmosphere seems to require it.

An offbeat vocal effect can have justification; but the composer has only to try singing it for himself to discover what he imagined dramatic is that, or on the other hand, ineffectual and ridiculous. What is more, he should be able to sing everything he writes no matter how grim his voice sounds. The music we best understand is the music we make for ourselves, and no composer can go far wrong if he estimates his vowels and consonants and prosody and all other attributes of song by letting them come naturally from his own vocal cords while in the act of composing. What he can do, his performer can do; but if he writes only what is theoretically performable, he is in for some jolts.

Setting words with a skill for declamation is said to be a rare gift, yet it is no more than notating words according to the laws of natural speech inflection. Irreproachable declamation is really no more indispensable to song than assigning practical vowels to appropriate notes. A poem, after all, is not "real life"—a song even less so. In this distillation of life, distortions are conceivable when they serve an expressive gesture. If a composer is going to distort the metrical values of a poem he should have good reason for risking loss of verbal comprehension.

The words of Art Song (how I hate that term!) are doubly hard to understand, even when they follow prosodic patterns, because the voice is taken out of normal speaking range. In jazz and folk songs, words are understood without effort, for these tunes are generally built within the limits of an octave which the singer transposes to his own speech range—and then emits through a microphone.

In verse, as in the prose of speech, phrases have an innate rise and fall which is rendered in the same way by most readers. In music, regular fidelity to this rise and fall makes for monotony, yet occasional consideration of it can be pertinent. The composer may disregard the effects of natural language for musical reasons, and such departures are part of the act of composition.

Now the question of accompaniment. Accompanists dislike the word and call themselves pianists. They feel that the best songs are a supple give-and-take between instruments of equal worth, and that an insensitive pianist will sabotage the greatest vocalist.

Accompaniment is classically a regulated pattern over which a voice moves. This is as true of, say, Schubert's songs as of his piano sonatas wherein the voice is not human. Accompaniment has evolved since the troubadours sang their tunes above a simple strumming, and instrumental sounds that used merely to sustain a voice are often now on equal terms with it, weaving in and out of, sometimes overwhelming, the vocal line. Piano parts of Debussy's late songs are virtuoso pieces; voice and keyboard have independent developments indicating a chamber duet rather than what we normally think of as a song.

Accompaniment reduced to its lowest terms does not, however, exist as a piece in itself, though a good vocal part retains its urgency even when performed alone. The composer may imagine that he conceives a work for voice *and* piano, but under our limited definition of song, it is music for voice *with* piano.

In the end, composition is choice, nothing more: choosing the right note to be sounded with the right tone in the right place at the right time, each choice presenting alternative decisions, other possibilities. But choices are not always conscious. I have mentioned inspiration as a presupposed faculty; and, when the tools of craft are well in hand, awareness of them has less importance than what they produce.

The majority of song composers write quickly: with the poem they have something to start with, the skeleton exists. If the composer has a good day this skeleton will acquire an inevitable flesh. He does not know the origin of this flesh, nor is he especially aware of its sequential growth.

His very first efforts doubtless came from sheer instinct without practical knowledge of the voice (except that which sang within him), or of musical form (except that which the poem seemed to indicate). Such songs can be quite good indeed, but this goodness troubles an untrained composer when he isn't sure why it is good. Probing the nature of song by studying formal vocal devices found in other people's music will not inhibit but release his ability. He will still write for the same "inspired" reasons, but with the assurance of an intervening knowledge without which he would have stood still.

Since the so-called born songwriter's early pieces have usually worked by instinct, he spends the rest of his life attempting to make tangible the fortunate formulas which originally appeared without his calling them. His young songs came to life, as it were, from the exuberance of first love. First love is unexpected revelation which seldom recurs except to saints and artists.

Song makers are so often reproached for not writing a "grateful" vocal line, or for misrepresenting a text, that they can assume the listeners do not hear as they do. There are as many reactions to music as there are people to hear it. The composer desires to bridge the gap between private conception and public reception. He does so by learning a recipe of indispensable ingredients. Later, if he is still around, he does it by trying to teach his interpreter to hear as he hears.

I have suggested that certain principles of songwriting become obsessive and distorted. These distortions are successful when their purpose is not esthetically gratuitous. The church music of Palestrina and his colleagues was less bound to words as literature than to their use for evoking the glory of God through choral counterpoint. A single syllable was strung out to such length that it could not be understood as having literal connotation. It was employed for its musical, and therefore religious, sound.

A modern example which gives a total interpretation of text at the expense of individual phrase comprehension is the setting by Boulez of René Char's *Le Marteau sans Maître*. The word values are so purposely deranged and the vocality so unnatural that the most agile enunciation could never project a literal sense. Boulez's intention was to interpret the poet, not the poem. He portrayed, in his way, a feeling for the author, using the words as a frame around his sound.

The opposite intention can be found in Thomson's setting of Gertrude Stein. The speech values are so exact, the melodies so "normal," the accompaniment so functional, that there is no question of each word being heard with the significance given by the poet. Or Satie, whose music on the prose of Plato allowed each syllable an ease of talk, brightened only by a discreet simultaneous French commentary on the old Greek.

Any words can be turned into song if the composer's aim is as sure as the text's. Celius Dougherty made a riotous encore out of the definition of Love as found in the dictionary.

Lou Harrison wrote a disturbingly effective essay on chlorophyll in Esperanto, then set it for eight baritones and orchestra. John Cage took a prose extract from *Finnegans Wake* and arranged it gorgeously for soprano on just three notes, accompanied by hand-tapping on all parts of the piano save the keyboard. Milhaud used words from a flower catalogue, and Bernstein from a recipe book, for charming cycles.

The writer of songs—by way of recapitulation—is a category of composer who can't always express himself on broader instrumental terrains, any more than a symphonist can necessarily make the lone lyric page a totality. Nor can he work without what he feels to be appropriate poetry, the test for which lies in his ability to add a fresh dimension by way of music (can he clarify a poem to an audience through a singer?).

Song is of greater magnitude than either text or music alone. The composer is concerned with words only insofar as they are related to music. Sometimes his comprehension of a poem is not fully realized until after he has completed the fusion. Speaking for myself, the only poems I've ever really "understood" are those I've put to music. This understanding resembles that of the astronomer for whom stars change their meaning as he approaches.

When the composer has decided upon a poem he should inquire as to whether it is in public domain or still subject to copyright laws.* He then

---

*Blushingly, may I append an appropriate morality-anecdote as antidote to the foregoing pedantry? . . . In 1948 I composed a setting of Edith Sitwell's *Youth With the Red-Gold Hair*. My publisher said: "Fine. Get the poet's O.K. and we'll print the song." I'd hitherto musicalized any words that appealed to me; my few songs already published had been to verse in public domain, examines the general tone of the text, sensibly, stanzaically, metrically. His music will move either with or against the normal flow of the poem according to what permits the most sensitive rendition. He takes care not to obscure comprehension of the words, but to illuminate them with regard to the dictates of rise and fall, of prosody and declamation, and of vowel and consonant properties.

The overall nature of the text determines the contour of melody. Extreme points of a song's melody are, in turn, determined not only by an inherent sense of "rightness" but also by knowledge of the most "telling" registers of the vocal range for which it's written.

Behind this melody occurs an accompaniment as a subsidiary part of song, though recently it has come to have almost equal value with the solo voice.

Any competent craftsman can fabricate an impeccable song in which every note is justified by some sort of musico-prosodic logic. One composer will undertake the writing slowly, with controlled manipulation not requiring "inspiration" (which comes in irregular spurts anyway). Another will produce his song in a fever of impulse with music spilling out all at once; in a single sitting, innately aware of his technical resources, he knits the sundry components of words and music into a coherent whole.

A professional has only a subconscious inkling of his working methods once they are ingrained. He is in the happy position of not being obliged to give himself an explanation for his individual choices if their sum total seems logical. It is for the theorist to inquire later into the reasons of choice; they may not necessarily jibe with those of the composer who may even have forgotten them.

No system guarantees a great song, although a well-trained musician may turn out a flawless one by academic standards. The artist's hand is not blessed every day. The magic touch cannot be willed. But without it a writer of songs—whether he has a dazzling technique, an intelligent conviction of "what should be," even an unquenchable inspiration—will deliver a stillborn imitation. A flawless song becomes great when it contains the breath of life.

Summer 1959

i.e., no longer controlled by international copyright laws. It hadn't occurred to me that living poets might have opinions—much less objections—about having songs made on their work. . . . I mailed a genteel request to Sitwell, and received no reply. After four months I wrote again— again no reply. In France a year later I stated the case personally to Sacheverell Sitwell and to Stephen Spender who, after hearing the music, promised to intercede. Still no answer. Once more I wrote. Silence. Eventually I received from the Sitwell editors a note to the effect that Walton was the only composer the lady favored, but that if I could persuade him to make an exception in my case, they might reconsider. Walton's secretary answered me from Ischia stating that the master was deep in *Troilus and Cressida*, but if I would write again in six months, etc. I wrote again in six months, and so did my publisher. No reply. Finally, exasperated, four years after my first inquiry, I sent off a letter of such ugly rebuke that Braziller's lawyer will not permit its reproduction here. Suffice that I demanded a simple yes or no. By return mail the attorneys responded: ". . . you complain that she has ignored your request to be allowed to use a poem of hers of which you had in fact made use before you asked. Dr. Sitwell receives a constant stream of requests from unknown persons who wish to hitch their wagons to her star and has in self defense been forced to a policy of ignoring them. . . ."

SONG AND SINGER

Songs and song recitals of our time have become trivial objects to almost everyone: to composer and manager, publisher and public alike. Singers themselves are still very much around, but have turned into a salable commodity. Big Business, in shelving the "miniature," has decalcified the performer's repertory and vulgarized his public image—because money is not carried on wings of song. When art falls to the low point of a curve as it has today, its smallest treasures are the first to break from the weight of false standards. Prizes for bad symphonies are higher than for good songs, although lengthy pieces make the average listener more uneasy than shorter ones. Most painting collectors prefer big canvases because they're worth more; and if large pictures delight while long music bores, the layman's criteria are nonetheless based (in art as in cigarettes) on size before quality. Musically those criteria are imposed by impresarios who disqualify voice recitals except for an occasional prestige venture. A few songwriters and concert singers still specialize, of course, though they are not in demand. But their specialty was once an invulnerable art whose periods of perfection coincided with the peaks of musical history.

The history of music is the history of song, since all music evolves from vocal expression; the Neanderthal probably sang his worship of nature before thinking of any other artistic utterance. Yet music is frequently claimed to have flowered last of the arts. Naturally its group expression, its instruments are prehistorical, and Grecian modes and flutes and zithers were not invented yesterday. Still, comparatively speaking, music as the formal tool of a single author *is* from yesterday.

One explanation lies in ancient man's exclusion of psychic exploration from the avowable pleasures of his artistic soul. His pyramids and sphinxes emerged from a balance between the human ideal and the tangible world, while music exploits effects without cause—which is why its power is as obscure as dreams. With the rise of Judeo-Christian culture, psychological rather than logical investigation was stressed. And so creative music, in keeping with the times, grew less concerned with clear-cut ideas. Words, of course, are clear-cut and logical, and all songs have words. In fact, most

Western music until modern times was fundamentally vocal—as though ancient man scented danger from afar, and foreseeing our hysteria felt obliged to link his abstract sound to the un-elusive verb. "What ancient man did create," says the poet Valéry, who advanced the above notions, "is nothing next to what he smothered within himself. If poetry attained full realization millenniums before music, the cause was its address to people who had no need of intense physical reaction in their enjoyment of art." I leave to others an enlargement of this theory. Whatever its time relation to the fellow arts, music's beginnings in any civilization are vocal.

Primitives gradually find melody by combining phrases which exaggerate the rise and fall of speech. Vocal contours depend on language and eventually give music a discernible national character. Since vocal music is the source of non-vocal music, speech inflection is the direct basis of all music of all cultures. And since music resembles the speech of a nation, it also resembles the people. People, therefore, resemble their music. Their religious beliefs (which are the origins of song) grow from fear of nature into praise of it, and hence into the melodized speech of tribal incantations which finally crystallize as highly organized chant.

Later Christian liturgy is not far from its Oriental predecessors. The pagan or folk music of the Dark Ages accompanied systematic bodily movement, not only of dance but of practical chores like spinning and chopping; hence regular meter. The religious or art version was reaction against such bodily movement and resulted in the melisma of Gregorian chant; hence irregular meter. (Irregular meter *and* a slower tempo, because of echoing cathedrals.)

Although medieval church music underwent meager development, the laity produced a race of nomadic recitalists called minstrels and troubadours. In the early 1300s they were domesticated (at least in Germany) into Mastersingers and organized guilds where apprentices learned the trade (not the "art") of song.

The Renaissance moved singing into even more secular routes, inventing the madrigal and eventually the single vocal line with instrumental accompaniment, a direct ancestor of modern song. This was perfected in Italy by Monteverdi and the elder Scarlatti, but declined around 1725 by becoming a mere frame around vocal gymnastics.

In England, Henry Purcell revitalized the art with a poignant skill unequaled anywhere, while in Germany of the next century, a literary flowering occurred attended by a corresponding advance in lyric music. The advance reached a climax most centrally in Franz Schubert, followed (as climaxes must be) by a rapid descent.

The history of music must not be considered an unbroken flow toward ultimate perfection. A chant of Gregory, a mass of Machaut, a motet of Gesualdo, a cantata of Bach or a lied of Schumann are each invariably a masterpiece—and irreplaceable. Each is a high note in music's story whose high notes have most usually been heard in the human voice.

After Schubert, then, another dark age awaited song. The darkness, to be sure, was occasionally shot with sunlight, for one cannot dismiss the vocal talents of Brahms or Wolf, of Ravel and Debussy. But the tendency was toward total eclipse as demonstrated by the puniness and near obsolescence of recent literature for the human voice. Ours is an instrumental age in every way.

And there, in a nutshell, is song's history.

What kind of people are those who sing?

Since Mozart's day prima donnas have been noted for their extravagant temperaments, for all we love in the legend of theater. Yet I can only judge from those around me who mostly seem loyal colleagues, hard workers and early risers.

Their body is their instrument, so singers require more steady health than other performers. The majority pamper themselves but have generous outgoing natures. They like to eat, drink, laugh, scream and kiss; they express emotion orally because they enjoy singing. When romance or digestion go wrong, these things said to stimulate creators depress singers, and the tension shows immediately to their public. So they keep themselves the most normal of artists.

At present they capitalize on normality to a monotonous degree. Latter-day divas are said to have followed fabulous conventions expected of them, and their wild self-indulgence served also as vocal expression. The acting of Jeritza, for example, was as brilliant in daily life as on the stage. With the exception of Maria Callas, few retain a semblance of fiery tradition, though Europeans are still more theatrical than Americans. Even in movie stars we admire homey humor before mysterious dynamism. The dynamic singer is vanishing as music becomes less a ceremony than an industrialized game.

Commercial spectacle, in replacing intimate ceremony, has all but killed the small recital both here and abroad. And record catalogues feature about 75 percent fewer songs than before the war. The public is after bigger game: it wants a voice backed by the sonorous gloss of orchestras and the visual sheen of décors. A singer who can still attract the public to his piano-vocal concerts does so uniquely through an established opera reputation. Usually the recital contains as many arias as songs.

Too many virtuosos lack curiosity about repertory other than for their own instrument, and singers lead the group. Curiosity may be less expedient than flair to great performance, but *some* intellect would aid in overall musicianship. Our singers are not so untutored as they once were (doubtless because of mechanical exigencies in all fields), yet they remain the least literate of musicians because of their medium's accessibility which offers them a less literate audience. Song is the most natural musical expression. Certainly our best jazz vocalists perform through sheer instinct, though their instrumentalists now are mostly conservatory graduates. If the jazz singer lacerates English prosody and ignores classical breath control, he nevertheless (or rather, she—for the greatest are women), *she* nevertheless works according to a long tradition and her every word is crystal clear. But the recitalist has forgotten traditions—not of singing, but of song.

Song has always bridged the gap between poetry and speech by combining two effects like a double exposure. Song is sound—a sound of greater magnitude than its separate components. Of course the sound of music—as opposed to rustling leaves or words of love—is sensual only secondarily. First it must make sense. Since composers today are less involved with sound itself than its means of production, their training in song is not much happier than the singers'. After the war, just as most authors eschewed the opulence of words, our composers lost the luster of notes, even in big forms. And only a handful of poets and musicians still concern themselves with vocal miniatures as did Schubert and Duparc, Burns and Yeats.

The scholastic trend encourages manipulation of massive structures, so young composers now have masterpiece complexes. Masterpieces are supposed to be long, yet one-page songs can indicate talent as effectively as interminable quartets. And all musical expression (if it is to have an effect as music) is basically a sung expression, whether it be a Stephen Foster tune or an electronic construction. He who composes graciously for any instrument need not be a performer, but must have imagination to sing within himself not only his songs but his symphonies.

The imagination of vocal composition has withered. The same fistful of songwriters existing twenty years ago still persists, but seems clenched tighter than ever. Younger men are not intrigued by word-setting, and when they employ the human voice it is less for verbal expression than for instrumental effect. That effect is shunned by most singers whose instruction has not even begun to explore the non-vibrato tone production which modern vocal music calls for. The singer and composer work as much at cross-purposes as do composer and audience. And all three seem to have renounced that sense of just plain dazzle from Rossini's time.

The art of serious music is not learned through education alone, of course, but through a sixth sense. Nor again is it an entertainment, which merely confirms rather than challenges. The art requires concentration, and concentration can be dull at times. But among other things music is fun (or should be) and is not all just scholarly sound.

The ceremony may be seen as well as heard. Stravinsky has organized works for their visible as well as their sonorous aspects. Presumably he does so to reinforce attention on the composition (since closed eyes make for wandering minds), although the ritual of music—from tribal dances to the Catholic Mass—has always involved the visual.

This is especially true as regards singers who, for better or worse, are indispensable to the art of song. They have even more need of stage presence than other executants since they can't beguile you with an instrument other than their own person. The greatest vocalists aren't necessarily the greatest performers, and conversely the most compelling ones don't always make the prettiest noises. When performance and sound are combined in a glamour buildup today as in, say, the case of Eileen Farrell, it means that she is a faithful wife who washes dishes like everyone else while producing sounds that nobody else can produce.

But with all the artless hominess of today's performers (or rather their managers), every good one, despite himself, retains an extramusical style: from his entrance on the platform to his moment of attack, he is an actor

presenting himself, a professional personality who at home may be dull as
dishwater. Personality is manifest, for example, through Lily Pons's demure-
ness, through Bernac's precision, Callas's bravura, Flagstad's "no nonsense"
style, Tourel's illusion of beauty, Della Casa's true beauty, Siepi's virility,
and so forth. As for Americans like Roberta Peters or Theodor Uppman,
they accentuate the kid-next-door approach. Involuntarily or studied, all are
showmen. Their audience is reassured when the musical movement arrives
because they know what they're doing and how to do it. Only when show-
manship dominates do they become caricatures like Anna Russell or
Liberace.

That magnetism is the executant's artistic projection of a driving interest;
stage comportment is an over-extension of his character. Such excitement,
however, cannot be taught, and its absence explains why many of our more-
than-capable students just never make the grade. Either they are too stable,
or too dull, or too intelligent, or too sure of themselves.

No virtuosos are sure of themselves, and most are afflicted by stage fright.
Their electricity comes from the sense of risk being run. The possibility of a
ceremony's getting out of hand (as at a bullfight) spellbinds the spectators.
They may be acquainted with the ritual's climax, but only the virtuoso can
lead them to it for only he knows how to get there, and he may never arrive.
Nothing is sure until complete. The interpreter's voyage exists in time so he
is prey to more perils than the creator. Sometimes he quite literally dies *en
route*. His is not the reason why. The difference between skillful amateurs
and magic professionals lies less in their understanding than in nervous feeling. The term *understanding* is vague anyway when applied to art. Complete
understanding is no more a requisite of musical performers than of actors.
The actor who overdoes his investigation of a playwright's motives turns out
to be a director, a critic or a ham. Great works possess too many levels of
diagnosis for one person to ascertain *and* interpret simultaneously. The performer's job is to project, not analyze. Analysis is for the musicologist and
the composer, and even the composer (if alive) is dumbfounded by the layers
of "meaning" a musicologist may reveal in his composition.

The public, of course, pays for performance more than for what is performed—so the performer capitalizes on that glamour of his. Which is why
composers so often resent interpreters. The gratuitously brilliant interpretation naturally sabotages composition as often as the inept one. But occasionally I wonder if truly excellent performance cannot do the same. In such a
case does the music itself thrill, or the person's manner of playing it?
Qualities of *vocally* performed music are particularly hard to judge. The sense
of song is expressed through words, and words have precise meaning no
matter how well or badly uttered. Even the wisest have difficulty divorcing
themselves from performance since the head finds less use for music than the
body. Saint Augustine, after desperate avoidance of the physical, could finally proclaim: "I am moved not with the singing, but with the thing sung."
Yet how can we know the dancer from the dance? And especially where the
human voice is involved, anyone has trouble disentangling the sound from
what is sounded; for here is the most emotional of instruments which all
others seek to emulate.

That emotional ingredient is why so many people shy away from a voice recital. They call it boring really because it strikes home, because they too can sing (in their way) and so can identify, and identification—as Gertrude Stein said—makes you "feel funny." But the funny feeling is a step toward appreciation and can be taken most easily through vocal music. One only regrets that today, with expanding audiences, we are persuaded to identify with the common. Songs, rather than transcending ordinary sentiments, now descend to reaffirm and justify them.

If the tune on paper were questioned, how would it answer? That "heard melodies are sweet but those unheard are sweeter"? For such melodies when brought to life sound far from the composer's first conception. Music lasts by itself and cares not who composed it; nor can music recall the thousand anonymous fingers and mouths which tamper with it, beautifully or badly.

Charles Ives, our musical Grandma Moses, once wrote that his songs had not been made for money, nor fame, nor love, nor kindling; in fact he had not composed them at all but merely cleaned house and proudly hung what was left on a clothesline for the neighbors to see. He explained his pleasure in contriving that which could never be sung. "After all," said he, "a song has a few rights the same as other ordinary citizens. . . . If it happens to feel like trying to fly where humans cannot fly, to sing what cannot be sung, to walk in a cave on all fours, or to tighten up its girth in blind hope and faith, and try to scale mountains which are not—who shall stop it? In short, must a song always be a song?"

Buffalo, 1960

LISTENING AND HEARING

"The ideal listener is one who applauds vigor-
ously."

—VIRGIL THOMSON

"What is the answer?" asked Gertrude Stein on her deathbed. There was silence. "Well, then what is the question?"—and she died.

The question, of course, has always been on the universal source and aim. It never changes. But history has provided ten thousand solutions through theology and science whose responses raise other questions; they are forever evolving, never complete. Alone the work of art satisfies, for its question and answer are mutually inclusive and form the one finished thing that exists.

Answers have less value than questions: we can learn them by rote. But curiosity indicates imagination, and imagination represents the first step toward good listening which will result in a comprehensibly musical reply—irrelevant to logic or moral persuasion.

Listening is easy. But true ease, like anything worthwhile, may be hard to cultivate. We hear all the time, even in sleep, though we don't always listen to what we hear. In music, as in living, fragments of question and answer might try the door of our consciousness, then pass unknown and leave us ignorant of what we've missed. Few people develop their capacity for perceiving what is always around; most ears follow a line of least resistance that allows only pleasant passive hearing. Active listening provokes reaction which is not always pleasant, for pleasure is the target of entertainment—a side issue of great music as of great crucifixions.

Since the larger public is passive, it might be desirable to cultivate a listening potential. But too much music is around today. Concentration grows implausible when accompanied by the unsolicited bombardment of Muzak wherever we go. Answers are there, but increasingly disguised by accumulation of rubble. Saturation desensitizes selection, and one cannot distinguish, or even knowingly hear. From self-protection we stop responding actively or passively. Or we stay home with our "serious" recordings which used to be a good proving ground but now demonstrate an obsession quite removed from the living core of art. Omnipresence of music derives not

316

from love of sound but from fear of silence. Sound has no meaning except in relation to silence. Ours is a century of racket—in all senses of the word. So when we finally come to the concert hall our reactivity is dead and the program goes in one ear and out the other.

Not that concerts make an ideal setting. They are a fairly recent addition to audience passivity. Hearing music for its own sake did not occur before the 1700s when it was a joint proposition between composer and performer and hearer, happening at home or at church. Music was either made by oneself or heard as a dedication to God's glory. The décor of discovery is significant: we may be more moved by a new piece in unexpected surroundings than in standard presentation. Solitary confinement inspires more propitious appreciation than the communal museum-jail. Having first heard Hindemith's Trombone Sonata with a temperature of 103°, I found it a masterpiece. Bartók's *Bluebeard* under mescaline was doubtful (but then so is all music). My first Piano Sonata (1948) might have turned out quite otherwise if I hadn't had chicken pox while composing it.

In America from 1925 to 1950 jazz fired the young to song and dance and jam sessions which again made them into dynamic contributors. Though not worshiping a special deity they were spontaneously reacting. But now jazz devotees (like concert publics) have renounced physical response and sit in "cool" absorption of their age's hysteria. We aren't allowed to dance to Ornette Coleman, but we do now to Rock. The weeks slide by like a funeral procession, but generations pass like a snowstorm.

Some people say they don't understand music but love it—or they know all about it except what they like—or they haven't learned to appreciate! Despite education we listen only to what we want to hear. Without formal coaching many perceive the maximum subtleties in jazz because it is of their time; they need not work at love. The attraction may be foreign to their parents, who had effortlessly digested the sonorous folkways of *their* heyday. A fashionable fallacy, in our passive age of the large audience, is that those elite communities of the past possessed deeper musicality by virtue of participation. Practical knowledge is urgent to creation but not to comprehension. Sensitivity alone arrives at an estimate of artistic worth. Love is sometimes wise to ignore rules, for technique may distract from effect. We can read with deep fascination of Oedipus or Burma without budging in time or space—without committing murder or building roads.

As for those who feel left out: why, after all, must everyone like music? That they are missing something is just the lover's opinion. Certain fine men simply don't need it, which doesn't signify a profound lack; they merely have other criteria and are honest about them. For that matter, there exists a probable boredom in most audiences most of the time with most music, especially the classics. However, they don't resent the classics because they are used to them and only *hear* them. Modern music usually impels listening, hence reaction. Most people hate to react—though nothing is more wholesome.

With artistic benefits and disadvantages of historic change there remain the same inherent levels of listening. But today for the first time civilization offers a minor role to art: the need is replaced by the romance of the atom.

Artists have reached a sort of impasse. Artistic distribution and consumption, on the other hand, are more avid than ever, though not very constructive. From the composer's viewpoint the impression is that, whatever the world's state, logical musical education should begin with works of the present as it always did in the past.

Music most comprehensible to people of today is music of today because it is penetrated by today, and literally no one can fail to perceive this on some level. I find it harder to identify with a Haydn sonata than with any modern score: I have a feeling for what my colleagues want to say. Today's music may be difficult because it is alive, and life is difficult. But this very difficulty talks to us even when we don't like what it says, whereas the classics approach us with the pacifying inactivity of corpses. We can know the past only through modern interpretations which change every day. The motionless unknown is judged by the fluid known.

I am not implying that Haydn's value has diminished; simply that we will never hear him with the ears of his time: ours are filled with intervening centuries of sound which Haydn ignored.

The average concert provides scant exposure to the contemporary. Impresarios sell the public what they suppose it wants: the "classical" repertory. The concert public has come to associate all music with this music. An overdose of the familiar is a drug dripping the danger of security which in art means being invulnerable. Those who interrogate the unforeseen are truly alive. Familiarity with the classics appears to justify evasion of the new. The classics only seem more comprehensible because they are heard oftener; in reality they are as removed as the communal belief in God which produced Renaissance art. We perceive such art with a far different esthetic from that of the people to whom it demonstrated a way of life.

Resentment of the new, then, rises from forced dissociation with the old. Yet our own composers, those of whom we should be proud, cannot reiterate. Expression today is more private than the mass celebration of God. Even the elevating powers of the past were less in theme than in treatment. Subject matter is never important—anyone can still praise the heavens if he wants to. Twisted wires, twisted toes, or twisted lives have the same skeletal connotations now as before, but are made timely flesh by Calder, Balanchine or Albee. An understanding of these treatments is latent, and emerges when the public frees itself from yesterday, not in erasing it, but in judging today by today's standards. The truths of the past are the clichés of the present. Periods of time will always be interactive whatever we decide, as Eliot pointed out when: "Someone once said: 'the dead writers are remote from us because we know so much more than they did.' Precisely, and they are what we know . . ."

If casual hearing is numbed by Muzak, and adventurous listening stifled by average concerts, where, then, do we find our new music and the peace to indulge in it? We can avoid Muzak in the silence of our home, then fill the silence with recordings of our choice. I have suggested that records, though an evasion of the miracle of accident, do supply a proving ground. If the average music lover lacks joys of even a hundred years ago when he himself played chamber music, today, nonetheless, he has access to a much larger repertory on discs; also the advantage of immediate rehearing, prerequisite to familiarity with the new. The majority of hi-fi enthusiasts, however, restrict their collection to the safe music of the usual concert. A safe work is one that tradition has frozen into a masterpiece, relieving us of our own decisions. Stereo addicts are frequently more concerned with the techniques of production than in the music produced. The most vociferous record public is, of course, made up of opera fans who are occupied first with a singer's reputation, second with voice production, third with the story and last but not most with the music. Music itself seems more sport than art, and the vast audience resembles that of a tennis match: heads move in hypnotic unison from left to right to left as a high C flies over the net to be whammed back by a rival coloratura. But for the exceptional listener—one with questions—records serve as introduction to unusual music, just as concerts introduce items with which he may grow more familiar through discs.

For not all concerts are "average," and even the average occasionally come up with something interesting. Concerts and records are the musical outlets of our time, and are less to be merely tolerated than put to good use. How shall we use them?

If acceptance of the classics has come through familiarity, the same will be true with our own music. Still, appreciation results from repetition only when we listen. To know a piece one must be on friendly terms with it. The structural elements of one language cannot be transferred to another. Thought produces grammar, and different peoples think differently. We don't understand a Frenchman, or even his culture, unless we have some knowledge of his spoken tongue. The knowledge brightens less through study than through exposure.

Exposure to music is active submission, though not always on subjective planes. Only superficially will it soothe the savage breast. Aaron Copland once caused a stir by stating he never cried when hearing music. He explained that while theatergoers may weep easily because of immediate human identification, the gifted listener only lends himself to music's power: "he gets both the 'event' and the idealization of the 'event' . . . even though the music keeps its 'physical distance.'"

Good music that summons no tears doesn't mean we are unmoved; the movement takes us away from (rather than into) ourselves. We are removed. If we do weep at a popular tune, that is because it beckons us into ourselves, reminds us of an extramusical past of situations which never return but which we hope to revive in the present. The "memories" are actually revised images existing in the present but associated with circumstances under which the tune was first heard. The images have nothing to do with the music, the past does not exist. Yet in such reveries many of us absorb music, osmosis-wise, involving the ego rather than abandoning it to the composer's. If we say: "I am hearing music and being moved," we are not wholly attending for we cannot do two things at once: we cannot be taken out of ourselves and contradictorily know we are taken out of ourselves. In identifying with a piece it is we ourselves and not music which concerns us. In reality (or unreality) we are divided between one present and another; the divisions are so small they seem to melt together. Scientists say we are given an infinite variety of ideas per second. Were it possible to grasp only one of them and prolong the present indefinitely, we might blast through dried oils to bare canvas where centuries ago an artist posed the soul by which we know him now: himself, the man!

There are tourists incapable of looking at a masterpiece for its own sake. They bow into a camera, snap experiences never had, then rush home and develop these celluloid events to see where they've been. Sometimes the film turns out blank. What we wish to keep we lose. When not urged to possess we are free to love. Concertgoers who seek or manufacture memorable experience have missed the point. Admission of this fact eliminates the need for tears at a symphony. The concept of a nonexistent past, or fears of a nonexistent future rising from past learning, make us cry. Apprehension is a waste of time—it is only now and predicts nothing.

The same is true of the performer who comes between us and the work he plays. When moved by his own performance he is a ham without the objective control of projection. His immediate feelings becloud our appreciation. The composer has not expressed his immediate feelings, for how could he weep and simultaneously have the *sang-froid* to notate his tears? Such a production would contain about the same sentimental authenticity as a high-school love lyric. Of the thousand reasons for audience emotion, not one may have been apparent to the composer.

A funeral march is not a funeral. Its author does not mean us to weep (even if *he* did), nor to blur our reactions dream-fashion. He clears the mist. If the gesture eludes us he is not at fault. What seems complex may be an ultimate plainness to which art transforms idea. But the nature-hating gimmicks of our society have unaccustomed us to simplicity. The gesture clarifies only what is contained within us: it is not in the music that we perceive what we hear. Sympathy between the outer sound and inner self ignites fireworks in some and lights no spark in others.

Scales of appreciation have as little relation to intelligence as facility for language has to musical gift. (There are brilliant musicians who just can't begin to master foreign tongues, and unmusical dullards who are proficient— though equally dull—in several languages. The separation between what is called an "ear" for language and an ear for music is really the difference between two brands of extroversion; ears themselves are all pretty much the same.) While enthusing over music, we sometimes see the so-called tone-deaf person looking as though he'd missed the point of a joke. Jokes can be explained, perhaps, but feeling art is the taste for a certain love. And love is the attempt to unfathom a mystery. When this succeeds, love dissolves. A superb paradox!

There is, probably, a comprehension that demands no set answers. The mystery of a masterpiece is never fully fathomed. In lacking the magic touch Clementi was monotonous where Mozart excelled, though as craftsmen they were on a par. No one will ever find sensible words for the difference between the great and the merely admirable. Which is why masterpieces, from one aspect, are all a bit boring: their multiple levels tax the effort of approach, and hard work is tedious. We often have greater affection for lesser products. We need not bother to decipher affection since total comprehension (assuming it's possible) sterilizes art. Besides, taste is unanalyzable. But if we dislike a work which we nevertheless feel to be great, we should know how to justify the opinion. This cultivation encourages the taste inherent in everyone. There is no good or bad taste, only taste. Unlike a bias, it seldom changes character, though sometimes it expands.

Can a listener let his mind wander, then come away the richer from subconscious exposure to music? Stimulus without concentration is useless for positive opinion, just as the beauty of dreams has small creative value next day. Like the churchgoer who gets only what he brings and brings only what he comes for, the concert-attender must attend for the concert. But as for being enriched (attentive or not), he will find that music—as opposed to church—is oblivious to persuasion or morality.

Unconscious listening is more dependable. Carlyle maintained that if you "see deep enough . . . you see musically; the heart of nature being everywhere musical, if you can only reach it." In signifying only itself, music becomes a language translatable by the universal awareness latent in everything. This most complex of expressions is also the oldest and so appeals to our most primitive level, inexplicable through reason. At that level we all hear music the same way though surface reactions vary with social advancement. Tears and concerts, for instance, are recent Western distortions.

Frequently an unskilled listener or child penetrates more directly than a dilettante into new works. Nothing in the ear structure rejects unusual sonority. Children won't complain louder about the worthwhile than about juvenilia: they like or don't, without censorhip or duty; only later do questions begin. We can grow nervous in wondering what art ought to be, and intellect alone will never inform us what it must be. No music is ahead of its time, but the public is often behind its time. The future doesn't tell. We must accept our music as it stands today, for the pronouncements of new decades upon our culture will rely on new tastes formed by the extramusical phenomenon of social progress. The sole formula a musical layman need observe is: the conscious repetition of exposure produces true opinion. "Mature artistic judgment can result only from the love of art," to quote Roger Sessions. "Any judgment in the absence of love is sterile and therefore false."

For the music student or practicing performer this love is presupposed and he must go beyond it. Perceptive acuteness of the untrained is fine, but may be deceiving. A little knowledge is dangerous, and it is only fair to offer formal encouragement to aptitude.

Formal encouragement means a technical sharpening of the ability to enjoy music. There are all kinds of enjoyment (gay, macabre, passionate, sadistic, innocent, even boring), but none of them is passive. Active enjoyment is the comprehension that begins with memory. A popular song is retained through reaction when we whistle or dance but, for the student, music is a rigorous game with complex interplay. The rules are not beautiful in themselves but in their productive understanding. The beauty of production lies in form which, with music, is ordering specific processes of repetition and variation. Anecdotes about a piece are often given to laymen as aid to recognition, but only ear-training for landmarks within a piece provides the familiarity of scholarly appreciation. Ear-training is usually imparted mechanically with no ends for the means. Though no end in itself, without it even the talented grow insecure while following scores. And there are hundreds of more-than-adequate performers who don't know technically what they're doing. Knowledge of harmony designates tonal location within a piece, and this is the essence of form (at least in standard repertory). Counterpoint study helps distinguish more than one voice: every note of a master can be accounted for. Instrumentalists should attempt formal self-expression so as to follow other music without getting lost. The ear is probably best trained through copying entire scores by hand, or even in actual composition.

The usual music student won't, and shouldn't be, a composer. Inspection of the problems will, in Schoenberg's words, "give him only one pleasure: [that] of balance between the joy he expects from music and the joy he actually receives." The advice is good for listening with new ears to old music. By what standards does he judge the new?

A trained musician can listen objectively most of the time. But whatever his opinion of a new work's quality, he cannot say its performance was good or bad without the standard of previous performances by which to compare it. The test lies in whether the piece holds his attention. If it does, he wants to see the score. Then if he is still interested, the music works and is "good" for him. Nothing of much importance is accomplished overnight, and love at first sight is rare. Love at first hearing is less indicative than involuntary concentration. Both trained and untrained listener can learn to love just as jokes can be explained. When he hears right he will progressively amend his tolerance level, not with the intention of accepting all, but of acquiring discriminatory judgment. He can readjust to almost any diet. Of course, whatever opportunities are offered, their results are unsure: a horse led to water won't always drink. The best education has been used for negative goals.

There will always be varieties of listener good and bad, logical and sensual, even impermeable. These last need not be morally obligated. As for the others, if they enjoy themselves no harm is done. Reactions are never the same; no psychologist is permitted to say our musical comprehension is off balance, or to know if his vision of blue is the same as our blue. There is no invariable listening method, no universal language on our conscious plane. But some education is helpful in shattering false illusions. The shock is short-lived when illusions are replaced by ideas of how to judge for ourselves. It's even better to be wrong than unopinionated. Freedom of choice is achieved by the labor of understanding.

Music must be a necessity we seek, not a luxury taken for granted. Anything is allowed the fool who sees nothing and the genius who perceives all. For the connoisseur a certain knowledge of certain rules for a certain time will be of eminent aid in resolving enigmas.

An American, Charles Ives, composed a work called *The Unanswered Question*. Being a masterpiece, it is an answer in itself. Gertrude Stein did not hear it in death—but we can, while very much alive. If we don't like it, we can listen again. Then again. Resolutions will come through music of the present. That is the only way to know the past.

Buffalo, 1960

COMPOSER AND
PERFORMANCE

When the final note of a composition is inscribed the composer's struggle is over and so is his creative pleasure. This work was accomplished mostly in silence and alone. Yet music, to have meaning for others, must be played aloud, and the road from composition to audition can be rough and long.

After the thrilling rosy shocks a young composer experiences in rounding up musicians to decipher his early efforts, he recoils before a challenge: that of procuring adequate professional hearings. His elder colleagues are of little use here, being too busy with the same problem and inclined to envy their juniors. Which is why so many composers pursue with ulterior motives the society of performing artists rather than of each other.

An "established" author of music knows rather accurately how his work-in-progress will ultimately sound, so is apt to lose interest at its completion, or at least after its debut; he is less intent on launching it than on starting something new. But the growth of a young artist depends on constant realization of his ideas; in order to learn, he must hear what he's written. This is easier said than done, especially when he writes for symphonic combinations. A piece commissioned for performance has smooth enough travel from manuscript to auditorium, though respectable execution is never guaranteed. When composed for its own sake, however, without anterior prospects of public presentation, the launching process of a new work—even by the famous—is complex, expensive and interminable.

Excepting drama, music is the only art to require mediation between producer and consumer; and drama is less bound to interpretation since it is more visual than visceral and makes sense to one who reads it. But silent score-perusal provides only a general approximation: music needs to be heard to be "believed." Before this century, creative musicians themselves were middlemen when improvising in a patron's parlor. In our specialized age, a composer is usually just a composer and requires an interpreter. If he hustles he can generally find a soloist who will give him at least one public audition. But for the average young hopeful's unsolicited symphony, the following

324

costly and time-consuming transactions occur between his last draft and first hearing.

Today a symphonic work of, say, twenty-five minutes takes anywhere from a month to three years to conceive, notate, revise and orchestrate. That is the engrossing period of composition. Afterward comes endless hackwork. If the full score amounts to three hundred pages, a union copyist will charge up to a thousand dollars for its transcription into what is called "autograph." So the composer does it himself on translucent paper suitable for the cheapest method of reproduction. This paper, at twenty-five cents a page, costs fifty dollars.

Music calligraphy, a grueling technique in itself, must be scrupulously adept or the performer will not consider the manuscript. An hour per page (or three hundred hours for the whole) is average copy time. Photo-offset duplication comes to around thirty dollars a copy. If the young musician can afford it he has five copies made, and mails them, along with engaging letters, to five conductors—reputedly champions of new music. A year later his scores may all be rejected and returned, and he will try his luck with other conductors.

If perhaps his work is accepted by even a third-rate orchestra, he is of course anxious to hear it. As the extraction of the separate instrumental parts is his own responsibility, this will involve either two hundred more hours of painstaking copy, or around seven hundred dollars to a professional copyist, plus additional reproduction costs.

When the great day arrives, he spends another hundred on train fare and hotel bills in the town where the orchestra has welcomed him with scant publicity, attends an insufficient rehearsal at which he's consulted with minimal deference, and takes a bow after the concert that is reviewed with speculative competence. Then the sound dies out forever, his work sinks into oblivion: a Society-for-the-Propagation-of-Second-Performances does not yet exist! The unknown hopeful has spent maybe three years of lonely labor on a single piece, and maybe fifteen hundred dollars for an hour's practical experience; many composers of parallel development don't even achieve this much. For better or worse he has learned something in hearing his music live once, but the procedure is discouraging. For solace he always has the dubious but tangible write-up which, however accurate, is no more than desultory comment on his deepest thoughts. Young composers understandably don't write large orchestral works much anymore. They compose for the excellent chamber groups in residence at colleges where America's most important musical activity takes place.

An uncommissioned work by the established composer is prey to a not dissimilar sequence, except that his publisher negotiates correspondence, exacts rental fees and reports the performance to the performing-rights society, which pays a regular stipend. When the piece is printed he receives royalties from sale to invisible artists who may turn their questionable renditions into a recording to be broadcast later on the radio, from which it will be taped by music fans for their private use. By this time the composer's germinal impulse is so far behind him that he recognizes his music as a long-lost acquaintance with whom he now has little in common. Sometimes he feels as though the vicissitudes occurring between creation and performance are hardly worth the trouble.

In any case, the definitive audition of all music transpires within the artist at work. No ensuing "live" representation coincides with this gestational notion—and it usually affords some shocks.

Composers are seldom surprised but often displeased with a performer's concept of their phraseology. They are often surprised but seldom displeased with a performer's concept of their tempo. Since music notation is inexact, all interpretation of it is different (occasionally better, usually worse) from what its originator had in mind. Nor is a composer's own public performance representative: he alters conceptions once his notes are brought from the introspective studio to expedient execution. These conceptions generally concern speed.

A metronome is an undependable criterion; the only designation which can't be misapplied is *presto possibile*. Tempos vary with generations like the rapidity of language. Music's velocity has less organic import than its phraseology and rhythmic qualities; what counts in performance is the art-istry of phrase and beat within a tempo. A composer is never sure of tempo before rehearsal, for preoccupation with such a detail during composition slackens creative flow. Writing time corresponds in no way to performance time, and intuitions regarding the latter are, at best, approximate. Notation of a scherzo can need many days and pages, though it plays a few seconds.

Slow movements are successfully written in one sitting, but the impulse in fast music presupposes pitfalls because inspiration can't be sustained for long. A too-eager composer inclines toward technical padding in rapid move-ments, and is wise to heed Hemingway's warning to Marlene Dietrich: never confuse motion with action. The pulse of creation is rarely identical to that of performance. (Francis Poulenc once told me: "Robert Shaw is not only my favorite choral conductor but my favorite musician of all time. His rendition of my music corresponds to the very action of the blood through my body!" Now this judgment from a composer is as rare as it is complimentary.)

Tempo indication is not creation, but an afterthought related to perfor-mance. Naturally an inherently fast piece must be played fast, a slow one slow—but to just what extent is a decision for players. If the composer happens to be the performer, so much the better. Rhythm and phrasing, nevertheless, do pertain to composition and are always misconceived (though sometimes beautifully), for as I say, notation is inexact.

When a composer determines his tempo as a final gesture to the product, he does so as an interpreter. Since tempo varies with the life of the times, his marking is inaccurate, his emotional conjectures will not have authentic translation into sound. The composer will never hear his music in reality as he heard it in spirit. Small wonder that his interest sometimes wanes when notation, or even formation, is accomplished. He prefers to compose some-thing new rather than pursue the hardships of attaining—and disillusion-ments in achieving—good performance.

✳

A moment back I mentioned that a composer's own performance of his music is not necessarily definitive. How often at parties he is confronted with requests like: "Do play us your new symphony!"—and when he explains that his symphony was not conceived for keyboard, and that anyway he doesn't recall how it goes, there's a disappointed reply: "You wrote it after all; you of all people should know it!" But on completing one piece he leaves it to begin another; it is his interpreter's job to master the technicalities and memorize the notes. Remember that composition and execution, though not mutually exclusive, do not go hand in hand. Some fine composers cannot play any instrument competently. And the true virtuoso-composer (Rachmaninoff, for instance) really has two professions: he must sit down objectively and *learn* his own music as he learns anyone else's: by practicing. As for obliging with a piano reduction of his symphony, or singing with skilled simultaneity the various male and female roles of his opera, his party-public must be equipped with a sophisticated ability for score-reading or they won't make head or tail of his behavior.

Musicians of the "popular" world maintain that composition and performance in a jazz solo constitute a single process; what is played is the same as how it's played. But this is not true formal creation any more than the improvised cadenzas in nineteenth-century concertos; it is only a technical trick demonstrating a facility for spontaneous variation on pre-composed tunes.

It may be that the expanding voyage from psychical germ to physical sound is necessarily a mutative process terminating, for a creator, in the shock of recognition. As with his audience, the initial visceral exposure to his composition is most decisive; and, like a jury, he cannot eradicate first impressions. The public, of course, does not experience this sonorous shock of recognition which is the relation between a seed's fertilization and its eventual blooming. Sudden wisdom gained at hearing thought in sound is not unlike the disturbing sensation most of us have experienced in unfamiliar situations: we feel sure this has happened before, but when?—in another life? Or like James Joyce who, confronted with the cold print in his first published book of love poems, exclaimed: "But these are not love poems at all!"

The public and composer hear in a less like fashion than members of the public among themselves.

The entire history of evolution is contained in the development of one human embryo. I like to liken the private and the public (the composer and his audience) to this process: a composer's work suggests the whole of creation as comprehended through Darwin, while the audience represents an embryonic version of evolution. No two listeners hear alike. Each takes away a shred of the composer's self. This shred is the listeners' own gestation, and though their pregnancy gives birth to children none of whom resemble each other, they all resemble mankind—that is, the evolutionary gamut. The most learnèd articles about music might not correspond at all to its composer's diagnosis; there is only one composer of the one work which has set off these multiple reactions, and by this time he is dead, or uninterested, or off somewhere writing something else.

He has gone away because the glamorous shock of recognition wears thin. He is soon accustomed to realities of "live" audition; these realities liquidate (or obscure) his first imaginary hearings by imposing one impression upon another. He can retrace the steps from conception, through birth, to performance (as Poe did in a post-mortem of his *Raven*, or Clouzot in his film on Picasso at work) only with an objectivity devoid of the "emotion" laymen are pleased to feature as artistic creation.

A second live performance, however, though possibly an improvement, seldom obliterates or holds surprises over the first. Since the composer is quickly used to the impurities of the initial aural surprise, a new and superior rendition can be disturbing when it does not match first impressions.

Most composers don't like concerts. Absorbed all day in their own music, by evening they aren't disposed toward anyone else's. Passive audience participation means sharing the breathing space, program-crackling, dubious thought waves and distracted coughing of strangers, most of whom, when they pay attention, admire performance and not subject matter. Since the impresario of management has become the chief star of the music world and dictates program-planning to performers, who in turn must mostly ignore contemporary composers, there is small adventure in concertgoing.

Management has arbitrarily determined the limits of taste; the more popular executant artists conform by becoming sportsmen rather than musical servants. Repertory has dwindled to about fifty proven masterworks of the past. So the public today, being more concerned with the playing than what's played, is less prepared to appreciate the three B's: Bach, Beethoven and Brahms, than the three C's: Casals, Callas and Cliburn. As for new composers, they are virtually left out in the cold, and have little wish to patronize recitals of famous artists who unfailingly execute (though each with a personal signature!) the identical, standardized program of other famous artists.

Many a good composer, then, hears less "live" music than the regular concertgoer, and some have a smaller repertorial knowledge of the classics than the average disc collector. The composer is, of course, for the most part, educated on classics like everyone else, but after a certain point such works no longer happen to be pertinent to his creative life. Being steeped in the music of his own time, he is prone to take the past for granted, with the result that years may go by without his sitting down to rehear, say, Beethoven's Fifth. This symphony, taken at long intervals, is likely to exude more rejuvenated meaning for him than for the lay public who hear little else and so have no point of comparison. (My own artistic education was the reverse of most in that the first valuable music I was exposed to was of my own century. And I loved this music to a point where the classics presented as formidable a blockade to me as the moderns do to others; I took the sound of my day by instinct, but needed education to the past: which demonstrates—despite the impresario's protest—that a capacity for understanding is strictly a matter of familiarity).

Vast knowledge is a quality of the dilettante; it doesn't necessarily make a finer artist and in some cases can inhibit him. When André Breton was asked why he never learned English during his years in America, he replied: *"Pour ne pas ternir mon français."* I have seen composers who, because they are so intellectually conscious of how a piece should go, and so avidly aware of the structural devices of others, become paralyzed when they undertake their own composition. Others are inordinately prolific, having unshakable faith in themselves rather than in the produce of others.

Unless he supports himself as critic or pedagogue, the only concerts a composer frequents are those devoted to the chamber music of himself and his colleagues, and even these prove trying. They are privately subsidized programs presented to small groups of modern-music *aficionados*. This elite public, in the trend of the times, also judges all music more by its performance than by intrinsic quality. In the case of a new work, only its composer is qualified to know whether performance is good or not; even *his* judgment is disputable since, like his audience, he has not the standards of previous performances by which to compare the present one.

When his own music is not in question, he still attends these small concerts less for enjoyment than to keep up, broaden his outlook, estimate his rivals, maybe plagiarize an idea or two; he is always in search of new material from either within or without. Sometimes he comes to renounce his confrères as sterile, and organizes a vogue for little-known but fertile masterpieces of the past. The novelty of thrill is increasingly rare as one catches up with existent literature, and it is seldom that a familiar work revives the intensity of its initial impact.

A musical author is less occupied with production of pleasure than with production, period. And he is less occupied with the product's being understood than with its not being misunderstood. His one aim is self-expression, and since this expression is communicable only through mediation, he can just hope for the best. But the best of performers (or mediators) remain servile to Big Business, and their volunteering of new music issues solely from good will toward the composer at the risk of diminishing prestige with their public. So, as they seldom learn such music, and then play it a single time, it has no occasion to mellow in their brain, much less in the public's. How, then, can audiences not misunderstand a work heard but once and under debatable circumstances?

The elite public is on the composer's side, the general public is for the virtuoso; though both (whether they know it or not) estimate creation by performance.

A composer shuns the big concert from boredom, and is present at the small one from sheer loyalty. If his work is represented on either, he is reluctant to attend because, although mediocre performance is out of his hands, he is always held responsible and condemned. His interpreter signals him to rise, and he must smile hypocritically in acknowledgment of the feeble and misdirected applause.

When communication of his music has possibilities for being reasonably faithful to his intentions, he is still reluctant to attend—for other motives.

There is a strange embarrassment in hearing one's music while others are present. A composer as audience to his own score usually doesn't listen to it so much as its interpretation: the recitalist's timing, phrasing, tonal beauty—or those many separate instruments uniting to raise life from a mass of black dots. In this he resembles the public which is alert only to performance, with the difference that the black dots are of *his* making—and he worries about them. In his nervousness over detail he hears only what goes wrong; what goes right is inaudible.

Audiences may get a better idea than the composer of his new piece in that they hear what "sounds" while he is aware of what doesn't "come off"; they absorb the whole while he hears separate parts and feels these parts are monstrously evident to everyone. If all goes well for the author, then he wonders if others are listening as he is. If they are not, he is nervous that they may have lost his message; if they are, he is nervous that they may have found his message. He perceives a spectral side of himself filling the hall with a sound he no longer controls. This is intensely personal: he feels disrobed, defenseless, imagining others know his secrets; he is as uneasy at the possibility of the audiences grasping the minutest discrepancy as at having his soul laid bare. There, of course, he is deluded: centuries will pass before psychologists decipher the symbolic tongue of music and expose, telepathically as it were, the creator's innermost thoughts. If music could be translated into human speech, it would no longer need to exist.

The ordeal over, the audience fixes the composer with bemused indulgence, somewhat astonished to find a man of flesh. Then they clap. Acclaim, though flattering and justified and even necessary, has no relation to the creative spirit. A writer is a writer only when he's writing. With the production behind him (the work of another man, so to speak) he feels public acknowledgment misplaced.

When his older works are played the composer hesitates attending because of a bittersweet nostalgia. There is little connection between initial impetus and final proofs: a publisher returns manuscript for correction, and the composer hardly recalls who wrote it! He may weep hearing his own songs, but it is less at the music's persuasion than from memory of himself as someone he once knew. That "someone" now is lost. The composer loses himself in each endeavor, and resultingly finds himself. Then he loses the music, for a printed song no longer belongs to its maker: he holds out his hand awhile, but the sound escapes, disappears, henceforth to defend itself without a parent's guidance. When his song arrives in a concert hall the parent is uneasy that this half-recollected child will misbehave.

How then, and when, can a composer actually sit back and enjoy his finished works? Probably the nearest answer is: when he is alone with a phonograph, and a recorded rendition he approves of. Speaking for myself, years of phonographic instruction have made me come rather to despise recordings, and to like collecting less than producing. Some musicians know all about music except how to make it, so are obliged to collect for pleasure. Most composers are too wrapped up in their craft to live as the pedant who moves all around an art without attaining its enigmatic heart.

But the phonograph is a necessary evil, and gives a composer the opportunity to hear his music without stage fright, or sitting in an audience and worrying over wrong notes. He has, for better or worse, an unalterable performance. We have observed that he quickly grows used to the first audition, and that no eventual superior performance can obscure this—nor even revive the period of formation.

Here is a personal example: In 1953 I wrote a twenty-minute piece for the Louisville Orchestra, which commissioned and recorded several such works yearly. As I was in France I was secretly relieved at not having to attend any rehearsals, performances or recording sessions, all of which can be painful. I first heard the work privately on the final recording sent to me, and was pleased to have notated my ideas succinctly enough for authentic transference into sound four thousand miles off. Qualifications I held about this performance were, as I played the disc over and over, gradually eliminated, or rather, absorbed into an overall effect as I now heard it undistractedly in sound. Perhaps I subconsciously concluded that these discrepancies were my intention. . . . The only "live" rendition I've attended of the work was under Eugene Ormandy with the Philadelphia Orchestra, which is reputedly the world's most sumptuous. By this time my Louisville listening habits were so solidified that I could only consider the golden Philadelphia tones as a kind of vague miscalculation.

So much for the sedentary sins of phonograph listening, and for the virtuous complacency it provides to both layman and composer. Live listening is naturally more exhilarating and instructive than records, but can be so wounding to the composer that he occasionally prefers to linger in the solitary realm of what Truman Capote names "sounds on the edge of silence."

But music, after all, is meant to be heard. (Stravinsky even maintains that all musical performance should be seen, and that closing the eyes during a concert makes one subject to irrelevant daydreams.) For the sake of a point, composers have here been shown more sensitive than they really are to the quandary of perfection. Like all artists, they are susceptible to appreciation and only hope for justifiable performance. Some feel greater joy in directing, conducting and organizing tangible manifestation of their work than in actual composing.

When he can, a conscientious executant should always listen to the originator, no matter how inarticulate the latter. Though a composer may be an unskilled interpreter, his private keyboard performance gives an instinctive hearer the clearest skeletal sense of his works. My ideal impression of all music is in my own mediocre playing and singing: imagination rectifies my technical inexactitudes. Another performance is more exciting, but completely divorced from me.

Composers are frequently interrogated about how it feels to hear their own music. Is it thrilling? For myself, though only a mildly curious auditor of a piece I've heard many times, I'm always uneasy. It is less disconcerting to accompany my songs onstage than to sit with an audience. As collaborative performer I am directly responsible for what is heard, so must concentrate on the business at hand. Hence I am not prey to the creator's distraction, nor do I even feel to be a composer while performing my own music. Whether my performance is capable is irrelevant to my nervous system.

Nerves apart, the composer doubtless has a larger, more extended post-creative thrill than any other artist in that his product alone involves double emergence: a "double birth," if I may say so, or a "double life"; the subjective birth through mind to paper, and the objective life through sound. Even a play has life on paper—but never music. Though one can scarcely say that music on paper does not exist; it simply has two existences while other arts have one.

To sum up: A composer's function has been purely achieved at the completion of a given work. From then on impurities arise. The music will not fully exist until sounded before some audience. When the composer is not his own interpreter he is usually entrepreneur for his auditions, a job both arduous and disheartening. When he performs himself, his conception is only one of many, and not necessarily the most authentic because (though he may be a fine conductor or instrumentalist) he cannot simultaneously be an author and an interpreter: one stops where the other begins. Nor is he used to listening to himself from outside; he hears primarily in silence. He is no more responsible for his own rendition than he is for that of others.

As occasions increase for listening dispassionately to his own music, he is less startled by disparities between what he hears and what he calculated. His calculations, however, are notated in an imperfect system, so while his music is played he always has suprises. They are pleasurable or not, depending on the variance of performing artists. Pleasant surprises are tastefully novel alterations of speed; unpleasant ones are betrayals of rhythm and phrase.

A performing composer can be his own worst enemy. Since a written sequence of notes is only theoretically explicit, its interpreter necessarily takes liberties. An available composer can be consulted at rehearsal, though he is never quite sure how his music should go; his job is to create, not to explain.

Composer and public are comparable to the evolutionary premise: ontogeny repeats phylogeny. All listeners contribute, in a sense, their individual definition of a given musical work.

Composers often avoid concerts because they are saturated with their own music, because they are weary of standardized programs exalting virtuoso rather than creator and because (when their works are represented) they are intimidated. The intimidation is either from dismay at a possible bad performance for which they are blameless, or from schizophrenia at hearing notes which no longer directly concern them and over which they've relinquished control.

They are usually a little impatient while their music is played: it sounds better or worse but never the same as what they heard in the inner ear. When impatience becomes gratifying, it's a transference of how they hope their audience is reacting. Their own reaction is doubtless most objective when alone with recordings.

Although acclaim is agreeable, it is foreign to the composer's basic elation. For that elation is exercised only in the hermetic act of writing music, and is of such unique magnitude and mystery that it is not only irrelevant but impossible to depict in words.

Philadelphia, 1959

ARTHUR HONEGGER

He had the kindest face I've ever known, and an unaffected intelligence which served as both balm and kindling to his dozen pupils—of whom I was one during his final years. Those years were nevertheless charged with both physical and moral torment which he dissimulated (at least with us) except for an occasional clenched fist or tired sigh. The quality of lucid restraint glimmered also through the surface fury of his art, and made him (thanks also to the somewhat sentimental and "visual" texts he often chose) the most accessible of so-called *modern* musicians for the general public.

For this reason, eleven summers ago, the French crowned Arthur Honegger (although he was Swiss) their National Composer, voting his music as that most likely to survive the millennium. The following autumn a curtain was pulled, not only on his life but on his work; nobody—not even the average Parisian to whom he was perhaps the one *known* composer—has talked much about him since. Those mid-fifties were already dominated by the traditional revolutions of the young even as Honegger and his friends had dictated the mid-twenties' tone, not so much in denigrating as in ignoring their elders. Nowadays the life span of new generations has shrunk to about five years, and musicians grow ever more quickly in and out of vogue. Unlike painters, death does not increase their market value. Except for Bartók (who was hardly cool in a debtor's grave before he was taken up internationally), no composer since the war has died with impunity—meaning with glory. Some, of course, like Griffes or Satie, are "discovered" by the intelligentsia a few decades late; others, like Ives or (to an extent) Poulenc, come in for revivals by the amateur. Neither category of listener seems yet inclined to disinter Honegger, although it had been his life's desire—and here maybe was his tragic flaw—to attract both the great mass and the elite through the same pieces.

Of those pieces, the one which most realized his desire, *Joan of Arc at the Stake*, seems now as frozen as a Griffith spectacular, featuring what Virgil Thomson once called "that least musical of instruments, the spoken voice." Yet Thomson cited *Pacific 231* as among the five most significant works of our first half-century. That piece has not, however, remained noticeably in the concert repertory, while performances of a gem like *Pastorale d'Été* are rare as hens' teeth. Certainly Honegger's String Symphony does not go unheard, and his oratorio, *King David*, is practically a staple in our more elegant Episcopal churches. Though all in all his music no longer fills a need for most audiences, particularly the young, and the young constitute the one public a *maître* most longs for.

This ostracism personally touched the gentle musician during his last years when (despite being such a vastly "appreciated" creator) he decided to publish some rather melancholy verbal reactions. These he modeled on Gide's *Corydon*, using as his duologistic foil Monsieur Bernard Gavoty who, under the pseudonym of Clarendon, is still France's most redoubtable old-guard defender. Their conversations now reach us in translation some fifteen years later with a resonance not unlike the music's: personal and poignant, bold and witty, a trifle old-fashioned.

The personal poignance lies in the composer's pessimism. "A few years hence the musical art as we conceive it will no longer exist," states Honegger, who goes on to deplore the performer's precedence over the composer: music now "comes nearer the domain of sport than of art." Not twice but twenty times he reiterates "that we are living in the last stages of our civilization; inevitably, these last moments are painful. They will be more and more so." He would advise young hopefuls against the profession of composer: "It is a mania—a harmless madness," a lifetime of dedication which will reap scant glory and even less money. The talks read like the laments of an unknown failure; indeed, the first five chapters are variations on the title "Complaints." Not until the book's halfway point does a certain humor appear, albeit ironic.

His bold wit stems from this irony. Arthur Honegger was the most withdrawn—the least *mondain*—of that group named *Les Six* who, as we know, were promoted by Cocteau in the twenties as *enfants terribles* of a compound mentality, but who in reality soon went their six separate serious ways. Honegger's way was not like Poulenc's toward the salon and Roman ritual via Diaghilev and Latin liturgy, but toward mass culture and the Protestant ritual via professional pedagogy and vernacular Old Testament sagas. He did once collaborate, and gorgeously, with the stylish Cocteau, though his constant unqualified admiration was for the prose-verse of the much stuffier Claudel. His recollections of these and other working unions are warmly recounted in later chapters, as are snappy judgments of Lady Music Lovers and the dubious necessity of snobbery.

If the book seems a touch old-fashioned it is not so much in his wise bromides about matters professional; composers when they're not composing have always voiced pretty much the same complaints in different words. Rather it is in his assessment of the future, i.e., our present. Sixteen years ago he declared: "I strongly fear that the twelve-tone fad—we already see its decline—may initiate a reaction towards a too simplistic, too rudimentary music. The cure for having swallowed sulfuric acid will be to drink syrup." Certainly he had a blind spot—or was it a pang of jealousy?—about the newest Terrible Children. Still, greater than he have uttered worse, and anything, even a shopping list, is important if scribbled by a genius. Whether Honegger was or not remains to be seen.

1966

THE BEATLES

I never go to classical concerts anymore, and I don't know anyone who does. It's hard still to care whether some virtuoso tonight will perform the *Moonlight* Sonata a bit better or a bit worse than another virtuoso performed it last night.

I do often attend what used to be called avant-garde recitals, though seldom with delight, and inevitably I look around and wonder: What am I doing here? What am I learning? Where are the poets and painters and even composers who used to flock to these things? Well, perhaps what I'm doing here is a duty, keeping an ear on my profession so as to justify the joys of resentment, to steal an idea or two, or just to show charity toward some friend on the program. But I learn less and less. Meanwhile the absent artists are home playing records; they are *reacting* again, finally, to something they no longer find at concerts.

Reacting to what? To the Beatles, of course—the Beatles, whose arrival has proved one of the healthiest events in music since 1950, a fact which no one sensitive can fail to perceive to some degree. By healthy I mean alive and inspired—two adjectives long out of use. By music I include not only the general areas of jazz, but those expressions subsumed in the categories of chamber, opera, symphonic: in short, all music. And by sensitive I understand not the cultivated listening ability of elite Music Lovers so much as instinctive judgment. (There *are* still people who exclaim: "What's a nice musician like you putting us on about the Beatles for?" They are the same who at this late date take theater more seriously than movies and go to symphony concerts because Pop insults their intelligence, unaware that the situation is now precisely reversed.) As to what occurred around 1950, that will be the starting concern of this brief essay, an essay with a primarily musical approach. Most of the literary copy devoted to the Beatles extols the timely daring of the group's lyrics while skirting the essential, the music. Poetry may be the egg from which the nightingale is hatched, though in the last analysis the nightingale must come first.

My "musical approach" will be that of what once was termed the long-hair composer, somewhat disillusioned, nourished at the conservatory yet ex-

NED ROREM

posed all his life (as is any American, of necessity) to jazz. It will not pretend to a total appraisal, only to the fact that I and my colleagues have been happily torn from a long antiseptic nap by the energy of rock, principally as embodied in the Beatles. Naturally I've grown curious about this energy. What are its origins? What need does it fill? Why should the Beatles—who seem to be the best of a good thing, who in fact are far superior to all the other groups who pretend to copy them, most of which are nevertheless American and perpetuating what once was an essentially American thing— why should the Beatles have erupted from *Liverpool?* Could it be true, as Nat Hentoff suggests, that they "turned millions of American adolescents onto what had been here hurting all the time . . . but the young here never did want it raw so they absorbed it through the British filter"? Do the Beatles hurt indeed? And are they really so new? Does their attraction, be it pain or pleasure, stem from their words—or even from what's called their *sound*—or quite plainly from their tunes? Those are the questions, more or less in order, that I'd like to examine.

Around 1940, after a rather undifferentiated puberty, American music came into its own. Composers burgeoned over the land which, then deprived of foreign fertilizer, began producing an identifiably native fruit. By the war's end we had cultivated a crop worthy of export, for every branch of the musical tree was thriving: symphonies of all shapes were being ground out in dozens; opera concepts were transplanting themselves into midwestern towns; and, for consideration here, vocal soloists were everywhere making themselves heard. On one side were Sinatra, Horne, Holiday, stylists of a high order, gorgeously performing material whose musical value (when not derived from the twenties of Gershwin or Porter) was nevertheless middling and whose literary content was dim. On the other side were specialized concert singers—Frijsh, Fairbank and Tangeman—who, though vocally dubious, still created a new brand of sound by persuading certain youngish composers to make singable songs based on texts of quality.

By 1950 the export was well under way. But our effervescence soon flattened when we realized that no one abroad cared much. Jazz, of course, had always been an attraction in the Europe that dismissed American "serious" music as not very serious; Europe, after all, was also reawakening after two numb decades under Hitler's shadow. But that awakening was into the past, namely into the dodecaphonic system which in America had atrophied, and in Germany had been forgotten by the war. This device (no, not a device but a way of thinking, a philosophy) was being revitalized not in the Germany where it had all begun, but in France, of all places! By 1950 Pierre Boulez had single-handedly cleared the path and set the tone that music would follow for the next decade throughout the world. And America took the cue, allowing her new-found individuality to dissolve into what ultimately became the bandwagon of International Academicism.

This turn of events surprised no one more than everyone, namely our most personal and famous composers. The lean melodism conscientiously forged by Aaron Copland, which had become the accepted American Style, was now tossed out by the young. The complicated romantic Teuton soup in which music had wallowed for a century was, in the twenties, reacted against either by the Spartan purification of a Satie or a Thomson (wherefrom Copland's "Americanism") or by the laughing iconoclasm of Dada which—though primarily, like Surrealism, a painters' and poets' medium—was musically exemplified in certain works of *Les Six*. Now in the fifties complex systems were revived, literally with a vengeance by certain of the middle-aged (Elliott Carter, Milton Babbitt, Arthur Berger, etc.) whom fame had bypassed during the Coplandesque forties, and by the young in general. If Dada randomness was reanimated by John Cage, this time with a straight face, Copland himself now chose to become re-engaged in serial formality, also with a straight face, as though intimidated by those deadly serious composers half his age.

These "serious" youngsters, in keeping with the times, were understandably more geared to practical concerns of science than to "superfluous" considerations of Self-Expression. When they wrote for the human voice (which they did less and less) it was treated not as an interpreter of poetry—nor even necessarily of words—but as a mechanism, often electronically revamped. Verse itself was no longer married *to* the music, or even framed *by* the music, but was illustrated *through* the music. And there was little use left for live singers.

Live singers themselves, at least those of formal training, weren't interested anyway. Modern music was too difficult. Besides it had no audience, and neither anymore did the classical song recital so beloved in the already distant years of Teyte and Lehmann. Young singers were lured away from *lieder*, from *la mélodie*, from their own American "art song," until not one specialist remained. They had all been seduced by the big money and hopeful celebrity of grand opera. Even today the few exceptions are European: Schwarzkopf, Souzay, Fischer-Dieskau. Our accurate Bethany Beardslee certainly makes no money, while her excellent West Coast counterpart, Marni Nixon, now does movie dubbing and musical comedy. But most modern song specialists have awful voices and give vanity concerts for invited guests.

Elsewhere was developing the Progressive, or Cool, jazz of Brubeck and Kenton and Mulligan, a rarefied expression that permitted neither song nor dance. The Hit Parade was defunct, Negro stylists out of jobs and vulgar vocalists of college bands in low esteem. Song was out.

Meanwhile the wall separating so-called classical from so-called jazz was crumbling, as each division sought somehow to join with and rejuvenate the other. Yet the need for "communication" so widely lamented today seemed to be satisfied less through music—any music—than through other outlets, particularly movies. Movies, in becoming accepted as a fine art, turned out to be the one medium which could depict most articulately the inarticulateness of today, even to intellectuals. Whereas the intellectualization of music had ironically alienated the intellectual and has not much interest for anyone else. Stravinsky, for example, may be a household word, but in fact little that he composed since 1930, and virtually nothing since 1950, is in the concert repertory anywhere. Stravinsky's recent music is heard exclusively when accompanied by the visuals of Balanchine, when performed biannually by Robert Craft (the presence of the master himself at these performances being the drawing card), or when conducted by the composer on Columbia Records with whom he has an exclusive contract.

I and a handful of songwriting friends (Paul Bowles, Daniel Pinkham, William Flanagan, David Diamond), who began in the forties, I consider as having come in at the end, as having attempted the irrelevant resuscitation of a creature with sleeping sickness. Most of us have written depressingly few songs lately, and those few emerged less from driving need than from ever rarer commissions extended by die-hard specialists. Since there's little money, publication, recording, performance or even concern for songs, our youthful enthusiasm for that most gently urgent of mediums has, alas, pretty much dampened.

But if the once-thriving Art of Song has lain dormant since the war, indications now show it restirring in all corners of the world—which is not the same world that put it to bed. As a result, when Song really becomes wide awake again (the sleep has been nourishing), its composition and interpretation will be of a quite different order and for a quite different public.

Since big-time vocalists like Leontyne Price are, for economic reasons, no longer principally occupied with miniature forms, and since "serious" composers like Stockhausen are, for scientific reasons, no longer principally occupied with human utterances (of which singing is the most primitive and hence the most expressive), and since a master like Stravinsky (who anyway was never famed for his solo vocal works) seems only to be heard when seen, the artful tradition of great song has been transferred from elite domains to the Beatles and their offshoots who represent—as any non-specialized intellectual will tell you—the finest communicable music of our time.

This music was already sprouting a decade ago through such innocent male sex symbols as Presley in America and Johnny Halliday in France, both of whom were then caricatured by the English in a movie called *Expresso Bongo*, a precursor of *Privilege*, about a none-too-bright rock singer. These young soloists (still functioning and making lots of money) were the parents of more sophisticated, more *committed*, soloists like Dylan and Donovan, who in turn spawned a horde of masculine offspring including twins (Simon and Garfunkel, the most cultured), quintuplets (Country Joe & The Fish, the most exotic), sextuplets (The Association, the most nostalgic), even septuplets (Mothers of Invention, the most madly satirical). With much less frequency were born female descendants such as Janis Ian or Bobbie Gentry (each of whom has produced one, and only one, good song—and who may be forgotten or immortal by the time this is read) and the trio of Supremes. Unlike their "grandparents," all these groups, plus some twenty other fairly good ones, write most of their own material, thus combining the traditions of twelfth-century troubadours, sixteenth-century madrigalists and eighteenth-century musical artisans who were always composer-performers—in short, combining all sung expression (except opera) as it was before the twentieth century.

For this expression one must now employ (as I have been doing here) the straightforward word *Song*, as opposed to the misleading *lieder* which applies just to German repertory, or the pretentious *art song* which no longer applies to anything. (The only designation in English that ever really distinguished "serious art song" from what used to be named "pop tune" was "recital song.") Now, since pop tunes as once performed by such as Billie Holiday and the Big Bands during an epoch not merely dormant but dead are heard not only in nightclub and theater but in recital and concert, and since those tunes are as good as—if not better than—anything "serious" being composed today, the best cover-all term is simply *Song*. The only sub-categories are Good and Bad. Curiously, it is not through the suave innovations of our sophisticated composers that music is regaining health, but from the old-fashioned lung exercise of gangs of kids.

That the best of these gangs should have come from England is unimportant; they could have come from Arkansas. The Beatles' world is just another part of the undifferentiated International Academicism wherein the question is to be Better rather than Different. It seems to me that their attraction has little to do with (as Hentoff implied) "what had been here hurting," but on the contrary with enjoyment.

No sooner does Susan Sontag explain that "the new sensibility takes a rather dim view of pleasure" than we discover her "new" sensibility growing stale. Her allusion was to a breed of suspiciously articulate composers—suspicious because they spend more time in glib justification than in composition—and who denigrate the *liking* of music, the *bodily* liking of it. Indeed, one doesn't "like" Boulez, does one? To like is not their consideration; to comprehend is. But surely fun is the very core of the Beatles' musically contagious expression: the Japanese, the Poles (who ignore the poetic subject matter of suicide and bombs) love them as much as their English-speaking fans; and surely that expression, by the very spontaneous timeliness of its nature, is something Sontag must approve of. The Beatles are antidote to the new (read "old") sensibility, and intellectuals are allowed to admit, without disgrace, that they like this music.

The Beatles are good even though everyone knows they're good, i.e., in spite of those claims of the Under Thirties about their filling a new sociological need like Civil Rights and LSD. Our need for them is neither sociological nor new, but artistic and old, specifically a *renewal*, a renewal of pleasure. All other arts in the past decade have to an extent felt this renewal; but music was not only the last of man's "useless" expressions to develop historically, it is also the last to evolve within any given generation—even when, as today, a generation endures a maximum of five years (that brief span wherein "the new sensibility" was caught).

Why are the Beatles superior? It is easy to say that most of their competition (like most everything everywhere) is junk; more important, their betterness is consistent: each of the songs from their last three albums is memorable. The best of these memorable tunes—and the best is a large percentage ("Here, There and Everywhere," "Good Day Sunshine,"

"Michelle," "Norwegian Wood" are already classics)—compare with those by composers from great eras of song: Monteverdi, Schumann, Poulenc.

Good melody—even perfect melody—can be both defined and taught, as indeed can the other three "dimensions" of music: rhythm, harmony, counterpoint (although rhythm is the only one that can exist alone). Melody may be described thus: a series of notes of varying pitch and length, which evolve into a recognizable musical shape. In the case of a melody (tune means the same thing) which is set to words, the musical line will flow in curves relating to the verse that propels it inevitably toward a "high" point, usually called climax, and thence to the moment of culmination. The inevitable element is what makes the melody good—or perfect. But perfection can be sterile, as witness the thousands of thirty-two-bar models turned out yesterday in Tin Pan Alley, or today by, say, Jefferson Airplane. Can we really recall such tunes when divorced from their words?

Superior melody results from the same recipe, with the difference that certain of the ingredients are blessed with the Distortion of Genius. The Beatles' words often go against the music (the crushing poetry that opens "A Day in the Life" intoned to the blandest of tunes), even as Martha Graham's music often contradicts her dance (she gyrates hysterically to utter silence, or stands motionless while all hell breaks loose in the pit). Because the Beatles pervert with naturalness they usually build solid structures, whereas their rivals pervert with affectation, aping the gargoyles but not the cathedral.

The unexpected in itself, of course, is no virtue, though all great works seem to contain it. For instance, to cite as examples only the above four songs: "Here, There and Everywhere" would seem at mid-hearing to be no more than a charming college show ballad, but once concluded it has grown immediately memorable. Why? Because of the minute harmonic shift on the words "wave of her hand," as surprising, yet as satisfyingly right as that in a Monteverdi madrigal like "A un giro sol." The notation of the hyper-exuberant rhythms in "Good Day Sunshine" was as aggravatingly elusive to me as some by Charles Ives, until I realized it was made by triplets over the bar; the "surprise" here was that the Beatles had made so simple a process sound so complex to a professional ear, and yet (by a third convolution) be instantly imitable by any amateur "with a beat." "Michelle" changes key on the very second measure (which is also the second word): in itself this is "allowed"— Poulenc often did it, and certainly he was the most derivative and correct composer who ever lived; the point is that he chose to do it on just the second measure, and that the choice worked. Genius doesn't lie in not being derivative, but in making right choices instead of wrong ones. As for "Norwegian Wood," again it is the arch of the tune—a movement growing increasingly disjunct, an inverted pyramid formed by a zigzag—which proves the song unique and memorable, rather than merely original.

The Beatles' superiority, of course, is finally as elusive as Mozart's to Clementi: they spoke skillfully the same tonal language, but only Mozart spoke it with the added magic of genius. Who will define such magic? The public, in realizing this superiority, is right, though not, as usual, for the wrong reason—as it was, say, ten years ago with Lolita. For while Lolita was accepted pretty much as just a naughty novel, the Beatles can legitimately be absorbed by all ages on all levels: one is allowed to dance or smoke or even have a funeral (playwright Joe Orton's in London) while listening to this music. The same public when discussing the Beatles does not do so by relating them to others, but by relating them to aspects of themselves, as though they were the self-contained definition of an entire movement, or as though in their so-brief career they had (which is true), like Picasso or Stravinsky, already passed through and dispensed with several "periods." For example, no sooner was the *Sergeant Pepper* album released than a quiver of argument was set off as to whether it was inferior to their previous album *Revolver*, or to *Rubber Soul*. The Beatles, so to speak, had sired themselves. But was "Eleanor Rigby" their mother or daughter? was "Michelle" their grandmother or granddaughter? and was the She of "She's Leaving Home" perhaps a sister, since she was the most recently born, or a wife?

And what's this one hears about their sound, those psychedelic effects produced from orchestration "breakthroughs" presumably inspired by Paul McCartney's leanings toward Stockhausen and electronics? Well, as first demonstrated in "Tomorrow Never Knows" and "Strawberry Fields," the sound proves less involved with content than color, more with glamour than construction. McCartney's composition has not been affected by these "innovations" which are instrumental tricks glossily surrounding the composition. Nor is any aspect of that composition itself more "progressive" than the Big Bands of yore, or the Cool groups of yesterday. The harmony at its boldest, as with the insistent dissonances of "I Want to Tell You," is basically Impressionist and never more advanced than the Ravel of *Chansons Madécasses*. The rhythm gets extremely fancy, as in "Good Day Sunshine," but nearly always falls within a ¼ measure simpler than the simplest Bartók of fifty years ago. The melodies, such as "Fixing a Hole" or "Michelle," are exquisitely etched, but evolve from standard modes—those with the lowered thirds and sevenths of the Blues. The counterpoint when strict, as in parts of "She's Leaving Home," is no more complex than "Three Blind Mice," and when free, as in "Got to Get You into My Life," has the freedom of Hindemith— which is really Bach without the problems, meaning without the working out of the solutions presented by the rigors of eighteenth-century part-writing. (The Supremes, not to mention instrumentalists like Ornette Coleman, go much farther out than the Beatles in this domain.) As for the overall form, the songs of *Sergeant Pepper* are mostly less complicated than those of previous albums which, themselves, seldom adventured beyond a basic verse/chorus structure. It is not in innovation that Paul McCartney's originality lies, but in superiority. It remains to be seen how, if ever, he deals with more spacious forms. But of that miniature scene, Song, he is a modern master. As such he is the Beatles' most significant member.

The lyrics, or rather the poems, of John Lennon have been psychoanalyzed beyond recognition. They are indeed clever, touching, appropriately timely and (which is most important) well mated with the tunes. Yet without the tunes, are they really all that much better than the words of, say, Cole Porter or Marc Blitzstein? Certainly Blitzstein's music succeeds in spite of the dated commentary of his words, and Porter's songs remain beautiful with no words at all. We are often told (for instance by Korall in *Saturday Review*) that the Beatles "are shouting about important things," but are these things any more pertinent than "Strange Fruit" yesterday or "Miss Otis Regrets" the day before? Was Peggy Lee's crooning "Where or When" less psychedelic than "Lucy in the Sky"? And even if they are, could that be what makes the Beatles good? While the film *Privilege* portrays a rock singer so subversive he requires total control, the fact is, as Gene Lees puts it, that "thus far no rock group, not even the entire rock movement put together, has made a government nervous, as Gilbert and Sullivan did." Even if, in a pinch, poems can be successfully political, no music can be proved to "signify" anything, neither protest, nor love, nor even bubbling fountains, nothing. John Lennon's words do indeed not only expose current problems ("A Day in the Life") but suggest solutions ("Fixing a Hole"); and the music—which is presumably set to the verse, not vice versa—works fine. But that music is stronger; and, like the slow and meterless Gregorian Chant which altered the "meaning" of the rapid and ribald street chanties it stemmed from, Lennon's words do or don't matter according to how they're sung.

With Billie Holiday it was not so much the song as her way with the song; like Piaf she could make mediocrity seem masterful. With the Beatles it's the song itself, not necessarily their way—like Schubert whom even a monster can't destroy. "Michelle," for example, remains as lovely but becomes more clearly projected when performed by a "real" singer like Cathy Berberian. Her diction (and the diction of nearly anyone) is better than theirs, at least to non-Cockney ears. Even if the words did not come second, the Beatles oblige you to judge the music first, by virtue of their blurred enunciation.

As for George Harrison's excursions into India, they seem the least persuasive aspect of the more recent Beatle language. Like McCartney with electronics, Harrison seems to have adopted only the frosting; but in pretending to have adopted also the structure, his two big pieces, "Love You To" and "Within You Without You," end up not hypnotic, merely sprawling. Harrison's orientalism is undoubtedly sincere but sounds as fake as the pentatonicism of Country Joe & The Fish. Debussy, like all his cohorts, was profoundly influenced by the Balinese exhibits at the Paris World's Fair of 1900, which inspired his *Pagodes* and *Lindaraja*. These pieces were as persuasive in the same genre as were the concert works many decades later by Henry Cowell or Harry Partch or even Peggy Glanville-Hicks. But whereas these sophisticated musicians without concern for "authenticity" translated Eastern sound effects into Western jargons and then spoke those jargons with controlled formality, Harrison still flounders for faithful meaning where it just won't work: good will and "inspiration" will never provide him with the background—the birthright—which of necessity produced the music he would emulate.

Ringo Starr's projects, when not involved with his comrades, are unknown, though he does seem to be learning to sing with what is quite literally an unutterable charm. Nor have I seen John Lennon's war movie. Thus far, however, when the Beatles are a conjointly creative process (even more than as a performing unit) they are at their most enticing.

Just as today my own composition springs more from pristine necessity than driving inspiration (I compose what I want to hear because no one else is doing it), so I listen—sifting and waiting—only to what I need. What I need now seems less embodied in newness than in nostalgia: how many thrilling experiences do we get per year anyway, after a certain age? Such nostalgia appears most clearly engendered by the Beatles. There isn't much more to say, since structurally they're not interesting to analyze: they've added nothing new, simply brought back excitement. The excitement originates (other than, of course, from their talent) in their absolutely insolent—hence innocent—unification of music's disparate components—that is, in using the most conservative devices of harmony, counterpoint, rhythm, melody, orchestration, and making them blend with an infectious freshness. (Parenthetically, their latest, "I Am the Walrus," seems a bit worrisome, more contrived, less "inspired" than anything hitherto. Though the texture may be Vaughan Williams with a Bebop superimposition and all very pretty, the final effect becomes parody of self-parody, the artist's realest danger. Though probably even the holy Beatles must be permitted an occasional stillborn child.)

The Beatles have, so to speak, brought *fiction* back to music, supplanting criticism. No, they aren't new, but as tuneful as the thirties with the same exuberance of futility that Bessie Smith employed. They have removed sterile martyrdom from art, revived the sensual. Their sweetness lies in that they doubtless couldn't care less about these pedantic explications.

If (and here's a big If) music at its most healthy is the creative reaction of, and stimulation for, the body, and at its most decadent is the creative reaction of and stimulation for the intellect—if, indeed, health is a desirable feature of art, and if, as I believe, the Beatles exemplify this feature, then we have reached (strange though it may seem as coincidence with our planet's final years) a new and golden renaissance of song.

1967

THE AVANT-GARDE AS DÉMODÉ

> Artists and intellectuals must deal with politics
> only insofar as it is necessary to put up a defense
> against politics.
>
> —CHEKHOV

Tantrums of the avant-garde no longer need the mass publicity they've
earned. The point has been proved, their rights have been granted, their
revolution is won—like it or not. Many of them do not like it: their work's
over, so their work must begin. Finally free, they still seem caged by bromides, for freedom and art are not synonymous.

The consumer-oppressor has paid the rebels' ransom, receiving little in
return beyond amateur admonitions that we are all artists. He finds himself
literally with his pants down. How, with current discouragement of analysis,
must he take this? By merely reacting, never questioning? If everyone's an
artist then no one's an artist.

I often betray but never defend my music: it must defend itself. Nor is my
responsibility to be knowledgeable or even interested in Where It's At. Artists are allowed intolerance of each other along with the world, as demonstrated both by me and by the young. My intolerance grows compassionate
at seeing youth's pat dismissal of the past: destruction of the traditional is
traditional. But my intolerance grows disdainful of contemporaries like
Lukas Foss or Julian Beck: iconoclasm is unbecoming to the middle-aged.
How can they keep up with every trend and still work with coherence?

"What do you think of modern painting?" Gertrude Stein's famous reply,
"I like to look at it," did not answer the question. She offered reaction rather
than opinion. With her as ally I reply, regarding certain modern music: I hate
to hear it.

What modern music? If once the world was balanced between church and state, today sacred and profane are one, as are classical and pop. In most of it the time-honored balance between reflection and antidote is uneven: art as society's mirror shimmers like Narcissus's pool wherein the Music Establishment is drowning without crying help.

That Establishment, so far as "serious" music is concerned, is maintained in our larger universities through foundation funds granted largely by academic colleagues. Musical art and academic concerns are, if not antithetical, no more synonymous than music and freedom, as may be seen in the advancing number of young and not-so-young composers whose need to vent genuine concerns is not counterbalanced by talent. Intellectual conviction is confused with expression, sound with sense. Commitment does not make music, yet the *fact* of commitment is persuasive enough to cause both paid reviewer and small paying public hesitation before disdaining the ever more predictably disorganized insults flung their way.

Most of these words apply to pop as well, except that pop's public is large. If in university music, emotion has been replaced with protest, students are not protesting these protests. Not that students find such protests irrelevant, they just don't find them—or rather, don't hear them over the thunderous sound of their rock.

To criticize a genre is specious, of course; one must determine only how well a work succeeds within a given genre, on its own terms. But inasmuch as any of this music aims at extramusical goals, it grows useless.

Still, as Wilde said, art is useless anyway. You can't eat it. You can't eat politics either. Some music *does* seem to be self-generating as well as beautiful. If kids today don't care about Art with a big A so much as events, it's another way of saying their art is nourishing. Works of art thus paradoxically become ornamental necessities or, like certain women, necessary luxuries.

That sentiment smacks of aristocracy. Risking the guillotine, I hold to it. Art has never been just anyone's property while retaining its property as art. The past four years have spawned ever fewer genuine works in any form; this, I feel, is due to the direct alliance of art with the New Left. If the state of body and soul appears better for it, the state of music as a lasting social contribution is worse.

Art and politics in America have never until recently been closely related. Not that artists lived in ivory towers, but their involvement was extracurricular. Even during the ironically stimulating Depression, the WPA made only nominal friends of politics and art. Nor did the war engender political American arts, perhaps because it did not physically concern us much. Nevertheless, by cutting us off from the cultural dugs of Europe it did wean us into an autonomous adolescence with new imagination added to old brute force. The imagination cultivated fantasy and reflection, dealing with crisis as nostalgia rather than as immediacy. But the youthful breed of novelist, composer and playwright spilled forth oceans of now classic masterworks.

The period thrived less than a decade. The young grew up. Their elders labeled them the Apathetic Generation, though in fact the Beatniks were driven with an urgency for natural emancipation. Their decade of the 1950s saw music's decline as a fine art, despite the rise of such distinguished craftsmen as Boulez. Nobody but his colleagues cared much. How could people *enjoy* Boulez's complexities when John Cage's fun was guaranteed culture, as was the simplistic sumptuousness of Elvis Presley who began to be sanctioned by the intelligentsia? The intelligentsia spokesmen had now replaced fiction with criticism. As escape from such critical reading one listened to the rhapsodic chants of Allen Ginsberg against backgrounds of a soon-to-be-outmoded form: jazz.

The Kennedys brought the initial conjoining of art with the political scene. However, government acceptance of artists—mostly famous performers—was less official (read financial) than social, as exemplified by invitations from Jacqueline Kennedy. Elsewhere emerged the Hippies, gentle offspring of the Beatniks—themselves heirs of Bohemia—whose art work, like their play (indeed, the two were one), was communal, thus political. This art was manifest in general by "new" mixed media and in particular by rock groups. Some inaudible signal, some psychedelic flare, caused the five invisible jars that once contained our separate senses to overflow into each other with orderly confusion. Yet the artful mixing of media for purposes of collective ecstasy predates the Catholic Mass. The originality of the best rock lay not in its presumed experimentation—what was called its *sound*—but precisely in its spontaneous reversion to simplicity as antidote to the "modern" music of concert halls which people were still afraid to admit they hated. Like most great art, the best rock was amalgamated, and quite unoriginal in style.

Rock's first function was to inspire again the visceral response of song and dance after the apathetic decade of head-in-hands listening to cool jazz or serial cerebrality. Its later function, with Lyndon Johnson's advent, was to speak out, tell it like it is. In this guise it became *the* art of our time, addressing itself to, and being accepted by, every social layer including classical composers trying to keep up. But gone now is the spontaneity. Arrived is a crass self-promotion so successful that it is bought and displayed as soberly by *Time* magazine as by the *East Village Other*.

Like the beaten-to-death Living Theatre, mixed mediators compare their arbitrary results with the calculated formality proceeding from professional creativity. In true revolutionary spirit, they seek to supplant the latter with the former, coexistence being alien to the anarchistic modes which amateurs invariably adopt when moving in. Certain delusions were essential for the elevation of mixed-media happenings to pretentious levels, one being the notion that group therapy can be Art. Another delusion, that mixed media was Revolutionary, therefore new, can be attributed to ignorance. But the grand delusion was that mixed media would, by sheer magnetic charm, destroy the performer-audience format forever.

The first delusion stems from the premise that any self-expression can be Art. This is definition by no definition: it can as easily be shown that no self-expression is art. Such a non-relative approach renders sensible discussion extinct. The second delusion forgets Barnum & Bailey, Dada, Scriabin, soundtracks (to keep merely within the last fourscore years). The third delusion ignores the diversity of human nature; some people still thrive on Vivaldi. Mixed media has merely acquired status.

Anxiety-stricken concert managers quickly point out that mixed-media groups sell and song recitals don't; they feel that the reason the public buys one is that it doesn't buy the other (a holdover from the one-car-family days when you bought one or the other, never both). The fact is, both managers and recording executives have been coasting on the tried and true for decades and have now reached the bottom of the hill. Who blames passengers for getting off? Since easy money has neither imagination nor responsibility, sooner or later a dead end is reached. But not before a try at cashing in on the *à la mode*.

Major recording labels, which can afford to take chances but say they can't, now promote contemporary music—though only of the far-out (read In) variety—advertising Boulez with the same crass hard-sell that Braniff Airlines uses for Andy Warhol. Such music is thus stamped with the Establishment seal, so the difficult becomes safe. Small companies like Desto, that cannot afford to take chances but do so anyway, are the only ones to record music of the so-called conservative (read tuneful) variety. Such music is thus necessarily adventurous, so simplicity becomes dangerous. If simplicity in "serious" music is eschewed by the avant-garde establishment, it is nonetheless the key to the best of our "avant-garde" rock, which is all that seems to matter anymore. But the best is ever rarer.

Like the jaded lover, the jaded music-fancier is one who too often has been forced to react in mediocre situations. At least once a day some friend exclaims, "Now hear *this*," as he puts on the first (and often last) platter by the "Swinging Doors" or the "Conniption Fit." Memory is a curse when revealing this week's totally different beat, sound or volume distortion as merely the same old beat, sound or volume distortion we begged the cab driver to turn off last week. The listener is jaded because his ears are literally, *medically*, in trouble.

My first article on the Beatles resulted from an appreciation for their quality. Quality was their originality, and as always quality transcended genre. Since the appearance of that article certain editors imagine me a Pop authority. But that scene interested me only during the brief moment when it contained *the pleasure of quality*. Until such a moment comes again I'll bide my time, as during the arid era between Billie Holiday and the Beatles.

It is no accident that the emergence of professional criticism as the preeminent literary form coincided with the rise of amateurism in the other arts. As current criticism feeds on the work of others even by denying that work, so current amateurism feeds off the past even by denying the past—a denial which becomes an end in itself. The cause of this dual rise (descent, really) is, of course, the worsening world situation. This situation has advanced scientific investigation, for better or worse, and the concomitant displacement of artists by scientists who are now possibly our best "creative" minds. Art is both mirror and antidote: it reflects the surroundings, then renders them bearable. A resolution to the sad Vietnam adventure may herald a renaissance as fructuous as the one after World War II. But we will no longer be adolescents.

1968

AROUND SATIE'S *SOCRATE*

". . . a freakish French musician, more inventor
than creator, Erik Satie . . ."
> —PAUL LANDORMY,
> *A History of Music*

"God will not be fooled; He hates literature. He
loved the blue eyes of Satie."
> —JACQUES MARITAIN

What used to be termed "modern" becomes, as we know, digestible to
laymen when superimposed on other mediums. Audiences swallow without
flinching music conjoined to film or ballet, music which in concert would
send them off screaming. Yet the famous riots all seem to have dealt with
visual or vocal music like *Salome* or *Pierrot Lunaire*. Are there non-program-
matic pieces that have impelled real scandals, other than scandals of boredom? Is it mischievous to suggest that the notorious rumpus at the première
of *Le Sacre du Printemps* was provoked less by Stravinsky's score than by
Nijinsky's terrible choreography?

Advocates of rock and of black folk music, both basically kinetic expressions, discuss the presumed complexity of their art as though complexity
were a virtue. Not only is complexity not a virtue (nor a vice), it is not an
element of rock or of black folk music. Simplicity is the necessary ingredient,
thus the true "virtue," of any music that moves us to song and dance.
Complexity deactivates the body—make us *débander*, as the French say—
because it stimulates the brain. Counterpoint, by nature abstract and by
extension "spiritual," is more complex, at its simplest, than the verbally
carnal and squarely rhythmic folk-rock. We don't naturally dance to abstraction. Rhythm, by nature less abstract, *can* lean in that direction: we don't
dance convincingly, or at least impulsively, to complicated (read irregular)
rhythms. No one has successfully choreographed *Le Sacre*.

Le Sacre has not worked as a ballet because hitherto its choreographers have
taken it at face value. (My most recent encounter: those Mickey-Mousing

351

bumps-and-grinds of Béjart's Chosen Virgin.) Any choreography which "explains" music on the music's terms is asking for pulverization. Dance must go against. Try this solution: cocktail-party intrigue with *Le Sacre* as background.

Or choreograph three stories—of ritual murder, of the building of the Boulder Dam, of life with Hell's Angels—and use Erik Satie's *Sarabandes*.

A triumph in style, among other things, Stravinsky's *Sacre* still sounds as fresh as the day it was born. This is the way with masterpieces. Yet it's unlikely, though unprovable, that anyone including the composer still hears it as it was heard then.

Now, a masterpiece like Satie's *Socrate*, is, in a sense, without style—without immediate location in time. Thus we probably do hear (and misunderstand) it the same way as on its birthday.

The rule, at least in our century, is that most new pieces sound dated sooner or later. Honegger, for example, or much of Copland. The rare ironic twist is in the piece which when first played sounded old-fashioned, but which now seems original. In America, Moore's *Baby Doe*, Barber's *Knoxville*, Bernstein's *Jeremiah*. In France, much of Poulenc. Though while the intent of the Moore-Barber-Bernstein work remains intact, we now read new motivations into Poulenc: as with Satie, we no longer admit his frivolity to be frivolity.

But we must earn the right to denigrate a master. We must earn the right to denigrate Satie who was not, properly speaking, a master. We must earn the right to declare him overrated, in the face of those who declare him underrated in the face of those who never rated him at all.

Since childhood I've known him. His *Gnosiennes*, *Nocturnes* and *Gymnopédies* joyfully saturated my adolescent keyboard practice long before Chopin displaced them. His *Socrate* is the one piece I've played every day for a decade without getting bored, the pleasure of expectation remaining always new. Then am I granted a right to state that, despite the Cage-Thomson-Milhaud sanction and syndrome (the "in" notion that Satie's undervalued), Satie may indeed be overestimated? (History forbids our pronouncing Beethoven a bore, Casals a Maharishi.) When folks easily declare that nine-tenths of the piano pieces or even *Parade* are silly, inept, unsatisfactory to the ear, we ask: Do you know *Socrate*? No, they answer. Now, *Socrate* is one of our century's five masterworks. Knowing, feeling this way, we may agree that *Parade* and nine-tenths of the piano pieces are unsatisfactory to the ear, inept, silly.

Satie never scared anybody. But certainly he did attract and influence his more celebrated peers because of his vitriolic anti-Wagner stance. Indeed, one thinks of Satie as older than Debussy, so great was his hold on the latter who first met him when Satie was earning a living as a café pianist. Actually Satie was born in 1866, four years after Debussy, though nine years before Ravel, both of whom had solid conservatory training and ultimately a fame far wider than their friend's. At age forty, when someone told Satie his music lacked form, he did apply for study with d'Indy, after which he composed his famous *Pièces en forme d'une Poire*. There began his series of cute titles, mostly defensive, one must conclude, since the music itself was seldom more cute than the Rosicrucian ritual which had previously influenced it. Knowledge, training do not of themselves make a better, fuller artist. The artist always finds before he seeks. Like Schubert, Satie knew as much as he needed to know to extract from himself what there was to extract and then write it down. His go at the Conservatoire in no way advanced him beyond his poignant titles. . . . Like everyone else, he became associated with Diagheliv during the teens of our century, collaborating with Picasso on two ballets, *Mercure* and *Parade*, the latter with a scenario by the young Jean Cocteau. He and Cocteau were eventually to become the father and mother of that twenties group who, for a while, called themselves *Les Six:* Germaine Tailleferre, Louis Durey, Francis Poulenc, Arthur Honegger, Darius Milhaud, Georges Auric. Toward the end of his life another group of his disciples (including Roger Désormière and Henri Sauguet) became known as the Arcueil School. Socially Satie was a wag, domestically a recluse.

His philosophy, in relating the conventionally unrelated (equating wit with sorrow as a qualitative expression, for instance) was not far from today's pop culture which makes the ordinary extraordinary by removing it from context. Elsewhere, conversely, like the surrealists, he treated his eccentric subject matter straightforwardly. Between the lines and among the notes of his compositions he often inserted little jokes, whimsical advice to the performer or "impossible" directions not unlike those Charles Ives was employing at the same time in America. No one would think of taking him literally. (When John Cage rented the old Living Theatre for a presentation of Satie's *Vexations*—a short piano work concluding with the words: repeat 472 times—hiring a relay of pianists to play the piece consecutively for sixteen hours, he produced a Cageian, not a Satie-esque, experience.)

Erik Satie's greatest work by far is *Socrate*, commissioned in 1919 by the Princesse Edmonde de Polignac, and composed originally for small orchestra with several human voices (which, however, never sing in ensemble). An equally, perhaps more, persuasive version is for solo voice and piano.

Socrate takes just over half an hour: fairly long as pieces go; as a program in itself, fairly short. Yet it is a totality, standing best alone. Nothing seems to "go" with it, least of all other works by Satie since, in a way, they are all contained within *Socrate*.

The texts chosen by Satie for his music were, of all things, from Plato's *Dialogues*, highly truncated and in French translation by one Victor Cousin of the Sorbonne. These the composer set to music without romantic affectation, even without vocal embellishment, but almost as they would be spoken. He set them, literally so to speak, with respect. Respect—that is, humility—is not a quality one especially associates with genius. Yet humility is precisely the genius of *Socrate:* the words of Plato are not illustrated, not interpreted, by the music: they are encased by the music, and the case is not a period piece; rather, it is from all periods. Which is what makes the music so difficult to identify. Is it from modern France? ancient Greece? or from the time of Pope Gregory?

I've said *Socrate* is one of the few pieces to which for two decades I've repeatedly returned without disappointment, the pleasures of anticipation remaining always fresh. But as this anticipation is not contained in highs and lows, for newcomers the music can feel static. In the academic sense *Socrate* has no development beyond the normal evolution imposed by the text. Hence the music moving forward seldom relates to itself thematically, though its texture remains almost constantly undifferentiated. The dynamic level never rises above mezzo-forte, with little contrast and virtually no climax until the final page when we hear forty-four inexorable knellings of an open fifth which denote the agony of Socrates who, in the last two bars, expires with a sigh. The harmony, mostly triadic, is rarely dissonant, and never dissonant in an out-of-key sense except in a single "pictorial" section, again from the end movement, when the jailer presses Socrates' legs which have grown heavy and cold from the hemlock: here the words are colored with repetitions of a numbingly foreign C sharp.

Wherein lies the genius, the ever-renewed thrill of expectation? It lies in the composer's absolutely original way with the tried and true. The music is not "ahead" of its time, but rather (and of what other work can this be said?) outside of time, allowing the old, old dialogues of Plato to sound so always new.

1968

PAUL BOWLES

In 1949, with the publication of his very successful *Sheltering Sky* at the age of forty, Paul Bowles became the author-who-also-writes-music, after having long been the composer-who-also-writes-words. That success brought more than a re-emphasis of reputation; from the musical community's standpoint it signaled the permanent divorce of a pair of careers. During the next two decades Paul Bowles produced fourteen books of various kinds, but little more than an hour's worth of music. Did he feel that one art, to survive, needed to swallow and forget the other? Surely he received in a year more acclaim for his novel than he had received in a lifetime for his music. This need not imply a superior literary talent; indeed, if history recalls him, it will be for musical gifts. It's just that ten times more people read books than go to concerts. Someday Bowles may fully release the underestimated musician who doubtless still sings within him. Meanwhile, perhaps chagrined by the underestimation, he coolly enjoys an international fame based solely on his books.

Composer-authors generally compartmentalize their two vocations, allotting parts of each year, if not each day, to each profession. But as authors their subject is inevitably music (as witness Berlioz, Schumann, Debussy, or today, Boulez, Thomson, Sessions), whereas Paul Bowles is a fiction-writing composer, the only significant one since Richard Wagner, and even Wagner's fiction was at the service of his operas. Except during the war years when he functioned as music critic for the *New York Herald Tribune*, Bowles's prose has been antithetical to his music. Whatever resemblance exists between the working procedures for each craft, the difference between his results is like day and night.

Paul Bowles's music is nostalgic and witty, evoking the times and places of its conception—France, America and Morocco during the twenties, thirties and forties—through langourous triple meters, hot jazz and Arabic sonorities. Like most nostalgic and witty music that works, Bowles's is all in short forms, vocal settings or instrumental suites. Even his two operas on Lorca texts are really garlands of songs tied together by spoken words. In 1936 Orson Welles's production of *Horse Eats Hat* became the first of some two dozen plays for which he provided the most distinguished incidental scores of the period. The theater accounts for a huge percentage of his musical output, and for the milieu he frequented for a quarter of a century, most latterly the milieu of Tennessee Williams whose works would never have had quite the same tonality—the same fragrance—without Bowles's music emerging from them so pleasingly. Indeed, the intent of his music in all forms is to please, and to please through light colors and gentle textures and amusing rhythms, novel for their time, and quite lean, like their author.

Paul Bowles's fiction is dark and cruel, clearly meant to horrify in an impersonal sort of way. It often bizarrely details the humiliation and down-fall of quite ordinary people, as though their very banality was deserving of punishment. Bowles develops such themes at length and with a far surer hand than in, say, his sonata structures. His formats in even the shorter stories are on a grander plan than in his music; at their weakest they per-suasively elaborate their plots (albeit around ciphers, and in a style some-times willfully cheap); at their best they transport the reader through brand-new dimensions to nightmare geographies. Bowles communicates the incommunicable. But even at their most humane his tales steer clear of the "human," the romantic, while his music can be downright sentimental. In-deed, so dissimilar are his two talents that it is hard to imagine him com-posing backgrounds to his own dramas.

Paul Bowles's real life is courageous and exotic. Whenever possible he has spent it in what we like to call backward countries with hot climates, es-pecially Ceylon and North Africa. Yet no matter how far afield he has wandered into the crowds of India or the deserted Sahara, he has maintained active correspondence with the West, specifically with American intellec-tuals who, since he seldom goes to them, cross oceans to meet him. Bowles, the social animal, has traveled Everywhere, known Everyone, and been much loved. His writings have dealt extensively with the Everywhere, but never until recently with the Everyone. Now here is his autobiography.

Without Stopping is curiously static but never tranquil, like Lewis Carroll's Red Queen. If in reality the author withdraws for long years of disciplined reflection in faraway lands, the effect from his book is of constant and vaguely futile comings and goings. *Without Stopping* is also curiously reticent, at least for a volume of memoirs. Obviously uncomfortable with the pronoun *I,* the autobiographer is revealed as far less rich and strange than the actual man. Here he denigrates his subject's "specialness." Scores of names are dropped with no further identification than their spelling, while close ac-quaintances vanish and die without so much as an editorial sigh from their friend. He displays no envy of competitors, no sign of carnal or intellectual passion. His one obsession would seem to be for investigation—not of the heart, which even his fiction avoids, but of the body as affected by foreign cultures, by the implacability of nature, exotic cuisine, ill health, hard drugs, but never, never by sex. If his novelist's reputation qualifies this printing of his journal, his novelist's morosely powerful voice remains mute. Occasion-ally we find a discussion, always objective, of literary method, but never of musical method. And his reticence rather grandly forbids display of the self-doubt which is an artist's *sine qua non.* Yet since Bowles is an artist, he is allowed his own rules. More than once he mentions his revulsion at the artist's visibility, be it through old-fashioned bohemianism or modern pub-licity. (On first meeting Stephen Spender in 1931: "I noted with disapproval the Byronesque manner in which he wore his shirt, open down to his chest. It struck me as unheard of that he should want to announce his status as a poet rather than dissimulate it; to my way of thinking he sacrificed his anonymity.") Why, then, write a book of this sort?

Could anyone not knowing Paul Bowles have the least interest in such a report? Maybe. Once we accept our disappointment at the low gossip con-tent and learn that the work is a cold fulfillment of a commission more than an inspiration, we can enjoy the elliptical levels of the writing. With the assurance of an aristocrat the author presupposes our acquaintance with his friends, with the books he likes, and with his own books and music and multilingual abilities. He assumes our knowledge of Jane Bowles's extraordi-nary creation, and, as with the subject of marital affection, deems it more tantalizing, and thus more skillful, not to spell things out. As for the heart, others have bled it to death, so why should Paul Bowles? when the descrip-tion of a jackal's wail or a Jalila trance or a Ceylonese temple filled with bats can be more terribly thrilling.

Still, the final crabbed product comes to less than the sum of its parts. The best of what is written here has been better written elsewhere by another Paul Bowles: the verbal landscapes. If he is not a human portraitist, he has, like some filmmakers, created character from scenery. Deserts, jungles, city streets are personages in his books as in his life, and he causes them to breathe and suffer and threaten us as only a god can do. But when discussing real people the effect is desperate, touching, even sad, sometimes humorous, though only secondarily the effect he intended, that is, a pose of non-involve-ment. That effect, which fills the novels, no longer seems viable for our troubled world—perhaps precisely because the world has turned into a Paul Bowles novel.

The best of Paul Bowles's early music contained a high-class appeal uniquely his own. Appeal has come to be considered a negligible ingredient in music. It would be interesting to see if Bowles could revive it, or if not, what dialect he might sing should he choose to sing again. The general public has forgotten his music, forgotten even that he was—is—a composer (our shyest composers must hustle ever more crassly to keep themselves known). Paul Bowles however has a built-in literary public who would receive warmly whatever he does. Let him finally reconcile his talents. For his music has had a long nap and might wake up refreshed, whereas his prose in this book seems momentarily exhausted.

April 1972

REMEMBERING A POET

Paul Goodman in his fiftieth year closed his journal thus: "I am not happy, yet as of today I would willingly live till 80. I have already lived longer than many another rebellious soul."

Growing Up Absurd had finally brought him major prominence, although he had been preaching (and practicing) its contents all his life. If he was not happy, nobody wise, with imagination and open eyes, can ever stay happy for long. But he was vital and fertile; more important for an artist, he was appreciated, even ultimately "understood," when last week at sixty he died, twenty years short of his goal.

It is 1938 in Chicago. Édouard Roditi and Paul Goodman stop by impromptu to see me (I am fourteen). From the back room I hear Mother say: "Sit down, young men, Ned will be right out." To prepare an entrance I wash my hair. By the time I emerge they have left.

Paul used to recount this episode as his most Proustian souvenir. I recount it as the first of a hundred occasions where narcissism made me miss out.

Yet I seldom missed out on Paul during the next years. To say that he became my most pertinent influence, social and poetic, would be to echo many a voice in the young groups who felt themselves to be as important to Paul as he was to them—the inevitable covetousness that comes when great men involve their entourage not only through their work but through their person. But that was long ago.

(At the end, in the melancholy of fame, Paul Goodman was admired by thousands who, paradoxically, did not know his name. His original notions, having become general knowledge, decayed into slogans which the liberated youth spouted back at him—to set him straight.)

My first songs date from then, all of them settings of Paul Goodman's verse. I may have written other kinds of song since, but none better. That I have never in the following decades wearied of putting his words to music is the highest praise I can show him; since I put faith in my own work, I had first to put faith in Paul's. Through Paul I wrote not only songs to celebrate Sally's smile, or Susan at play or prayers for the birth of Matthew Ready (now gone too), but an opera *Cain and Abel*, a ballet (with Alfonso Ossorio), choral pieces, backgrounds for the Becks' theater, and nightclub skits. He was my Goethe, my Blake and my Apollinaire.

No one will deny him as a serious thinker: the coming weeks will bring homages emphasizing his contribution as sociologist, city planner, psychotherapist, linguistic theoretician, political and educational reformer. All will mention *Growing Up Absurd;* some will talk about his diary, *Five Years*, which juxtaposes tracts on creative method with bodily encounters; a few will applaud his novels (is that what they are?), *The Grand Piano, The State of Nature, The Holy Terrors* and *The Dead of Spring*, a tetralogy on an iconoclast's passage through the Empire City. But if he was that rare thing among radicals today, an educated poet, who will yet bring up the poetry? A disconcerting number of fans, even among his friends, did not realize he wrote poems.

That was partly his fault. Hardly modest, Paul nevertheless did not stress the sheer variety of his talents. Like Jean Cocteau (the strongest of his early influences) who classified his own output—fiction, movies, plays, ballets, drawings, paintings, criticism and pure life—under the one heading *Poésie*, so Paul Goodman called himself a humanist. "Everything I do has the same subject," he would say, a quite European non-specialist attitude for one so American—or rather, so New Yorkish.

Yet his poetry is not the same as his other works. It rises higher, and will be viewed as individual long after his thrilling but didactic ideas, pragmatic and doctrinaire, have been absorbed, as they will be, into our anonymous common culture.

Let me stress his frivolity, a quality contained in all artists, since all art is made from the contrasts formed by an ability to express relationships between the superb and the silly. Paul's was not the simplistic sexual frivolity of a Mick Jagger, nor the thunderous German-joke frivolity of a Beethoven, but the high-camp spiritually practical yet sad frivolity of, say, Haydn, Voltaire, Gogol, Auden, Billie Holiday.

Did you know he actually wrote music too? Not very inspired, sort of Brahmsian and technically childlike. Like fellow composer Ezra Pound, he confused homemade discovery with professionalism, though any well-trained nonentity could have done better. Still, his writing *about* music, critically and philosophically, was less dumb than any layman's since Thomas Mann.

With all his heterogeneity he never became (though for a time it threatened) a pop figure with catch phrases, like McLuhan or Buckminster Fuller. He was too compact for love at first sight.

He was aloof and cool—traits not unusual in philanthropists, beginning with Freud. He never ceased to intimidate me because he was, and remains, The One whose stamp of approval I seek; childhood idols can never have clay feet. When the demands of glory grew, his warmth was directed more to-

ward groups than toward individuals. I received his new poems then only
through the mail. We had grown so apart that, on phoning ten weeks ago to
ask about his health, I half hoped he wouldn't answer. But he did.

"Should we be worried, Paul?"

"Yes, we should." Yet gently he added: "Nice to hear your voice, kiddo." I
sent love to Sally, and we promised ourselves an autumn reunion.

If Paul can die then anyone can die, even God, and whom can we fall back
on now? In 1939 he concluded an epitaph for Freud:

> . . . suddenly dead for all our hopes and fears
> is our guide across the sky and deep,
> this morning a surprise for bitter tears,
> a friendly dream now I am asleep.

Paul Goodman was a household poet, a poet who did not rework verse into
Eliotian cobwebs of intricacy, but composed on the run, for immediate
occasions, in the manner Frank O'Hara would make popular. Two examples:

In 1947 John Myers was madly trying to turn Mary's Bar on Eighth Street
into another Boeuf sur le Toit. For the opening Paul and I concocted three
Blues which John and Frank Etherton intoned in the styles of Mistinguett
and Stella Brooks. Heartbreaking. But hardly the speed of that clientele. At
2 A.M. Eugene Istomin took over the keyboard of an upright casserole and
amid the fumes of laughter and beer performed *Gaspard de la Nuit*. Incredibly,
that *was* the speed of the clientele. Next day Paul made a first-class translation of the second-class prose-poems, by one Aloysius Bertrand, which had
first inspired Ravel's piano cycle, and for years Istomin reprinted these translations in the program of his international tours. (And those blues today? In
the back of a trunk. But maybe the words and music would be the speed of
our new clientele!)

Janet Fairbank was a youngish soprano who during the war years gave
concerts of new American music, a specialty no less rare then than now. She
was our sole voice, our outlet. We all collaborated on many a song that Janet
sang; indeed, it was she who premièred my setting of Paul's soaring words
that still so grandly extol his beloved Manhattan, *The Lordly Hudson*. The
evening she died, twenty-five years ago this month, Paul appeared on my
doorstep with a poem. "Here," he said, "make some music out of this."
Three short stanzas describe how Janet sang our songs because she loved to
sing, how we loved to make up songs for her to sing, how she is now mute
and we are dumb. Too soon the final lines evoke Paul Goodman himself,
with their question from the impotent survivor confronted with a dying
fellow artist.

> . . . If we
> make up a quiet song of death,
> who now shall sing this song we made
> for Janet Janet not, because
> (no other cause) she loved to sing?

August 1972

REMEMBERING GREEN

At Rizzoli's while searching for quite another book my hand fell upon Julien Green's latest *Journal* (1966–72) which I bought on the spot. Spent the whole afternoon reading it. Or *re*-reading. The emphases, identical to those of past volumes, could have been composed in 1926. Yet such preoccupations are close to my own, or any working man's, not in color but in stress and distribution. By mid-adolescence we know what we are, then spend our remaining years resigning ourselves to that knowledge. Yes, we may come to learn new things, but we will observe them through our unchanging lens. Short of conversion we stay forever the same. Even conversion is horoscopically preordained. Our truths are not discovered, they are realized: they come from within, from our knowledge.

Thus I am the same person as he who two decades ago first came upon Green's journals, meeting old friends again in turns of phrase, in paragraphs rich with familiar nightmare. Those perpetual obsessions with sin and the true way, with prayer and dream, with shop talk (Jesus talk) among clerical friends! If in this *Journal* Julien Green continues, through his specific belief in God, to miss more general points at every corner, in his fiction this very "miss" provides the Julienesque tonality, the singular Greenery. Surely if one-track-mindedness empties the spirit of humor, it does fill the mind with an explosive physicality which remains the *sine qua non* of virtually all large souls. (Humor is not physical but intellectual, and multiple-track-minded.)

Green's is a stance which no resident American, even a learned Italo-American Catholic, can comprehend; there is no room for comprehension, only for blind belief ripened for this convert who feels himself a nineteenth-century poet mislaid as a prosifier in the twentieth. Famous French dramas like Gide's *Saül* or Sartre's *Le Diable et le bon Dieu*, Green's own plays or Mauriac's novels are bizarre for us because we are not involved with redemption, much less with going to hell. Emancipated Frenchmen (the Surrealists, for instance) always deny God, whereas for even the most retarded of American literati God is not there to be denied. (Should one of them convert, he usually leaves the States.) That God is the same to all is as demonstrable a fallacy as that music is a universal language.

(Sincerity versus artistry. If you can locate a copy, read the Cocteau-

Maritain correspondence of circa 1924. The poet's grief at Radiguet's death renders him vulnerable to the theologian who "leads him back to the sacraments." Maritain sees squarely ahead, Cocteau's glance veers skyward; Maritain labors for his trust in the Lord; Cocteau takes trust on faith and garnishes it with gargoyles. For Maritain religion is salvation, for Cocteau it is subject of rhapsodies. Maritain may plod toward heaven, yet Cocteau now dancing in hell wins hands down, for his imagination erupts from within while Maritain's appears superimposed from without—a label stamped by the Red Cross. The church never "took" for the inspired Jean; not for a minute do we Believe his Belief, but we believe it, since it is poetry. Still, the myth is ingrown in the French who take it for granted and are less stifled by Christ than we by Freud. The Vatican for centuries supplied a nest for a poetry grander than our Baptists and Mormons could dream of.)

I do not believe in God, though I do believe in the belief in God when expressed believably by plebeian practitioners or revolutionaries, or fantastically by saints and artists. So here I sit absorbing fatuities that occasionally, when they pass the buck to God, seem unfeeling. Reiteration of faith is suspect to infidels: it never seems to go beyond itself, but proves itself only through the self-hypnosis of that very reiteration, not through good acts. A believer is narrow, an artist is wide. Julien Green, being both, becomes a magnet between, attracting the unwary. Which explains why it's impossible to put down this trying tome.

Moved, I finish his diary (the twentieth of Green's books I've read) and momentarily indulge in the dangerous practice of feeding on the past, on a friendship that no longer exists with a man I'll probably never see again.

If I demurred nearly two years after coming abroad in 1949 before reading the famous writer, it was because he was somehow confused in my mind with Elliott Paul. Then during the fall of 1950, while I was convalescing from a primitive hemorrhoidectomy in a Moroccan clinic, Robert Levesque brought me *Moïra*. What an experience! to meet my double in a trance. Narrated in the compact Gallic language, the subject matter treated of American disorder: sexual guilt of, and murder by, a horny inarticulate red-haired youth in a Southern university. New World puritan frustration described via the mother tongue of Mallarmé. Green speaks American in French, the opposite of, say, Janet Flanner, who speaks French in American.

Thus runs the gist of a note received in November 1950:

> Very few letters have ever pleased me quite as much as yours and I do not want to wait to thank you for it. It is so direct, so friendly and so sincere. I think that only an American could write such a letter and I am only sorry that you did not write it sooner, but you had not read my book.
>
> So glad you liked *Moïra*. Much of it is autobiographical. I knew Prailean very well (although I regret to say it was months before I could nerve myself to speak to him. We then became and remained good friends). I also knew Joseph and that disgusting little prig David.

Now I shall look forward to seeing you in January. You have my address. Now here is my 'phone number: Littré 48–55. I am always at home in the morning and at meal times. If I like your music as much as your letter you will have to count me as one of your fans! Many thanks too for the picture which I like very much although I wish it had been larger. My greetings to Robert Levesque. It was nice of him to remember me.

Best wishes to you and I hope *à bientôt*.

(He signed Julian when writing in English, but I continue to call him Julien *à la française*.)

(Am I sincere? Sincerity, as opposed to honesty, is a minor virtue, no more than meets the eye, black and white, a bit right-wing. . . . He can only be disappointed. Or sad. The wounds of unrequited love lie less in the broken heart than in the fact that one's judgment is contradicted.)

On the third day of the new year 1951, rectal region still swathed in cotton like an imported peach, I flew from Casablanca to Amsterdam with Julius Katchen who was including my "Second Piano Sonata" on his Dutch tour and wanted me along to take bows. (Incidentally, my agenda notes a meeting with Klemperer, and two dates with Mengelberg to go over scores, on January 6 and again on January 10. These dates were doubtless arranged by Julius, a powerful star then in Holland; but despite my well-known total recall, I have no recollection of these men.)

Re-established in Paris on the 12th, I made the acquaintance, in the Bar Montana, of the actor Jean Leuvrais who would for a while become my closest friend in France. He was then playing his first lead role, opposite Mademoiselle Jany Holt, in Mauriac's *Le feu sur la terre* which I saw next evening, a Saturday, at the Théâtre Hébertot. Sunday I moved to the Hôtel du Bon La Fontaine, then dined chez Marie Blanche de Polignac for the first time. On Monday I met Julien Green.

It rained viciously (like a pissing cow, as the French say) during the beautiful ten-minute walk at noon from Rue des Saints-Pères to the three-story house in Rue de Varennes which Julien Green occupied with his sister Anne (whom I never met during many a subsequent visit) and the debonair Robert de Saint-Jean. I recall the rain specifically as a blight to my appearance. Eyes looked down on me already as I crossed the courtyard like a wet rat, so there was no time to comb my hair before the front door opened.

At fifty-one, the age of wild oats, Julien's social pattern still centered, as it had for decades, round individual visitors received two or three afternoons weekly, one-shot interviews with thesis-writers or adapters of novels, or *tête à têtes* with regulars like the Père Coutourier so in vogue then—and in *Vogue*—as official shepherd to recalcitrant celebrities, a sort of upper-class Billy Graham.

We had Cinzano (Julien never drank), went to lunch on the upper floor of the Maintenon, Boulevard Saint Germain, finished a bottle of Bordeaux, returned to Rue de Varennes where Julien watched me drink more Cinzano, switching then to Cointreau, all the time speaking of mutual literary infatuations, mostly of the Old Testament which he was pleased to know I knew. The rain stopped. With my last liqueur a shaft of sunshine like a finger of the Lord entered the library, whereupon my host asked if I would don a djellaba which he brought out, a vast velvet apparel with red stone ornaments and a hood. Berobed thus, glass in hand, I sat sainted in a circle of light, while Julien's voice from the shadows, serene and nervous, questioned me. The sunshine gradually faded. Something happened.

At five he canceled an appointment with Jouvet (*Sud* was being considered by l'Athénée), and we left instead to hear a run-through of my sonata five blocks away chez Julius Katchen. More apéritifs, Rue Cognacq-Jay, where Jean Leuvrais also came to meet me before going to his theater. Instant mistrust of Jean by Julien. ("I can size up the French bourgeois perhaps more easily than you." But a few seasons later Leuvrais was to star in Green's play *L'Ombre*. By such ironies do shadows lighten our small world!) . . . Next morning a gift was delivered to the desk of the Hôtel du Bon La Fontaine— *"par un monsieur de bien en tenue sombre."* A plaster cast of Chopin's hand.

Astonishment pushes me to record what seems unnecessary. My old agendas show so many crucial people being met in so short a time! So many hangovers with which I nonetheless coped! Here in my own library twenty-two years later I am assailed not by memory but by the actual smell of each *cuite*, by the touch of Jean Leuvrais's large hands on my neck, or Julius's hands on the keyboard there across the room, sounds of honey and iron. And the sound of ice cubes and Julien's reticent laugh. . . . Today I am just three years younger than he then, and am sometimes prey to visitors like this, whom I discourage with as much fright as he encouraged them with charity. Julien has turned gray now, I'm told. Jean Leuvrais is lost. Julius has died. Auden, in a poem unwritten when these souvenirs were real:

> Flash-backs falsify the Past:
> they forget
> the remembering Present.

On 18 January 1951, he sent me a little book, "the story of a shy boy," with the admonition: "Don't read it now. Wait until you have plenty of time," adding that he had been thinking about me. "Will you remember your promise to call me up? I love and admire your music. There are many things I want to tell you."

The little book was a new edition of his 1930 memoir, *L'autre sommeil*. I read it on April 15 in the waiting room at Marignane before boarding a plane for Casablanca. En route, I translated three extracts, and during the following week in Marrakech composed a baritone cycle on this English prose, calling it *Another Sleep*.

That early spring of 1951 Julien showed me Paris through his eyes. For one who virtually never writes about food, he had a passion for little sandwiches and cakes, English style, and we visited the hundred teahouses of Paris, the libraries and gardens, zoos and byways of the third *arrondissement*. His handsome stoical eyes could ferret out madness through a sunlit pane, yet much of what he found naughty was so innocent! For example, at his local bookstore he bought me an under-the-counter *Fanny Hill*. The clerk said, "I'll put it down as *Jane Eyre*." . . . Vicarious, he enjoyed my accounts of drunkenness and orgies (exaggerated), hoping nevertheless that I read the Bible each night. Each night in fact I would meet J. L. at the Théâtre Hébertot.

I meanwhile forced him occasionally into *my* Paris despite his contention that anyone seen with me was automatically compromised: A musicale at Marie Blanche's, a lunch with Marie-Louise Bousquet on Île Saint-Louis, the recital of Julius Katchen (*Paris-Match* pictured me in my silver necktie seated between Julien and Robert de Saint-Jean like proud parents), or my shoddy hotel room where he now saw Chopin's hand, broken, upright against the mirror with a cigarette between two fingers. I remember an afternoon chez Henri-Louis de la Grange with Menotti and Julien as sole audience to a concert of my songs by Nell Tangeman. And on another Tuesday, February 20, shaken from seeing Gide in state. And yet again the next afternoon between my rendezvous with Henri Gouin and Nadia Boulanger. Indeed, my agenda indicates a meeting every few days until March 10, a Saturday, when my involvement with Marie Laure began.

In April I spent my first fortnight at Marie Laure's *Saint Bernard* in Hyères, which became the scene of my most productive years. Julien, in Monaco to receive an honor from Rainier, drove over with Charles de Noailles to pass a weekend with us. But we did not then, nor ever again, resume the unset pattern of our first rainy day. A cooling off began. Which is when I returned to Morocco until September.

In June he thanked me for the translation of *Another Sleep*, adding: "I think it might be easier to sing the words if a few changes were made; perhaps we can go over it together. Of course I am dying to hear the music which, I am sure, is very pretty. Has it occurred to you that we might leave the words in French? It seems to me that, had I written the book in English, I would have said something else, totally different perhaps."

A triumph of tact, while stating plainly his doubts! Today in re-examining the score I too have doubts, not about the words or the music or their combination, but whether the text as I used it was actually by Green.

The set of songs, *Another Sleep*, has been performed only twice: by Bernard Lefort in Salle Gaveau in 1954, and by Donald Gramm in Town Hall in 1956. The music is perhaps too "sensitive" but I remain fond of it. However, my translations are not good, nor are they really Green, nor yet me. The effect is bastardly. Still, I'd have liked to publish the cycle if I had received permission to use the words. What words? Correspondence about them was resolved by silence, and my hunch is that Julien did not want to be identified with the texts of my songs.

As to his suggestion that "we might leave the words in French," I can only reply that in French I would have composed "something else, totally different perhaps."

(In an essay, "The Poetry of Music," I have discussed the problem of multilingual composers. Frustration awaits the American impelled to write songs in French, for those songs will seldom be heard. The rare French recitalist who programs an American song will make an effort to learn it in

English. Meanwhile, American singers find it more "legitimate" for their French group to be by Frenchmen. I am not the first to suffer from this irony. Yet the suffering is mild. Since few vocal concerts are given in any language by anyone anywhere anymore, little loss comes from indulging the unsalable challenges this precious medium provides. So I continue to write to whatever texts appeal to me.)

On the bus he sits across from a young redhead ("hair the same gold as the edge of his Bible"). When the boy gets off, he follows. When the boy walks faster, he likewise. When the boy finally stops in a doorway, he asks: Why do you let strangers chase you?

"Your letter touched me very deeply and I am glad you wrote," he himself wrote in November 1951. "I have been unwell and am not feeling quite myself yet, but someday, when you come back, we must see each other again."

Cemeteries, which Julien finds unbearable, are for me always cheerfully tranquil. I feel protected, not by the past but by the casualness of the present. No effort is made there, not even by the gardener mowing the lawns, the gardener more beautiful than his roses. I, who so fear death, find nothing fatal about those lawns, just peace, while Julien quotes Maeterlinck: The dead would not exist if it weren't for cemeteries.

He is concerned and cultured. Strangers who write him usually seem concerned and cultured. Strangers who write me are madmen. Disconcerting: the possibility that not opposites but similarities attract.
No denying that his *oeuvre* spills forth with obsessional folly, yet those who write to him identify with *him*, not with his characters, and he, though melancholy and visionary and godly, is not crazy.
(What is crazy? Let the night-nurse decide. Norris Embry, mortally bored by his continuing incarceration in an Annapolis "mental" hospital despite his pleas of normalcy, finally pointed to the door and shrieked: "Rabbits! here they come!" For that he was given an A.)

I wrote him from Marrakech and in February 1952 he answered. "Your letter touched me almost as much as it surprised me. Not for one minute did I ever suspect you cared for me as you seem to now. Perhaps I lack intuition, but never mind: what remains in my mind is what you wrote and you may be sure that I will always think of you."

Who guides my hand? His art is wrenched forth by some Doppelgänger.
I am clear about the Me who writes my music (with prodding: he loves to nap). That Me is me, though different from the Me typing these words. The composer never strikes a pose, yet I know him less well than I know Me.
Long long ago, toward 5 A.M. Heddy de Ré and I passed out cold while listening to Suzanne Danco sing Ravel's *Asie*. Ten hours later we awoke, the floor still soggy with beer, Danco still singing. At nine times an hour we had

heard through our dreams ninety identical performances of *Asie*. That evening I lent Julien my journal—this journal. He found in it a Me he neither recognized nor liked. Manipulator? Crybaby? In the published *Paris Diary* did he read a confidence betrayed?

Intermission. Daily finger-stretching on Debussy's *Études*, and practice on my own *Gloria*, which Phyllis Curtin and Helen Vanni record in two weeks. Now the typewriter's propped on our red dining-room table so I can look out upon the synagogue roof, and onto the (for a change) unpolluted topaz sky. These clean late summer days bring Taxco into the room, sometimes Marrakech, never New York, and flood the floor with dying sun. Beyond the synagogue murmurs Central Park, where the dozen alleyways around Bethesda Fountain reverberate, identical to Morocco's Place Jemâa-el-Fnâa with seven simultaneous orchestras, and here as there the laughing sickly smell of cannabis. But there as here resounds the exasperating noise for its own sake, transistors carried like static-purses, or unembarrassed cyclists, radios on their handlebars, broadcasting sheer din that rises to a thousand-decibel level, then fades as hairy thighs whiz by. I love the apartment and the city. But no American—not Paul Goodman nor any pop singer—has evoked with love or loathing this New York with the same devotion the French singer shows for his Paris. Villon, Balzac, Edith Piaf, Julien Green.

I have not seen Julien Green since the mid-1950s. Between then and the mid-1960s I've had four or five letters, all of them replies to professional inquiries. Occasionally when in Paris I telephone and he says he'll call back and doesn't, or a female voice explains that he is away. Meanwhile I keep in touch through his novels, his autobiography and through journals like the current one telling me about deaths, ever more frequent, of old friends or forgotten acquaintances. Among those pages my name remains invisible as by a determination to efface an identity that was ever conjoined to his own.

I had committed the unforgivable by nourishing his predecision of who and what I was, knowing the predecision to be untrue. For I was not always kind—though was the nourishment in fact so unkind? Yet even without nourishment, any predecision must become untrue, since the actual behavior of others cannot coincide with our fantasy about that behavior.

There's a distinction between the impression we think we give and the impression we do give, and neither relates necessarily to what we are. Julien writes continually of himself without revealing himself. The impression he would give, in words written and spoken, is of a magnanimity which strikes outsiders as old-maidish. If most people's character is revealed through their eyes, Julien's is revealed through his mouth which is thin, intelligent, withholding and sly.

At the MacDowell Colony I once composed a brief piece for strings, *Pilgrims*, on a notion which had long been floating in my brain: an impression that through music the strangeness of Julien's first book, *Le Voyageur sur la terre*, could be transmitted without words. The piece was later published with a cover of pale green on which, in deep green, the title, an epigraph, and appropriate credits are printed. For his seventieth birthday in 1970 I mailed a copy of this music to Julien Green. But he never answered.

The preceding pages are appallingly niggardly. I re-read them and squirm. Though Green may be the most unusual author of our day, I've shown here not my reaction to his value, only his to mine, and none too well. I've not "seen" him, but strived to show that he saw me. To acknowledge this in no way exonerates me, although the present sentence is a plea for indulgence.

Every artist, to be identified as such, does his unique number. Julien's number is honesty—an unflagging refusal to compromise. Now, every artist is honest, whether he tries or no, and for some the very act of compromise is artistry. (Julien might contend that compromise never tempted him, so why talk of "refusal"?)

My number is faking the shallow. But admitting to superficiality doesn't render one less superficial, only more self-serving. Can I prove I'm a fake? The admission, however, is far from my music, for there I'm too lazy for whoredom or gluttony; I compose only what I want to compose.

A fan letter today compliments me on my "Memoirs." Between diaries and memoirs lies the difference of years, the difference between now and then. I am incapable of the memoir as genre, as these diary pages on Julien Green precisely prove. Waste of retrospect. A retrogression. Failure. (Yet might not the seconds between these parentheses and that failure already place the failure in the past?)

September 1972

INDEX

Abercrombie, G., 21
Abravanel, M., 183
Achard, M., 83
Addison, A., 231
Adler, R., 293, 294
Adler, S., 65
Aeschylus, 206, 218
Agee, J., 238
Ajemian, M., 168
Akhmatova, A., 163
Albee, E., 97, 318
Allen, B., 231, 265
Allen, W., 167
Ameling, E., 93, 249, 250
Ames, E., 102
Ames, W., 226
Amiel, H. H., 211
Amram, D., 30
Andersen, H. C., 198
Anderson, M., 20, 244
Andrew, 241–42, 245–46
Annunzio, G. d', 139
Ansermet, E., 188, 253
Antheil, G., 285
Antonioni, M., 44, 70, 80, 88, 256
Apollinaire, G., 108, 280–81, 283, 301
Ardrey, R., 210
Arendt, H., 200
Aristophanes, 136
Armstrong-Jones, Anthony (Tony), 212
Arthur, E. (E. Forrestal), 54
Ashbery, J., 96, 109, 228, 245
Asher, A., 76
Ashton, F., 210
Auber, D., 285
Auden, E. (E. Mann), 200
Auden, W. H., 33–35, 99, 110, 168, 173, 191, 195, 200–8, 214, 215, 224, 228, 302, 359, 364

Augustine, St., 314
Aumont, J.-P., 100
Auric, G., 27, 50, 61, 172, 176, 178, 181, 182, 185, 241, 282, 353
Auric, N., 50, 59, 178
Austen, J., 244, 275
Axelrod, George, 211
Axelrod, Ginette, 211
Ayen, Duchess d', 288

Babbitt, M., 153, 193, 232, 295, 339
Bacall, L., 67
Bach, J. S., 22, 44, 108, 191, 216, 218, 252, 262, 274, 276, 294, 311, 343
    appreciation of, 65, 328
    N. Boulanger and, 139, 141
    greatness of, 36, 61, 139, 193
    keyword for music of, 275
    Messiaen and, 277
    music of, in films, 79, 182
    playing Debussy like, 150
    simplicity in music of, 94
Bacon, E., 226
Badings, H., 230, 231
Baksa, R., 231
Bakst, L. N., 130
Balanchine, G., 64, 130, 292, 318, 340
Baldwin, D., 249, 250
Baldwin, J., 97
Balthus, 36, 61, 93
Balzac, H. de, 49, 69, 273, 367
Bankhead, T., 212
Barab, S., 153
Barber, S., 23, 27, 28, 158, 231, 238–39, 241, 264, 281, 352
Bardac, E., 259
Barnes, D., 123
Barney, N., 131, 133
Barrault, J.-L., 166, 179
Barrymore, L., 42

Bartók, B., 24, 147, 197, 199, 317, 334,
        343
Basie, Count, 21
Bathori, J., 124
Baudelaire, C., 103, 114, 134, 211, 233,
        249, 255, 273
Baudrier, 277
Beardslee, B., 103, 231–32, 339
Beatles, The, 45, 179, 210, 337–45, 349
Beck, J., 346, 359
Beckett, S., 60
Beeson, J., 30, 231
Beethoven, L. van, 18, 24, 39, 40, 83,
        139, 156, 172, 173, 179, 224,
        266, 291, 292, 295, 328, 359
    banality in, 286–87
    Bizet and, 270
    charm of, 43, 199
    Coward on, 210
    Debussy compared with, 149
    Fifth Symphony of, 94, 190
    Goldbeck on, 253
    greatness of, 61, 102, 191, 207, 273
    improving on music of, 288
    learning music of, 22
    overestimating, 352
    percussion approach of, 19
    Poulenc and, 288
    Shaw and, 216, 218
    Stravinsky and, 193
    vocal music of, 196, 228, 260, 305
    C. Wagner and, 136
Béjart, M., 284, 352
Bellini, V., 305
Bellow, S., 117
Beman, R., 21
Bennett, A., 128
Benois, 187
Bentley, E., 100, 215
Berberian, C., 232, 344
Berg, A., 91, 154, 194, 196, 199, 242,
        261
Berger, A., 191, 339
Bergery, B., 133
Bergman, I., 80, 186, 292
Bergsma, W., 231
Berkeley, L., 231, 240
Berlin, I., 210
Berlioz, H., 60, 211, 215, 234, 249,
        250, 253, 275, 355
Bernac, P., 27, 227, 238, 250, 314
Bernanos, G., 198
Bernhardt, S., 177, 191

Bernstein, L., 29, 141, 204, 210, 264,
        280, 281, 286, 308, 352
Bert, L., 226
Bertolucci, B., 80
Bertrand, A., 360
Bettis, V., 33
Beydts, 236
Biesel, C., 21
Billings, W., 240
Bischoffsheim, M. T. (M. T. de
        Croisset), 55, 56, 176
Bishop, E., 245
Bismarck, O. von, 135
Bizet, Geneviève (G. Strauss; G.
        Halévy), 264, 269–71
Bizet, Georges, 262–73, 289
Blesh, R., 30
Blitzstein, M., 91, 158, 205, 230, 231,
        238, 270, 271, 343–44
Bogart, H., 67
Boito, A., 255
Bok, Mrs. (Mrs. Zimbalist), 221
Bolcom, W., 30
Bonazzi, E., 265
Bond, C. J., 238
Bonds, M., 17, 20–21
Bonnard, P., 128, 130, 131
Borges, J. L., 43, 186, 258
Borodin, A., 163
Borowski, F., 264
Bosset, V. de, 186
Bouis, A., 164
Boulanger, E., 139
Boulanger, L., 123, 138, 139, 141
Boulanger, N., 20, 44, 123–24, 138–43,
        152, 167, 176, 181, 265, 279, 365
Boulez, P., 42, 58, 95, 130, 154,
        165–71, 179, 186, 255, 284, 286,
        348, 349, 355
    Barber and, 264
    N. Boulanger and, 142
    intellectualization of music and, 338,
        341
    Jacobs and, 151, 152
    Rosenthal on, 285
    Stravinsky and, 187, 191, 193
    vocal music of, 228, 231, 242, 308
Boultenhouse, C., 73
Bour, E., 278
Bourdet, D., 246
Bousquet, M.-L., 51, 365
Bowles, J., 33, 75, 206, 207, 234, 357
Bowles, P., 33, 42, 130, 206, 226,

228–30, 233–34, 240, 295, 340, 355–57
Boyle, K., 86, 104
Brahms, C., 191
Brahms, J., 19, 52, 60, 68, 187, 196, 204, 216, 228, 260, 262, 273, 311, 328
Braque, M., 210, 251, 283, 294
Braziller, G., 56, 309*n*
Brennan, M., 68
Breton, A., 173, 329
Bridges, J., 63, 82
Brian, 74
Britten, B., 25–27, 110, 162, 194, 203–6, 210, 216, 228, 231, 240, 245, 248, 263, 279, 286, 294
Brod, M., 97, 284
Brooks, S., 360
Brown, E., 226
Brown, F., 184
Brubeck, D., 339
Bruckner, A., 43, 274
Bryant, A., 86, 87
Bryn-Julson, P., 232
Bucht, G., 230
Buckley, W., 103, 177
Bufano, R., 198
Bülow, H. von, 135, 136
Burns, R., 313
Burris, Mrs., 69, 76
Burroughs, E. R., 294
Busoni, F., 30, 183, 273
Bussine, 249
Butor, M., 57–58
Byron, Lord, 191

Caballé, M., 95
Cadman, C. W., 228, 235
Cage, J., 19, 45, 130, 167, 232, 308, 339, 348, 352, 353
Cain, J. M., 191, 240, 246
Calder, A., 318
Calderón de la Barca, P., 136
Caligula, 39
Calisher, H., 75
Callas, M., 47, 210, 264, 312, 314, 328
Callendar, N. (H. Schonberg), 113, 294
Calvé, E., 216
Campion, T., 195, 302
Camus, A., 185, 198
Canteloube, 238
Capote, T., 32–33, 37, 331
Capucine, 211

Capra, F., 69
Caravaggio, P. da, 68
Carissimi, G., 45
Carpenter, H., 20, 39, 202, 205, 207–8, 262
Carroll, L., 232, 356
Carson, J., 33
Carter, E., 93, 114, 139, 140, 142, 146–48, 151, 167, 181, 182, 232, 245–46, 251, 294–95, 339
Cartier-Bresson, H., 51
Caruso, E., 23
Casa Fuerte, Y. de, 230
Casadesus, G., 30, 149
Casals, P., 76, 94, 191, 294, 328, 352
Cavett, D., 37, 91, 97, 103
Cervantes, M. de, 258
Cézanne, P., 93
Chabrier, A. E., 260, 273, 288
Chamberlain, E., 136
Chanel, C., 127, 129, 130, 187
Chanler, T., 139, 226, 228, 231–33, 235–36, 238, 264
Channing, S., 118
Chapelier, Mme., 169
Chaplin, C., 23, 97, 147, 172
Char, R., 228, 308
Charcot, J., 275
Chaucer, G., 228
Chausson, E., 269, 273
Chekhov, A., 163, 224, 346
Cher, 33
Chesrown, M., 66
Chevigné, A. de, 262
Child, J., 118
Chigi, Count, 27
Chopin, F., 19, 22, 26, 45, 78, 156, 216, 221, 271, 273, 274
  feminine soul of, 179
  music of, in films, 79
  Poulenc and, 276, 288
  songs of, 196, 242, 247
  Stravinsky and, 187–88, 193, 194
Citkowitz, I., 235–37
Claoué, Y., 184
Clarendon (B. Gavoty), 335
Clark, K., 131
Claudel, P., 60–61, 67, 129, 187, 335
Clementi, M., 320, 342
Cliburn, V., 328
Clouzot, G., 328
Cluytens, A., 287
Cocteau, J., 35, 47, 55–56, 80, 81, 97,

Cocteau, J. *(cont.)*
    107, 127, 130, 131, 284, 290,
    335, 359
  Auden and, 200, 201
  N. Boulanger and, 138
  Coward and, 212–13
  Maritain and, 361–62
  music and, 172–85
  Poulenc and, 178, 184, 263
  Satie and, 281, 282, 285, 353
  Stravinsky and, 187, 191, 198
Colbert, C., 212
Coleman, O., 317, 343
Colette, 67, 102, 128–30, 146, 279–80,
    285, 290, 302
Collins, J., 45, 95
Connolly, C., 200
Conrad, D., 133
Conroy, F., 81, 82
Cook, B., 91
Cook, G., 20–21
Copland, A., 19, 39, 93, 97, 138, 165,
    191, 233, 264, 279, 319, 352
  N. Boulanger and, 123, 142
  film music of, 181
  influence of, 153, 235, 236
  rejection of, 338–39
  Stravinsky and, 28, 197
  vocal music of, 228, 235–38
Coppola, P., 278
Corneille, P., 55
Cortes, R., 226
Country Joe & The Fish, 340, 344
Couperin, F., 154, 236, 274, 276
Courbet, A., 43
Cousin, V., 353
Coward, N., 89, 172, 176, 209–14
Cowell, H., 226, 344
Craft, R., 75, 83, 186–89, 205, 340
Crawford, B., 23
Crawford, J., 84
Crawford, R., 124
Crespin, R., 241, 286
Creston, P., 175
Croisset, E. de, 167–68
Croisset, F. de, 176
Croisset, M. T. (M. T. Bischoffsheim),
    55, 56, 176
Crompton, L., 216
Crosland, M., 184
Crumb, G., 175, 232, 295
Cuénod, H., 41, 189
Cukor, G., 211

Cumming, R., 229, 231
Cummings, E. E., 228, 230, 231, 237,
    263
Curtin, C. M., 243
Curtin, P., 229, 231, 233, 241, 243,
    245, 249, 367
Curtiss, M., 269–72

Daley, R., 87
Dali, S., 56, 251
Damase, J.-M., 268
Damrosch, W. J., 228
Dana, R., 226
Danco, S., 366
Daniel, O., 154
Darrieux, D., 57
Darwin, C., 327
Daudet, A., 264, 271
Davies, P. M., 232
da Vinci, L., 172, 212
Davis, B., 80, 178
Davis, G., 206
Davis, Mrs., 19
Day, J., 51
Dean, W., 267, 270
Debussy, C., 17–20, 22, 27, 73, 101,
    203, 217, 227, 269, 270, 272,
    279, 294, 355, 367
  bias toward, 273–77
  Boulez and, 166, 167
  Cocteau and, 183
  as critic, 215
  Fauré and, 259–61
  Flanner and, 132
  Jacobs as interpreter of, 149–52
  learning music of, 19, 20
  nature celebrated by, 277
  Pelléas and Mélisande, 251–58
  as pianist, 28
  Poulenc and, 178, 184, 263, 289
  prose of, 42
  Ravel and, 161, 286–88
  Rosenthal on, 284
  Satie and, 274, 275, 289, 352
  songs of, 232, 247–50, 254–56, 302,
    305, 307, 312, 344
  Stravinsky and, 131, 187, 193, 197
  20th century opened by, 192
  women as interpreters of, 124
DeGaetani, J., 232
Degas, E., 51, 167
de Gaulle, C., 133, 191
de Gaulle, Y., 55

Deharme, L., 57
de Kooning, W., 45
Delacroix, E., 211, 250, 253
De la Mare, W., 202, 233
Delannoy, J., 230
Delibes, L., 268
Delius, F., 20, 247
Della Casa, G., 314
Del Tredici, D., 30, 168, 232
Désormière, R., 353
Dewey, T., 54
Diaghilev, S., 129, 161, 173, 175, 186, 187, 213, 264, 282, 335, 353
Diamond, D., 30, 139, 226, 231, 278, 291, 340
Diana, Princess of Wales, 212
Dickinson, E., 42, 202, 237
Dietrich, M., 212, 244, 263, 326
Dillon, M., 207
Dinesen, I., 26, 177
Disney, W., 186, 199, 285
Dlugoszewski, L., 30, 124
Dominguez, O., 54
Donizetti, G., 256
Donne, J., 113, 226, 228
Donovan, 340
Dougherty, C., 226, 235, 308
Dowland, J., 195, 232, 240, 302
Dreyfus, A., 271
Drouet, M., 47
Dryden, J., 302
Du Bois, W. E. B., 20
Duchin, E., 127
Duff, J., 211
Duke, J., 226, 234–35
Dukelsky, V., 27
Dunham, K., 20
Dunkel, P., 241
Dunphy, J., 33
Duparc, H., 247, 269, 313
Dupont, J., 59
Durey, L., 178, 353
Durk, D., 115–16
Dutilleux, H., 231
Duval, D., 281, 286
Dvorsky, M. (J. Hofmann), 18
Dylan, B., 340

Eames, W., 216
Eastman, J., 232
Eberhart, R., 204
Eddy, T., 25
Edmunds, J., 226

Edwards, A., 128–29, 131
Einstein, A., 35
Elgar, E. W., 216, 217, 256
Eliot, G., 60
Eliot, T. S., 58, 200, 202–4, 207, 218, 302, 318
Elizabeth II, 212
Ellis, A., 96
Éluard, P., 176, 228, 301
Embiricos, P., 71
Embry, N., 366
Entremont, P., 287
Epstein, J., 105
Esty, A., 230–31
Etherton, F., 360
Etherton, J., 360
Euripides, 182

Fairbank, J., 225–27, 229, 338, 360
Falla, M. de, 251
Fantozzi, W., 21
Farr, N., 226
Farrand, N., 278, 291
Farrell, E., 91, 313
Faulkner, B., 33
Faulkner, W., 60
Fauré, Gabriel, 27, 42, 139, 140, 142, 185, 216, 247–50, 254, 259–61, 265–67, 269, 274, 276
Feeney, L., 228, 232, 233
Fellini, F., 80
Ferrand, G., 51
Ferrier, K., 139
Feuillère, E., 61
Février, J., 27
Fine, I., 191, 231
Fine, V., 118, 229
Finney, R., 142
Fischer, B., 34
Fischer-Dieskau, D., 229, 339
Fitch, C., 213
Fizdale, R., 130–31, 175
Flagstad, K., 314
Flanagan, W., 56, 61, 158, 229, 231, 278, 291, 292, 340
Flanner, H., 134
Flanner, J., 102, 132–34, 362
Flaubert, G., 274, 280
Fleiner, L., 24
Floyd, C., 231
Fonteyn, M., 210
Forrestal, E. (E. Arthur), 54
Forster, E. M., 105, 215

Fort, P., 184
Forte, A., 187
Foss, L., 28, 30, 231, 346
Foster, S., 235, 313
Fourtine, H., 52
Fox, G., 70
Françaix, J., 142
France, A., 65
France, C. de, 150
Francine, 42, 100, 101
Franck, C., 265, 271, 274, 277
Franklin, B., 42
Frescobaldi, G., 81, 252
Freud, S., 124, 137, 162, 167, 192, 202,
    359
Frielicher, J., 118
Frijsh, P., 226, 234, 238, 249, 250, 338
Fromm, P., 223
Frost, R., 202
Frost-Jones, H., 148
Fuller, B., 359

Gabin, J., 54
Gabis, S. (S. Rhoads), 23, 24, 77–78,
    150, 153, 168
Gallet, L., 271
Galli-Marié, C., 266
Galway, J., 292
Ganz, R., 19, 21
Garbo, G., 112
Garden, M., 28, 124, 256, 264
Garfield, J., 84
Garrigue, J., 156
Gauthier, E., 227, 229, 278, 291
Gavoty, B. (Clarendon), 35
Gendron, M., 139
Genêt, J., 176
Gentry, B., 341
Geoffroy, G., 54
Gershwin, G., 30, 210, 225, 276, 303,
    338
Gesualdo, C., 311
Gide, A., 40, 54, 69, 86, 105, 116, 127,
    131, 140, 165, 173, 185, 187,
    211, 215, 279, 294, 335, 361
Gideon, M., 30, 229
Gielgud, J., 292
Gieseking, W., 28, 149
Gifford, B., 105
Gilbert, W. S., 268, 302, 344
Gillette, P., 226
Ginsberg, A., 251, 348
Glade, C., 262, 263

Glanville-Hicks, P., 229, 344
Glass, P., 295
Glazunov, A., 163
Gluck, C., 279
Godard, J.-L., 252
Godowsky, L., 149, 152
Goehr, A., 230
Goethe, J. W. von, 196, 206, 228, 271,
    302
Goetz, H., 216
Gogol, N., 163, 359
Gold, A., 130–31, 175
Goldbeck, F., 252–54
Golde, M., 69–70, 77, 101, 105, 154
Goodman, B., 252
Goodman, P., 48, 55, 72, 154, 170, 177,
    181, 200–1, 227, 228, 245, 278,
    291, 358–60, 367
Goodman, S., 358, 360
Goosens, E., 27
Gottlieb, J., 139
Goudebet, M., 129
Gouin, H., 365
Gould, G., 30
Gounod, C., 216, 217, 236, 247, 259,
    260, 269–71, 273
Goya, F. de, 271
Graffman, G., 23
Graham, B., 363
Graham, M., 23, 61, 64, 93, 117–18,
    191, 140, 342
Gramm, D., 24, 27, 40, 229, 231, 241,
    365
Grandma Moses, 83, 115
Gravys, R., 230
Gray, Francine, (see Francine)
Greco, El, 44
Greco, J., 184, 244, 287
Gregory II, 311, 354
Greeley, Reverend, 71
Green, A., 363
Green, J., 69, 76, 134, 175, 211,
    361–68
Greenough, V., 41
Greuze, J. B., 55
Grey, M., 124, 250
Grieg, E. H., 22, 217
Griffes, C. T., 20, 39, 240, 334
Griffith, D. W., 334
Grosser, M., 169
Gruen, J., 229, 230
Guilbert, Y., 217
Guitry, S., 49, 172

Gysin, B., 36

Hager, M., 226
Haggin, 75
Hahn, R., 175, 238, 268, 274, 281
Haieff, A., 176, 191, 197
Haines, W., 226
Halévy, D., 270
Halévy, F., 269–71
Halévy, G. (G. Bizet; G. Strauss), 264,
    269–71
Halévy, Léon, 270
Halévy, Ludovic, 270
Hall, Mrs. R. J., 124
Halliday, J., 340
Hammarskjöld, D., 105, 204
Handel, G. F., 216, 217, 236, 244, 285
Hanson, P., 230
Harbaugh, R., 19
Harbison, 295
Hardwick, E., 35
Hardy, T., 118, 202, 228
Harrell, M., 226
Harris, R., 39, 139, 237
Harrison, G., 344
Harrison, J., 84
Harrison, L., 30, 152, 226, 295, 308
Hasselmans, Mme., 259
Haydn, F. J., 21, 30, 192, 242, 259,
    288, 289, 318, 359
Hayward, S., 96
Heifetz, Y., 24
Heine, H., 228, 261
Hell, H., 178
Hellman, L., 102
Helm, E., 231
Helps, R., 30
Hemingway, E., 81, 89, 326
Henahan, D., 293–95
Hentoff, N., 341
Henze, H. W., 179, 205, 210, 232
Herrick, R., 228
Hillyer, R., 231
Hindemith, P., 26, 175, 183–84, 317,
    343
Hitchcock, A., 109, 168
Hitler, A., 42, 135, 162, 165, 201, 338
Hoffman, J. (M. Dvorsky), 18
Hofmannsthal, H. von, 279
Hoiby, L., 30
Holden, W., 211
Holiday, B., 21, 64, 108, 244, 250, 338,
    341, 344, 349, 359

Holman, L., 21, 244
Holmes, J., 17, 32, 33, 37, 43, 57,
    61–63, 68–72, 74, 76, 78, 96,
    114, 115, 286
  animals and, 70, 79, 107
  on being deluded, 47
  and discrimination against homosex-
    uals, 105–6
  and Grandma Moses, 83
  on harmony, 18
  on Judas, 110
  on looking one's age, 101
  Paris trips of, 165–67, 283–84
  sadness and depression of, 69, 108–9,
    111–13
  on suicide, 37
Holt, J., 363
Homer, 136, 185
Homer, L., 228, 238
Honegger, A., 50, 168, 177, 178, 184,
    282, 334–36, 352, 353
Hope, B., 212
Hopkins, G. M., 172, 238
Hopper, H., 37
Horgan, P., 184
Horne, L., 292, 338
Horne, M., 91, 264
Horne, W., 226
Horowitz, V., 21, 149, 151, 167
Houseman, J., 63
Howard, L., 80
Howland, A., 226
Hughes, L., 20
Hugo, J., 36, 52
Hugo, Valentine, 184
Hugo, Victor, 217, 249, 273
Hundley, R., 229
Hunter, A., 21
Hurok, S., 56
Hurst, F., 291
Hutchins, R., 71
Huxley, A., 58, 215
Huysmans, J., 88

Ian, J., 340
Indy, V., d', 271
Ionesco, E., 77
Isherwood, C., 99, 103, 105, 204
Istomin, E., 23–24, 52, 56, 150, 153,
    289, 360
Ives, C., 36, 167, 235, 237, 264, 274,
    283, 294, 315, 323, 334, 342, 353

Jackson, H., 226

Jacobs, P., 28, 149–52
Jacobson, R., 262
Jaffe, S., 68
Jagger, M., 64, 359
James, H., 40, 69, 71, 95, 198, 218
Jenkins, N., 153
Jeritza, M., 312
Jewell, I., 68
JH, see Holmes, J.
Johnson, E., 228
Johnson, L. B., 348
Johnson, T., 293, 294
Johnson, V., 100
Joio, N. D., 226
Jolivet, A., 277
Jones, C., 231
Jones, J., 134
Jourdan-Morhange, H., 124
Joyce, J., 169, 228, 235, 237, 327
Jullian, P., 35

Kael, P., 73, 190, 293
Kafka, F., 40, 43, 45, 97, 218, 263, 284,
    285, 301
Kallman, C., 33, 200, 204–7
Kapell, W., 24
Karajan, Mme. H. von, 210
Karloff, B., 97, 284
Katchen, J., 287, 363, 364
Kavafian, A., 25
Keller, G., 244
Kelly, G., 140
Kennedy, J. (J. Onassis), 81, 348
Kennedy, J. F., 177, 305, 348
Kenton, S., 339
Keogh, T., 33
Kern, J., 235, 280
Kierkegaard, S., 62, 205
Kinsey, A., 30–31, 89
Kirchner, L., 30
Klemperer, O., 363
Kligman, R., 118
Koch, K., 203, 230
Koch, S., 184
Kochno, B., 55, 264
Kolb, B., 30, 32, 124, 223
Koussevitzky, S., 132, 187
Kramer, H., 86
Kunst, B., 87

Labisse, F., 61
La Forge, F., 235
La Grange, H.-L. de, 365
Lahr, J., 105

Laing, R.D., 82, 203
Lamont, R., 77, 81, 83
La Montaine, J., 231
Landormy, P., 351
Langland, W., 231
Lansbury, A., 77, 91
Latiener, J., 23
Latouche, J., 33, 112, 176
Laughton, C., 65
Laurencin, M., 281
Lautréamont, 160
Layard, J., 203
Lederman, M., 230
Lee, G. R., 205
Lee, G. V., 215
Lee, N., 30, 139, 151
Lee, P., 344
Lees, G., 344
Lefort, B., 365
Lehmann, L., 234, 339
Leibowitz, R., 142, 264
Leigh, V., 212
LeMasle, R., 52
Lenin, V. I., 163
Lennon, J., 343–44
Lenya, L., 183
Lerberghe, C. van., 249
LeSueur, J., 68
Lessard, J., 226
Lettvin, T., 23
Leuvrais, J., 363–65
Levesque, R., 362
Levin, M., 105
Leyland, W., 67
Liberace, 314
Libman, L., 188, 191
Lichtenstein, R., 36
Lifar, S., 182
Lipatti, D., 139
Lipkin, S., 23
Lipton, M., 64, 263–64
Liszt, F., 19, 26, 28, 128, 135, 187,
    216–18, 265, 288
Lockwood, N., 226
Lockspeiser, D., 19–20
Long, M., 27, 124
Lorca, F. G., 232, 233, 238, 251
Loriod, Y., 28, 148
Lott, F., 286
Louis XIV, 191
Louÿs, P., 89
Lovell, B., 115
Lowell, R., 47

Lowenthal, J., 24
Lucarelli, B., 241
Ludwig I, 136
Luening, E., 226
Luening, O., 226
Lunt, A., 212
Lunt, L., 212
Lutcher, N., 154

Maar, D., 56
Maazel, L., 291
MacCarthy, D., 211
McCarthy, M., 57, 86
McCartney, P., 343, 344
McCullers, C., 206
MacDonald, J., 85
Machaut, G. de, 45, 228, 288, 311
McIlhenny, H., 117
Mackail, J. W., 254
McKuen, R., 92
MacLeish, A., 233
McLuhan, M., 114, 359
Maeterlinck, M., 183, 252, 254, 256,
    302
Mahler, G., 43, 151, 160, 291, 294
Mallarmé, S., 127, 129, 228, 243, 248,
    250, 261, 362
Malraux, A., 163
Malraux, M., 167
Mandelstam, O., 186
Manet, É., 43, 95
Mann, E. (E. Auden), 200
Mann, G., 205
Mann, T., 58, 173, 191, 200, 207, 215,
    359
Manziarly, M. de, 124
Marais, J., 176–77, 184
Maralda, F., 263
Margaret, Princess, 212
Margollies, M., 21
Maritain, J., 351, 362
Markevitch, I., 140, 282
Marlowe, S., 169
Marshall, M., 240
Martin, F., 231
Marty, J.-P., 139, 283, 286–91
Marx, K., 38
Marx Brothers, 67, 280
Masselos, W., 28, 151, 153
Massenet, J., 256, 268, 271, 275
Mathis, J., 242
Matthew, St., 116
Maugham, W. S., 213

Mauriac, F., 69, 361, 363
Maurice, J.-C., 168
Mayakovsky, V., 162
Mdivani, R., 129
Menuhin, Y., 139
Meilhac, H., 270
Melville, J.-P., 118, 176
Mendelson, E., 202
Mendelssohn, Fanny, 125
Mendelssohn, Felix, 22, 125, 196, 217,
    273
Mendès, C., 249
Mengelberg, J. W., 363
Menotti, G., 23, 210, 229, 231, 365
Meredith, B., 147
Mérimée, P., 267, 268, 272
Merman, E., 91
Messager, A., 257
Messiaen, O., 28, 58, 142, 146–48, 151,
    242, 248, 264, 274, 277
Meyer, M., 27, 28
Meyerbeer, G., 217, 270
Meyerhold, V., 163
Michaux, H., 169
Michelangelo, 228, 270, 294
Milhaud, D., 37, 50, 61, 62, 178, 187,
    230, 231, 277, 282, 300–1, 308,
    352, 353
Milhaud, M., 178, 197, 243
Miller, A., 198
Miller, G. (G. Rorem), 18, 21, 72, 78,
    114, 119, 246
Miller, P., 228–29, 232
Millet, J. F., 151
Millett, K., 69
Miranda, A. M., 286
Miró, J., 134
Mishima, Y., 64
Mistinguett, 360
Mitchesky, Princess R., 139
Mitropoulos, D., 153, 230
Modigliani, A., 283
Molière, 225, 248
Mondrian, P., 97
Monet, C., 68, 250, 253
Monreal, G., 57
Montesquiou, R. de, 35, 36, 213, 248
Monteverdi, C., 45, 91, 140, 256, 277,
    311, 342
Moore, D., 226, 352
Moore, G., 249
Morgan, H., 244
Morgan, R., 82, 125

Morgenthau, A., 153–54
Morley, S., 211
Morton, J. R., 30
Moss, H., 63–64
Mostel, Z., 155
Mothers of Invention, 340
Mozart, W. A., 19, 29, 32, 105, 155,
    160, 185, 210, 216, 217, 259,
    266, 294, 305, 312, 320, 342
Muggeridge, M., 75
Müller, W., 260
Mulligan, G., 339
Murphy, N., 133
Murphys, G., 131
Murray, N. D., 102, 134
Musgrave, T., 43
Mussolini, B., 187
Mussorgsky, M., 19, 162, 197, 232,
    275, 288
Muzio, C., 243
Myers, J., 71, 112, 360

Nabokov, Natalie, 169
Nabokov, Nicolas, 184, 191, 205
Nabokov, V., 26
Nadar, 78
Naginsky, C., 226
Nancarrow, C., 30
Napoleon I, 191
Nat, Y., 24
Natanson, T., 128
Neveux, A., 166
Nevin, E., 228
Neway, P., 153, 229
Newlin, D., 229
Nicolson, H., 205, 211
Nietzche, F., 136, 215, 267
Nijinsky, R., 19
Nijinsky, V., 19, 187, 198–99, 351
Nin, A., 75, 211
Nixon, M., 339
Nixon, R. M., 72, 73, 96, 97, 165, 284
Noailles, Countess de, 35, 55–56, 365
Noailles, M. L. de, 33, 35, 49, 51,
    53–57, 68, 72, 79, 80, 107, 116,
    127, 131, 176–78, 183, 264, 265
Noailles, Vicomtesse de, 288
Noguchi, I., 61
Nolte, A., 22, 23
Nordica, L., 228
Novak, K., 211

Oberlin, R., 39
Paderewski, I. J., 18, 28, 286

Painter, W., 130
Palestrina, G. P. de, 156, 228, 275, 288,
    388
Panzéra, C., 250
Parker, W., 25
Parry, C., 218
Partch, H., 30, 83, 344
Pasternak, B., 163
Pastor, F., 23, 221
Pastré, L., 55, 80
Pater, W., 301
Paul, E., 362
Payn, G., 211
Pears, P., 27, 205, 238
Péguy, C., 131, 141, 177
Penny, H., 54, 71
Peretz, M., 81
Pergolesi, G., 196
Perle, G., 30, 153, 295
Perrin, J., 57
Persichetti, V., 231
Peters, R., 314
Petit, R., 182
Pfitzner, H., 260
Phelps, B., 72
Phelps, R., 53, 55, 62, 72, 102, 133, 184
Piaf, E., 217, 282, 344, 267
Picasso, P., 36, 40, 82, 93, 125, 127,
    173, 174, 180, 186, 187, 191,
    198, 207, 282, 283, 292, 328,
    343, 353
Pickens, Mrs., 19
Pinkham, D., 30, 226, 231, 340
Pinter, H., 36
Piston, W., 139, 236, 237
Plath, S., 125
Plato, 65, 289, 308, 353, 354
Plimpton, G., 177
Podhoretz, N., 86, 105
Poe, E. A., 285, 288, 328
Polignac, Comtesse de, 140
Polignac, M. B. de, 51, 363, 365
Polignac, Princess E. de, 124, 288, 353
Pollock, J., 95
Pommey, L., 249
Pommier, J.-B., 287
Pompidou, G., 142
Pompidou, Mme. G., 167
Pons, L., 314
Pope-Hennessey, J., 54
Porter, A., 75, 191, 241, 245
Porter, C., 338, 343–44
Porter, Mrs. C., 288

Porter, Q., 226, 230
Poulenc, F., 27, 40, 50, 54, 130, 170,
 176, 191, 238, 268, 271, 280–91,
 294, 326, 334
 bias toward, 274, 276–77
 Cocteau and, 178, 184, 263, 289
 Esty and, 230, 231
 Honegger and, 335
 journals of, 211
 Ravel and, 287, 288
 Satie and, 276, 352, 353
 Stravinsky and, 192, 196–98, 276,
 288
 theater pieces of, 278, 280–83, 287,
 290, 291
 vocal music of, 91, 116, 228, 231,
 232, 241, 248, 250, 260, 261,
 263, 301, 342
Pound, E., 42, 58, 172, 173, 215, 359
Powell, J., 244
Presley, E., 340, 348
Price, L., 27, 237, 264, 340
Pritchett, V. S., 271
Prokofiev, S., 24, 28, 161, 265, 266, 275
Prokosch, F., 238
Proust, M., 35, 37, 58, 97, 99, 119, 127,
 130, 159, 173, 207, 215, 248,
 270, 271, 288, 291, 296
Puccini, G., 232, 275, 276, 279, 305
Pugno, R., 139, 140
Purcell, H., 216, 226, 236, 240, 286,
 302, 311

Quine, D., 211

Rachmaninoff, S., 18, 19, 22, 26, 28,
 30, 228, 327
Racine, J., 182
Radiguet, R., 45, 138, 160, 184, 362
Rainier III, 365
Rameau, J. P., 275
Raphael, 45, 137
Raphling, S., 231
Rauschenberg, R., 169
Ravel, É., 285
Ravel, M., 17, 19, 22, 32, 39, 47, 84,
 111, 130, 151, 177, 191, 194,
 227, 269, 272–80, 284–91, 343,
 360
 Auden and, 202
 banality in music of, 286–87
 bias toward, 272–76
 Cocteau and, 183
 and composing at the piano, 26

Debussy and, 161, 286–88
 as pianist, 28
 private life of, 289–90
 Satie and, 287–88, 352
 seriousness in music of, 97
 M. Sert and, 128
 Stravinsky and, 187, 192, 193, 196,
 197, 279, 285
 theater pieces of, 278–80, 282, 287,
 290–91
 vocal music of, 247, 248, 250, 259,
 260, 302, 311, 366
 women as interpreters of, 124
Ré, H. de, 51, 52, 366
Ready, M., 358–59
Reardon, J., 91
Rebikov, 255, 270, 275
Rechy, J., 211
Rédé, A. de, 281
Redlich, G., 21
Reed, R., 77, 80
Reese, G., 47
Reeves, G., 234
Reger, M., 274
Reid, C., 242
Reinhardt, M., 128
Reis, C., 230
Reiter, J., 270
Reiter, M., 270
Réjane, 127
Renoir, A., 127, 248, 253
Resnais, A., 282
Reverdy, P., 127
Reyer, C., 231
Rhoads, S. (S. Gabis), 23, 24, 77–78,
 150, 153, 168
Rhys, J., 68
Rich, A., 97
Richard, Mrs., 124
Richter, S., 216
Rieti, V., 27, 231
Rilke, R. M., 57, 158, 238
Rimbaud, A., 47, 71, 93, 160, 166, 167,
 169, 228, 290
Rimsky-Korsakov, N., 187, 285, 288
Ritman, B., 61
Robbins, J., 206
Robeson, P., 163
Robinson, E. A., 235
Robinson, F., 96
Rochberg, G., 114, 168, 169, 246
Rockefeller, J. D., 211
Rockwell, J., 244

Rodin, A., 57
Roditi, É., 50, 358
Roerich, N. K., 187
Rolland, R., 163, 173
Ronsard, P. de, 248
Roosevelt, F. D., 156
Rorem, G. (G. Miller), 18, 21, 73, 78,
    114, 119, 133, 246
Rorem, N., 18, 20, 21, 23, 32, 73, 114,
    119, 133, 263
Rorem, R., 18, 133
Rose, B., 191
Rosen, C., 151
Rosenstiel, L., 141
Rosenthal, C. (C. Verneuil), 283–86
Rosenthal, M., 231, 268, 283–86
Rossini, G., 217, 223, 247, 269, 313
Rostand, M., 213
Rostropovich, M., 130, 210
Rota, N., 27, 80
Rothschild, E., 19
Rothschild, N., 17, 19, 20
Rouault, G., 250
Rouché, M., 290
Rousseau, J.-J., 211
Roussel, A., 154
Rubinstein, Anton, 18
Rubinstein, Artur, 28, 140, 210, 292
Rubinstein, I., 124
Russell, A., 314
Ryan, D. D., 72, 84

Saby, B., 152, 168
Sade, Marquis de, 131
Sagan, F., 160
Sager, G., 53
Saint-Jean, R. de, 177, 363, 365
Saint-John Perse, 127, 233
Saint Laurent, Y., 287
Saint-Saëns, C., 141, 259, 260, 268, 271
Samain, A., 249
Sand, G., 137, 271
Sanders, G., 150
Sarfaty, R., 229, 231, 265
Saroyan, W., 233
Sarraute, N., 56, 57
Sartre, J.-P., 48, 79, 187, 361
Satie, E., 30, 54, 65, 97, 127, 130, 156,
    185, 187, 285, 287–91, 334, 339
  Cocteau and, 175, 179, 183, 184
  Debussy and, 274, 275, 289, 352
  Poulenc and, 276, 352, 353
  Ravel and, 287–88

Rosenthal on, 285
Socrate of, 351–55
Stravinsky and, 197, 199
theater pieces of, 278, 281–83, 287,
    290, 291
vocal music of, 232, 255, 256, 308
Sauguet, H., 59, 80, 184, 230, 231, 268,
    353
Scalero, R., 22–23
Scarlatti, D., 26, 247, 311
Schmitz, E. R., 23
Schnabel, A., 24, 30
Schoenberg, A., 28, 30, 65, 84, 97, 151,
    153, 155, 166, 179, 196, 199,
    215, 261, 322
Schonberg, H. (N. Callendar), 113, 294
Schubert, F., 60, 83, 194, 207, 210,
    216, 272, 273, 353
  interpreting, 27, 47, 287
  songs of, 58, 185, 196, 243, 260, 302,
    307, 311, 313, 344
Schumann, C., 148
Schumann, R., 22, 42, 151, 196, 215,
    228, 251, 260, 271, 273, 287,
    288, 311, 355
Schumann-Heink, E., 228
Schuyler, J., 230, 233
Schwarzkopf, E., 229, 234, 339
Schweitzer, A., 76
Scriabin, A., 20, 28, 161, 277, 348
Scribe, A. E., 271
Seeger, P., 124
Serkin, P., 41
Serkin, R., 23, 40, 41, 151
Sert, J.-M., 129
Sert, M. (M. Godebska Natanson Ed-
    wards Sert), 124, 127–31, 191,
    288
Sessions, R., 28, 236–37, 295, 321, 355
Sévigné, Marquise de, 42, 269
Shakespeare, 45, 84, 124, 136, 150, 179,
    185, 195, 228, 233, 254, 266,
    270, 302
Shapero, H., 191
Sharp, C., 125
Shaw, G. B., 163, 173, 198, 215–18,
    296
Shaw, R., 326
Shostakovich, D., 45, 160–64
Shostakovich, M., 161
Sibelius, J. J. C., 228, 305
Sibilat, M., 269
Siepi, C., 314

Siloti, K., 197
Sills, B., 93
Simenon, G., 67
Simon, J., 41, 288
Simon, N., 71
Simon and Garfunkel, 340
Sinatra, F., 191, 338
Singher, M., 256
Sitwell, E., 302, 308n
Sitwell, S., 309n
Skelton, G., 136
Smit, L., 30, 191
Smith, B., 156, 345
Smith, G., 197
Smith, M., 263
Smyth, E., 217–18
Socrates, 105, 110, 138, 170
Solzhenitsyn, A., 163
Sondheim, S., 32, 91, 225
Sontag, S., 36, 37, 57, 92, 97, 341
Sophocles, 185, 198
Souzay, G., 229, 249, 250, 283, 339
Sowerby, L., 21
Spender, S., 117, 203, 206, 309n, 357
Spirito, R. di, 226
Spohr, L., 270
Sprigge, E., 184
Staël, Mme. de, 111
Stalin, J., 162, 163, 165, 167
Stanislavsky, C., 163
Starr, R., 344
Steber, E., 237
Steegmuller, F., 130, 184
Stein, G., 65, 125, 134, 169, 212, 228, 234, 277, 308, 315, 316, 323, 346
Stein, J., 51
Steiner, M., 80, 178
Stern, I., 52, 210
Steuermann, E., 30
Stevens, W., 32, 147, 208, 231, 296
Stich-Randall, T., 95, 249
Stimer, D., 230
Stockhausen, K., 30, 179, 340, 343
Stokowski, L., 47, 153
Strauss, É., 269
Strauss, G. (G. Halévu; G. Bizet), 264, 269–71
Strauss, R., 22, 111, 194, 231, 247, 277
Stravinsky, I., 22, 26–28, 39, 42, 58, 130, 154, 168, 186–99, 207, 217, 264, 275, 331, 343
  Auden and, 205, 206
  N. Boulanger and, 139–42

Boulez and, 187, 191, 193
Cocteau and, 174–75, 179
critics of, 294
Messiaen and, 277
percussive approach of, 19
Poulenc and, 192, 196–98, 276, 288
Ravel and, 187, 192, 193, 196, 197, 279, 285
Satie and, 282, 351, 352
M. Sert and, 127, 131
Shostakovich and, 162, 163
vocal music of, 305, 339–40
Stravinsky, V., 186–89
Streisand, B., 91
Styron, W., 86
Sullivan, A. S., 268, 302, 344
Sully Prudhomme, R., 249
Summer, D., 91
Supremes, The, 341, 343
Sutherland, J., 91, 210
Swanson, H., 20, 230

Tailleferre, G., 50, 124, 177–79, 230, 231, 353
Takemitsu, T., 118
Talese, G., 86
Talese, N., 244
Talma, L., 124, 139
Tangeman, N., 61, 139, 226, 249, 263–64, 338, 365
Tannenbaum, B., 17, 21–22
Tashi, 118
Taylor, P., 198–99
Tchaikovsky, P. I., 39, 105, 196, 216, 265, 305
Tchelitchew, P., 71, 176
Tebaldi, R., 255
Tennyson, A., 104, 228, 301
Tessier, V., 264
Teyte, M., 227, 339
Tharp, T., 43, 64
Thomas, D., 196, 208
Thompson, A., 19
Thompson, K. (K. Harbaugh), 19
Thompson, R., 231
Thomson, V., 25, 33, 42, 49, 52, 100, 102, 134, 177, 245, 282, 288, 308, 334, 339, 355
  Boulez and, 169
  Carmen and, 264, 266
  as critic, 215, 292–94
  Debussy and, 151, 255
  Fairbank and, 225, 226

Thomson, V. *(cont.)*
  Great Master syndrome and, 93
  on listening, 316
  Messiaen and, 277
  Piaf and, 217
  as pianist, 28–29
  Satie and, 352
  Stravinsky and, 194
  as teacher, 23, 138, 144–45, 233, 271
  vocal music of, 228, 230, 231, 237,
    240, 308
Thorne, F., 30, 153, 295
Tiepolo, G., 95
Tolstoy, L., 36, 294
Toscanini, A., 34, 161, 162
Toulouse-Lautrec, H. de, 127
Tourel, J., 29, 189, 226, 227, 263, 314
Tovey, D. F., 215, 296
Trapp, J., 56
Truffaut, F., 282
Tuchman, B., 153–54
Tureck, R., 108
Turgenev, I., 259
Turner, C., 264
Turner, J. M., 253
Tyler, P., 70–73

Uldace, P., 130
Uppman, T., 314
Uris, D., 240

Valéry, P., 128, 140, 195, 251, 311
van Gogh, V., 227
Van Horne, H., 22
Vanni, H., 367
Varèse, E., 58, 166
Varèse, L., 169, 230
Vega, G., 72, 74
Verdi, G., 19, 71, 150, 197, 217, 232,
    254, 255, 269, 271, 295
Verlaine, P., 243, 248, 259–61
Vermeer, J., 95
Verneuil, C. (C. Rosenthal), 283–86
Verrett, S., 264
Veyron-Lacroix, R., 264
Viardot, P., 249
Vidal, G., 92, 97, 105
Vilallonga, J.-L. de, 57
Vilallonga, S., 57
Villon, F., 172, 283, 367
Vilmorin, L. de, 177, 243
Viñes, R., 27
Vivaldi, A., 276, 349

Volkov, S., 161, 163–64
Voltaire, 359
Voorhees, E., 77
Vreeland, D., 95
Vuillard, E., 68, 127, 130

Wagner, C., 135–37, 186, 187
Wagner, R., 28, 42, 59, 110, 162, 210,
    215, 216, 218, 271, 273, 352
  Bizet and, 265, 270
  Nietzsche and, 136, 267
  vocal music of, 196, 232, 256
  C. Wagner and, 135–37, 186, 187
Waldman, A., 64
Waley, A., 228
Wallace, H., 163
Walters, B., 96
Walton, Sir W., 302, 309n
Ward, R., 231
Warhol, A., 290, 294, 349
Webb, C., 212
Weber, B., 153–59, 230, 231, 295
Weber, C. M. von, 45
Webern, A. von, 45, 152, 167, 186,
    232, 254, 261
Webster, Dr., 78
Wehr, W., 36
Weill, K., 91, 183, 184
Weisgall, H., 30
Welles, O., 355
West, M., 46
West, R., 212
Wharton, E., 95, 118
White, Edmund, 86–89
White, Erick, 191
Whitman, W., 103, 228
Wigman, M., 40
Wild, E., 25
Wilde, O., 71, 89, 97, 129, 180, 213,
    224, 279–80, 292, 347
Wilder, T., 51
Williams, T., 117, 228, 230, 292, 356
Williams, V., 345
Williams, W. C., 208
Willkie, W., 162–63
Windham, D., 165
Wittgenstein, L., 27–28
Wolf, H., 260, 274, 311
Wolff, B., 246, 265
Wolff, C., 278
Woolf, V., 211
Wuorinen, C., 30, 187

Wyatt, J., 68
Wylie, E., 123

Yates, P., 192–94
Yeats, W. B., 207, 228, 251, 301–2, 313

Yevtushenko, Y., 163
Yradier, S., 266
Yudina, M., 163

Zimbalist, Mrs. (Mrs. Bok), 221